ain't but a few of us

ain't but a few of us

willard jenkins, editor

black music writers tell their story

DUKE UNIVERSITY PRESS *Durham and London* 2022

© 2022 DUKE UNIVERSITY PRESS

All rights reserved

Printed in the United States of America on acid-free paper ∞

Designed by A. Mattson Gallagher

Typeset in Warnock Pro, Meta Pro, and Helvetica LT Std
by Westchester Publishing Services

Library of Congress Cataloging-in-Publication Data

Names: Jenkins, Willard, [date] editor.

Title: Ain't but a few of us : black music writers tell their story /
Willard Jenkins, editor.

Description: Durham : Duke University Press, 2022. |
Includes index.

Identifiers: LCCN 2022020093 (print) | LCCN 2022020094 (ebook)

ISBN 9781478016397 (hardcover)

ISBN 9781478019039 (paperback)

ISBN 9781478023661 (ebook)

Subjects: LCSH: African American journalists—Biography. | Music
journalists—United States—Biography. | Jazz—United States—
History and criticism. | African Americans—Music—History and
criticism. | African American jazz musicians—Biography. | African
American musicians—Biography. | BISAC: MUSIC / Genres & Styles /
Jazz | SOCIAL SCIENCE / Ethnic Studies / American / African
American & Black Studies

Classification: LCC ML385 .A38 2022 (print) | LCC ML385 (ebook) |
DDC 780.89/96073 [B]—dc23/eng/20220713

LC record available at https://lccn.loc.gov/2022020093

LC ebook record available at https://lccn.loc.gov/2022020094

Cover art: *Left and right:* The hands of the musician. Photo
by Suteishi/iStock. *Center:* Hand of a person writing on paper.
Photo by cottonbro/Pexels.

contents

acknowledgments

This book is dedicated with thanks to my brother, George L. P. Jenkins, who was there at the earliest stages, shared my earliest music obsessions, and represents our loving ancestral parents, Annalouise and Willard Jenkins Sr., who encouraged our love of music; to my wife, Suzan Jenkins, daughters, Iyesha and Tiffany, and grandson, DQ, for their continued support and inspiration; and to the memory of Randy Weston and the African Rhythms family for such powerful ongoing inspiration in my writing/editing efforts. Thanks also to Frank Alkyer of *DownBeat* magazine and Lee Mergner of *JazzTimes* magazine for their support of the work and the anthology section of this book; and to all of the contributors to our series of *Ain't But a Few of Us* interviews—collectively, your stories were the inspiration behind this book!

introduction

WILLARD JENKINS

Yes, this is a book about one important sector of the music industry, examined from a race perspective; it is a book about race examined from the viewpoint of those who write about jazz and in many cases also chronicle other jazz-informed music. How did we arrive at this unprecedented examination? And what about that curious title, *Ain't But a Few of Us*? The title is a straight lift from the colloquial speech that black jazz musicians and fellow travelers along the African American trail have employed across the ages. The first time I heard it uttered, it stuck. Before or after some long-forgotten performance, the late vibraphone innovator Milt Jackson uttered the phrase in warmly greeting his fellow jazz master and bop-era survivor, the saxophonist Jimmy Heath—as in, "Man, ain't but a few of us . . ." (presumably, from their era left). So it was that the phrase became a compelling sobriquet for what is to follow.

For this observer, recognizing that, where it concerns writing about jazz music and its many extensions (and, some would argue, about *any* music), there truly *ain't* but a few of us—or to extend the theme further, *ain't but a few of us* who have been granted access—has been a bit more of a convoluted journey. That journey for me began as a youth coming up in Pittsburgh and living my preteen years through marriage and young fatherhood in Cleveland and Kent, Ohio.

I grew up with a jazz-devoted father and a jazz-welcoming mother: Dad a lifelong newspaperman, Mom an early childhood education professional, both proud college grads. Dad was a record lover, while Mom appreciated most of what he laid on the turntable. And I say she appreciated *most* of it, because I do recall certain things entering the collection that she would humorously side-eye and designate as "that way-out stuff"—for example, a record by the pianist Bobby Timmons, a trio record titled *In Person* that Dad picked up and that forever mesmerized me with Timmons's evocative intro to "Autumn Leaves," with Ron Carter on bass and Albert Heath on drums.

Influenced by Dad's records and, later, when we moved to Cleveland (I was eleven), by my immersion in the city's twenty-four-hour, commercial jazz radio station WCUY (a dinosaur in today's radio universe), I cultivated a deeper schoolboy appreciation for instrumental music than was evidenced by most of my peers. Even in the case of the dominant pop music of the day—the various singing groups like the Temptations, Impressions, O'Jays, Spinners, Marvelettes, and the Supremes, or James Brown, Marvin Gaye, and later Parliament-Funkadelic, the Ohio Players, and so on—I developed what I suppose was an unusual fixation on the instrumental underpinnings of those tunes, the first in my crew to recognize James Jamerson's Motown bass greatness long before knowing his name. (Remember Motown's and other pop labels' ongoing conceit: album jackets lacked instrumentalist credits.) Clearly, an appreciation for that largely instrumental music known as jazz was brewing.

The fever started with records, particularly following Christmas of 1961 when Dad bought one of those huge old console entertainment units—more furniture than audiophile item—that delivered the magic of stereophonic sound to our living room. My younger brother George and I loved spinning that innocuous test record that came with the unit, just to get that glorious stereophonic sound in our ears. Dad's LPs became ever more alluring.

Perhaps the sheer variety of jazz sounds that entranced my ears suggests that WCUY was the real culprit, but one of Dad's records in particular proved especially fascinating, and turned out to be a sort of pathway to expanding my jazz personnel consciousness. It was an otherwise mundane-looking black-and-white-jacketed number titled *The Best of Argo Jazz*. This was the kind of sampler that record labels released on a fairly regular basis back then to further promote the brand and their artists; also the kind of record often found in then-burgeoning stereo shops as demonstration records.

Easing that compilation album onto the turntable, I was charmed by the exquisite elegance of James Moody's tenor sax essaying "I Remember Clifford" with a lush orchestral string backdrop. To my preteen ears *this* was classical music, hip and elegant by turns. I still have that record—beat my brother to it when Dad passed—and have to chuckle whenever I drag it out these days and hear the snaps and pops throughout that Moody track; residue from where my undisciplined young hands would snatch up the tonearm to repeatedly experience those gorgeous introductory chords.

There were endless aural fascinations on that sampler, and useful additional details were discovered in the jacket information. There were no personnel listings, but the jackets from each artist's track were on display: a (pre-Rahsaan) Roland Kirk wielding three horns simultaneously on *Introducing*; Ahmad Jamal grinning out from his *Happy Moods* cover; Al Grey (whose track is a definitive swinging shuffle) perched astride a stool in elegant suit and plaid vest, trombone resting at his side; Art Farmer and Benny Golson (in the Jazztet) relaxing and smiling amid some cityscape, looking like Mad Men of jazz in suits and ties on the cover of *Big City Sounds*; and Lorez Alexandria elegantly wrapped in come-hither glory on *Sing No Sad Songs for Me*.

Thus commenced the record jacket curriculum of my jazz education, particularly from those records that proffered what were referred to as "annotated notes" and detailed personnel listings. If someone other than the leader on a given record date truly stood out to those young ears, he or she became the focus of subsequent record-hunting expeditions. The expansion of my knowledge of who was who in this music called jazz, and the growing thirst for those new sounds, continued to escalate.

Fast-forward to college days, when I became a sort of go-to guy for new records in my circle at Kent State University—both jazz and otherwise—particularly among my Omega Psi Phi brothers. My insatiable thirst for the latest sides knew few bounds. My lack of wheels for the thirty-five-mile foray north to Cleveland's record stores was no impediment; I'd resort to commandeering the cars of girlfriends or underclassmen (thank you, Bro. Tim Moore) for the trek. In those days, records were often released regionally in increments rather than according to the nationally orchestrated release practices still to come, and so the latest would arrive in Cleveland record stores before they'd trickle down to Kent.

In particular the latest Miles Davis records became an insatiable passion once an aware upperclassman named Larry Young hipped me to *Miles Smiles*. And by then James Brown (what a band!), Sly Stone, Jimi Hendrix, Cream,

Earth, Wind & Fire (I was the first on campus with their original Warner Bros. launch), Parliament-Funkadelic (actually Parliament *and* Funkadelic, before it became clear that they shared personnel in George Clinton's brilliant marketing scheme), Led Zeppelin, and all sorts of progressive rock–related music (particularly when that music bore some elements of instrumental prowess, which those bands certainly did) had also deeply invaded the consciousness, stoking the growing record collection. Remember, unlike the singing groups of grade school days, these were self-contained bands that played their own instruments!

The kid lost his mind when Miles jumped into the electric pool with *In a Silent Way*, followed by the landmark *Bitches Brew*. Upon their respective release dates I commandeered a ride and hustled up to Record Rendezvous, in downtown Cleveland, to cop each of those—quick, fast, and in a hurry!

The times were indeed a-changing, and along with Kent State's growing antiwar movement—which would culminate in that infamous day May 4, 1970, when four KSU students were gunned down by the Ohio National Guard—black student consciousness was growing in that roiling era. A small group of my peers founded Black United Students (BUS), and the collective consciousness of our black student body grew exponentially.

In 1968 the Oakland Police Department was recognized in the black liberation movement for its open oppression of the Black Panther Party in its California birthplace. The OPD got the bright idea to make Kent State part of an audacious national recruiting tour. Our Black United Students organization was having none of that, and we fomented a Thursday afternoon demonstration that escalated from sit-in to outright takeover of one of the KSU administrative buildings.

By that Thursday evening, we had been alerted that the campus police, assisted by the Kent PD and Ohio state troopers, had begun to encircle the building with buses, with the clear intent of forcibly ousting us from the building in a mass jailing. We quickly hatched a plan to march out peaceably and avoid whatever bloodshed, not to mention parental disapproval, might have resulted from that forced removal and arrest. By the weekend, our righteous anger continuing to escalate, we developed a unified plan to further demonstrate our grit and opposition by marching on campus that Monday and symbolically walking out.

Our show of determination and numbers proved successful. We developed a manifesto of demands, most of which were met by an administration eager to avoid an escalation of black student hostilities. Our demands included an insistence that Kent State develop a black student center and black studies curriculum (today's Center of Pan-African Culture, which houses the school's Department of Africana Studies).

That progress spurred the publication of our black student newspaper, the *Black Watch*. Having always enjoyed writing, I signed up. Early on I sought insights from writers I'd been devouring in the jazz prints, like Dan Morgenstern, Leonard Feather, Ira Gitler, Martin Williams, Alan Heineman, and Frank Kofsky—to try my hand at writing about the joys and occasional missteps of jazz music. Thus began my jazz writing pursuits, contributing record reviews to the *Black Watch*.

As my writing persevered, lo and behold, an exceedingly pleasant development arose for this broke college student: completely unsolicited, major record labels like Atlantic Records began sending me their latest releases to review! Another revelation was that, suddenly, I qualified for occasional press accommodations at jazz performances, at places like Cleveland's now-legendary Smiling Dog Saloon. It was there that I at long last witnessed the glories of Miles, Mingus, the earliest incarnations of Weather Report and Return to Forever (Brazilian edition, with Airto and Flora), Herbie Hancock (Mwandishi septet edition); spent a glorious evening with the Thad Jones/ Mel Lewis Orchestra on a rare foray away from their traditional Monday nights at the Village Vanguard; and experienced a mind-blowing month-long residency by the Sun Ra Arkestra (in full force, with costuming, dancers, June Tyson singing, and backdrop films illustrating Ra's Egyptology), among other live performance revelations. Space was indeed the place! It was on; clearly this writing about jazz might lead to something!

A bachelor's degree in sociology bought me a ten-year career in public service. But my newspaperman dad came to the rescue. He had matriculated as a typographer and proofreader through the black dispatch (from Cleveland's *Call & Post* to the legendary *Pittsburgh Courier*) and on to Pittsburgh's late *Sun Telegraph* afternoon daily, as part of the first wave of professional African Americans working at daily papers, to the *Cleveland Plain Dealer*. We landed in Cleveland, through his industrious typographer's union, when the *Pittsburgh Post Gazette* bought out the *Sun Telegraph*, a sale portending the end of the two–daily newspaper towns. Dad hooked up his postgrad wannabe-jazz-writer son with a man named Bob Roach, the editor of the *Plain Dealer*'s weekly *Friday Magazine* entertainment section.

At the *Friday Magazine* I became a weekly contributor, one of *two* regular jazz writers—the other being the late former WCUY jazz DJ Chris Colombi, who contributed a weekly record review column. My assignments were to preview the upcoming weekend's or the following week's jazz performance activity around town. I was mentored a bit in this jazz writing endeavor by an elegant Frenchman with a prodigious record collection, named Bernard Laret, who covered jazz for the rival afternoon paper, the *Cleveland Press*. During that Sun Ra residency, Arkestra members stayed in private homes on Cleveland's east side, and some stopped by Bernard's home for conversation while I was there on one of my pilgrimages.

Now I truly had carte blanche to descend upon jazz performances, not only citywide but all around northeast Ohio, which was particularly useful when nearby Akron hosted two jazz clubs for a hot minute: one was The Bank, so called because its venue was a former savings and loan, where I had my first Art Blakey and the Jazz Messengers sighting (the Bobby Watson and James Williams edition).

Initially the greatest resource for those weekly newspaper preview pieces was the Smiling Dog Saloon, where the owner Roger Bohn was beginning to branch out into jazz concert production at the old Allen Theatre downtown. He presented several iterations of Miles's murky, early 1970s prehiatus electric jazz unit (in the time of Mtume, Pete Cosey, Michael Henderson, Reggie Lucas, Al Foster, Sonny Fortune—and one edition boasting three guitarists!). One such tour stop yielded my only interview encounter with Miles. Bohn's Allen Theatre efforts also presented a particularly sublime evening with the Keith Jarrett Quartet that featured Dewey Redman, Charlie Haden, and Paul Motian.

The Dog had a great run, but like most jazz clubs it flamed out, the end arriving in 1975 amid pointed opposition from its residential neighbors, opposition served up with an entrée of racial tension. The Smiling Dog was located on the near West Side, just west of downtown and the Cuyahoga River. Back then East was black, West was white, the river being the line of demarcation; gentrification and other factors have changed that equation in twenty-first-century Cleveland, but in those days that was the rule—and never the twain should meet. Given that the Dog was dedicated to jazz, there were more than a few black folks who ventured over to the West Side in search of great sounds; a few, mind you, not exactly a torrent. Seems those relative few sufficiently raised the hackles of the Dog's neighbors to put the heat on their city councilman. The heightened pressure ultimately got the best of Smiling Dog ownership, and the legend was shuttered. The unfortunate upshot was a drought of touring jazz greats passing through town.

In 1974 a new avenue for expressing this writer's commitment to the music opened up when my old friend and Omega brother Mike Brown bequeathed his WKSU (the radio voice of Kent State) program slot to me; thus was born the weekly Exploration Jazz show. Radio became a new expression for my sense of the music and an additional perch from which to observe the comings and goings of the art form. That volunteer radio pursuit continues today with the Ancient/Future show on WPFW in Washington, DC. A subsequent opportunity to teach jazz survey and jazz history courses at Cleveland State University (at the invitation of Dr. Ed London and the resourceful multisaxophonist-composer-educator Howie Smith) further broadened my immersion in the music.

All these developments, as well as a significant new brick in the foundation that would arrive shortly thereafter, were satellites to the core of my entry point in the jazz crusade: the writing quest. My approach to writing about jazz has always been more about story, history, atmosphere, and an enthusiast's conveyance, with occasional editorializing on elements affecting the overall jazz condition. My sensibility has always been more about seeking converts to the music, and decidedly not about impressing musicians and fellow writers with any measure of technical music acumen. Says here the average jazz enthusiast, or the simply curious, aren't that interested in chord sequencing or any other measure of music science reportage.

Meanwhile my writing endeavors were branching out to a variety of so-called alternative weeklies, which were either citywide or neighborhood-oriented tabloids whose minuscule pay for articles (if anything!) at least granted a certain amount of precious editorial freedom, important for someone developing their craft. Not to mention access to the latest records and press list admission to performances. Eventually my writing opportunities expanded a bit nationally, with assignments from *Cadence* magazine and eventually *JazzTimes* (then still a tabloid) and *DownBeat* magazines. Those opportunities helped grow my perspective to regional live jazz pursuits—for example, a particularly transcendent Sonny Rollins stand in nearby Akron, OH, at a short-lived joint called the Nightclub; or in occasionally traveling to some concert presentation by the exemplary University of Michigan student jazz presenting organization called Eclipse Jazz in Ann Arbor (including another memorable Sun Ra sighting).

Eventually such forays encouraged annual trips to New York for George Wein's post-Newport uprising festivals (when unruly fans drove the Newport gentry crazy and Wein had to vacate that tony burg for a minute), whether it was Newport–New York, the Kool Jazz Festival, or the JVC Jazz Festival. This was also a time when New York's downtown scene was blooming with original expressions, whether that pursuit meant hanging out at Sam and

Beatrice Rivers's Studio Rivbea, Rashied Ali's Alley, the Ladies Fort, Tin Palace, Joe Papp's Public Theater, or old standbys like the Village Vanguard and the Village Gate. So a night at Wein's festival might start with a 7:00 p.m. concert at Carnegie Hall or Lincoln Center and end at 3:00 a.m. nursing a beer in a club or holding up a wall in some steamy loft.

Those New York trips took this writer out of the northeast Ohio cocoon to inevitably encounter other jazz writers covering Wein's festivals, critics I'd known vicariously through the pages of *DownBeat* and other prints: men like Dan Morgenstern, Leonard Feather, and Ira Gitler, and peers like Gary Giddins, Howard Mandel, Lee Jeske, Art Lange, Fred Bouchard, Michael Bourne, and others—none of the above, mind you, were black, nor were there any women writers to be seen in those press sections or lurking around backstage chatting up the headliners for interviews. Special mention must be made here of the George Wein organization's longtime, no-nonsense publicist Charlie Bourgeois for granting festival access to a greenhorn from Cleveland.

Reading about jazz became an expanded pursuit, revealing important archival contributions from African Americans: Amiri Baraka (née LeRoi Jones), A. B. Spellman, Ralph Ellison, Albert Murray, and the contemporary writings of Stanley Crouch, Ron Welburn, and next-gen peers like Don Palmer, Nelson George, Vernon Gibbs, my homeboy Robert Fleming, and later Greg Tate, brothers of my approximate generation versed in jazz, whose prose encompassed other branches of the black music tree. Granted those weren't the writers I encountered on those festival assignments sitting in adjacent press rows at the concert halls where the major Wein festival performances occurred.

My writing exploits advanced, including scoring not only some national print assignments but also international opportunities via *Jazz Forum* (published in Poland—not sure whether my accumulation of Polish coin-of-the-realm zlotys remain in my account there!). A major addition to my jazz exploits came when concert presentation was added to the mix via the Northeast Ohio Jazz Society. An informal group of enthusiasts had founded that late nonprofit organization in 1977, seeking a means of addressing the lack of touring jazz artist performances coming through Cleveland after the passing of the Dog. Connections with still more jazz writers resulted. It was beyond apparent that there were only a small handful of black writers covering jazz in newspapers and magazines, or for that matter authoring jazz books.

Opportunities for black writers on jazz expanded a bit with the 1979 launch of the *Jazz Spotlite News*, published by the jazz enthusiast and gig presenter Jim Harrison. *Jazz Spotlite News* was one of what has been a minuscule number of jazz-oriented publications that actively sought the black perspective on jazz. Preceding the *Jazz Spotlite News*' black slant on jazz had been such other worthy and lamentably short-lived efforts as Amiri Baraka's *Cricket* and Ron Welburn's *The Grackle*. Succeeding the *Jazz Spotlite News*, with a similar Afrocentric orientation, were the California-based *Jazz Now* and, later, the Brooklyn-based *Pure Jazz*; both provided vehicles for black jazz writers. Recognizing the disparity of black pens chronicling jazz, I contributed enthusiastically to each of these publications, continuing to write about jazz as a freelancer, including in the *Plain Dealer*.

I eagerly departed my social services career in 1983, to assume a hang-fly, one-year contract, funded by the National Endowment for the Arts, to conduct a jazz community needs assessment in the former Great Lakes Arts Alliance region (Illinois, Indiana, Michigan, and Ohio). As part of that assignment, I interviewed jazz musicians, educators, performance presenters, radio broadcasters, and whatever journalist-critics I could find in a given community, be they local newspaper writers or freelancers like myself. Despite frequent oral history interview trips to regional cities with historic African American jazz lineages—like Chicago, Detroit, and Indianapolis—I encountered few, if any, regularly contributing African Americans writing on jazz, not even when those cities had a weekly or monthly black newspaper or tabloid; sadly, in their modern evolution those black dispatches were increasingly indifferent to jazz coverage.

In 1985, as a consequence of its undeniably compelling results, and with the tacit encouragement of the National Endowment for the Arts, that needs assessment morphed into a full-time position at the merged Midwest regional arts organization known as Arts Midwest. From our new Minneapolis base, we established the country's first regional jazz service program. As a result of the merger of two former regional arts service organizations, our region had now expanded to include the Upper Midwest states of Iowa, Minnesota, North and South Dakota, and Wisconsin. The black population of those states was not as deeply rooted as in those original four Midwestern states; there would be no revelation of additional black jazz writers in this new territory.

Among other developments at Great Lakes Arts Alliance, and in addition to those fact-finding and needs-assessment trips, I published a quarterly jazz newsletter. I set out to eventually expand the *Jazzletter* beyond my own writing to encourage a broad sampling of bylines. This was important because, despite the evident lack of diversity in who was covering jazz, there was also no evidence of any outreach on the part of the traditional jazz prints to expand the diversity of their contributor pool, nor any sense of their recognizing this disparity. The eternal puzzle: a music, born largely out of the African experience in America, reported on journalistically by people almost totally outside of that experience!

At Arts Midwest, which encouraged a fully vested Jazz Program as part of the merger, the quarterly regional *Jazzletter* continued to cast its net wide for aspiring jazz writers of any stripe, including black and women contributors (the gender gap in jazz writing—food for another meal—has always been even broader than the ethnic diversity gap); only a few black or women contributors answered that call from this vast region. The *Jazzletter* was one cornerstone of our program of services to the jazz community, which also included producing technical assistance workshops around the region, writing a series of professional development booklets, and building a regional jazz database. The *Jazzletter* began to gain some visibility and traction, at least in our region, and it led to our producing the first regional jazz media conference.

Held in 1987 on the campus of the University of Illinois Chicago, the conference—which featured guest speakers, workshops, panel discussions, and performance opportunities—had a mission to serve as an initial gathering of regional jazz media personnel and resources, to be joined by writers and jazz radio broadcasters from around the country to interact and share ideas with our regional conferees. The assembled writers seized the opportunity to begin discussions that resulted in the formation of the Jazz Journalists Association (JJA), which carries on today under Howard Mandel's leadership with an international membership and which pre-pandemic produced the annual Jazz Awards show in New York City.

Throughout this time, I continued to keep mental notes on the few black music writers I read or otherwise encountered on travels. One such writer was the Harlemite Clarence Atkins, who at the time contributed writing on jazz to the historic black dispatch the *Amsterdam News*. When Mr. Atkins passed in 2004, a modest sum of funds was earmarked by the JJA to support young black writers interested in jazz. In 2006 the JJA created a limited Clarence Atkins scholarship fund with the express purpose of assisting a handful of young, aspiring African American music writers to attend a national arts critics' conference in California. (Two recipients of that Clarence Atkins fund subsequently contributed to the *Ain't But a Few of Us* interview series.)

Fast-forward to 2010 and a lot has gone down in the ensuing years, but the number of black writers on jazz in the mainstream jazz prints and general interest publications remained modest. Continuing to ponder the relative scarcity of black music writers, I began a series of interviews with African American writers on my blog, the *Independent Ear*, at the Open Sky Jazz website. Interest in the series, which was fueled by assorted conversations and a specific set of emailed questions, was quite significant and encouraging, certainly judging by the comments section; instant feedback being one of the benefits of our twenty-first-century electronic media universe.

As opposed to conventional interviewing—with a recorder and an ensuing arduous transcription process—our methodology involved emailing questions to participating writers. This afforded the participating writers more time to broadly express and edit their contributions before submitting their responses for editing and publication in our series, and it allowed us to achieve a broader geographic outreach. Our interview questions included common inquiries and were also more often than not tailored to the specific writer.

Back at Arts Midwest, because we were the only regional arts agency (or state arts agency, for that matter) with a Jazz Program, I became a sort of go-to "jazz guy" for arts councils and arts service organizations around the country, including being asked to represent the art form on numerous funding panels. That work began to expand my multidisciplinary arts perspective, with a particular eye toward multidisciplinary audience development initiatives, feeding the viewpoint that audience development remains a major pursuit for those presenting jazz. I began to write from a broader arts perspective. My writing focus has often been less on the personalities of jazz and the science of music than on more systemic matters.

These broader jazz industry perspectives have included that abiding interest in audience development, perceived disparities in how jazz musicians and bands so seldom operate in a manner befitting the need to grow the jazz audience, and other issues relative to jazz preservation and the vehicles and venues through which the music is disseminated to the public. For that wider lens, I have to point to my years in arts administration and eventually in jazz presenting; those respective stations have clearly colored my overall sense of the art form.

The online *Ain't But a Few of Us* series of interviews and dialogues commenced on May 21, 2009, with the author, poet, and arts administrator A. B. Spellman, author of one of the foremost books of jazz artist interviews, *Four Lives in the Bebop Business* (1966), subsequently abbreviated and reissued as *Four Jazz Lives* (2011). The four subjects at the core of Spellman's book are Herbie Nichols, Jackie McLean, Ornette Coleman, and Cecil Taylor. The tone and tenor of those interviews suggests that Spellman may well have been seen by his interview subjects as a somewhat sympathetic inquisitor—a black jazz writer—with subsequent suggestions that Spellman may have elicited a deeper sense of response because of who he was. (The same held true in Arthur Taylor's important book, *Notes and Tones*.)

Our initial interview with Spellman was published with the subtitle "How Black Jazz Writers Persevere," which would be altered in subsequent installments to "Black Jazz Writers Tell Their Story." The introductory paragraphs in the original *Ain't But a Few of Us* online series provided the reader with the following context relative to our mission:

> Despite the historic origins of this music called jazz, a unique development of the African experience in America, the ranks of black critics and journalists covering the music has always been thin. Black jazz writers have been inspired through the years by the examples of Ralph Ellison, Amiri Baraka (formerly LeRoi Jones), Albert Murray and more recently Stanley Crouch . . . and few others. The Jazz Journalists Association has a handful of currently active black writers on its rolls. Major jazz festivals such as Montreal, Monterey, Northsea, and Umbria, which have long been annual congress for jazz writers who generally operate pretty much in splendid isolation, rarely find more than one black writer in their coverage pool.
>
> Your correspondent has been writing about the music from various perspectives since my undergrad years in the early 1970s at Kent State University. In that time I've been privileged to have numerous off-the-record conversations with artists who have occasionally questioned why there are so few black jazz writers. In that spirit we began a series of conversations posing the same set of questions to black jazz writers on how they got started and their perspective as members of a tiny subset of the fraternity of jazz writers.

A. B. Spellman was an apt starting point, as I had known him and his activist wife Karen Spellman from around the Washington, DC, arts and culture environs. A.B. is greatly respected as a keen observer of the music, from his days contributing to *Metronome* and *DownBeat* magazines to his authorship of *Four Lives* and his work as a published poet. I had also known A.B. from my arts administration work; he retired from a distinguished career at the National Endowment for the Arts, where he continued to champion jazz artists and was one of the catalysts behind the NEA Jazz Masters program. Upon his retirement from the NEA, then-chairman Dana Gioia introduced the A. B. Spellman Award for jazz advocacy as part of the annual NEA Jazz

Masters program to provide fellowships to those who have contributed indelibly to jazz from off the bandstand.

For the second and third installments of the series I purposely sought out dialogues with two younger jazz writers with whom I had enjoyed a friendly and mentoring relationship. John Murph and Eugene Holley Jr. had worked with me at the former National Jazz Service Organization, and both have continued their jazz writing. Murph has worked as a regular contributor for the two mainstream jazz periodicals, *DownBeat* and *JazzTimes*, as well as for *Jazzwise* in the UK and various crossover publications both online and in print. Murph, a proud gay man, has written perhaps the most definitive article to date—included here in the anthology section—on openly gay jazz musicians. The second contributor, Eugene Holley Jr., has written for both traditional and online publications on jazz, including more recent contributions to such general readership outlets as *Publishers Weekly*, the *Village Voice*, *Ebony*, Amazon.com, the *New York Times Book Review*, and the broad-based music magazine *Wax Poetics*. Holley's rangy choice of music subjects is something of a hallmark of the writers who have contributed to this series of dialogues, most of whom cover other musical genres and additional areas of interest, including sports, cuisine, wine, and politics.

As the series has evolved, the goal has been to include black writers from several different perspectives and stations in the media pursuit. Additionally, I sought contributions from fellow travelers for whom writing about the music represents part of a diverse portfolio of other related work, including from broadcasters, arts presenters, and full-time educators—none are full-time jazz writers.

The range of writers contributing to our series has been broad: including book authors, newspaper and periodical contributors, online media journalists, black dispatch scribes, educators, and publisher-editors. This book represents a variety of viewpoints and vantage points, but inevitably the dialogue leads back to considerations of that specious, man-made construct known as race.

In his contribution to the extensive compilation and anthology *The Oxford Companion to Jazz* (assembled by jazz musician-scholar Bill Kirchner), the writer (and contributor to *Ain't But a Few of Us*) Ron Welburn notes the development of jazz criticism at its beginning stages, ironically nominating the great early twentieth-century African American proto-jazz pioneer bandleader and military officer James Reese Europe as the first jazz critic. Welburn writes, "As other writers were practicing the jazz essay, they seemed ignorant of the essence of jazz performed by blacks, missing altogether the performances of King Oliver, Louis Armstrong, Fletcher Henderson, Jelly Roll Morton, and Duke Ellington. Not until 1933 did a lengthy appreciation of Ellington appear, by Walter Hobson for *Esquire*.[1] Would this have been different had blacks been writing about jazz?

Welburn does cite a handful of black jazz writers: "Although most commentators acknowledged the African American roots of jazz, few African Americans wrote about it with critical depth."[2] He goes on to cite Dave Peyton (for the *Chicago Defender*, 1927–1938) and Lucien White (for the *New York Age*, 1913–1927), both of whom discussed jazz more as a social phenomenon than in purely analytical terms. One exception among Welburn's citations is Frank Marshall Davis, whose examination of jazz recordings was syndicated in the 1930s by the Associated Negro Press. Otherwise, by any measure, white writers have thoroughly dominated the writing of jazz journalism, criticism, and history.

Bob Porter, a white writer, wrote in the preface to his valuable 2016 book *Soul Jazz: Jazz in the Black Community, 1945–1975*, "You can find contemporary jazz history texts with no mention of Buddy Johnson, Illinois Jacquet, Gene Ammons, or Donald Byrd; successful jazz musicians whose popularity drew largely from the black community. And this situation seems likely to continue; there is little variance in the telling of jazz history."[3]

The anthology section of this volume is by no means complete, and it does suggest the need for a more expansive anthology of black writings on jazz. The goal was to represent historic black writings on jazz as well as the contributors to our original *Ain't But a Few of Us* series, including essays that reflect an assortment of viewpoints on jazz from a black perspective, and especially further inquiry into the dearth of African Americans writing on jazz. Also represented are black jazz writing forerunners, including several historic figures, and black musicians who have contributed to the dialogue, the latter culled primarily from the mainstream jazz prints. The goal of our anthology is to present contributions on jazz by black writers from several perspectives, including previews, reviews, recordings reviews, and editorials on the general jazz condition.

notes

1. Ron Welburn, "Jazz Criticism," in *The Oxford Companion to Jazz*, edited by Bill Kirchner (New York: Oxford University Press, 2005), 748.

2. Welburn, "Jazz Criticism," 749.

3. Bob Porter, preface to *Soul Jazz: Jazz in the Black Community, 1945–1975* (Bloomington, IN: Xlibris, 2016), ix.

1

roundtable

ERIC ARNOLD, JORDANNAH ELIZABETH, BILL FRANCIS,
STEVE MONROE, RAHSAAN CLARK MORRIS,
ROBIN WASHINGTON, AND K. LEANDER WILLIAMS

We begin with a lively "roundtable" Q&A with several of the writers who contributed to the unprecedented dialogues we originally published in the *Independent Ear*.[1] We begin here in part to illustrate the key points of inquiry in our series with black music writers who have chronicled their sense of jazz and jazz musicians, in part for the sake of brevity, and in part to further exemplify the scope of our inquiries.

What originally motivated you to write about music?

ERIC ARNOLD (SAN FRANCISCO BAY AREA): When I was in college at UC Santa Cruz I read LeRoi Jones's *Blues People* in my African American Music course, taught by Nate Mackey, a professor who was also a jazz radio DJ. At that time I was also deejaying on the college radio station. I started writing for the school paper and just went on from there.

1. The *Independent Ear* is an independent jazz column published at http://www.openskyjazz.com.

JORDANNAH ELIZABETH (BALTIMORE, MD): I had been booking shows for a few years in Denver and then in New York City. I was just overwhelmed and wanted to do something a bit more private that would keep me involved in the music industry and community. I started a music blog and record label called the *Process Records*. The music blog became a bit more popular, and all the friends I'd made began to do interviews with me, for example, the Black Angels. I was able to start my professional writing career from blogging on my own site and writing on Medium.com back when it was really exclusive. But I had always dreamed of being an author, so writing about music was really natural.

BILL FRANCIS (BROOKLYN, NY): My father was a jazz musician as well as one of the legendary Tuskegee Airmen. From an early age, jazz has been part of my world. In college, while playing in a jazz fusion group, hearing and meeting some of the greatest jazzmen of the day (e.g., Herbie Hancock, Freddie Hubbard), I realized that jazz was much more than a music genre; it was a culture and an important part of African American history.

STEVE MONROE (WASHINGTON, DC, AREA): I was working for the sports desk of a daily newspaper and wanted to shift to features, to cover music, theater, the arts—to do profiles of interesting people, especially those in the black community of Rochester, NY, where I was located. While writing features, I started covering all kinds of music, and since I was a jazz fan, I became especially interested in the jazz performers who came through town, and I reviewed and interviewed the ones I could, like Dizzy Gillespie, Billy Taylor, Ron Carter, Bill Evans, Grant Green, and many others. The first review and profile I did was of Phil Woods, and I was fascinated by the stories he told of Charlie Parker and how he was so influenced by him. That started my jazz reviewing and writing career, in the mid-1970s. Up to then I was just a fan, but I became interested in reviewing and profiling the greats of the music, the trends, because it was such an original American music and had so many genres to cover—from soul jazz to avant-garde, from the vocalists to the whole swing, big band thing.

RAHSAAN CLARK MORRIS (CHICAGO, IL): The thing that motivated me and got me thinking about writing about jazz in the first place was Amiri Baraka's essay "Jazz and the White Critic," published in his collection of essays *Black Music*, from 1968. The thought occurred to me that black folks should be in control of their own culture and of how it is appraised and critically approached. I always thought it was the highest order of cultural arrogance to assume that someone from outside a group that had been culturally dispossessed could come in and present criticism of that culture, especially because of the pre-1960s American separatism that had gone on for so long. Baraka's argument made the most sense to me, especially if you go from the lead point that this music comes out of the black experience in this country.

ROBIN WASHINGTON (DULUTH, MN): Speaking primarily of *"My Favorite Things* at 50," it's my favorite piece of music and I wanted to share everything about it with as broad an audience as possible.[2] My intent was to give listeners the backstory and ingredients to the piece to let them form their own opinion, which is the way I approach all works of criticism. Once that happens, though, I doubt many listeners would be able to just walk away from it.

K. LEANDER WILLIAMS (BROOKLYN, NY): I wrote about music in college, but I'd started thinking a lot about different sounds as a teenager. The woman who was really responsible for my jazz curiosity was my best friend's mom, a worldly sista' whose LP collection was different from my parents'—which I guess brings us back to aesthetic differences. I was initially attracted to the visual style of jazz LPs—cool-looking black folks dressed in great clothes. My friend let me "borrow" several records out of his mom's collection—*Kind of Blue, Carmen McRae Sings Lover Man, Thelonious Monk and John Coltrane, Mingus Mingus, Time Further Out,* and an Art Blakey Jazz Messengers record with "I Hear a Rhapsody." It turns out that she had been a radio personality in a past life; she had photos of herself with Duke Ellington.

When you first started writing about music were you aware of the dearth of African Americans writing about music?

ERIC ARNOLD: Not really, but that became obvious later on.

JORDANNAH ELIZABETH: No, I didn't have a huge support system. I knew I was a good writer and that my friends and readers would like to read about underground bands. Writing is a comfort zone that no one can make uncomfortable for me, so it was a decision of self-care.

BILL FRANCIS: When I began writing professionally as a reporter and music columnist at the *Kansas City Star*, there seemed to be few African Americans getting mass exposure for writing about any serious subjects. At

2. *Editor's note: "My Favorite Things* at 50" is an October 2010 public radio documentary that Washington wrote and produced, on the occasion of the fiftieth anniversary of John Coltrane's famous recording, and the recipient of the National Association of Black Journalists Best Radio Documentary citation.

the time, Baraka's *Blues People* was my only inspiration for thinking I could make a difference as an African American jazz journalist.

STEVE MONROE: No, but since, in the 1970s, there were only a few African Americans writing professionally even about general news and features to some extent, including sports and business in most media, I didn't think much of it back then.

RAHSAAN CLARK MORRIS: I could tell from the tone of the writing, and from some of the allusions in the writing, that there weren't that many brothers or sisters writing about the music.

ROBIN WASHINGTON: By no means does that mean that non-black writers are incapable of accurately or even emotionally conveying the essence of the music or of the artists' lives, but you always have to be cognizant of the legacy of some white writers who have done so much damage in the past. I don't think that statement needs to be qualified.

In researching *"My Favorite Things* at 50," I made a point of reading Cuthbert Simpkins's biography of Coltrane before reading Lewis Porter's Coltrane biography, and even went back and forth between Simpkins and the work of Ingrid Monson, who I featured in the documentary. Interestingly, Monson, who is white, speaks more directly about race in jazz than many writers who seem to avoid the issue. I also stopped researching at a certain point, letting Coltrane's own words, the music, and my own interviews take dominance over secondary or tertiary sources usually written by non-black writers.

K. LEANDER WILLIAMS: I was aware of it, but it had as much to do with the lack of African Americans writing about pop music and rock (which I also cover) as it did with jazz. It kinda felt like there was a schism that was generational. You had people who were dealing in academic ways with jazz and the blues because they were older, but were not necessarily wanting to get their hands dirty on the contemporary forms of blues—like hip-hop. It always felt like a continuum to me, fruit from the same tree. I had also begun listening to a little African pop music at that time.

Why do you suppose that's still such a glaring disparity—where you have a significant number of black musicians, many of them in the vanguard of several genres of music, but so few black media commentators on the music?

ERIC ARNOLD: I think there's always been a certain amount of cultural appropriation going on with respect to black music; you can look at Baraka's essay "Jazz and the White Critic" for a historical reference. There are so few black-owned media outlets—that's one reason. And for most white editors who want to cover black music, I don't think they really see a problem with having non-black writers write about it because they're not really aware of the cultural nuances. Cultural appropriation is not really something white people take seriously; there's no impetus or motivation to be culturally authentic.

JORDANNAH ELIZABETH: Young black people don't grow up with the *New York Times* coming to their door. In a place like Baltimore, we watched the nightly news, which doesn't highlight local musicians and the arts very well. So, black kids don't even know that a music critic exists. It's about access. Who could afford twenty-five cents for a paper back in the day when families were struggling to put food on the table? And now, who has time to read *Pitchfork*, when sites like the *Shade Room* have a true tone that connects with the black voice? There is a disconnect between music publications, black life, and access.

BILL FRANCIS: There is no mystery about that disparity. It is a direct result of African Americans and other minorities being greatly underrepresented in the ranks of publishers, editors, and producers at newspapers, magazines, and television. Whether it's jazz, culture, or everyday life, African American stories are seldom told in the media, and it is even less often written or produced by African Americans.

STEVE MONROE: I think that for many parts of black America, if not all of America, jazz has become something of an archaeological dig for those who have the time and intellectual leaning to pursue that type of thing, and most of those people with that luxury are not black Americans.

ROBIN WASHINGTON: I've served for years on the boards of the National Association of Black Journalists and its umbrella organization, Unity Journalists of Color, both of which can cite endless data about the lack of people of color in the media in general. It's across the board in the journalism business, even in areas like sports, where African Americans dominate those being covered. Newspapers, magazines, and broadcast media have all made efforts to increase diversity and have gone a long way since 1968, but have not kept pace with the increasing diversity of the nation as a whole.

More particular to jazz writing is the inequity in the academic world that spills over into journalism. Jazz is picked apart, studied, and at times even reassembled in the academy by people who indeed become experts and qualified critics; but there too the legacy of institutional racism results in far more white scholars than black. I'm immensely impressed by those white jazz scholars who have done research to unearth previously unknown aspects of the music and the composers' lives; yet far too frequently I find myself explaining things about black music to white devotees that seem to have been obvious to me since childhood. It's simply part of the idiom I grew up with and that others who "discover" the music in adolescence or beyond did not.

Do you think that disparity, or the dearth of African American jazz writers, contributes to how the music is covered?

ERIC ARNOLD: Absolutely! A lot of times the whole notion of race as it relates to music is deemphasized or tokenized. I think this extends past jazz into all genres of black music. In general, the lack of cultural diversity among music writers affects a lot of aspects of how music is perceived, what can be said—and what *isn't* said.

JORDANNAH ELIZABETH: Amiri Baraka said everything I'm going to say. White jazz writers don't have the emotional, experiential, existential, historical connection with jazz. I got my experience through following bands, listening to my elders, and really reading and studying on my own. I have some talented jazz musicians in my family, and my grandfather played me records as a child, so I really grew up with it and understood it. I didn't become a jazz writer until I was mature. I was twenty-nine when I really started breaking through. It takes time. The music is complex, and I think the disparity comes from the fact that jazz is very sacred to some; you've got to have a level of intellect, maturity, and poise to be taken seriously. It's just a strange thing to pursue for anyone, let alone a young black person with a lot of options. It's even harder to pursue for a young black person who has very few options.

STEVE MONROE: I have had to fight to get review or profile space for jazz in the black media outlets I have contributed to—and that's even when I was doing it for free! So if we can't get jazz covered prominently by black publications, what chance is there for it in the larger media world?

ROBIN WASHINGTON: It's obvious that those with life experience in any condition would reflect that experience more authentically than those who didn't have it. Again, that's not saying that every black writer is inherently qualified to write about or even understand jazz, or that white writers cannot, but the odds are greater that they will have a closer connection to it.

K. LEANDER WILLIAMS: Any time an aesthetic is underserved there's going to be a disparity. But as I said earlier, in the current climate, where there's not much jazz coverage of any kind, that'd be a hard thing to even quantify. I started out by talking about aesthetics, and yes, we could run down the reasons I'm drawn to things that swing, that are blues-centered or whatever—as opposed to someone else's preference for jazz that's less so—but we're currently at this place where all forms of jazz are pretty much neglected, no matter who's playing or covering it.

Since you've been writing about serious music, have you ever found yourself questioning why some musicians may be elevated over others in the media, and is it your sense that this has anything to do with the lack of cultural diversity among the writers covering the music?

JORDANNAH ELIZABETH: No. Music is business. The music business is run in a country that legalized segregation and is aggressive against reproductive rights. If you make music in a sexist and racist culture, that's how the infrastructure will be.

BILL FRANCIS: Even more than a lack of African American writers with jazz in their souls, it is the lack of black editors to champion greater diversity in the stories assigned that relegates jazz to second-class status commercially in America.

ROBIN WASHINGTON: What I do find consistently irksome is how a white expert in something black can with a straight face tell a black colleague he or she is wrong without stopping to listen to what that person has to say. No better, or worse, example of this is in the only negative criticism I have received on "*My Favorite Things* at 50," which was from the NPR music director in rejecting the piece for a national feed. The reason given was that *My Favorite Things* was not Coltrane's most significant work and not as deep as *A Love Supreme*. Well, I know that—and those exact words were in my script for the documentary! But the point of the piece was to bring Coltrane to a general audience—exactly the intent of an NPR hard feed—as opposed to something only of interest to jazz aficionados. You could never attract a general audience by saying, "Hey, come listen to a piece about Coltrane's *A Love Supreme*, whereas you can (and I did) garner mass appeal by making the same pitch with *My Favorite Things*—a song that everyone knows and that most people like even if they've never heard of Coltrane.

K. LEANDER WILLIAMS: There's a subjective component to any writer's taste or analysis. I'm sure folks have looked at stuff I've championed and thought, "Huh?" I have no qualms about bumping my taste up against anyone else's though. And if as a writer I can't be persuasive or convince an editor that my taste is something to be valued or curious about, well then the editors will continually go back to the same well, or remain in the comfort of their preexisting social networks and frameworks.

What is your sense of the indifference of so many African American–oriented publications toward black music beyond the popular realm?

JORDANNAH ELIZABETH: I write for *New York Amsterdam News,* a black paper in Harlem. I'm happy and write about serious music and issues. I've had a good experience, and I can't speak on black publications that don't cover serious black music and jazz.

BILL FRANCIS: Black publications could take the lead in educating and promoting jazz, as not only America's only true original art form and an important part of our heritage, but as an unrivaled improvisational music experience. But the marketing realities in America require deep pockets and a deep commitment on the part of minority publishers whose bottom line is usually more tenuous than their white music publication counterparts.

K. LEANDER WILLIAMS: I'm not so sure that African American publications ever truly felt committed to covering jazz, but the reasons today seem more about what's perceived as popular or mass-cultural, whereas decades ago my sense is that the indifference had more to do with the implication that the jazz scene was a magnet for deviant behavior or bad role models. For quite a while the black bourgeoisie didn't seem to think jazz and the blues were "positive" enough.

How would you react to the contention that the way and tone of how music is covered has something to do with the ethnicity of who is writing about it?

ERIC ARNOLD: I don't think that's contention, but fact. Let's just say something gets lost in translation culturally.

JORDANNAH ELIZABETH: I think black men, women, and LGBTQ writers should be hired in droves. There can't be fair and balanced perspectives without voices of all nationalities and backgrounds—Asian, Afro-Cuban, African, etc. Good tone comes from unique styles and analysis.

BILL FRANCIS: I have no doubt that if there were more African Americans writing about the music and being read, the tone of jazz journalism would be far different and more accessible. Think of what major league baseball was before Jackie Robinson, or the NBA before Connie Hawkins and Dr. J. That's what jazz journalism is for the most part today without the major influence of black writers.

RAHSAAN CLARK MORRIS: A writer who comes from the same background as the artists involved would by nature be more sympathetic to what the artist is up to than someone who does not come from that environment.

K. LEANDER WILLIAMS: I think that's true about anything. Only folks who think a certain way about capitalism are covering business for the *Wall Street Journal*.

What obstacles have you encountered—besides difficult editors and indifferent publications—in your efforts at covering music?

ERIC ARNOLD: The worst is when you pitch a story to a newspaper and they pass on it, and then sometime later one of their white staff writers writes a story on the same or a similar topic that's not as good as what you would have done. That happens a lot.

JORDANNAH ELIZABETH: I used to have a lot of trouble working with male editors. Now, I've learned how to communicate. They are a bit more rigid than women editors and tend to have a little less imagination and enthusiasm. They take fewer risks, but now in the wake of the disparity of black women writers there seems to be a bit of a change of heart, and male editors are beginning to really look at our résumés and not just at our gender and skin color. But men have been an obstacle via jealousy and competition as well. We as music critics are in this together, and it should be about the artists and not how many bylines we get.

STEVE MONROE: One obstacle is venues that see you as a fan who just wants to get in free and not as a journalist covering a legitimate news story; that has bugged me in the past. Some venue owners see the music and the people who make it not as real stories worth telling or being covered by journalists: they're just entertainers, and everyone must pay, regardless of whether they're covering or not—they don't see the value of the publicity and marketing from what I and others may write.

K. LEANDER WILLIAMS: It was my own fault, but Don Pullen didn't like the way I approached him for an interview at first and almost wouldn't talk to me. It was between sets at Condon's in Union Square, and I didn't quite know how to get to him because he seemed busy socializing and I didn't want to intrude. Then, as he was walking by the bar, I kinda moved into his view, introduced myself, and said, "I'm gonna want to talk to you a little bit later, before you leave, is that cool?" He looked at me a bit weird and kept moving. So after the next set he shot me another weird look and kinda disappeared. I found out he was downstairs. When I came down and asked, "Mr. Pullen, is it okay if we talk now?" He looked at me and said, "Now that's more like it. I don't know who you are." He was great after that, and I learned a lesson.

BILL FRANCIS: One big issue concerns convincing publications that stories about jazz and jazz musicians can be compelling for their readers; this is a constant frustration to overcome. Like jazz musicians, jazz journalists who are committed to writing about the music must constantly work to stay positive in the face of the reality of their standing in the music marketplace and journalistic hierarchy.

ROBIN WASHINGTON: I'll talk about the difficult NPR editor again. A hard feed from NPR would mean all stations would air it more or less at the same time, coming on one prominent show like *Morning Edition* or *All Things Considered*. Having gone this route and been rejected meant I had to market the Coltrane documentary individually to stations, which is a bit of work and a lot of time that as a daily newspaper editor I don't have. As I said, about three dozen stations picked it up, including major jazz stations, and several made a major production of it by interviewing me or scheduling relevant programming around it. In the end, it felt like the show was on tour and it actually wound up being more fun than the one-shot of a hard feed.

In your time writing about music, what have been some of your most rewarding experiences?

ERIC ARNOLD: Hearing Oumou Sangare jam with a bunch of folks in a small club in Essaouira, Morocco, was pretty special!

JORDANNAH ELIZABETH: I've been embraced from day one. I think being embraced by Michelle Coltrane after years of admiring and writing about her mother, Alice, was the most rewarding. Seeing Michelle and Ravi Coltrane perform Alice Coltrane's music was amazing. Becoming a mentee of Greg Tate was amazing as well.

BILL FRANCIS: As a resident of Brooklyn, I've frequently written about the vibrant jazz scene there, including several stories about the wonderful Parlor Jazz phenomenon of top-flight live jazz being hosted in people's homes. Being privileged to hear, get to know, and spread the word about incredible artists such as Mem Nahadr, Carla Cook, Cal Payne, or Onaje Allan Gumbs, whose music and talents warrant much greater recognition than they have been afforded, have been among my most rewarding experiences as a writer.

STEVE MONROE: My interviews with Grant Green, Earl "Fatha" Hines, and Keith Jarrett (though he was not the easiest person to interview!) were so educational early on, they remain special. The violinist Joe Venuti was another, again because I was so young in terms of covering music. I was impressed with how patient he was in talking about his music and life. Knowing and covering the late Buck Hill all those years, and Nasar Abadey, and the veteran folks around DC, has been an ongoing treat. Sonny Rollins concerts at Blues Alley and Wolftrap have to rank as outstanding encounters. I have to add that seeing Charles Mingus and Sun Ra opened my ears to more than just bebop. And long live DC Space, where I heard Don Cherry, resulting in my getting more into the freer genres of the music.

RAHSAAN CLARK MORRIS: I was doing the lights for the Chicago Jazz Festival one year, and I had been talking to Famoudou Don Moye about doing an interview with him and Lester Bowie, covering their performance of Lester's Brass Fantasy band. As I was watching the rehearsal in the afternoon, a woman wearing a light straw hat came down stage right in a wheelchair. I recognized her almost immediately: it was Melba Liston. I found out later from Bowie that she had done a lot of the charts for the band and she was just checking out the rehearsal. I asked if I could take her picture and she graciously consented. After I got my camera out Lester and Rufus Reid came up and I took a shot of all three of them. It is one of my favorite shots. I noticed people asking each other, "Who was that woman in the wheelchair?," and I just smiled to myself.

ROBIN WASHINGTON: Producing *"My Favorite Things* at 50"—in addition to the wonderful reception it received on stations coast to coast, putting it together was simply magical. Normally in documentary work, I transcribe every word of my interviews and write by laying down a sound bite from the interview subject, followed by a line of narration of my own. In this case, I'd lay down music or the interview bite, then would take a microphone and start recording my narration "live" without having written it first, going through several takes until I got it right. It was very much like creating improvised jazz.

K. LEANDER WILLIAMS: I'm just glad I can say I saw quite a few geniuses in the flesh. I've had the opportunity to hear (and sometimes hang out with and talk to) folks like Jaki Byard, Abbey Lincoln, Tommy Flanagan, Lester Bowie, Sonny Rollins, Dewey Redman, Cecil Taylor, Don Pullen, Geri Allen, and Jackie McLean. When I started writing, you could still see genius musicians show up and sit in on each other's gigs in New York. David Murray might be sitting in with the Mingus Big Band, or Barry Harris would get up from the piano at Bradley's in the middle of a tune and James Williams would sit down and start playing. The first time I heard Brian Blade was when he dropped in for a Kenny Garrett gig. And to this day one of the best shows

I've ever seen is one of the first jazz gigs I checked out: Henry Threadgill, Fred Hopkins, and Andrew Cyrille—basically Air without Steve McCall—in a little bar in Times Square. They grooved and flowed for nearly two hours; Henry's horns and stuff were laid out on the pool table. That kinda thing just doesn't happen anymore.

2

the authors

PLAYTHELL BENJAMIN, HERB BOYD, KAREN CHILTON, FARAH JASMINE GRIFFIN, ROBIN D. G. KELLEY, TAMMY KERNODLE, GUTHRIE P. RAMSEY JR., GENE SEYMOUR, A. B. SPELLMAN, AND GREG TATE

The interview participants in this section—some of whom have also operated as freelance writers or newspaper reporters or columnists at key points in their writing pursuits—have contributed to jazz documentation as long-form book authors, and as such have operated in a different sphere from freelancers, newspaper reporters, and columnists. Theirs is the relative "long game" of jazz literature, another sphere in which African American authors on the subject of jazz music remain the exception rather than the rule.

Playthell Benjamin

Playthell Benjamin reserves his greatest current writing enthusiasm for his online journal *Commentaries on the Times*. His commentaries on political and sociocultural matters, arts and culture, and sports and other resonant topics of the day can also be heard on his award-winning WBAI radio programs. The Pulitzer Prize nominee has contributed to the *Guardian*, the *Observer*, the *Sunday Times* of London, the *Village Voice*, and the *New York Daily News*. He is the coauthor of *Reconsidering the Souls of Black Folks* on the W. E. B. Du Bois classic.

I grew up in St. Augustine, Florida, in a world surrounded by music; my aunt was a classically trained pianist and a choirmaster. In the music culture I grew up in, everybody played classical music, jazz, and rhythm and blues. Music appreciation was part of the curriculum in school. All my life I have been in love with music, and I really don't make a distinction about great music—I like Mozart as much as I like Monk. I sang in the choir where we sang Bach, and I also sang in a rhythm and blues group where we sang tunes by the Moonglows, the Five Satins, and Hank Ballard and the Midnighters. I grew up in a musically rich world.

I discovered modern jazz in school. The first music teachers we had taught classical music. Then we got this music teacher who said, "I want to introduce you all to some other great Western art music." He put on Max Roach and Clifford Brown's "Move." I was trying to play the trumpet, and hearing Clifford Brown—and thinking about the fact that this cat was playing like this without any sheet music—was demoralizing, so I turned to the drums. That's why I love Wynton Marsalis so much: because I see how easefully he does certain things on the trumpet.

I wrote a piece on Wynton Marsalis and the art of the trumpet. It's a defense of my position, which is that Wynton Marsalis is the greatest trumpet player to ever pick up the horn—period. What I'm saying to people when I talk about Wynton is this—there's the art of jazz trumpet, and then there's the *art* of the trumpet. And what I'm talking about with Wynton is the *art* of the trumpet. I'm not arguing that Wynton Marsalis is the greatest jazz trumpet player ever, because it's hard to prove something like that. When you get to the masters, it's a question of what you like. There are techniques to playing the trumpet that you can evaluate objectively.

The guy who introduced us to jazz, Chuck McClinton, was from Pittsburgh and went to Tennessee State. He would tell us about Hank Crawford—he used to call him Benny. He'd say, "You all want to see a great musician," he said, "Benny Crawford, a guy I graduated with from Tennessee State, he can play anything; he can play a double reed, bassoon, oboe, all of the reeds—he just happened to settle for the alto saxophone." And after a few bars you can hear him, because nobody sounds like Hank Crawford.

The school Ray Charles went to is in my hometown. The first time I saw Ray Charles, he was playing a recital of Chopin, produced by the Chopin Society in St. Augustine. Ray Charles could play everything. When he left there, Ray Charles would come back every year and play a dance. So I was inundated in this whole musical world and ended up playing drums.

I went to Florida A&M in 1959 with the intention of playing football, didn't make that, and then I decided I wanted to make the drum line and got my heart burst even further because there were so many great drummers and musicians who went there—a lot of guys who had been out on the road with bands. As these bands were breaking up, they were coming back to school to get their degrees. So there was that environment.

We once drove a thousand miles to see Miles Davis and John Coltrane at the Village Vanguard—I wrote about that experience—we went because Cannonball Adderley had joined that band. I thought Miles was cooler than God! The way these guys played, I thought there was majesty and magic to it. What I saw in these musicians was an image of real black male dignity and power. To me, musicians were heroes.

The first piece I wrote about jazz was in the 1970s for a black musicians' conference at the University of Western Massachusetts. My piece was later published in *Freedomways*. That first piece was inspired by the collapse of the jazz radio station WRVR. I was sitting at home writing when WRVR went off the air. I was listening to "Goodbye Porkpie Hat" by Mingus, with Eric Dolphy, and then the next tune was, "Do You Love Country Music?"! I thought WRVR must have gotten knocked off the air, and that it would come back shortly.

So I'm sitting here waiting, and one country tune after another is played, and I'm saying, "What the fuck is going on?" I tried to call WRVR but the switchboard was swamped. The Sonderling radio chain had bought WRVR from Riverside Church. A tractor trailer pulled up to the place, and they unloaded the music library of all the jazz and replaced it with a country music library and replaced the people with new people. They turned it into a country station overnight! I was so upset about it that I lapsed into despair, sitting there wondering what could I do. Then I wrote this piece for *Freedomways* called "Will Jazz Survive?: Notes on the State of a Great American Art."

I was a history professor with a great interest in politics; I think about things in terms of their political, economic aspects. So when I set out to write this music piece, I saw it as an essay on the political economy of culture. Jazz was the subject, but I wanted to know: how do you determine which art forms will survive and which ones will not? It was this impetus that caused me to write about this music. It took me in some interesting areas, because for one thing it required me to define the difference between jazz and classical music, talking about the differences in the cultural establishment's response to it. Then I wrote another piece for a journal at the University of Massachusetts called "Western Culture Revised: A Century of Afro-American Music." My intention was to show how Afro-American music changed the sensibility of Western culture.

As far as black music writers, I had known A. B. Spellman, Stanley Crouch, and Clayton Riley, and beyond that I didn't think about it a lot because I really had not read a lot of the jazz literature. By the time Jazz at Lincoln Center arose, I had come across texts like *Black Nationalism and the Revolution in Music* by Frank Kofsky. I had already begun to see from previous study that there was this whole history of white artists basically stealing Afro-American cultural materials. In fact, Harold Cruse wrote about this in *The Crisis of the Negro Intellectual* when he talked about how white artists based their work on the filching of black cultural ingredients.

Then I read James Weldon Johnson's *Black Manhattan*, and he has this description of the Marshall Hotel, where all these black musicians used to stay and have jam sessions, and they would put bands together to go to Europe or around the country. It was owned by Jim Marshall, a black guy, and was down in what they used to call Black Bohemia.

Johnson described what life was like there. It was a wildly creative place. He talked about whites coming down to the Marshall Hotel looking for Negro "stuff," as he called it. White girls came down looking for Negro lovers; white performers came down looking for black "stuff" to use in their acts. I basically came to see this whole tradition of white artists covering the work of black artists—and in that segregated society, they were able to come observe what black artists were doing and then present it as if it were theirs. Nick LaRocca, of the Original Dixieland Jazz Band, got to make the first jazz record because Freddie Keppard didn't want to record—because he thought people would be able to steal his shit. But Nick LaRocca claims that he never heard black musicians play. The more authentic white band, the New Orleans Rhythm Kings, admitted they were playing black music and apologized for not being able to play it as authentically as black musicians, and they were better musicians than the Original Dixieland Jazz Band.

When the Jazz at Lincoln Center program began, I saw the outrage on the part of white jazz critics that they hadn't been consulted. In the meantime,

I came across Kofsky's book, and something he said that really struck me was that white Americans had two attitudes about jazz: if they were not in the jazz world, they would admit that jazz was Negro music but deny that it was serious art; and if they were involved in the jazz world, they would admit that it was serious art but deny that black people created it.

I began to examine this more closely, and I saw it very clearly represented in the opposition to Jazz at Lincoln Center and the way they tried to say it was not authentic because they were not consulted. Stanley Crouch, Albert Murray, and Wynton Marsalis—three black men—created that program. At the time, I had a program on WBAI, I was a columnist in the *Daily News*, and I was a feature writer for the *Village Voice*. I wrote about Jazz at Lincoln Center for the *Guardian,* the *Observer* of London, and in the *Sunday Times* of London. For a while, I was JALC's major defender in the media.

On WBAI I used to have a segment on my show, introduced with these Baroque fanfares that Wynton plays—and when you heard them, you knew what was coming—in which I would announce "a flagellation in absentia." If a critic wrote something that I found offensive or silly, I would challenge them, I would summon them to come on the program to defend their positions; if they didn't come, they'd get a flagellation in absentia. I'd play this thing and whip their ass anyway, or I'd write a piece and dog them.

Peter Watrous, the *New York Times* jazz critic, showed up one day. He had torn his ass with me because we'd both covered a concert at Lincoln Center—I was writing for the *Times* of London. Dianne Reeves sang, and Peter Watrous wrote that she couldn't sing! I was so pissed off, I summoned him. He's the august *New York Times* critic, and he knew me, so he came. I thanked him for coming and I said, "Listen, I regret that this is the case, but since your colleagues are too cowardly to appear on the air, you're gonna have to take the whippin' for all the white folks: all the sins that your white colleagues have created you'll have to take the whippin' for them all." And I beat him up for writing that stuff.

I saw an active need to write about this music. I had read Albert Murray's great book *Stomping the Blues*, which I thought was head and shoulders above anything I had seen from white writers. I used to read Stanley Crouch all the time, a person I really got to know well. I first met Stanley when he was a writer in residence at Claremont College, and in 1968 I went out there to do some lectures on black history.

Crouch was trying to play the drums at the time, and I began to see his column "Crouch on Jazz" show up in *Players* magazine. I said, this guy can really write. So I watched him when he came to the *Voice* and wrote a lot of great things on jazz. We had some differences about the music, differences that I wrote about at length in a collection for a book I had been writing called *Open Letters to My Ex-Friend Stanley Crouch*, some real serious critiques of his whole method of looking at art, which also included some of his opinions on jazz. Like his attitude on Miles Davis, for instance . . .

I didn't set out to be a jazz writer. I've written about classical music, rhythm and blues, Latin music—writing about music is something that just happened because I'm such a music lover and was dissatisfied by the way certain questions were treated; so I began to write about it myself. Of the over six hundred essays in my blog *Commentaries on the Times*, a good many of them are about music; the rest are on politics and some sports.

It's hard to make a living writing about jazz: the publications are white-owned, and I think they prefer white writers. I know a lot of black people who can write about jazz, people like Herb Boyd. If somebody offered Herb Boyd a job writing about jazz, he'd write a lot of great pieces. If you're black and you write about jazz, it seems like an act of charity, because you're not going to get paid. Jo Ann Cheatham published *Pure Jazz* magazine with virtually no resources. If you make a living from writing, it would be hard to make a living on the kind of money you could make writing about jazz. If you look at all the major publications, their jazz critics are white.

I saw a review of Stanley Crouch's Charlie Parker book with one line that said, "Mr. Crouch does not like to get his knees dirty, he has not climbed through any archives looking at the details or records that would tell us what one expects to find in a serious biography." And it is described as a literary biography, which makes me kind of suspect. In the historical profession, the literary men are suspect. The fact is, that's how they happened to develop a methodology for historical research, because the first historians to become quite influential were literary men, men like James Ford Rhodes, who wrote an eight-volume history of the United States. Literary men have different values from historians. Historians are interested in finding out everything that you need to know to determine what happened in a particular event.

Historians have ways of weighing evidence—primary, secondary, tertiary, and what have you. So a historical text written by somebody like Robin Kelley, who wrote the Monk biography, has to meet those standards. A literary work is different: it's subjective, and it's impressionistic. Much of what Stanley writes has been judged on style rather than substance. A lot of these writers cannot withstand rigorous scrutiny.

Professor Bernard Bell, the emeritus professor of literature at Penn State, wrote the masterwork on Afro-American literature, *The Afro-American*

Novel and Its Tradition. Bernard Bell describes Stanley's style this way: he says that Stanley is essentially a poet who uses his command of language to so mesmerize the reader that they don't notice there's no gravitas to his arguments. I think that is a good explanation of a lot of what Stanley writes.

If you look at the book Stanley and I wrote together on Du Bois, *Reconsidering the Souls of Black Folk*, you can see the difference. First of all, I wrote four-fifths of the book. You can see it because my stuff is under my name and his stuff is under his name, and if you look you will see that I do all the heavy lifting. What Stanley basically does is riffs. I would write an essay and send it to him; it was supposed to be an exchange, but I never saw his essay at all until the book was published. I began saying that the reason why I didn't see it is because he knew that, had I seen it, he would have suffered an egregious ass-whipping in the pages of this book—so I never saw it until the book was published. But he saw mine, which is why, if you look at the introduction in the second—paperback—edition of the book, you will see that he practically fawns over me about my essay. I view that as self-serving, as an attempt to explain away his paltry contribution to the text. He talks about how he intended for me to write most of the book, but that's not so; that's just how it turned out.

Stanley's a great writer, even though he's sometimes too clever by half—his prose can become overly decorative at times. One professor friend of mine describes his prose as gothic rococo. I sometimes think Stanley spends too much time trying to find a clever way to say something rather than say something of substance. I expected that his Parker book would be elegantly written, I expected that it would make many allusions because he's a poet—he's great at creating allusions, making metaphors—and that it would be an interesting read. But it would be more of a literary essay than a scholarly work like Robin Kelley's Monk book.

There's a unique book, published by a group affiliated with the United Nations, that only goes out to the heads of state and the ambassadors of every nation affiliated with the UN and is not commercially available; it has writers from all over the world, including some heads of state. They want pieces with an international perspective, so they approached me about writing a piece. "Jazz around the World" is an unusual piece because, as always, I'm interested in jazz as much as a cultural phenomenon as a musical one.

One of the reasons I wrote this particular piece is that I had been in Spain and was on a panel discussing jazz. One of the people on the panel was this philosopher who was really quite famous in Czechoslovakia and had been imprisoned for things he had written about jazz and society. He and his circle found in jazz the antithesis of the totalitarian state; they found jazz to be an art that celebrated freedom. They developed a philosophy around it that landed them in jail, because at one point the communist line was that jazz was the music of a decadent, bourgeois civilization—just like Adolph Hitler had regarded jazz as part of a black and Jewish conspiracy. So this guy got in a lot of trouble. I had never heard of him, but we ended up on this panel together, and it was fascinating.

When they asked me about this, I started thinking about this piece, "Afro-American Jazz and Black South Africa," written by a black South African, where he talks about how modern South African culture was inspired by jazz musicians; I published it on my site. This is what I love about writing online: it's a multimedia forum. I'm absolutely fascinated by this online forum. What I want to do is create a body of work online that historians will look at as a primary source. Journalism is the first draft of history, and I'm writing *Commentaries* like Frederick Douglass, describing what is going on in our times.

I'm motivated to write about jazz because I love the music, but it's usually a particular event that causes me to write about jazz. Like I wrote this feature piece in the *Guardian* on Wynton, and this was when there was all the discussion about Jazz at Lincoln Center. It was a review of a performance as well as a discussion about what Wynton meant in terms of this music. I wrote a piece in the *Sunday Times* of London, called "School for Cats," about Betty Carter and her Jazz Ahead program at the Majestic Theater in Brooklyn. I interviewed Betty and a lot of the musicians who were just getting started back then, like Cyrus Chestnut, Adonis Rose—there was a whole group of young people that I met then that would go on to become real superstars in the music.

I wrote a piece called "Night of the Cookers." Sometimes I write a piece because I'm so impressed by a performance. I just stumbled into Dizzy's one night—I didn't even know the Cookers were playing—and I wrote that piece because I thought it was a great performance and it deserved a good review—as in, somebody should preserve what's happening here—so I came home and wrote this piece.

I came upon a video of the ceremony celebrating the hundredth birthday of Louis Armstrong that was held at the Jazz Institute at Columbia, and Bob O'Meally had Stanley Crouch and Wynton Marsalis there. So I wrote a piece about that and put the video at the bottom of the piece. It could be any kind of inspiration: if I come across a piece of music I really like, or some problem—some issue—might cause me to write about jazz. I just write about jazz naturally when an issue comes up that moves me, but I don't regard myself as a jazz writer as such.

I wrote a piece on Valaida Snow that Jo Ann Cheatham published in *Pure Jazz*. I just came upon Valaida; she was a genius, one of the greatest artists of the twentieth century, and I didn't know anything about her—I stumbled upon her. My daughter had a book on dancers, and I wondered how many of them I could find on YouTube. So I checked, and I found all of them, and I discovered Valaida Snow. Shortly after that, I was reading Stanley Dance's *The World of Earl "Fatha" Hines*, and I came across these extraordinary things that Earl Hines was saying about Valaida Snow.

First of all, Earl Hines used to play for Bojangles Robinson, who didn't like drummers—he felt they got in his way. So when Earl Hines said that this woman was damn near as great a tap dancer as Bojangles, that caused me to sit up and pay attention, because he knew what he was talking about. Louis Armstrong said that Valaida was one of the best trumpet players he'd ever heard; they used to call her Little Louie. I saw that she could arrange, she could do this, she could do that—Valaida Snow could sing, dance, act, play about six or seven instruments, and really do it! I became fascinated with her, and that's how that piece came into being. I write about music when the spirit moves me.

In "Jazz around the World" I argue that jazz as a cultural artifact is an art form that has achieved the American ideal in a way that no other American cultural expression has, in a way the political system has never been able to achieve. Jazz is a system that is completely democratic, which values individual freedom and promotes innovation in its very form. When you listen to ragtime and you know what was happening in the history of the United States at the time, you can see that this music is the perfect music for this civilization.

Jazz is the quintessential American art. I have known, since I was a teenager, that jazz is a great art form. There were people who could play classical music and yet who couldn't play jazz, and I knew that it was different; that's what led me to ask: How is it different from European music, and why is it great? Those are the kinds of questions I'd ask.

I'm writing a piece on a night I spent with John Coltrane. When I was about twenty-four or twenty-five years old, John Coltrane came to a speech of mine, some speech I was giving on Africa—and he showed up! This was in Philadelphia on Ridge Avenue. John Elliot Churchville had organized this event where I was speaking. And since I had been a radio show host, it was publicized on the radio that I would be speaking.

Trane said he was driving along and just heard about it. He was home visiting his mother, who lived on Ridge Avenue, not far from where we were. He heard about it and decided to come. I didn't even know that he was there until I got through speaking because the place was packed. And then John Churchville ran up on the stage and said, "Brothers and sisters, the greatest black artist in the world is in here tonight, brother John Coltrane." I couldn't believe it, because to me John Coltrane was a god-like figure.

Trane came up to me and he said, "Young brother, all of our people should have heard what you had to say tonight," and he offered me a ride home in his station wagon. We sat up and talked all night long, and I asked him to come and talk to my class in the morning. He said, "I can't say it like that; I say it all with my horn." He told me that what he was playing was his feelings about what was going on. When you hear something like his composition "Alabama"—I once heard Elvin Jones tell Gil Noble about when they first performed it. They were in Japan; Jones said Trane started playing it, and I think they played it for a couple of hours. Elvin tells this story about how he saw an angel descend from heaven and hover over Trane. It's a strange, strange story, but he swears this was what he saw, because he thought that John Coltrane was some sort of angel that came to earth to enrich.

There are two forms of virtuoso music, music that requires real virtuosity on your instrument: European classical music and jazz. Until the invention of jazz, there were no other terms used in complex instrumental music. It was black musicians who developed terms like *swing*, *groove*, and *funk*, these kinds of things—real musical terms that mean something to the musicians who are performing. So if you play any of the major European instruments and are really interested in the challenge of being a great instrumentalist, there are only two forms of music that you can go to—either European classical music or jazz. What happened with modern European music is that it became a technical exercise that composers were writing to impress their colleagues, not to appeal to an audience. Some of that happens in jazz, and it particularly happens with what's called free jazz.

When I've written about jazz, it has been more about self-motivation than about an assignment. I came across this European intellectual who said that if we had continued to listen to classical music, we would have all committed suicide; jazz was this new life that virtually revitalized the European intelligentsia after the devastation of world war.

Herb Boyd

The writer Herb Boyd, of Harlem, NY, is one of the relative handful of living veteran black music scribes. Herb got his start in the second half of the twentieth century covering Detroit's historically rich music scene. I first became acquainted with Herb Boyd via his writings on Detroit and on the many great musicians who make that city one of the key incubators on the jazz history continuum. Boyd is cited by several of the contributors to this dialogue as one of their inspirations among African American music writers.

As a teacher, Herb Boyd helped establish the black studies curriculum at his alma mater, Wayne State University. He later helped develop the jazz studies curriculum at Oberlin Conservatory.

Herb Boyd is an award-winning author and journalist who has published numerous books, including a collaboration with the late NEA Jazz Master Yusef Lateef on the multi-instrumentalist's autobiography. He has also authored biographies of such historic world figures and kings of the Harlem community as James Baldwin and Sugar Ray Robinson, as well as countless articles for national and international magazines and newspapers.

With Robert Allen, Boyd coedited the essential anthology *Brotherman: The Odyssey of Black Men in America*, which won the American Book Award for nonfiction. In 1999, Boyd won three first-place awards from the New York Association of Black Journalists for his *Amsterdam News* contributions. In 2012, Boyd published the book *By Any Means Necessary: Malcolm X Real, Not Reinvented*. In 2014, Boyd was inducted into the National Association for Black Journalists Hall of Fame.

Like much of my writing, writing about jazz was either by default or it emerged organically, out of my desire to report. As a young person I attended events, including political rallies and concerts, and later I would invariably be asked what happened. Sometimes my exuberance and storytelling was so vivid and passionate that I was compelled to document these events, mainly as diary entries. Those journal or diary entries evolved into stories I shared with friends who felt they were worthy of being published.

By the time I served in the US Army and then later attended college at Wayne State University, that habit had evolved to full-blown attempts at journalism, something I relished doing and something that came relatively easy. I loved writing, and I loved jazz, and in time the two blended almost imperceptibly. Before long, I found myself writing about the concerts I attended, and, like my other jottings, folks thought they were good enough to be submitted to various publications.

As far as music writing, I had no real idea who was writing about the music, or why, when I got started; I'm still trying to understand my own instinct and desire to report. Of course, after submerging myself in the world of jazz, it became apparent that not only was there a paucity of African American writers on the music, there were only a few devoted whites interested in writing about the music—at least writing in a way that appealed to my own nationalistic tendencies.

I recall the first *DownBeat* and *Metronome* magazines I bought as a teenager, and among black artists, only Lionel Hampton, Duke Ellington, and Billie Holiday were receiving consistent coverage. Otherwise, it was white musicians on the cover and being featured throughout those magazines in lead articles. And if the subjects were white, it was pretty clear there was little likelihood that the writer would be black—that just didn't happen.

I began writing about jazz or serious music for *The South End*, the student newspaper at Wayne State University, and the *Fifth Estate*, an early alternative paper in Detroit. They gave me the opportunities that evolved into a long stint as a correspondent in New York City. Depending upon the editor, I've written features and several cover stories, mostly on ideas they proposed.

One of the most rewarding features I wrote for *DownBeat* was a piece on Stanley Turrentine and Ray Brown, both of whom were from Pittsburgh. For *Emerge* magazine I did one of the last interviews with Dizzy Gillespie, along with Max Roach. Those two assignments, with four giants of the music, will always be precious moments. Getting musicians to cooperate, and adjusting to their schedules, has always been part of the challenge of this writing. Of course, working with Yusef Lateef on his autobiography stands as a memorable milestone as well.

Beyond jazz and music in general, there is a scarcity of black writers, period—no matter the topic or genre. You can count the number of blacks writing about business, world politics, economics, or science—whether in newspapers or magazines or as authors of books. I think if the overall pool of black writers were larger, there might be more black writers covering issues and subjects across the board proportionately, and serious black music might be a beneficiary. Even so, finding a few more writers seriously concerned about our music's history and its current status could be more challenging than in other fields, since there's no real demand for it; few publications are interested in jazz or black music.

The relatively small number of black writers being published on the subject of jazz absolutely contributes to how the music is reported. With a larger number of black writers, the possibility of a wider distribution of interests would emerge; though again, there's no guarantee of this. For example, just because we have a number of Historically Black Colleges and Universities doesn't mean they will have an interest in jazz, and sadly, very few have music programs with an emphasis on jazz.

The tone of the coverage of the music, in terms of whom and what is covered, may be a critical issue and a consequence of the small number of black writers covering the music. So much of the direction of music and culture in America is at the mercy of market forces. There are very few radio stations where you can hear so-called avant-garde music, and this may be based on the station's orientation to mainstream jazz, which used to be, in another day and age, progressive or advanced. To this degree we can be thankful that some outlets have finally caught up, though far too much of the programming features artists like David Sanborn, Kenny G, Diana Krall, and the like.

There may be a connection between who is writing about the music and how the music is covered, but the major concern is the extent to which the publication has an editorial stance that is sympathetic to the music. Currently at the *Amsterdam News*, as it has been for the last quarter century, we've had three columnists who deal with classical and jazz—and this is quite unusual for a black publication. Even with that, the jazz writer's column is limited in space, and there is a tendency to key his coverage to performances, rarely delving into pertinent issues about the music.

As for the bulk of the so-called black dispatch, if the *Michigan Chronicle*, the *Chicago Defender*, and the *Pittsburgh Courier* are representative of the African American press over the last generation or two, then jazz is virtually nonexistent—and I mean jazz of any style. The most we've been able to hope for is coverage of rhythm and blues, music reflective of the historic examples of Motown and the Philly sound. And even this is sporadic and usually only presented in association with a concert or an advertisement supplement in the black press.

Karen Chilton

I met the writer Karen Chilton at a book signing for *African Rhythms*, the autobiography of Randy Weston (arranged by Willard Jenkins), at the African American gallery MoCada, located in the gentrified section of downtown Brooklyn adjacent to the

Barclay's Center. In addition to a theatrical career and her other work as a writer, she is the biographer of two exceptional, under-recognized black women jazz artists, the vocalist Gloria Lynne and the virtuoso pianist-vocalist Hazel Scott. The latter's career was somewhat unfairly overshadowed by her roller-coaster, society page–chronicled marriage to the larger-than-life Harlem congressman and clergyman Adam Clayton Powell Jr.

As we swapped stories about our book odysseys in pursuit of chronicling the rich lives of underrated (or at least under-considered) African American artists, things were remarkably simpatico between us. That kinship and sense of parallel pursuit began with our shared challenges of convincing would-be agents and publishers to take on book projects involving noble artists with richly detailed careers who nonetheless hadn't led the lurid existence of rampant dissipation, up-from-the-gutter careers, or the kind of controversies that seem all-too-magnetic to agents and publishers as sales hooks.

Clearly there was a connection between her detailed travails at getting published to those of other contributors to this dialogue, though hers was a slightly different career path. She had written about music, but mainly in sidebar situations or as a supplementary income toward her career goals as an actor-playwright.

I never set out to write books, much less books about jazz. When I moved to New York from my hometown of Chicago in 1992, my sole intention was to be an actor, to perform in the theater and write for the stage and for film. The only writing I had ever hoped to publish were my stage plays. And while I've had the great fortune of achieving much of what I've set out to do, my journey has been anything but predictable. It's been one surprising turn after another.

I believe the first twist in the path came when, after studying classical piano from ages five to seventeen at the Chicago Conservatory of Music, I decided to cast it all aside and study business management and economics in college. I still have no reasonable explanation for *that* decision, but I have since found solace in a quote by the playwright Edward Albee: "Sometimes it's necessary to go a long distance out of the way in order to come back a short distance correctly."

For years I worked as a freelance writer. My philosophy was, "I write to support my acting habit." An actor's life is a performance of pure grit and unbidden tenacity—and lots of downtime. While a writer may wait on an editor or publisher to greenlight a project, nothing and no one has the power to control your putting pen to paper. It's a much more autonomous existence. An actor waits by the phone for an audition or for word on a gig; a writer . . . *writes*. There is some self-satisfaction and gratification in productivity, in creation—even if the pages collect dust over time.

Freelancing for magazines was at best flimsy; good work if you could get it. Because I always loved music, and jazz in particular, I opted to do music reviews and features on musicians. During this time, I met a woman one night who had chased me down in a Barnes & Noble, asking if I knew any *women* who wrote books about jazz. In retrospect I don't really know why she was so drawn to *me* in the midst of a very crowded bookstore. All she said was, "You look like you would know."

We've discussed it over the years, and we've both decided it was serendipity, kismet, divine providence. When she approached me, I promptly told her I didn't know any women jazz writers and pointed her in the direction of the store's information desk. I think I even made some snide remark like, "Jazz books are written entirely by men, and most of them aren't even American."

That brush-off was simply a reflection of my overall feeling of frustration and discontent with the way jazz isn't embraced in the country of its origin, with the ease with which American publishers seem content to publish works about black artists and black life from the perspective of non-black writers. I am quick to ask: what could this European white man know about being a black American woman—a black man—a black musician? As an avid reader of books on jazz and musicians' biographies, that's been a point of contention with me for many years. Those outside of our experience have told so much of our history; that becomes problematic when it is the only perspective that gets any light.

The woman chasing me down in Barnes & Noble turned out to be Gloria Lynne's publicist, Dell Long. She gave me her card and asked me to call her if I knew anyone that might be interested in coauthoring Ms. Lynne's memoir.

At the time, I was working a temp job at a major record label that I thought would send me straight to an asylum. I was doing mundane administrative work. It paid the rent, but I had been in New York City just a few years, and every day that I walked into the BMG building I knew that I hadn't come this far, hadn't taken this big a leap of faith, to be shuffling papers, scheduling other folks' travel, and answering somebody else's phone. On the upside, I worked for a very cool top exec who was quite self-sufficient and didn't mind me working on my stage plays on company time. He liked the fact that I always "looked busy."

The very next day after meeting Dell, I called her and boldly suggested myself for the job of coauthoring Gloria Lynne's memoirs. I had about five years' worth of feature articles on all kinds of musicians—from Youssou

N'Dour to Jon Lucien to Seal—to demonstrate as samples. I submitted my materials to the literary agent representing the project but was promptly turned down for having no track record as an author.

I sent a thank-you letter to the agent for even considering me and offered, "If you don't find what you're looking for, feel free to call me back." Six months later, I was called back and offered the gig. Seems Gloria Lynne had chosen me! She liked my writing style, and she said she wanted to tell her story to another black woman. I found out later that Gloria had been working with a white male writer that she was uncomfortable with and had dismissed.

It was a baptism by fire, to be sure. The writing came easy. It's all storytelling to me. Being an actor and writer are extensions of the same gift, the gift of telling a story well whether it's on the page or on the stage. And Gloria Lynne had a fascinating life story, which made my creative work a pleasure trip. The countless hours we spent together over her kitchen table were more fun than any two people ought to have. But dealing with the rigors of actually getting the book published—the publisher, the agents, the editor, the production team, the publicists—was quite overwhelming.

Gloria and I both had a very steep learning curve; this was new territory for us both. Our deadline was in just a matter of months, so we really had to hit it. There were plenty of challenging moments along the way. If I had to give an overall description of our experience, I would say: it's like being invited to a party, but once you arrive you get the distinct feeling that no one really wants you there.

Our interactions with the publishing staff were strained at best. When we had questions or needed assistance or support, we were generally met with dismissal and exasperation, or simply ignored entirely. I remember once, after expressing my discontent with some production issues surrounding the book, instead of getting an answer to my question, I was told simply, "You're lucky to even have a book." Lucky? The assertion, the tone and meaning, were clear: "We're doing you a favor, so you have no right to complain about anything." Now what do you call this kind of treatment? How do you label it? Were their other authors treated with such hostility? Was it personal? Should we not expect a certain level of respect and decorum?

Black folks know this scenario well. There were many occasions where incidents took place that gave both Gloria and me pause, but they weren't things that we could easily explain to our agent or editor without sounding histrionic or just plain crazy. So we repressed our anger, vented to each other, and pressed on.

Gratification for us came later. For Gloria Lynne, it was the appreciative response to the book that she received from her friends and fans. For me, it was Gloria's love of the book. She was extremely pleased with what we achieved; she would read the book all the time, and let me know, always, how much she appreciated my work. In the end, that's all that really mattered.

There have been certain impediments along my road to writing about black music, to be sure. For reasons beyond my comprehension, women typically are not expected to know about music, especially not jazz. It's akin to a woman knowing a lot about sports (which I love as well); you're treading on male-dominated territory. You're sometimes treated like an interloper. I'm speaking in generalizations of course, but those attitudes do exist. So it becomes a question of our credibility. It arises particularly when trying to get interviews with musicians on the front end, and trying to get publicity for your own work in major music journals on the back end.

In the case of the Hazel Scott biography, the publishing scenario was almost comical, because at first, editors would ask, "Hazel Scott, who is *she*?" Then they'd look at me and say, "*And who are you?*" While researching the Hazel Scott biography and simultaneously looking for a publisher—which took nearly five years—one editor, a woman at a very prestigious house, seriously questioned whether or not I'd be sufficiently objective in my approach. So how does one respond to that? Say exactly what's on your mind and burn that bridge down to a crisp then and there, or smile politely and leave? I left.

American publishers, and perhaps even the American public, are comfortable with books about African Americans—our culture, our art, our music, and our history—being written by non-black writers. It's as if the black American experience is open to any and all purveyors, unless you're black; everyone gets to have their say about us, unless it is *we*. I can't think of another group of people in this country whose culture has been co-opted with such regularity; we are constantly being dissected, examined, and explained—it's so commonplace that being a black writer documenting the experience of one of your own is almost exotic, requiring a different set of rules, a new set of expectations.

Complicating matters further, bias exists within our community as well. A female African American editor responded to my Hazel Scott book proposal by saying: "This would be a great book *if* it was written by someone else." Someone else like whom? You catch it from both ends some times. Judging from the number of books being published today by African American writers, what I'm saying may sound ridiculous to some, but I'm not talking about the ultimate output (or the quality of the output) but about the sheer madness that many black authors encounter on their quest to find a publisher. It's a largely unknown part of the story.

Depending on the subject matter, it can take years to find a publisher, a daunting task for any author. I knew from the outset that selling the idea of Hazel Scott was going to be challenging, so I continued to compile research while simultaneously seeking a publisher. When I circulated my Hazel Scott book proposal, the reaction was very similar from various publishing houses: editors were very excited about the prospect of telling this story of an unsung, under-recognized musician, and the project would make the rounds, only to die in marketing.

When the sales and marketing departments ran the numbers on how books by and about black women sold, inevitably the deal fell through. They made sweeping generalizations about the sales potential of *Hazel Scott* based on how other books sold in the marketplace, about not just jazz women but about *any* black woman—living or dead, from any time period.

Once the numbers came back looking less than promising, the proposal was ditched. No matter how thorough, well-researched, and in-depth the proposal, no matter the target market or the innovative marketing techniques you planned to employ upon publication, no amount of explanation could sway them to contract. After nearly five years of searching for a publisher, the University of Michigan Press came through. To get there, I went through three literary agents and almost fifty publishers. And by this time, I *was* an author with a track record. It still didn't matter.

I'll never forget the filmmaker Melvin Van Peebles telling me, when I was just beginning work on Gloria Lynne's book: "Karen," he said, "I've been asked to prove myself over and over and over. And you will be too. So get ready. And write anyway." This he said while sitting in his home office surrounded by framed accolades lining the walls—Drama Desk Awards, OBIES, the French Legion of Honour—evidence of a career so expansive it is beyond comprehension.

I know a handful of African American authors who haven't gone through any of these travails. They have editors they trust and admire, publishers they're committed to and who are committed to them. I look forward to that kind of experience, that level of support and spirit of collaboration.

Fortunately, I felt very much at home writing both books. By virtue of my own life experience and my being a performer, I intrinsically understood the demands and challenges of these women's careers. As a biographer, you're obsessed with the idea of "getting it right." That can be an overwhelming thing, holding someone's life in your hands and crafting a narrative that is a truthful representation.

With Gloria Lynne, I had her there with me if I ever needed additional clarity. It was just a matter of picking up the phone. With Hazel Scott it was much more difficult, since she had long ago passed. There were so few people around to talk to who knew her intimately. Her running buddies were Dizzy Gillespie and his wife Lorraine, Duke Ellington, Billie Holiday, Lester Young, Mary Lou Williams, and Lena Horne. Fortunately, her son Adam Powell III was extremely generous, sharing his mother's memorabilia with me, including her personal writings, which included the beginnings of a memoir she had been working on before her death in 1981.

I also had the pleasure of interviewing people like Mike Wallace (of CBS's *60 Minutes*), who was a lifelong friend of Hazel's, as well as her ex-husband Adam Clayton Powell Jr. The jazz pianist Marian McPartland, Matthew Kennedy (the former director of the Fisk Jubilee Singers and a fellow Juilliard alum), Murray Horwitz (cocreator of *Ain't Misbehavin'*), and Father Peter O'Brien (the longtime manager of Mary Lou Williams) all provided in-depth interviews.

Getting interviews and gaining the trust of interviewees was probably my most challenging and time-consuming task. Because I am not affiliated with an academic institution or a major newspaper or magazine, my requests for interviews were often declined, if not ignored completely. It's a question of credibility and of circumventing whatever preconceived notions someone may have about your common hurdles. Whatever people's reasons were for questioning that credibility, only they knew. I had to do some extra convincing and cajoling in order to gain access to information. I certainly couldn't say I'm an actor who happens to write jazz biographies as a side gig (I made that mistake once, and I'm still waiting for that musician to return my call!). That was one of my greatest disappointments with the project. I felt that Hazel Scott deserved better. If they couldn't submit to a five- or ten-minute conversation for my benefit, surely they could have done it for her.

I have several theories as to why black writers have such difficulty chronicling jazz and jazz lives, some that I've tossed around with other black writers who write about jazz. But I've yet to come to any conclusion that I can feel good about. I remember having this discussion with a black male writer who was working on a book about some of the musicians from the Free Jazz era, and we were sharing our war stories. In his estimation, many back musicians were simply unaccustomed to being interviewed by black writers. They've grown used to the embrace of European and Asian audiences, so suspicion arises when one of us talks about documenting their story. This writer believed it was simply world-weariness on their part, that they were just too tired of going through so much BS in their own business to spend time trusting their stories to yet another writer—whether of the same race or not.

Is there a general fear or distrust of writers, a concern of being misrepresented, misquoted, misunderstood? Perhaps. Of course there are some truly great black writers who continue to do great work on the subject. That doesn't discount the fact, however, that the gathering of research—including interviews with prominent jazz artists—remains a constant challenge. Even among writers, there can be a reluctance to share information. The only thing I know for sure is that being a black woman writing about jazz can cause some real upset. You are challenged about everything: the subject matter itself (Why are you writing about *her*?), your prowess (Who are *you* to be writing this?), questioning the credibility of your subject (Well, she wasn't as good as so-and-so, and that's who deserves a book!), and even your own level of credibility is repeatedly called into question (Who are *you*? This would be a great project for so-and-so; he or she could give it some legs.).

I recall that one of the constant questions that arose from potential publishers were the facts surrounding Hazel Scott's death. They seemed to hunger for something more scandalous, more titillating than her being diagnosed with cancer and simply passing away. They wanted to know if there were drugs involved, any alcohol addiction, any physical or emotional abuse in her past? They seemed to expect and crave this kind of sick, twisted stereotypical pathology. And when I announced that none of that was part of her story, they quickly lost interest.

What can you do? Keep going. Write anyway, as Melvin Van Peebles told me. Write anyway. Being a writer is an amazing thing—a gift, a joy, and a blessing. Spending time documenting the music and the artists that you admire ain't nothing but love. It's the thing that enables us to bear the brunt of ignorance, arrogance, envy, and apathy that often come with the territory.

Jazz remains the greatest music. Because the contributions of many of its artists are so gravely overlooked and under-documented, it makes completing a work on one of its legends always feel like a victory. Even if your book lands on the dusty bottom of a bookstore shelf, or in the back corner next to the outermost window under the single shelf dedicated to

"Music," you can always count on that precious handful of people who will seek it out, discover it, love it.

Farah Jasmine Griffin

Farah Jasmine Griffin is the author of *"Who Set You Flowin'?": The African-American Migration Narrative*, as well as such jazz-related volumes as *If You Can't Be Free, Be a Mystery: In Search of Billie Holiday*. With Salim Washington, she coauthored *Clawing at the Limits of Cool: Miles Davis, John Coltrane, and the Greatest Jazz Collaboration Ever*. She is a professor of English and comparative literature and African American studies at Columbia University, where she has also served as the director of the Institute for Research in African American Studies and is a member of Professor Robert O'Meally's Jazz Study Group at Columbia.

To a large degree, Farah dates her gateway to writing about jazz to her unusual volume on Billie Holiday (2001), though she's been a jazz enthusiast since her childhood explorations of her dad's record collection. This passage from her treatment of Billie—which has many biographical elements but is more a beautifully drawn literary treatment—is illustrative: "Billie Holiday has been the conduit through which many singers have discovered their own unique sound. She has certainly played a similar role for me, for to write about her is a constant state of discovery. She accompanied me through my early efforts as an aspiring writer, through my academic training, and now she has become the subject that allows me to enter the world of writing about the music I love. She has done so for others as well."

The first thing I ever wrote about music wasn't for publication; it was a paper that I wrote for class as an undergraduate in a literature class at Harvard. I had a literature professor who was German who specialized in African American literature. His was the first class I ever took in African American literature; I had been reading it since I was in junior high school but I'd never taken a class, it had never been taught to me. He used this anthology and the anthology started with the spirituals. So I wrote a paper for that class about the spirituals, more about the poetry of the spirituals than about the music.

Then later on, in graduate school, I wrote a paper for Cornel West on the blues. There was an article that had just come out by Hazel Carby, a woman who later became one of my teachers. She had written on blues women and how the classic blues women talked about issues that the women who wrote about intellectuals wouldn't touch. They sang about sexuality, sang about poverty, and all of this; I wrote an essay on the impressions we could learn about black people's lives through these blues women and what they were singing.

Growing up I listened to a lot of R&B, and post-bebop jazz, but I had never really listened to the blues in that way; that was the first time that I really took my time. At the time, I didn't think I'd be writing about music, but those classes gave me a chance to write about spirituals and the blues.

I was reading everything. It was after I had written my dissertation, and after that became my first book. I was trying to write about the ways black artists talked about the way our people migrated from the South to the North. I wanted to see how they talked about it and everything: like, did they paint about it, did they write short stories about it, did they write scholarly works—and what kind of music, how did the music reflect on that experience? For me the music was one part of our larger culture and history; it wasn't devoid of these other things. I felt like, if I'm going to write about black cultural history, I have to take the music seriously. The goal was to write a form of history about black people, and the music was one source.

I never thought, "Oh, I'm going to write about the music separate from all of this other stuff." The music was a gateway, a basic part of this black life. My first real publication—which was a kind of cultural history about African Americans—included a lot about music. Someone who read the book, and who I respected a lot, said to me, "As I was reading it, I wanted to hear more of what you have to say about music."

My dissertation turned into my first book, *"Who Set You Flowin'?": The African American Migration Narrative*; it was about the ways that African American artists talked about migration. There are tons of blues lyrics about migration, and then there's Stevie Wonder's "Livin' for the City," but I also wrote about Richard Wright, James Baldwin—I read hundreds of books and listened to a ton of music around that, and that was the first piece I wrote on music.

The music that I wrote about in *"Who Set You Flowin'?"* was everything from the blues to some stuff on Stevie Wonder and finally on hip-hop. I had been thinking about music, thinking maybe I wanted to write more about music; thinking about this project I might want to do on Billie Holiday that was like a dream project. But I still hadn't yet decided. I didn't really have the chops to write about music; I thought I had to learn more.

I was trying to think of what my next project would be, and during the time I was writing that dissertation I felt like I missed a whole stage of black popular music because I stopped listening to it. When I was writing the dissertation and the book, I just started listening more and more to jazz; I listened to a lot of John Coltrane. It was hard for me to come out of that mindset and listen to contemporary popular music because to me it all sounded very repetitive—I was really bored by it. So I feel like I missed a certain section of R&B.

After that—this was the early 1990s—I was thinking about what I would write next. So I reread Amiri Baraka, Ralph Ellison, Albert Murray, A. B. Spellman, and those kinds of people. They were so seductive because they wrote so beautifully. I was just starting out as a young professor, and there was a project that I thought was a good career move, a kind of literary, theoretical book, but I knew I was going to be bored to death by it. So I decided that, with all of these notes I had been taking, and kind of obsessing about Billie Holiday, I would write about her. But I also knew that in order to write about her I needed to learn a bit more about the music I had been listening to. I needed to learn more about it and take it more seriously.

So I listened and read a lot; I even took some music lessons. I used to play the flute, but I didn't know music theory. My first introduction to music was through my father: he was a big fan, so I inherited all of his records. At this point I had friends that were musicians, and I would just follow them, listen to them, ask them questions, and they were so generous. They not only taught me, they encouraged me just to trust my ear.

I'd say, "What is this, what are you doing?" And they'd say, "Just follow your ear . . ." They knew that I had an interest in writing about music, but mostly they knew that I loved the music—that's how I ended up meeting most of them. I also wanted to know what I should be listening to. I remember saying to one of them, "I don't know anything about music theory," and they'd say, "A lot of people who know stuff about music theory can't write about this music; they're too busy caught up in the music theory."

They were encouraging me because there weren't that many black people writing about music, because so much of the writing about music was not really understanding the context out of which the music was emerging. Some of them were people who were also doing some writing about music themselves, but most were not. They really wanted more black people to be writing about the music. So that was my experience.

I had a friend, Salim Washington, a musician who was also in school and was involved with Robert O'Meally and the Jazz Study Group at Columbia; this was after I'd started trying to write about the music. He said, "There's this group of people who you need to meet, they're all doing really similar, interesting things," and so he brought me into the group. I had by then already started writing on my own.

I taught myself and was taught by people from asking questions. I did take a jazz class in Philly from a brother, who has since died, who used to be on the radio in Philly at the Temple University station WRTI. Harrison Ridley taught that class at a community college at night, and that's the only jazz class I ever took, once a week for five weeks. My classroom was the other writers I was reading and the musicians.

I knew I wanted to write about Billie Holiday; I'd been listening to her for what seemed like my whole life, and she really felt like my own. I read everything I could find that had been written about her, but then I became very discouraged because I felt like it had already been done. And then I decided that I was not going to write her biography, because there were Billie biographies out there, and some of them were good, but I was really interested in what I thought I heard in her music versus what I felt were the myths about her. I felt like most people—not jazz fans, but most people in general—knew more about the myths than they knew about the music, so I wanted to juxtapose. How do you know what you think you know about Billie Holiday, and what kind of work does that icon do versus the story that we hear?

That seemed like it was a more complex tale: there is somebody who left a body of work for us to listen to; I wanted to share what I learned about listening to this body of work; and then also what I learned by looking at the way she's represented, separate from the music she produced. Somewhere in between we might get closer to who she was. So I looked at her, I looked at the movies about her, I looked at the way she was used in advertising, I looked at the way intellectuals wrote about her, the way poets wrote about her. And in every one of those chapters I also tried to listen to some part of that vast body of work that she left us. That body of work told us a lot about her as a woman, told me a lot about African American life, told me a lot about the struggles that we all have, just trying to live.

So that was the angle I took, and it also opened me up to listening not just to Billie; she became like a gateway. I wanted to listen to the people who came before her and listen to the people who came after her. It was through her that I started seriously listening to tenor saxophonists, to the musicians that she said influenced her and to the musicians who say they were influenced by her. It just opened up a whole world. What was so exciting about it was that there was no closure: I was never going to know everything, there was always something to learn, and I felt like my brain was just exploding because I was constantly discovering what had come before but also listening to what people were doing now, and it felt like a journey that had no end.

I did the research and wrote it in about five years. But when I look back on it, I had been thinking about it for so long. I looked back on when I wrote the prospectus for my dissertation, and the first draft of the proposal had a chapter on Billie Holiday—and I had completely forgotten that. And then I remembered when I started looking at the stuff I had been collecting about her for years, even before I went to college, and I certainly had been listening to her all along.

Like I said, my father was my introduction to many things, my introduction to history and music and politics and all things that he loved, and then he died when I was nine years old. Billie was the only woman he used to talk about. He'd talk about Miles and Trane and Monk and Bird—he'd talk about all of these people, and she was the only woman. I think that stood out, and there was probably some record of hers among those records. I remember those records very clearly, and after he died I used to just play those records over and over again.

She was part of his pantheon, and then right about the time he died *Lady Sings the Blues* came out, with Diana Ross, there were all these articles about Diana Ross but also about Billie Holiday—so I remember reading all of those. I think it was just something visceral. And her voice—even as a girl I was captivated by her voice, and I didn't understand why. I remember thinking, "She's not Aretha, she's not even Roberta Flack, but why am I so enamored by this voice?" And I realized that I was listening to late-period Billie Holiday.

A lot of the reissues that came out around the time of that movie were late Billie Holiday. I remember an aunt had *Lady in Satin*—I remember that album cover—but there was something so compelling about her voice, so I just started listening and listening and I just think her voice expressed to me a sense of loss, even then, when I couldn't articulate it. It was much later on that I heard a younger Billie, and I said, "Oh, that's a different Billie Holiday, that sounds flirtatious." And then I got it: *Here, she actually sounds like a horn.* While I thought Sarah Vaughan's voice was just so pretty, so beautiful, and Ella's voice made me so happy, I just kept coming back to Billie Holiday—and hers was *the* voice.

Robin D. G. Kelley

The author and sociopolitical commentator Robin D. G. Kelley is currently the Gary B. Nash Professor of American History at UCLA. Formerly a professor at USC and at Columbia University's Center for Jazz Studies (where he held the first Louis Armstrong Chair in Jazz Studies), Kelley has written extensively about both jazz music and hip-hop.

Robin Kelley's jazz contributions have included the definitive biography of the great Thelonious Monk, *Thelonious Monk: The Life and Times of an American Original*. In 2010 Kelley followed his acclaimed Monk bio with the insightful book *Africa Speaks, America Answers*, profiles on the explorations of four musicians deeply invested in Africa in both their lives and music, including two American-born artists who have sought to explore the African essence of their music (the pianist-composer Randy Weston and the bassist-oudist-composer Ahmed Abdul-Malik) and two African artists who brought that heritage to their unique jazz explorations (the Ghanaian percussionist Guy Warren, née Kofi Ghanaba, and the South African vocalist Sathima Bea Benjamin). Kelley found common ground with A. B. Spellman's *Four Lives in the Bebop Business* in the development of this book.

Kelley has contributed to numerous newspapers and periodicals on jazz and other subjects, including the *New York Times*, *Rolling Stone*, *Code Magazine*, *Utne Reader*, *Black Music Journal*, and *Boston Review*.

My motivation to write about serious music stemmed from having grown up with music. I was introduced to this music initially through my mother, who arranged for me to have trumpet lessons with Jimmy Owens when I was in the second grade, in New York in 1969. As I got older, my tastes branched out, but I never lost a connection with the music because of my older sister, who also loved the music. But my love for this music was reborn after my mother married a white jazz musician. By that time, I was playing piano by ear and some bass, but I never really studied with anyone. Under my stepfather's tutelage, and thanks to my sister's prodding, I got deeper into the music then labeled avant-garde—Ornette Coleman, Cecil Taylor, Albert Ayler, and so on, in addition to Mingus, Monk, and Miles.

When I got to college and decided that I wanted to become a historian, I considered writing about the music but was pulled more into politics and social movements. I did write (bad) poems about and inspired by these artists, but not much else until the early 1990s. I began playing more, reading more, and of course listening a great deal, but I also started writing about hip-hop. That gave me the confidence to write about a variety of black musical forms. I never became a "critic" in the formal sense, but I began exploring broader social and historical questions pertaining to "jazz" in both my published essays and the classes I taught.

I don't think of myself as a critic simply because I don't review works by artists—performances, recordings, and so on. Of course, there are exceptions, but my "reviews" are few and far between, and I don't feel like I have the proper background to critically appraise any work. My approach to writing about music is as a historian interested in the intersection of the social, economic, cultural, and aesthetic—in other words, the context in which artists are trying to say something, what they are attempting to express with their music, and the milieu in which their work is heard, consumed, appreciated, or challenged. I came to hip-hop *after* jazz. Jazz is the music of my roots, my foundation, and I spent more of my teenage years listening to Mingus and Coltrane and Cecil Taylor and reading biographies of jazz musicians than I spent dealing with popular music.

When I began reading about this music, it was mainly for pleasure. Whereas most readers choose fiction for their light reading, I had a jones for biographies of jazz musicians; most were terrible, but that didn't stop me from devouring them. I quickly learned that there were very few black writers in the field.

There have always been black jazz writers and critics—obvious figures include Albert Murray, Ralph Ellison, Marc Crawford, and certainly Amiri Baraka, who may be the most consequential jazz critic of his generation. Before all these folks, you had black writers like Onah Spencer, who I believe was *DownBeat* magazine's first black writer. But pick up *DownBeat*, from its inception in the 1930s through today, and the vast, vast majority of contributors have been white men. Some have been quite brilliant, like Marshall Stearns, but almost all of them, particularly from that first generation, came out of the Hot Jazz Clubs that popped up in the United States and Europe, including George Simon, George Avakian, George Frazier, John Hammond, and others.[1]

They were usually politically progressive, often Jewish, college-educated record collectors. These clubs may not have been exclusive, but they were not going out of their way to recruit black members. They were the ones who not only created the mainstream jazz press, but they also became record producers.

1. *Editor's note:* Others, including that other notable pioneer of European jazz criticism and journalism, Hugues Panassié, who was president of the Hot Club de France.

This is not the whole story. The heart of the story can be found in the black press, where African American art critics, often responsible for all forms of music and other expressive forms of culture for their publications, wrote very important pieces about the music. I think of the writings of Herbie Nichols, the genius composer and pianist who wrote regularly for the *New York Age* and the short-lived, black-owned *Music Dial*. Nichols also wrote for *Rhythm Magazine*, a black entertainment publication that carried excellent articles on jazz. There is an entire history of black jazz writing waiting to be unearthed. It would be something to put together an anthology of the best of this work.

I was fortunate that one of the first books I read written by an African American writer on jazz left a huge impact on me, A. B. Spellman's *Four Lives in the Bebop Business*, a bona fide classic. It is perhaps the most honest account of the jazz world from the perspectives of working, struggling, innovative black artists. He asks the critical questions not just about how one creates this music but about how one survives, and about what resources one derives from the communities that raise these artists.

In my Monk bio you will see the influence: follow the money, pay attention to what musicians think about everything—not just about music—be attentive to the price one must pay to make new music. Spellman's approach shaped my approach to Thelonious Monk's life.

With *Africa Speaks, America Answers*, I tried to follow the *Four Lives* framework, with intersecting histories and biographies. The difference, of course, is that my four subjects crisscross the Atlantic, and the book is as much about Africa as it is about the United States. And I thought it was important to include a woman, Sathima Bea Benjamin, because there were so many things she faced that the other artists never had to deal with.

There were fundamental texts that served as my models for writing, but I quickly discovered that they were the exception, not the rule. I was blessed to become friends with the late Marc Crawford, one of the unsung black critics of this music; he really inspired me and is responsible for my decision to undertake a book on Thelonious Monk.

I first met Marc in my "other" scholarly and political world. We were both members of the board for the Abraham Lincoln Brigade (the Americans who fought Franco on Spanish soil during the Civil War in Spain from 1936 to 1939) Archives. When I joined the board, he was the only other black person on it, so he drew me in like a long-lost brother. I recall during a meeting break he started scatting Ellington's "Cotton Tail," and I think he had broken into a Johnny Hodges solo, and since I loved the music, that was the beginning of our jazz connections. Thanks to Marc, I began writing on African Americans in the Spanish Civil War, which was a central chapter in my book *Race Rebels*.

Marc never talked about himself or his work, but I began to look him up and discovered that this same Marc Crawford had written so many important articles about jazz in *DownBeat* and *Ebony*; he had written liner notes for many jazz greats, including Clark Terry. Before I had a chance to express my embarrassment, he asked, "What are you doing for lunch tomorrow? I'm meeting Clark Terry—why don't you join us?" Just like that. It is still one of the highlights of my life, listening to two great masters reminisce about the music I love, while I sat there, tongue-tied, in awe, imagining what the black Village scene must have been like in the early 1960s. (At one point, Marc asked me to help Clark with his memoirs!) To top it all off, when lunch was over we all paid a surprise visit to the trumpeter and bandleader Jonah Jones, who lived in my apartment building in the Village at the time. We continued to talk about jazz on and off over the years, and as a result of Marc's encouragement, I decided to write a book on Thelonious Monk. Indeed, it was Marc who put me in touch with T. S. Monk and family. Although Marc never had a chance to see the book completed, I could not have done it without him.

The fact that you have so many black musicians making this music, but so few black writers on the subject, has to do in part with the establishment; it's hard to be a member of the club. By club, I mean those able to write for the big national and international jazz publications. I think this might be changing, but that has more to do with the internet and the opening of other spaces. I suppose for a minute I was a member of the club when I wrote a few pieces for the *New York Times*, but I never felt like I was a complete member. I was there only by the good graces of John Rockwell. As soon as he left the editorship of the Arts & Leisure section and they brought in Jodi Kantor as editor, the NYT kicked me to the curb.

Thanks to John Rockwell, I contributed several pieces to the *Times*. He generously invited me to write because I was pushing for more diverse voices on that page. I never felt censored or pressured to do anything, and I always worked closely with Fletcher Roberts, an African American editor on the paper. I understood how privileged I was, especially given how few of us were writing for the *Times*. But then I proposed writing a piece about the history of jazz in Brooklyn and its renaissance in the community through various clubs, churches, and the Central Brooklyn Jazz Consortium, among other elements.

The main argument or discovery was that black folks in Brooklyn were taking jazz back through cultural institutions that are not necessarily on the "downtown" radar. The piece was written and ready to go, but then John Rockwell was replaced by the then-twenty-eight-year-old Jodi Kantor, and she nixed it; said something like, "Who is going to believe black people are so into jazz?"—or it could even have been, "Who cares?" I don't remember; all I know is that my writing for the *Times* ended then and there.

I remember a poem the late Jayne Cortez used to perform, where the line was, "They want the oil / but they don't want the people." Of course, she meant this literally as well as figuratively. It applies to the music, too, indirectly. For many black intellectuals, the music and the people, the music and the context, the music and the community are inseparable. Once you separate these things, it is easy to make the case that jazz transcends race and history—it is a way of claiming jazz's universalism, but based on a skewed definition of *universal* as "without connection."

For me, and for other writers I'm sure, this connection is essential. This is why we tend to move our sites out of the space of performance, recording, and even the tour bus, and into the spaces of living. When we do that, we learn that, historically, few jazz musicians fall into the category of the solitary, tortured, individual artist but come from a community—a community that nurtured, taught, and profoundly shaped the musicians' path. It allows us to see more clearly the process or pedagogy, or how this music and the values that go along with it are learned, passed down—and how this music is consumed and engaged. Jazz musicians play for audiences who share a history, sometimes share inside knowledge.

The last part of the Brooklyn jazz piece and the NYT rejection of it relates to the dearth of African American writers on the subject of jazz; to put it more directly, in some cases black writers want to look at questions of race, politics, and power and to place this music within its broader context. I've found some resistance to this, mainly from those who think music is pure and that any discussion of politics, race, and power is an imposition. What I do find interesting is how eager many musicians are to discuss these issues.

A number of black scholars and writers were part of the beginnings of our efforts at Columbia. There was a wave of attacks on those of us involved with the Center for Jazz Studies at Columbia. We were seen as upstarts who know nothing about the music, armed with all kinds of poststructuralist theories and cultural studies ideas that have nothing to do with jazz. This was an unfair assessment, and I remember Farah Griffin, Brent Hayes Edwards, Robert O'Meally, myself, and others getting this kind of silent treatment.

Indeed, some of the people who are now my champions did not think much of my work or ideas, especially after I published my NYT piece on Miles Davis. When the Monk biography came out, it was like I was vindicated, but that doesn't mean that our entire multidisciplinary "new jazz studies" project was vindicated.

I don't think there is a whole lot of interest on the part of young black writers and scholars in jazz. I've taught courses on jazz and politics, the anthropology of jazz, and a seminar on Thelonious Monk, and the number of black students who take these courses or are interested is quite small. In fact, my biggest frustration with some of the African American students is that they wanted to talk about hip-hop and nothing else. And those who are calling themselves music journalists and critics—and there are a lot who've passed through my classes or my office—are committed to writing about hip-hop and popular music but not much more. Our collective musical literacy is quite low.

I think all of us—at least among Americans—need to take responsibility for our lack of musical, and for that matter poetic, literacy. Music has ceased to be an essential part of our education. It is a combination of budget cuts and priorities. In our neoliberal moment, education has become either a training ground for market-oriented competition on a global scale or a holding cell for the prison-bound—not much in between. Arts education has deteriorated, or it has become, for the younger ones, merely a means of self-expression and narcissism rather than a body of knowledge or a mode of interpretation.

So my students don't know how to read a poem, and even those who play an instrument do so in such a mechanical way that they have no philosophy of music. Indeed, we have no philosophy of anything, because no one reads philosophy! Therefore, as writers we have to do two things: first, dumb down any critical discussion of actual music and music-making; and second, find a whole lot of adjectives to describe what we hear and make it appealing to readers without ever having to analyze what we're hearing. This is why the music schools and programs put together by, say, the AACM in Chicago and elsewhere are so important for creating a new generation who can *think* about music.

While I do write about serious music, I do so as a historian rather than a critic. I don't write reviews of shows or recordings, and the few times I have written on contemporary developments in the music—like my NYT piece on DJs and jazz—I hardly pay attention to what critics are saying about the contemporary scene. In other words, I don't know who is being elevated over whom at the moment, except when I listen to the jazz station in Los Angeles, KJAZ, and have to endure endless recordings by Jack Sheldon but virtually nothing by Thelonious Monk, let alone Cecil Taylor.

I know in principle that a lack of cultural diversity among writers has a negative impact on any kind of writing or critical engagement. The lack of intellectual diversity does, too. What I mean is that not all writers are critics, and sometimes the issues are not about who is better than whom but about what a particular artist is trying to do and what it teaches us about the music and the world we inhabit. This is exactly why I appreciate the work of Stanley Crouch and Baraka, not to mention Robert O'Meally, Farah Jasmine Griffin, John Szwed, Guthrie P. Ramsey Jr., Krin Gabbard, George Lewis, Eddie Meadows, Kyra Gaunt, Tammy Kernodle, Salim Washington, Dwight Andrews, Eugene Holley Jr., Willard Jenkins, and many others who are trying to say something other than this is a great recording and this is not.

The concerns I raise here are very good at trying to address that, and these writers that I've cited are very good at trying to address them. These are scholars who understand that everything has context and that what is behind the music is not just sound and performance but people with ideas, memories, experiences, and a philosophy about music in which justice, freedom, originality, and community take precedent over individual glory.

Unfortunately, the neglect of jazz by African American publications has been going on for a long time. In writing Monk's biography, I scoured the black press for material—which again, is almost always ignored by other writers, scholars, biographers—and found what I think of as a forgotten legacy of black jazz writers. We need to deal with *Rhythm Magazine*, a black-owned but short-lived publication. Herbie Nichols wrote for them, and he wrote a regular column for the *New York Age*, as did John R. Gibson, among others.

Few know about Nard Griffin's little book *To Be or Not to Bop?*, published in 1948. Dizzy Gillespie stole the title for his memoir from Griffin. We haven't paid attention to the brilliant writing of Frank London Brown, better known to us as a novelist, who was also a fine jazz writer and an excellent singer himself. There were also many black women writing about this music in the black press. Most people have never heard of Eunice Pye of the *LA Sentinel*, or Joy Winstall of the *Pittsburgh Courier*, or Phyl Garland of *Ebony*. But over time, black publications withdrew from writing about this music and instead fell for the celebrity trap. I think they thought they were losing their readership, and, truth be told, they were competing with mainstream magazines and newspapers that had their own critics.

Through interviews and inquiries, I've made many friends with some amazing artists, and nearly everyone demonstrates a level of generosity and intelligence that hardly comes across in the mainstream reviews. I can name many, but the relationship that has been most transformative for me has been getting to know Randy Weston. I've always loved his music since I was a teenager, but meeting the man, benefiting from his insights, his deep commitment and love for all people, especially for Africa and its immense history, his politics and deep knowledge—he's like the father I wish I had. He is a model musician and composer and a model human being who always has kind and thoughtful things to say. And he's down with the people!

If I were in a position where my job was to review musicians I've met and befriended critically, I suppose that might be a problem. But I see myself as a historian charged with documenting and understanding the music's history, meaning, influences, and contexts—not judging it for its worth. Truth is, if the critics had not already determined its importance, I could not make the case to write about these artists as historically significant. Seriously, who would question Randy Weston's musical value, even those who hate the fact that he consistently insists on the music's African foundations?

In my writing I focus on rethinking and revising the history of serious music, and sources therefore continue to be a problem. We need more archives and oral histories. It is incredibly hard to write this history, especially of those artists who have remained under the commercial radar. I think about George Lewis's magnificent book on the Association for the Advancement of Creative Musicians, *A Power Stronger Than Itself*, and what a tremendous contribution he made. Just look at the footnotes, and you'll see why it took so long and just how hard he had to work to reconstruct that story!

My book on Monk tries to do the same, especially when I try to give little capsule biographies of the folk who rarely made the history books—like Little Benny Harris, Denzil Best, Danny Quebec West, and Vic Coulsen, or even the better-known figures like Herbie Nichols. I fought hard to tell their stories, and some reviewers will complain about the "dizzying" detail in my book! But these stories have to be told, and reviewers, editors, and readers don't have the patience to engage the bigger, more truthful picture. It's easier to play into the cult of the individual and write about what's genius and jacked up about an artist—instead of the community that made the artist who she or he is.

For the first five years of the Monk book project—despite Marc Crawford's exuberant introduction—the Monk family was not interested in dealing with me. I almost gave up, but then when they launched a website and needed material, I volunteered to give them everything I had (about five boxes worth of stuff). This is when I met Toot, T. S. Monk, Thelonious's son, and we got along very well, had friends in common. I did not think he realized I was black, and he was a little shocked when he saw me. I do think this made a difference. And he never tried to control what I wrote, no matter how critical I may have been. But then, well into the research, I was hit by a car while leaving the Institute of Jazz Studies in Newark! That set me back two years as I dealt with my injuries. Then I got a divorce and moved west, which slowed me down. In the end, I got the book done, but it took all of fifteen years.

Tammy Kernodle

Some years back, at a jazz education conference, I walked into a presentation by Tammy Kernodle. Such sessions often had a tendency to be dry as dust for all but the most ardent researchers and academics, but there was something different about this one. For one thing, the rare African American jazz researcher was presenting this session, in an academic domain with a narrower participation by women of color than even jazz journalism and criticism. And besides that, she had a certain authoritative presence that drew me into the room. Her research subject was the great Mary Lou Williams, one of the vastly overlooked jazz masters—at least until Dr. Tammy Kernodle, and a crew of other women dedicated to uplifting Ms. Williams's considerable contributions to the music, began their quest.

With a PhD in music history from the Ohio State University, Tammy Kernodle is currently a professor of musicology at Miami University, Ohio. She is the author of the biography *Soul on Soul: The Life and Music of Mary Lou Williams*. She has also served as the associate editor of the three-volume *Encyclopedia of African American Music* and the senior editor for the revision of the *New Grove Dictionary of American Music*, and she has also served as the scholar in residence for the Women in Jazz Initiative at the American Jazz Museum in Kansas City.

When I was student teaching in a school whose student population was 90 percent black—but where the faculty and staff of color constituted only 2 percent—I found, in trying to create lesson plans that went beyond the standard Western canon, that there was a small body of scholarship that focused on the development of African American music, but that there was not much in the way of public school curriculum. I really wanted to do more than just show up and do the typical "Beethoven Was Black" lecture. I wanted to expose them not only to African American concert composers but also to jazz musicians and other forms of popular culture. I was already investigating graduate programs and decided to delve deeper into what musicology was about. I applied and was accepted to a graduate program in the Midwest and arrived to find that most of my peers were writing dissertations on the Renaissance.

The resistance I experienced from some of my professors in studying and writing about the music of African Americans only inspired me to pursue it even further. I realized that the only reason why an educated, trained professor would stand in the front of a class of graduate students and say that "no American, no black, and no woman has ever made any substantial contribution to music" was because, first, his training was limited, and he had never been exposed to anything beyond the Western canon; and second, the body of literature that framed the canon, or the central focus of most music history or music courses, needed to be expanded. So I found my purpose in the attempts to suppress my passion for writing about and teaching black music, both concert and popular.

My writing has one purpose—to expand our understanding of the historical and musicological contexts that have been framed in and through the American experience. I want to write about excluded and ignored artists in the canonical history. I don't write just to write or publish just for the sake of having another line on my resume. I'm very strategic, and the subject matter must resonate with me. I grow through the writing I do.

I think part of the problem with having so few black writers covering music is that you have diversely trained people out there writing about music and—because our methodologies, approaches to analysis, and use of language is dictated by our training—some get excluded from certain opportunities. I'm amazed at how sometimes a cultural theorist or scholar in the area of English or women's studies will get a music writing gig from a certain publication or institution in lieu of a person trained as an ethnomusicologist or musicologist. Now, I'm not saying that those individuals are not capable of writing about music, but their approach to it is completely different. Sometimes the prose or narrative takes on a colloquial tone that fails to frame the performance aesthetic of musicians in a language that is comparable to scholarship on concert or classical music. Those individuals become the central or sometimes the only black voices heard, as opportunities are not filtered to individuals who have different training or experiences with the music.

I think the road to writing on music in major publications (trade magazines, etc.) is circuitous for many black scholars. I'm not hating on anyone (trained or untrained), because I can appreciate anyone who takes the time to accurately and seriously write about music, especially black music, and not trivialize it. I also believe that, unless we develop a passion for writing and analyzing the world around us instead of pushing young people to choose a profession that's going to pay "big," there's going to be a dearth of black music writers.

I believe the dearth of African Americans writing in jazz is one of the very reasons why some musicians have been excluded from serious discussions regarding the evolution of jazz after 1965, and is why we see the repeated deification of certain artists. I think that there are certain aspects of the history that require a nuanced reading that can only be gained through lived experience.

Jazz has become canonized in such a way that many believe that we have not progressed beyond certain genres and musicians. I'm waiting to see the history expand to more coverage of regional scenes and musicians who are shaping the music where they are. Before Hurricane Katrina, the HBO series *Treme*, and the rising popularity of New Orleans musicians like Trombone Shorty, who was *really* talking about the contemporary New Orleans jazz scene? I have yet to see one jazz history book revisit New Orleans after the closing of Storyville. My point is that we need writers, who have evolved organically from or forged relationships with communities and musicians that are often ignored by the cultural industry, to continue to expand the historical context.

It's always baffled me how someone like Wynton Marsalis could be elevated as "the voice" of jazz, when individuals like Bertha Hope, Billy Taylor, Carline Ray, or Roy Haynes who lived and experienced the music as it was developing are never quoted or even talked about. I don't have a problem with Wynton, but his lived experience in jazz begins in the 1970s, if not the 1980s. What can he tell you—that extends beyond what you can read—about the rent party culture of Harlem during the 1940s?

I've sat at the feet of Billy Taylor and heard him talk about hearing a young Thelonious Monk play at a rent party. Taylor left this earth without ever recounting much of the history he was a part of in the public forums that have been granted to musicians who give you a bunch of repeated anecdotes, sound bites, and stories. The same can be said for Carline Ray, who played with the International Sweethearts of Rhythm and worked extensively with Mary Lou Williams in the 1970s and early 1980s.

How many writers are going to take the time to develop relationships with pioneering musicians? I'm not slamming Wynton, because I believe he does take the promotion of jazz very seriously, but the history of jazz will not be complete if we continue to privilege the voices of some musicians over others. I'm not going to get into the gendered aspects of jazz writing; that's a can of worms that reflects a narrow viewpoint among black *and* white writers.

Many of the African American–oriented publications are no longer black-owned. So the diverse and organic coverage of our community has been diluted down to whoever or whatever is popular. They are struggling for relevance against the *People* magazines of the world. So unfortunately they replicate the templates of white-oriented magazines. I look at old issues of *Jet* and *Ebony*, and I'm amazed at the amount and range of coverage that black music received. Popular culture in the form of rap, R&B, and soul are advanced as "authentic" representations of blackness, which means we have regressed in our own understanding of who we are and what we do.

Outside of *DownBeat*, did any black publication discuss Jason Moran's appointment as the artistic director of Jazz at the Kennedy Center? Is anyone talking about black singers on the operatic stage? No, but go through the last few years of *Ebony*, *Essence*, or *Jet* and you will see Beyoncé at least three times; Kerry Washington from *Scandal* at least three times. But where is Angela Brown? Where is Audra McDonald, who made history at the Tony Awards? You won't see them, because that's not who we as a community embrace or offer as examples of success. More importantly, in general we are a public that wants small bits of information that are accessible through our smartphones and tablets. We engage completely differently with the published word today, so in order to remain relevant, these publications have to tap into what interests the prominent demographic. It's a real conundrum.

I think there are instances where it's true that the tone of serious music coverage has much to do with who's writing, but overall I would not apply this to every situation. I've read the work of some white writers who I would have sworn were black because of their treatment of the subject matter.

Some of the rewards of my writing about music have included meeting the family of Mary Lou Williams shortly after one of my first articles on her appeared in a journal. During the Q&A segment of a public lecture I gave on Williams, her niece stood up and thanked me for my work. She said that I had captured the essence of her aunt and her passion for music. Man, it almost took me out. I don't know how I held it together. That was priceless to me! And that's because those were the people who knew her most closely. I've had a lot of people over the years come to me and say, "Thanks for writing about black women musicians the way you do; I so appreciate your work," and that's what makes it all worth all the struggles I have sometimes in finding resources or finding the right way in which to describe the music.

By contrast, family members, and their perspectives on their relative's life and music, can be an obstacle. Sometimes people have their own agendas, and they believe they can dictate what you write, even if it's not true. My earliest work was on the operas of William Grant Still. Initially, his daughter was a supporter of my scholarship (she provided me with many of the materials I've used in my work), but when she realized I was not willing to repeat some of the commonly held beliefs that circulated among her family members (because there was no definitive truth), I became her mortal enemy. My work never dismissed these beliefs, but I could not in good conscience substantiate them.

She first wrote a letter to my alma mater requesting that they rescind my thesis because it was "blasphemous" and defamed the legacy of her father's memory; then when she was ignored, she launched a tour, complete with the five-page, single-spaced typed letter that she sent me. I know this sounds crazy, but it's true! I would get messages from people who would say, I went to this conference, and Judith Still was there, and she had this display that had her letter to you, and so on. I wanted to go straight gangsta' on her, but I realized that I was not the only scholar she was targeting.

Over the years I would randomly receive these letters from her, harassing me further. I never responded. One other scholar actually hired a lawyer; I didn't, because Ms. Still's plan of discrediting me only made my scholarship more popular. But it took a mental and spiritual toll on me, and I grew to hate the music of William Grant Still. She is one of the very reasons why I and many other scholars no longer write on Still. But that's the price you pay, when dealing with individuals who have their own readings of their family member's life and music. What was most distressing is that she took issue with two pages of a seventy-page-plus document. Nothing I wrote maligned her family or her father's music. She just read what she wanted to in those pages.

I learned from that scenario that integrity is more important than popularity, but there's a cost. She reached out to me a few years ago about participating in a conference on Still, but she specified that she wanted me to present on women musicians. I never replied! I didn't go either, because I knew I probably would have caught a case if I were in the same room as her. While I still try and reach out to living musicians and their family members, I'm more aware of the challenges that sometime come with this.

The only other obstacle I've faced in my writing pursuits is people wanting to be paid for being interviewed. Even when I explain that I'm writing for scholarly journals, I've had people blow me off when I can't pay them for simply relating their experiences. I experienced a lot of that when writing my book on Mary Lou Williams. I really tried to talk to as many of the musicians who played with her as I could. Some were cool; others were just plain rude when they learned I had no budget to pay them. That attitude is one of the very reasons that I haven't seen anyone write on them or mention them in jazz history books.

Guthrie P. Ramsey Jr.

A true music Renaissance man, the musicologist-pianist-composer-author-educator-bandleader Guthrie P. Ramsey Jr. is a professor of music at the University of Pennsylvania. As an author he has contributed *The Amazing Bud Powell: Black Genius, Jazz History, and the Challenge of Bebop* (and produced the companion documentary film *Amazing: The Tests and Triumph of Bud Powell*) and *Race Music: Black Cultures from Bebop to Hip-Hop*. As a musician, he is the leader of Dr. Guy's MusiCology. Dr. Ramsey's late father-in-law is Amiri Baraka.

Writing about serious music, for me, was an outgrowth of my interest in the music histories of black people. With more scholars and writers turning to writing about all kinds of popular music, I believe it's necessary to consider forms of music that lie somewhat outside of the political economies of major culture industries. Although I understand that my interest in "serious" cultural activities limits my audience base, I think it's still necessary to highlight and investigate the work of those musicians who are not, have not, and probably will not be in the Top 40.

My first published writing effort was in the realm of what I would call historiography, meaning that I had always been fascinated with the music writers. Coming up, my whole life being musical, I was totally involved in the sound and the musicians. When I became a scholar, I began reading the histories of people writing about African American music from the mid-nineteenth century to the present. I felt like my writing was trying to make sense of the patterns in that writing, so my writing really was more literary-focused than musically focused.

My first book, *Race Music*—when I started in earnest writing about a range of music and about what I would call serious black music—was definitely a part of that. I also included pop music in that book because I didn't really see the divisions, but I had to recognize the divisions that others saw in order to be legible, to be heard. I had to show that I understood how most people engage these topics as being separate, but in fact I see the connections in them.

I was not aware of the scarcity of black music writers when I first began writing about music. I didn't realize this until I started doing the research for an article I published in 1996 about black music historiography. The article traces writings about black music research from the late nineteenth century to the 1960s. It was amazing to learn how few writers of color were allowed *access* into the major vehicles for music criticism.

Opportunity breeds the numbers. One of the first studies I did was a discussion on black music faculty in US university departments of music. We sent out a survey instrument that tried to learn what the real numbers were. What we learned was that most of the black or African American people who were getting degrees in music were gravitating toward either music education—training to be music teachers—or performance careers. There were very few being trained to be music scholars and writers; that's just not where people were being directed or funneled to.

I think it's about access. If nobody is telling you that music writing is a viable career option, then you don't even consider it. A recent example of the attitudes of those who should serve in mentoring or advisory positions came recently, when I was in Chicago golfing with a high school buddy who was always on the athletic side. He went on to play ball in college, but he told me that when he was around one of the school counselors or coaches, he was told, "I didn't know that you guys wanted to go to college"—which was just stunning to him!

Many of us aspiring musicians were hanging around Chicago State, Northeastern Illinois University, and Governors State University, each of which had African American jazz band directors. There's no reason why any of those black musicians should not have been at a music program in college, if for no other reason than to get a degree and then decide what to do with it. At that time, I know many of us didn't even think that was an option.

Traditionally, we have been funneled into music education to be teachers, and most black families who get the money together for a family member to attend school, they're not going to say, "Be a writer; be an artist." They're going to tell you to get a job, and if education is where the jobs are, then that's where most people go. And even with performance: how many of our performers go through formal training and then get to the point where they evolve to the possibility of an operatic career, then graduate and try to build those careers? How many roles are they actually going to get? So once again—access.

I believe that people, and particularly artists and writers of color, are systematically blocked from participating. It's clear to me as well that the digital age has opened platforms for those who have been ignored by traditional outlets. I'm happy about this turn. Although the older, more established venues for writing still carry the prestige of a particular brand of cultural capital, younger black writers are bringing strong cultural criticism and analysis, particularly to hip-hop-oriented musical styles. I'm not sure I can say the same for jazz; that is to say, I know of fewer online sites with robust conversations focused on jazz. But the internet has opened new avenues to music writers of color. It seems these days to be more like the days of the 1940s and 1950s, when music magazines like *DownBeat*, *Metronome*, and some other outlets were allowing writers to contribute who didn't necessarily have specific training in music writing but who were music enthusiasts that could write.

They had opportunities, and they made them; their writing is what we look at as the bedrock, the beginnings, the foundation of jazz writing. This is something that was critiqued by Amiri Baraka, because he saw himself as being kind of exceptional by design, when there weren't a lot of people writing, who had access to those platforms, who could bring the cultural sensibility to the writing, another angle. I don't think it's the only angle but it should be in the mix.

Now you have total access: all you need is an email account and access to the internet, and you can put your ideas out there. You may or may not be getting paid for it, but your ideas still circulate. What it has done is create a very robust and broad conversation about hip-hop culture. This has kind of exploded into full-blown careers for writers writing about hip-hop, and these writers are not just from music disciplines: they're from English, they're from communications, they're from anthropology, they're from history departments at their schools.

I think jazz had a little shine, like hip-hop has now, but what's interesting to me is that jazz is over a hundred years old, and hip-hop is almost fifty years old, but everybody's writing about hip-hop—both in the popular press, in the blogosphere, and in academia. Because the access is there, more writers can fill in and create.

One of the things I've learned as I talk to people about all of this work that's exploded around rap and popular music is that it's key that the music is more readily available across the globe, and across the United States—you can live in rural Washington state and you're going to hear the latest Jay Z record, but you may not know about the new Kendrick Scott record or the new Branford Marsalis or Esperanza Spalding.

As a young person explained to me, writing about hip-hop or pop music allows them to be part of a larger conversation with people who don't live in their specific locale, so they know they're responding to the same thing that somebody is in New York or DC. So that's the attraction. I asked the question as to why everybody is focusing on hip-hop, and that was this person's reaction: "This is how I can talk to other people beyond my locality, because these other things are not getting here."

I live in Philadelphia and New York, so I get to see the latest exhibitions, plays, and music as they're being workshopped, let alone when they finally make it to Broadway. So I don't necessarily have to focus on hip-hop and pop music, because I can make connections with people, I can have face time with a real arts community because this is where I live—so it's a little different for me.

I do think that the lack of black music writers contributes to how the music is covered, but until we get these writers of color in place, we'll never know what might change. That's why it's important to achieve this; then we'll know what the difference will be. I'm always clear about how commercialism and corporate powers have the means to push one artist over another. The extent to which any writer—of whatever identity—can be bought or sold is also in the equation of who gets play in the market. Cultural diversity means a diversity of perspectives, not just of a specific cultural perspective but of a political and critical perspective as well.

I think it's both a matter of writers being bought or sold, their opinions and subsequent writings being based upon commercial considerations of the marketplace or of publication, and a matter of a lack of diverse viewpoints among the core body of music writers. What I mean by bought or sold is that, if I hear something that I really dislike, it's going to be very hard for me to go to a major outlet and say that I want to write about how much I hated this or how off it was, or why this artist did this or that. So I think that, the way the structure is set up, there are only certain things that you're allowed to write about in order to get published. And I would push it further to say that there are probably a limited number of ways in which you're allowed to talk about them.

That's what makes the blogosphere a little different, because you do get this diversity of different perspectives when people are not being paid: they don't have an editor telling them what they're allowed and not allowed to say; it's just a different scenario. So even though as a historian I love to engage historical texts—from *DownBeat*, from *Esquire*, *Billboard*, or whatever—I know that what I'm reading was allowed by their editorial policy to get published, or was what that writer needed to write in order to put food on the table that week, and not necessarily some unbiased opinion about whatever musical object they happen to be discussing. What I read is always bound up in historical, political, economic, and personal networks of circumstances that I'm also reading and digesting as "truth."

The indifference of black publications toward jazz is a problem on two levels. First, many African American–oriented publications apparently have to focus on getting capital, and that seems to drive content choices. The other issue is one of education. Like the broader population, the people deciding on content issues are likely unaware of the scope of creativity among black musicians playing serious music.

One way to close that awareness gap is through education. In my classes, I make students aware of the wide variety of art-making among black artists, that it is not always about Jay Z or Beyoncé's latest records, that there are other artists, who we might consider alternative, who are doing important work, and sometimes that work is in multimedia spaces like museums. My classes go to museums, to galleries, to exhibitions as part of a history of jazz course, trying to get the students to understand the relationship between a piece of music and a painting or a sculpture. I believe that the students who spend sixteen weeks with me are going to leave with a different idea about how important it is to engage a wide variety of artistic practices. I think it is important that they actually experience the art for themselves. I see that as the kind of activism that will change attitudes.

It's about not only allowing people to experience a wide variety of things in a setting that they should appreciate because it's good for them, but letting people know how it can relate to what they already know—this is what you can gain from engaging this art practice. All I'm trying to do when I educate is to reproduce or model for my students how I engage art.

I get my most profound thoughts when I'm standing in front of what I consider to be a profound piece of art. That's the thing that really gets me thinking on a high level about things; I start thinking about freedom, hope, and all the other things we think about life. I just try to set students up to have that experience as well. It's not about trying to change their personal reactions; it's about trying to get them to understand how what they think about a great piece of art is actually part of a larger social world. And that world can either connect them to people or it can help them to understand why an artisan or musician in the 1920s did something and how it was perceived. Education is about opening students up to that. I started my blog *Musiqology* because, if you have internet access, you can learn what I'm doing in my classes; sometimes I share the syllabus, or sometimes I share a lecture or other things we're thinking about.

The greatest reward for me personally has been when students or readers tell me that what I've written has opened their ears to experience the music. Oftentimes in music history courses it was about introducing students to great work and works that have been considered masterpieces. What I have learned is that students need to understand more about what it took to make that thing: everything that made that music resound so importantly when it was made, and what has made it retain that importance, although in changed form, in the current moment. That means there is a whole lot of unpacking that needs to be done in order to get them to understand that. That's particularly important in an age where students have access to so much more information than I did when I was their age because of technology. Another great thing is when students let me know that what I've written helps them to understand the commitment level it takes to build a career in serious music.

Since most of the work I've done has been from an academic platform, I've not encountered the same kinds of discrimination as independent writers. However, I do believe that the vetting processes of the academic publication system can suppress some of the more radical ideas that writers may have. For the most part, however, I've managed to say what I wanted to in my published work.

I was a musician who got a teaching gig, fell into research, and fell into the scholarly life. I had done so little writing outside the academy that when the blogosphere started in earnest I didn't even understand that the writers were making pitches to editors about what they wanted to write; I thought that, if you were a writer, they would find you and come to you with assignments. I started my blog because nobody had contacted me about writing.

And then I learned that the writing and publishing end of the business is a little different. It's not like I don't respect those other writing vehicles, like hard copy periodicals, but it just wasn't something that I had done or been asked to do, so I didn't focus on that kind of writing.

Gene Seymour

Born and raised in Hartford, Connecticut, Gene Seymour says he literally bit and clawed his way through the public school system. He managed, against what he characterizes as overwhelming odds, to edit his high school newspaper before moving on to the University of Connecticut. There he received a BA in English literature, thus all but assuring him a six-figure salary for life, or so he naively believed. He settled for two years of what he characterizes as aimless wandering before finding his way to the daily *Hartford Courant*, where he began a thirty-year career in newspapers that would take him to the *Philadelphia Daily News*, and the New York City and Long Island editions of *Newsday*.

Seymour paid his dues covering schools, police departments, and whatever he could pick up off the streets. By the time he got to New York, he'd evolved into writing regularly about movies, TV, and jazz music—in descending order of importance to his editors, and in ascending order to himself. Along the way, he published a young adult's history book, *Jazz: The Great American Art*, and published articles on various topics for, among others, *The Nation*, the *Washington Post*, the *Los Angeles Times*, *Film Comment*, FI *Magazine*, *American History*, *Book Forum*, CNN, and, significantly, a jazz column for the late *Emerge* magazine. For the African American monthly *Emerge*, he contributed the column "Just Jazz." Seymour is currently a freelance writer and teaches writing and media courses on the university level.

He was one of only four African American writers to have contributed to the massive (852-page) and allegedly comprehensive *Oxford Companion to Jazz* anthology—out of sixty total contributors.

For as long as I can remember, my imagination has been stimulated more by what I heard than by what I saw, even though my very first ambition was to be a cartoonist. Sound, as opposed to noise, has been my muse, my joy, and, every once in a while, my terror. (Pitched at just the proper angle, the memory of the lone sound of a muted tympani accompanied by an ominous voice during a radio or recorded fairy tale could keep me awake all night.)

Growing up in a four-room housing project apartment, it was easy for all manner of sound to seep into my bedroom, even with the door closed. So when my father would play Miles Davis, Stan Getz, Clifford Brown, Lee Wiley, Charlie Parker, J. J. Johnson, Gerry Mulligan, Oscar Peterson, Sarah Vaughan, and others while I was supposed to be sleeping, I was highly susceptible to their facilities and their force.

From that time on, music became both a wellspring and a refuge, a place where I could shape my own dreams and narratives to fit the soundtrack. Still, it never occurred to me that the sounds themselves could be subjects for my own narratives until I haphazardly encountered such myriad texts as Amiri Baraka's *Blues People*, Martin Williams's *The Jazz Tradition*, Ralph Ellison's *Shadow and Act*, and the sundry scattered journalism of Nat Hentoff, Whitney Balliett, Leonard Feather, Ira Gitler, Dan Morgenstern, and others. And it wasn't until I found even more idiosyncratic sensibilities writing about jazz and popular music—from Albert Murray to Robert Christgau, from Lester Bangs to Al Young, from André Hodeir to Greil Marcus—that I started believing that music in general and jazz in particular could be places where the critical imagination could run wild and free. Somehow, some way, I still do.

To put it simply, each of these writers made music personal. They weren't afraid to call upon their erudition, education, and individual voices to evoke what the sounds they heard meant to them. If, for instance, Greil Marcus wanted to expand his discussion of Randy Newman's songs, he'd reach up and grab what he believed were relevant references to Raymond Chandler. Al Murray likewise brought his main literary men—Hemingway, Mann, Faulkner—into his tough-but-tender examination of the blues-as-catharsis.

Musicians tend to dismiss—or worse, detest—such a grab-bag approach, because they believe it gets too far away from the music. But if these writers made music vivid to me by using what they knew in their essays (and isn't that what jazz improvisers do anyway?), then why shouldn't I try to make vivid to others what I loved to listen to?

The death of Amiri Baraka made me renew my appreciation for his *Black Music* collection of jazz journalism, which simmers, vibrates, and explodes with the same relentless energy and individual style as the other writers I mentioned. *Black Music* may in time come to be regarded as a more lasting and valuable work than his classic *Blues People*. (That book, by itself, got a lot of black writers thinking that they, too, had the right and even the duty to tell their versions of blues history.) But *Black Music* seems to me to be livelier, a more distinctive expression of Baraka's narrative, poetic voice—and it brings to subsequent generations of readers the excitement of being alive in the mid-1960s and experiencing a generation of black jazz musicians grabbing hold of what was then called the "New Thing."

It always seemed to me more curious than enraging, when I was growing up, to find printed discourse on African American music in which African Americans themselves rarely if ever participated. (And this applied to just about every other subject you could think of beyond one's personal experiences of being black in America.) Most of the problem was that black folk were rarely, if ever, invited to participate in the discourse—which should not have stopped us from joining in anyway. At no time did it ever occur to me that I *couldn't* or *shouldn't* express myself about music in any forum.

Look around and tell me if you see *any* mainstream outlets with *any* regular commentary about jazz. And the few music publications that are left look as if they're nervously staring over a precipice—which they are. And let me tell you what they're up against: for as long as I've been professionally writing about the music, I've spent an inordinate amount of time struggling to convince readers and editors alike that jazz is neither a trip to the dentist nor a complex code whose secrets are out of reach to all but either select or mutant beings. (And, just so we're clear, it's not just white folks who show resistance.)

Sometime in the midst of my *Newsday* years, I did a multipage section introducing jazz and its glories to novice readers. A decade passed, then five more years, before another editor, a black woman, said to me, "You know, we really should do a take-out, introducing readers to basic jazz"; this was posed as a condition for my writing more jazz articles. So it was and so it shall continue to be for the dwindling years of print journalism's primacy. In fact, for whatever it's worth, I think it's precisely this attitude toward jazz that has helped push print media to the brink of extinction.

When I finally got the chance to write about jazz in New York City on a regular basis in 1990, I carried with me what I now regard as romantic notions about cultural reporting for daily newspapers; I thought that as a critic of the arts in the nation's largest and most influential center for culture, you would be able, even mandated, to try getting as far ahead of the crowd as you were able and stake your claim to discovering whatever trend or artist seemed ready to illuminate the horizon.

For the first few years at *Newsday*, it was pretty much as I imagined, as editors seemed to welcome any and all aspects of jazz reviews and interviews, from Anita O'Day to Cecil Taylor, Sun Ra to Sonny Rollins, Don Byron to Gerry Mulligan, Cassandra Wilson to the Microscopic Septet, David Murray to the unavoidable, inevitable Brothers Marsalis. But somewhere along the way, the New York newspapers, especially our much-maligned "tabloid in a tutu" (*Newsday*), started getting nervous about their readers' attention spans drifting waywardly toward less challenging, less subtle content.

By the late 1990s, it became less important for a culture journalist to be even slightly ahead of the curve. The powers that be wanted you to be *on* that curve, holding on for dear life and making sure you mentioned enough names that our readers easily recognized—as opposed to introducing them to new, obscure, but potentially exciting artists. This wasn't just true of jazz but of all the other arts as well.

The moment I realized things had changed came in the summer of 1993 when I was assigned to profile the actor Blair Underwood, then a regular on TV's *LA Law*. He was appearing in the New York Shakespeare Theater production of *Measure for Measure*. Naturally I had to see the production before the interview, so I made the trip to Central Park one hot night and came away with my mind blown; not by Underwood, who was fine, though in a relatively minor role, and not even by Kevin Kline. The highlight was a barn-burning, senses-shattering performance by another young black actor, Andre Braugher, who was back then known only for playing a quiet, scholarly foil to Denzel Washington in the movie *Glory*.

I went back to my editors and insisted that *this* was the guy we should be writing about because he could very well catch fire as a result of this play. But they were adamant about my doing the Underwood story because, well, *he's* the one who's on TV *right now*, as it were. And perish the thought that we should give our readers Somebody They've Barely Heard Of, no matter how great an actor he is. (Braugher's time for big take-out stories would come soon enough when his own TV show, *Homicide: Life on the Street* made him a star.) We could have been there first with the news on Braugher!

I know this gets us off the music track, but I'm telling this story to illustrate how newspapers not named the *New York Times* were becoming less interested in telling people what they didn't know and more preoccupied with reassuring their audiences of the validity of their (mostly pop) culture tastes. In this time continuum, jazz, delicate and vulnerable even in the best of times, never stood a chance. This was why I kept encountering editors who, unlike their predecessors, didn't grow up listening to, or who weren't even much aware of, the music. They kept asking me to write stories that would introduce our readers to jazz to justify their letting me write about it even on a semiregular basis.

To broaden the point I made about the insidious effect of this point of view on the rest of the news business, imagine editors in other departments and other desks declining to pay or bring attention to certain matters that, however minor they may seem on the surface, could be proven crucial to society and democracy with a little extra reporting. But these matters may be too far ahead of the curve—or, to echo what many mainstream editors believe about jazz, too old and passé to care much about. Which, come to think of it, is the kind of thing people say about print media too.

Obviously the internet is the new Wild West of personal expression. But beyond a handful of worthy efforts in this direction and maybe a few others, I don't see too many black music writers making a prominent space for themselves on the web. I do my part, but I also have an audience that (such as it is) wants to hear me jabber about movies and TV, so it's not *just* jazz.

I have noticed how musicians have taken to the internet to pick fights and raise hell; I'm thinking in particular of Nicholas Payton's provocative #BAM (Black American Music) blog, which has included savvy, sometimes incendiary, views of black pop and jazz. It'd be nice to have a countervailing voice to Payton's that was just as provocative and challenging.

About the small number of black writers on the subject of jazz, let me cite two quite different, yet equally important, books by African American writers that have come out in the last few years: George E. Lewis's *A Power Stronger Than Itself* and Robin D. G. Kelley's *Thelonious Monk: The Life and Times of an American Original*. Both are historical works, one (Lewis's) written from the inside and the other (Kelley's) written mostly from the outside. Yet both achieve greater legitimacy as jazz history because they are written from a black perspective.

Has any white critic more passionately or incisively evoked the thrust, diversity, and legacy of the black avant-garde in the Midwest than Lewis? Could Monk's somewhat complicated family life, both as a child and as an adult, receive more empathetic treatment from a white writer than from Kelley? It's possible, but even if that hypothetical writer were able to gain the trust and access from Monk's family, I'm guessing he or she would still find more psychic territory closed off.

My overall point here is that, without a greater African American journalism presence in jazz history, the intimate and profound transactions between black culture and jazz music would be undervalued, if not undocumented. Looking back over several decades, I'm struck by how much of that emotional transaction has been more thoroughly covered by generations of

African American poets than by journalists. Langston Hughes and Amiri Baraka are the most obvious examples. But one also thinks of Larry Neal, Bob Kaufman, Michael S. Harper, Jayne Cortez, Al Young, Quincy Troupe, Nathaniel Mackey, Cornelius Eady, and many more who have had an unsung influence on their white counterparts, many of whom have in recent years engaged jazz tropes, imagery, and subject matter. This is yet another aspect of jazz history that could only be brought to light by an African American sensibility.

It may overstate matters somewhat to say that *only* an African American sensibility could bring this influence to light. But it does seem to me that Billy Collins, Philip Levine, the late William Matthews, and other white American poets have used jazz thematically—and, at times, even semiformally—and that they might not have felt inspired to do so without the trail being cleared, so to speak, by many of the African American poets I've cited here. If I had the time, space, and, most of all, the money to go to graduate school for an advanced English degree, I could make such connections, speculative or otherwise, into a thesis. For all I know, there may be a grad student who's doing exactly that—and it's altogether possible that it may not necessarily be an African American student, but a white, Latin, Native American, Hindu, or Arab student.

African American poets, more than African American critics, have been writing about the emotional connections between black music and black audiences for generations. Rappers, mostly the Roots and A Tribe Called Quest, have carried this tradition past the millennial door hinge, but for how much longer?

I don't necessarily find myself questioning why certain musicians may be elevated over others, with regard to the small number of African American critics. At least not as much now as I might have if I'd built this career sixty, fifty, or even thirty years ago. As the first century of jazz wound down, it became clearer that all of us—musicians, producers, journalists, and aficionados of varied colors and creeds—were all crammed together on the same shrinking sea craft and that whatever wave caught that vessel had to carry all of us, as long as it didn't sink us.

At this late hour, are we really going to begrudge Diana Krall for getting all the gigs and the love that Dianne Reeves doesn't? Because from where I sit, neither one is really getting the props they deserve. (Let Krall play more piano and do less retro-purring.) If the latter is the best that music marketers can do with her, then they deserve everything that's been coming to them over the last couple decades. I'm far more frustrated that neither Don Byron *nor* Anat Cohen can attract more attention, not just for reenergizing the jazz clarinet, but also for their freewheeling eclecticism and witty showmanship.

My sense of African American publications is that they've never felt truly, madly, deeply obligated to cover jazz or any other serious music beyond those artists whose level of wattage made them impossible to ignore, making them as culpable as other mainstream magazines. I didn't learn about Ornette Coleman, Charles Mingus, or Cecil Taylor from reading the John Johnson publications (*Ebony*, *Jet*, et al.). I learned all that stuff from Chicago's other mid-twentieth-century publishing tycoon-visionary: a fella by the name of Hugh Hefner, whose *Playboy* jazz poll was more conscientious about keeping tabs on the annual rise and fall of jazz's fortunes than any other mainstream publication. (See, some of us *did* read the articles.) In fact, when I had my monthly "Just Jazz" column for *Emerge* magazine, my editor, the late George Curry, compared what we were doing to the *Playboy* magazine of the 1950s and 1960s.

I arrived at *Emerge* because someone at *Newsday* talked up my jazz pieces to George Curry, whose reputation had been known to me favorably from his work with several magazines and newspapers. Mr. Curry invited me to DC and told me about the kind of magazine he wanted *Emerge* to become. All I needed to do, I then supposed, was tell him that there was a great void in the lives of African American readers that *Emerge* was destined to fill—or words to that effect. Whatever I said, it worked, and though meeting their monthly deadline became a challenge at roughly the same time that my daily workload at *Newsday* became more daunting, I have no negative experiences to report of my time at *Emerge*.

George Curry may have ruefully remembered the times when I dragged my feet with a column, but we parted friends. He gave me the freedom to do whatever I wanted with my allotted space. I can only now imagine the pressures that he and the other editors might have been under to feature "contemporary jazz" players more accessible to the magazine's readers than, say, Henry Threadgill or Horace Tapscott. But they let me write about them and anything else I cared about during a given month. I especially appreciated the tough-love editing they gave to my one-and-only cover story for the magazine, a 1999 piece on Duke Ellington's legacy on the occasion of his centennial. The *Emerge* gig was too short, but it was sweeter than anything I could have hoped for from a national magazine.

It's easier to talk with musicians than it used to be. They're younger, more media savvy, and more articulate about the elements of their craft than their predecessors might have been. I remember a dismal interview

I had with Benny Carter, in which he responded to almost every topic in a curt, monosyllabic, or evasive manner. The man was in his ninth decade and had better things to do than talk with me.

What remains somewhat of a problem is musicians' belief that we journalists can't possibly be as sophisticated or knowledgeable about the music as they are—and thus we are suspect. I used to tie myself in knots over this issue until I eventually realized that, in the end, I wasn't writing *for* these musicians; I was writing *about* them for people like me who were simply curious about the music they loved without reason.

I've noticed in recent years that on those rare occasions when I'm covering a club gig or concert, the musicians, when notified I'm there, seem glad to see me. Some of them remember my previous lives and welcome me as they would a long-lost relative. But I think there's more to it than that. They're not living in a plastic container. They know how the media universe has been contracting and that a newer, less familiar, and more chaotic entity of information-gathering is assuming greater dimension and power. It's harder than ever for jazz musicians to make joyful, novel noises and have them widely publicized and recognized as such. So I'm thinking, or maybe dreaming, that whatever grievances musicians may have had against writers may be softening by necessity. I still believe there's mutual wariness between the factions.

There are a lot of things the musicians know that we don't. On the other hand, those of us with long, broad experiences listening to and writing about music can tell musicians many things they may not know, or even suspect, as to how their sounds are coming across to the audiences who still show up, paying their admission, buying drinks, and awaiting transport. In this still-nascent age of digital everything, musicians and journalists need to let down their force fields to lower frequencies and recognize that we're all in the same small, jammed, imperiled boat trying to keep it from being swamped or sunk. That's how I see it now; in a couple years I may feel altogether different.

It seems that access to any and all cultural outlets—mainstream, boutique, online, or analog—is more limited than it's ever been in my lifetime. And where it was once true that you had readers who were always attentive to whatever stirrings could be found in the more obscure and eclectic corners of music, I'm not sure we live in that world anymore, beyond whatever somebody finds popping up on any number of "delivery systems"—or what I call water-based forces such as clouds, streams, and so on. In short, I don't know exactly where editors and publishers believe the "cutting edge" of anything is any more, and the scourge of social media has leveled things off to such an extent that it's just as easy for an opinion, informed or not (likely the latter), to get shot down in midair before it even has a chance to settle and grow in people's minds.

There's far less money, and maybe a little more love, involved with covering jazz than with the movies. The stakes are higher, the pressure greater in the more prominent realms of show business than they are in jazz. And that relative lack of size and pressure may allow for more collegiality between journalists and artists in this field. I like to think that there's a recognition among all of us in jazz, from the club owners to the school masters to the booking agents to the music distributors to the record producers to the musicians to the unions to the historians to the bloggers and onward, that despite our differences, we're all involved in keeping this delicate, beautiful flower called jazz fed, watered, warmed, and, whenever necessary, shaded.

A. B. Spellman

Throughout our ongoing series of dialogues with African American music journalists, critics, and authors, several key books and writers have been common citations for their mentoring influence on succeeding generations of black music writers. One such writer and one such volume is A. B. Spellman and his essential 1966 book *Four Lives in the Bebop Business* (reprinted originally as *Black Music: Four Lives*, and more recently reprinted as *Four Lives*). The book profiled four somewhat disparate artists: the pianist Cecil Taylor, the saxophonist Ornette Coleman, the saxophonist Jackie McLean, and the pianist Herbie Nichols. Spellman discovered common threads between them, not least of which was initial public neglect of their immense artistry.

Another contributor to this book, Professor Robin D. G. Kelley, author of the seminal Thelonious Monk biography, directly credits Spellman for the four-artist profile methodology which Kelley subsequently engaged in his exceptional book *Africa Speaks, America Answers*.

In the case of the Herbie Nichols chapter in *Four Lives*, at least up until Mark Miller's informative 2009 book *Herbie Nichols: A Jazzist's Life*, Spellman's dialogue with Nichols remained the definitive piece on this somewhat mysterious, neglected pianist-composer, whose writings are represented in the anthology section of this book.

Since Spellman's interview with Nichols, at least one group of contemporary musicians—the Herbie Nichols Project, originally led by the late pianist Frank

Kimbrough—made a point of investigating and performing the modest but unfailingly rich book of compositions that the pianist left here for us to learn. The case could be made that, absent Spellman's *Four Lives* chapter on Nichols, the pianist may have faded still deeper into obscurity. Even Mark Miller's book is rife with references to Spellman's interview.

A North Carolina native and a graduate of Howard University (where fellow poet and erstwhile jazz writer-commentator LeRoi Jones, later known as Amiri Baraka, was a classmate and a running buddy), Spellman first published as a poet, the 1964 book entitled *The Beautiful Days*. His most recent volume of poetry is *Things I Must Have Known*. He taught African American studies at Harvard from 1972 to 1975 and subsequently embarked on a long and fruitful career as a high-level administrator at the National Endowment for the Arts (1975–2005) during which time he championed jazz music and jazz musicians.

While at the NEA, Spellman was a particularly influential voice in the Endowment's development of the NEA Jazz Masters program, which since 1982 has been the highest honor the United States bestows upon master-level jazz practitioners. On Spellman's retirement from the Endowment, the NEA chair Dana Gioia designated a new advocacy category of the Jazz Masters program as the A. B. Spellman Award in recognition of those who have achieved jazz mastery in advocacy and support roles beyond the bandstand. Ironically, three such recipients have been former *DownBeat* magazine contributors and editors: Nat Hentoff, Dan Morgenstern, and Ira Gitler—Morgenstern having first invited Spellman's initial *DownBeat* contributions.

The witty, erudite A. B. Spellman's career as a music journalist (he is careful to make the distinction between journalist and critic) began in 1958 and included stints at *Metronome* and *DownBeat* magazines, among the mainstream jazz prints. He wrote for LeRoi Jones's journal *The Cricket* and for a time published his own *Rhythm* magazine, though that publication was not about music.

The simple answer as to what motivated me to write about serious music, in the beginning, is that I discovered that I could write about music and I had the opportunity. LeRoi Jones (aka Amiri Baraka) introduced me to Dan Morgenstern, who was then the editor of *DownBeat* (circa the late 1950s, early 1960s), and Dan let me write a piece introducing Archie Shepp, then made me a regular reviewer.

You know the old saw that, if you remember the 1960s, you probably weren't there? Well I was there, but I truly have no recollection of the editors at *DB* or how I went about placing articles. I only remember writing record reviews for them and can't name the specific records. I think I got a lot of the "out" records. I have a much better memory of *Metronome* because I had a more personal relationship with Dan Morgenstern, who gave me my first shot at jazz writing. I never thought I was a token black writer, though I was very much aware that LeRoi Jones and I were the only black jazz writers on the scene.

A new and stronger motivation set in with the so-called "New Thing," which was resisted mightily by the mainstream critics who had defended bebop. I'd leave the Jazz Gallery or the Village Vanguard limp in the knees after having John Coltrane blow my sinuses out, only to subsequently read in *DownBeat* how unmusical, even destructive of jazz, his playing was! I could only conclude that either I was tone deaf or those cats were, and I trusted my ear; so I wrote in self-defense. I wrote one line in particular that was quoted often: "What does anti-jazz mean and who are these ofays who've declared themselves the guardians of last year's blues?"

I believe that was my first record review. Shortly thereafter I decided to stop reviewing LPs that I didn't like and to put my energy into advancing good music—unless, perhaps, it was something that the jazz press was making too big a deal about.

I seldom went to the DB office, so I never discussed the Trane differences with them. I did write a piece in the *Kultur* quarterly that Jones edited in which I wrote about a concert of Coltrane's in the context of the anti-jazz controversy. My line about "last year's blues" was a good line, I think. I also quoted the DB review of *Now Is the Time*, which acerbically put down Bird, Miles, and Max Roach.

I stopped writing about jazz because I was frustrated by my limitations. I didn't know enough music to do the kind of technical analysis that I thought was needed. What I was writing seemed to me to be at best journalism, at worst fan mail, so I cut it loose and hoped that some other brothers would step in. Sorry, but I don't see a lot of other brothers with musical backgrounds who are picking up the slack. There are some academics, like the group around the *Black Music Research Journal* in Chicago; I'd like to see their prose in a popular journal where they wouldn't have to write in such a dry manner.

When I first started writing about jazz, of course I was aware of the shortage of black writers covering the music. There was me, LeRoi Jones (not yet Baraka), some of the belles lettres pieces of Ralph Ellison and Albert Murray, and not much else. I'm not sure why that's still such a disparity: the number of significant black musicians making serious music versus so few black writers on the subject. There are people who are competent to write sound criticism in the colleges and universities; I'm thinking about folk like those who publish in the *Journal of Black Music*—but they stick to the academics. There are more conservatory-trained African Americans now than there ever have been, but they don't write. Black jazz musicians don't write either—and they should!

Billy Taylor's book on piano jazz was very thoughtful, very useful. James Reese Europe wrote some things. Bill Dixon, who used to work with Archie Shepp and organized the October Revolution in Jazz, has written. Of course we can't forget George Russell's writings on theory. I was very impressed with George Lewis's *A Power Stronger Than Itself*, about the Association for the Advancement of Creative Musicians (AACM), a book with true depth and scope. He didn't leave it to some outsider to write that history, to his great credit.

With *Four Lives in the Bebop Business*, I chose Ornette Coleman and Cecil Taylor to profile because I thought that the avant-garde needed to have its champions defended, that there was not enough consideration given to how serious art was made in the environment that jazz musicians inhabited. Jackie McLean, I thought, was a bridge between the avant-garde and mainstream jazz, especially considering the music that Jackie was making in the mid-1960s. I thought that Herbie Nichols was in danger of being forgotten.

As to whether the lack of African American writers contributes to how the music is covered: it certainly does. This is not to slam the many good white authors who have written about the music; without them there'd be very little documentation at all. But damn! This is music that came out of us; this is our synthesis and exposition of our American urban presence; but except for some extremely valuable autobiographies, for the most part intermediated by whites, the people who have lived closest to the experiences of the major makers of jazz have been silent. The opportunity is diminishing as the potential inventory of African American critics is rising, as the black documentation in jazz is declining with each generation, for the jazz training opportunities for school-aged whites by far exceeds those for blacks.

All art criticism is subjective, no matter how objective connoisseurs pretend to be. Put another way, criticism is essentially the defense of taste, and taste is a cop and blow proposition, as we used to say. A diversity of writers would make for a diversity of opinions, which would give readers choices, which would affect the roster of success. Any way you cut it, there really is no truly objective response to such a subjective medium as art.

I know, there have been artists who tried to make art objectively, as well as critics like the structuralists and deconstructionists who tried to be objective in their analyses, but I don't buy it. There are too many approaches to making music for anyone to stand outside of everything and claim a complete rationality of judgment, too many ways of making jazz. Sooner or later we all come back to standards of some kind, and where do these standards come from? Some undiscovered corner of our brains? I know that there are some very good musicians playing smooth jazz, and there's an enormous audience for it, but I can't imagine trying to make critical choices about it because I just don't like it. I've never seen a critic write, "I hated this concert because I don't like this kind of music, but it was very good nonetheless."

As far as the absence of jazz writing in the African American–oriented prints, the answer is obvious: the African American commercial press is out to make money like the rest of the commercial press, and the money is with popular culture. The not-for-profit black press is small and poorly subscribed. That's our fault for not supporting it.

I moved to Atlanta for a while in 1967, which pretty much cut me off from jazz sources, though it did gain me a terrific wife. That was the biggest part of the reason that I never finished the Billie Holiday book, the other being that I stopped liking her as a person the more I learned about her. Soon thereafter I was at the NEA, which didn't leave me any time to write.

During my time writing about serious music, as far as rewarding experiences, nothing compares with having experienced John Coltrane live. I've written about that so much that I'm reluctant to go over it again. I would also add the following names: Lucky Thompson, Sonny Clark, Fats Navarro, Hassan Ibn Ali, Wynton Kelly, Tina Brooks, and Martial Solal—I'll try not to wake up tomorrow with more names in my mind!

Greg Tate

The late Greg Tate (who joined the ancestors in 2021), in addition to his writing exploits, was the leader of the burning, probing, inquisitive, boundary-free ensemble known as Burnt Sugar, which grew out of the Black Rock Coalition, which Tate cofounded. As a writer, Greg wrote for a variety of publications; his byline became quite prominent during his days as a frequent contributor to the *Village Voice*, where he was a staff writer from 1987 to 2003.

In his later years Tate taught a course on Amiri Baraka's music writing. The class was called "The Loud, Black, and Proud Musicology of Amiri Baraka" at Yale University. The course engaged Baraka's books *Blues People*, *Black Music*, and *Dig*. A steadfast chronicler of many forms of black music, Greg Tate was indeed a journalist-provocateur. Two collections of his writings have been published by Duke University Press: *Flyboy in the Buttermilk: Essays on Contemporary America* (2015), and *Flyboy 2: The Greg Tate Reader* (2016).

Reading Amiri Baraka's book *Black Music* and *Rolling Stone* magazine when I was about fourteen encouraged me to become a vinyl collector and a music journalist. I was very aware of the lack of black music writers, because in my teens I came to know who all the black journalists who had ever written for *DownBeat* were: Baraka, A. B. Spellman, Bill Quinn, and W. A. Brower. Being a DC native, I knew about the *Washington Post*'s Hollie West, and I knew Phyl Garland had done some things at *Ebony*. But even on the R&B/hip-hop side, outside of the black press there are few black music writers being published.

To this day I think *Rolling Stone* hasn't published more than five black writers in its history—Nelson George, Cheo Coker, Touré, myself . . . The *New York Times* still has never had a regular black jazz writer.

I think the lack of black music writers is because, by and large, music editors aren't interested in diversifying their writer rosters. Hip-hop music, when it was younger and fresher, marked the first time in African American history where the majority of writers covering it for the *Voice*, the *Source*, and *Vibe* were black. The ratio there flipped once corporate interests took control over the creative aspects of that music—so that now, at many major hip-hop publications, the writers are non-black.

The cultural ignorance of non-blacks about black culture and hip-hop created openings and opportunities for black writers at the birth of hip-hop, when the fan base was largely black. Once that changed and the music became more predictable and redundant, the most talented, most thoughtful black hip-hop writers became less interested in writing about it.

I think what's interesting is that even when I was at the *Voice*, none of us—with the exception of maybe Stanley Crouch and Nelson George—had really ever decided on music journalism as a career. Even with those guys, it was pretty typical of the group of writers I came in with that people would branch out into writing about film or music, or take on book projects, become editors of magazines, start magazines—so it was a pretty intellectually and creatively diverse group.

You look at someone like Thulani Davis, who is a novelist and a playwright, has written librettos for composer Anthony Davis, and who has had pieces produced at the Public Theater. Look at Lisa Jones, Amiri Baraka's daughter: she's a scriptwriter who wrote things that got produced, and she also wrote four of Spike Lee's making-of books, including the one on *Do the Right Thing*. Scott Coulson-Bryant was instrumental in the formation of *Vibe* magazine. Dream Hampton is considered one of the premier hip-hop writers of her generation, but she came to New York to go to NYU film school. She's made a few films and she's done a lot of the writing for the BET Awards show. So that group, as they matured, it seems like the development of the kind of hip-hop they were interested in writing about began to diminish—so folks just moved on to other forms of written expression.

Of course with jazz, the problem is that so few educated African Americans even support it—preferring black pop over jazz; this is somewhat analogous to the Ivy League–educated Euro-Americans who would consider themselves stupid for not knowing what Richard Serra or Gerhard Richter are up to, yet feel no shame in not keeping up with the symphonic tradition.

Certainly Cornel West refers to himself as an "intellectual jazz man," and you have other people like Houston Baker, who has written a book on the blues and critical theory. Robin Kelley is another one: he wrote the book on Thelonious Monk. I'm thinking of that generation that came through, whose intellectual maturity occurred in the 1970s, when you pretty much understood black music, particularly jazz, to be part of the black liberation project. I think that was very much the thinking of that age, and it really manifested itself in the music itself, in the post-Coltrane music that was being made on the funkier side of fusion—Herbie Hancock, Norman Connors, and a lot of the collectives like the Tribe, the Awakening, Doug and Jean Carn, Horace Tapscott, and so forth. But I think people very much had the sense of the music being at the center, and even at the front lines, of the grassroots politics of the era. Of course Baraka had a huge impact on a whole generation of black intellectuals' thinking about the music as being "political" and being indelibly connected to what we call struggle and movement.

I think who is writing—and the lack of black writers—affects all aspects of the news! But the real problem with jazz is that it's no longer a form of expression where what black musicians do or don't do matters to most black Americans. Jazz has more meaning for black Americans as a history lesson than as a living, breathing cultural experience. It's not on black radio or TV programs, or in black schools, neighborhoods, or churches, so it's pretty irrelevant as far as the modern black experience goes. The question is how much longer contemporary jazz will even be considered a "black" art form in America. The notion of black jazz actually has more weight in London now than in the fifty states of the union. The lack of cultural diversity among music writers is an editorial politics problem. Wynton and the Jazz at Lincoln Center guys make all the real money in American jazz; I don't know that any jazz musicians not in that band, regardless of skin color, will ever make what those cats make, not even if they had three lifetimes.

Jazz might as well be dead as far as the majority of black Americans at every class level are concerned. If culture is defined as what people do, then we can say that, in significant numbers, black people don't do jazz anymore.

If you talk to some of those elder black folks who do come out—especially when it's a free situation like the Charlie Parker Jazz Festival or the Clifford Brown Jazz Festival, they'll tell you that they don't go to jazz clubs, not because of economics but because they feel alienated by the environment; it does not feel like the environment in which they came to love, appreciate, support, and engage with the music—I'm talking specifically about the clubs downtown, because if I'm going to support contemporary jazz musicians it's going to be at a Village Vanguard, a Smoke, and so forth.

But what's great about what's happened in the last ten years in Harlem is that there's just more venues now that actually do provide occasions for folks to hear jazz, whether it's the Apollo's salon program, or Harlemstage, or the Schomburg—and then some of the newer venues as well, like Red Rooster, do jazz practically every night. Certainly, in terms of Harlem, the situation has changed.

My parents are from the Memphis of the 1940s and 1950s, when Beale Street was hot, and my mother went to high school with Phineas Newborn, Frank Strozier, Hank Crawford, George Coleman, and Charles Lloyd. Pops said, "When we were coming up, the musicians were not placed on a pedestal above the community, they were part of the community, and you went to see them, and they were in the black community." You could go to a bill with like six or seven acts for a dollar. I think economics is a factor for some black folks, but if Beyoncé is playing at one of the stadiums in New Jersey or somewhere, folks will save up for that $200–$300 ticket—that will be where their entertainment dollar will go. We find the money to support the things that we have a taste for. I think the economic question is not so much, what's the problem?—I think there's just something about the way jazz has been separated from the black community's consciousness in terms of culture.

One of the things that Baraka and those guys did in the 1950s is they brought Archie Shepp and Sun Ra uptown to play on flatbed trucks, and folks were digging it. I grew up in DC, so I grew up hearing all the music of all eras in a black context—whether it was going to see Cecil Taylor or Basie at the Smithsonian, or going outside to hear Dexter Gordon or Betty Carter at Fort Dupont Park, or going to see Al Green at Carter Barron, there was just live music all over the place. The first place I saw Sun Ra was at a joint across the street from Howard University called Ed Murphy's Supper Club, and it was full of folks from the community. The New York experience of supporting the music has been very different. We lost a lot of those venues because of economics, gentrification—now there seems to be a swing in the other direction, so there are places in some of our major urban centers for folks to go and hear the music. Certainly in New York we've seen a real turnaround.

But also look at the Kamasi Washington situation, which just points to the fact that, at the end of the day, it's really going to be the musicians who turn the tide through how they connect with their particular generation. The thing with Kamasi is, with a lot of us who follow the jazz press, we read the articles, and a lot of the musicians also saw the press; but a lot of the younger people I know listen to NPR, and when *The Epic* came out, they went out and got the three-album set and that's all they played every morning. That's got nothing to do with hype, because certainly, as hard as a lot of us have been trying to hype people—if that's all you needed, a whole bunch of cats would be better known. But there was something about Kamasi's music. That music is not a jazz/hip-hop hybrid; Kamasi is coming right out of the music of Sun Ra, Horace Tapscott, Pharoah Sanders, McCoy Tyner, Charles Tolliver—Kamasi is coming right out of that 1970s tradition, what people now call spiritual jazz, cosmic jazz, or pan-African jazz.

Kamasi just picked that up, and that was the aesthetic. Those brothers could have gone a lot of ways with the music, and they chose something that is really reflective of the neighborhood, if you think about it. They're really playing the Leimert Park tradition. It's in the oral tradition of the music, the music being what my father talked about as a community enterprise. When I went to see Kamasi at the Blue Note, I said, "Man, I ain't seen this many folks under thirty coming to see anything at the Blue Note, probably since Wynton Marsalis, Steve Coleman first came out." But I think that's where you get into the real mystical qualities of the music, because I think those things are the community source, something that's coming through that music that is really attracting younger folks too.

Not to be vague, but I'd say that the way and tone of how serious music is covered has to do with who's writing about it—which is true of any writing about anything; if you're asking whether a black or a white writer is covering the music, I'd say look to the individual before the ethnicity.

My interviews with Miles Davis, Ornette Coleman, Wayne Shorter, Marion Brown, Henry Threadgill, Dexter Gordon, and Betty Carter were highlights of my writing career. Pulling together a tribute page to Lester Bowie, after he passed—which involved many of his generational cronies, like Don Moye, Oliver Lake, Henry Threadgill, and Butch Morris, respected elders such as Max Roach, and Lester's wife Deborah and his good friend Thulani Davis—was another high point.

I can't say I've encountered any real obstacles in writing about serious music. I've been pretty blessed, since I spent most of my music-writing career at a publication that for years had two of America's best jazz journalists (Stanley Crouch and Gary Giddins) on staff: the old-school version of the *Village Voice*.

3

black jazz magazine editors
and publishers

JO ANN CHEATHAM (*PURE JAZZ*), JIM HARRISON
(*JAZZ SPOTLITE NEWS*), HAYBERT HOUSTON
(*JAZZ NOW*), AND RON WELBURN (*THE GRACKLE*)

The contributors to this section represent the brave world of self-publishing
a jazz periodical and all of the marketplace stresses and obstacles that en-
tails. It should also be noted that to a man and woman, these contributors
recognized the monocultural, one-sided proposition inherent in the history
of jazz periodical publishing, not to mention the phenomenon of swimming
upstream represented by the daunting prospects of periodical publication.

It should be further noted that one common theme in this section—in
some instances stated more emphatically than in others, to be sure—is that
these editor-publishers' determination to publish on jazz, and their subsequent odysseys, came from a desire to provide a more welcoming vehicle for
jazz writers of color and, in at least one case, as a means of achieving some
measure of gender equity in the ranks of jazz writers.

Jo Ann Cheatham

Jo Ann Cheatham joined the ancestors on January 2, 2016, at age seventy-three. Ms. Cheatham was a true rarity, likely the lone African American woman to publish and edit her own glossy jazz periodical. She was founder of the Brooklyn-based quarterly *Pure Jazz*, the crowning manifestation of what she felt was her true calling: to preserve jazz as an American classical music. Under Cheatham's leadership, *Pure Jazz* was particularly proud of emphasizing the unique contributions of black women to the history of jazz, another mark of distinction. Since her passing, Ms. Cheatham's family has announced plans to continue publishing *Pure Jazz*, including continuing to solicit articles from past magazine contributors.

Jo Ann Cheatham was a founding member of the Central Brooklyn Jazz Consortium (CBJC), an organization whose mission is to preserve and promote jazz in Brooklyn, with a particular emphasis on the borough's rich jazz history. An educator, she taught photography among other disciplines to children in the New York City public school system. This true Renaissance woman worked alongside Joan Maynard, the founder of the Society for the Preservation of Weeksville and Bedford-Stuyvesant. She also worked with the writer, producer, and actress Vy Higginson as the circulation manager for *Unique New York Magazine*.

INSIDE THE PAGES OF *PURE JAZZ*

At twenty-six glossy pages, the Spring 2012 issue of *Pure Jazz* features the NEA Jazz Master Roy Haynes on the cover, with a profile by Ron Scott. Inside are feature articles on Nina Simone, a reprint of Martin Luther King Jr.'s jazz-centric reflections to the 1964 Berlin Jazz Festival, an article on Philadelphia vocalist TC3, an interview with the hip-hop pioneer Fab 5 Freddy, and an excerpt from an oral history interview with Freddy Braithwaite for Brooklyn's Weeksville Heritage Center.

Recognizing the long-standing jazz and poetry coupling, the issue includes two poems, including "Drum Roll/New Sheriff in Town" as a tribute to President Barack Obama. There's a review of the trombonist Delfeayo Marsalis's album *Such Sweet Thunder*, as well as the self-explanatory LP column "Vinyl Man." The publisher Jo Ann Cheatham penned the column "With the Music in Mind," which in this issue features Sun Ra.

For this particular issue, *Pure Jazz*'s advertising profile includes book advertisements and an ad for Pacifica radio station WBAI's program "The World of Jazz"; several musicians post ads for their latest recordings; the actor Rome Neal advertises his weekly Banana Pudding Jazz gig at the Nuyorican Poet's Café; and *Ain't But a Few of Us* contributor (and frequent *Pure Jazz* writer) Playthell Benjamin advertises his *Com-*

mentaries on the Times blog. The Brooklyn jazz presenter and Bed-Stuy community hub Sista's Place is also an advertiser.

For twenty-seven years I was an educator in the New York public school system. I was a substance abuse prevention specialist. Then I got involved with the drummer and dancer Scoby Strohman after he came to my school for a program. During the time we were together we talked about my publishing a jazz magazine. I had worked on three children's magazines before that. But after being with this jazz musician I decided to do something for adults and publish a jazz magazine.

In 1999 I got involved with the Central Brooklyn Jazz Consortium, which was just getting started. I went to one of their meetings at Sista's Place and joined the CBJC efforts. One of the other women from that organization, Rosalyn Blair, was presenting a program called "Jazz: The Woman's Viewpoint"; she wanted to do the same things for black women that Cobi Narita was doing with her Women in Jazz organization. Not long after that, I decided I was going to start publishing *Pure Jazz* magazine. But I didn't realize until 2013 that there were no black women who consistently wrote about jazz!

I came to that awareness after attending a meeting. I ran into the bassist Reggie Workman, and he and his friend Francesca were going down to Jazz at Lincoln Center and gave me a ride in a cab. I was talking with Francesca about how women don't necessarily write about jazz, something I had never really thought about previously, but it was real motivation.

I never thought about *Pure Jazz* being a concept, but the scholarship of the black people who've written their stories for *Pure Jazz* leaves a legacy, one which no other magazine has chronicled, documenting the experiences of black people in jazz. *Pure Jazz* is designed as a vehicle for African American jazz writers. Despite all good intentions, I've still never had black women writers!

Except for being funded for about five years by the Brooklyn Arts Council, I've worked this whole *Pure Jazz* enterprise myself. The opinions of other cultures about this magazine are really not important to me. I've stuck with *Pure Jazz* because I really believe that jazz music belongs to our people.

I've invited writers to write as extensively as they feel is necessary to make their points. I would rather the articles be as lengthy as they tend to be, because they give you a certain depth, a certain time and space. But again, what continues to have my head in a tailspin is that black women don't write about jazz consistently! I published an issue focusing on Abbey Lincoln, and a sister wrote in that issue, but I still have not had any consistent women contributors to the magazine.

I attribute that disparity to the fact that men tend to harass women in the music; men don't want to truly understand women. There are a lot of things that happen to women in the jazz industry that don't happen to women in other industries. Women have known abuse, and other things that have happened to them, that they're not going to put down on paper. Some women are also reluctant to talk about their men in public. It's just shocking to me that there are no black women writers' voices on jazz from the 1930s; none even from the 1960s!

I've frequently written for *Pure Jazz* myself; in fact, I have a monthly column called "With the Music in Mind," and I wrote a couple of pieces I called "Jazz ala Mode," discussing current CDs. I also wrote an article on the trumpeter Maurice Brown, a piece on the Brooklyn saxophonist Jeff King, and an article on the Brooklyn jazz performance space Sista's Place.

Perhaps because I was so close to him, Scoby Strohman always told me that there are things African American musicians will tell black writers that they won't tell other writers. But there are also certain things a musician might reveal to me that, if they were of a negative nature, I wouldn't put in a piece. I've found some resistance from people who are close to the artists, particularly musicians' wives. With some artists, if you want to interview them you've got to go through their management; but if I want to interview someone I'm going straight to the artist, not their management, because I don't get the same flak from the artists.

As for why there are only a relative few African Americans writing about jazz, they keep us bridged off. Early on, black writers didn't write very consistently about jazz; from my research it seems we didn't feel scholarly enough to write about ourselves. We as a people weren't scholarly about writing about jazz.

When I wrote an article on Thelonious Monk's widow Nellie Monk—a black woman writing about a black woman in jazz—all of a sudden *Hot House Magazine* published a feature on Jazz Women, but it was all white women! We once featured a record column in *Pure Jazz* called "Vinyl Man Spins," and then suddenly they started running a vinyl records column in *DownBeat*! A lot of people copy what I do; they don't want to talk about it, but they copy it. I think at the beginning it had to do with keeping control of the music and saying what they wanted to say about it. And beyond that, it's all about finances.

Record companies buy ad space in different magazines. We don't do it because we don't have the money to buy ad space. People who do the kind of work I do don't tend to have a whole lot of money. But other jazz businesses, like the Blue Note label, have the money to buy what they want; they made a lot of money off people like Coltrane and Monk. That's how the mainstream jazz magazines cover what they want and maintain the control of the industry.

One of the obstacles I've encountered in publishing *Pure Jazz* is the lack of consistent assistance. Because of the way the arts funding system has changed over the years, and because we lack dependable funding, I don't have a proofreader, a social networking person, a researcher—those are all resources I just don't have, and they're crucial to the successful management of *Pure Jazz*.

On the positive side, our Abbey Lincoln issue was especially rewarding. I knew Abbey, but I wasn't close to her. From time to time I would go to the Blue Note when she was there and go to the green room and talk with her about the weather. I followed her all along her journey, through all the things that happened to her. I went to see her when she was in the nursing home, and I was there at her funeral services at Abyssinian Baptist Church. I guess because I loved Abbey I expected more to be written about her during her career. You just didn't see much written about Abbey, and that's why I chose to write about her in *Pure Jazz*, so that at least some place, some time, somebody wrote about Abbey. It was such a crowning achievement issue because it was about Abbey.

Our other crowning *Pure Jazz* achievement was our Amiri Baraka issue. All these years I've been following poetry, I've always been inspired by Amiri Baraka and his cadences. I was never scared of Abbey, but I was scared of Amiri Baraka! I finally got up enough courage to ask him to write an article for *Pure Jazz*. I gave him some copies of the magazine at the Vision Festival, and he said he would write something. I asked him to write an article on the fiftieth anniversary of his classic *Blues People*, on why he chose to write that book in the first place and what he felt was its ongoing relevance; he wrote the piece, and I was proud to publish it! Each issue of *Pure Jazz* is almost like a crusade in terms of truly getting it done.

Jim Harrison

How the late Jim Harrison (who joined the ancestors in 2021) came to publish *Jazz Spotlite News* is a classic story of a jazz enthusiast morphing into an activist and reacting to the scene to fill a perceived gap. In its relatively brief shelf life of ten quarterly issues, *Jazz Spotlite News* became a haven for aspiring black jazz writers—this writer included—as well as for musicians who could document the scene and its players in deeply personal ways, and overall for a black perspective on the jazz scene from a decidedly New York–centric point of view. We owe much of Jim Harrison's activism, including his tabloid publishing exploits, to the late NEA Jazz Master saxophonist Jackie McLean. There was a period in the early 1950s when Jackie McLean didn't have his cabaret card, which in effect banned him from playing clubs in New York City. That prohibition spurred Jim Harrison's presenting and later his publishing aspirations.

INSIDE THE PAGES OF *JAZZ SPOTLITE NEWS*

Jazz Spotlite News was a lively tabloid chock-full of articles on the musicians and the music from an unabashedly black perspective. The Fall 1980/Winter 1981 issue (vol. 2, no. 2) features two relatively under-sung but productive hard bop players, the trumpeter Bill Hardman and the tenor man Junior Cook, under the headline, "Preserving the Hard Bop Tradition." Inside are articles on artists as diverse as Lionel Hampton, Carmen Lundy, Mal Waldron (interviewed by noted poet/jazzoet Nathaniel Mackey), and a tap dance article penned by the terpsichorean Tina Pratt on "The Vanishing Artist and His Art," as well as a short profile on Ms. Pratt herself.

Notable also is the number of women contributors and commentaries on women's jazz pursuits. An example of the latter in this issue, "A Woman's Jazz Loft," on the nascent development of a performance space in Boston, specifically devoted to women in jazz, whose performance series was bannered, "Jazz Women in Concert." Included also are profiles of unsung women jazzers like the keyboardist Dee Myers, and a full two pages devoted to pieces contributed by the vocalist Stella Marrs.

Included also is a four-page profile of Barry Harris, a close associate of the publisher Harrison. Prominently featured are city and regional column reports (Philadelphia, New York, Jersey City, DC, Cleveland, and Detroit). The New York City column was, notably, a contribution by the veteran jazz producer Billy Banks. The early black musicians union local of Kansas City is sketched, as is "Jazz Radio Houston," a report on that city's KTSU-FM, which broadcast from the campus of Texas Southern University, an HBCU. Though bop and hard bop are *Jazz Spotlite News*'s stylistic bread and butter, the editorial range is also on display in a review of the edgy composer Julius Hemphill's saxophone opera *Long Tongues*.

Musicians were always welcomed with column inches in *Jazz Spotlite News*, including Frank Foster, Larry Ridley, Benny Powell, Johnny Hartman (writing on the recently passed bop singer Joe Carroll), and the Eddie Jefferson vocalese protégé George V. Johnson Jr.'s DC-centric column.

Me and a friend of mine were really into Jackie McLean; we used to have these record sessions and used to play Jackie's records all the time. So one day I said to him, "Boy, I sure wish there was something we could do for Jackie," because at that time, without a cabaret card, he couldn't work that often in New York. He could probably do Birdland maybe once or twice a year. So my friend said, "Why don't you form a fan club for Jackie?" I said that's a good idea, so then I formed this fan club, and the whole purpose of it was to be able to hear Jackie. The first time I presented Jackie, it was amazing to be able to get up onstage and say, "Ladies and Gentlemen, here's Jackie McLean"—that really knocked me out, to be able to present my favorite artist in concert.

Jackie turned me on to Slugs because he lived right around the corner from there. He knew the people at Slugs, and around 1964 they were just starting to book acts in there on a regular basis. I started doing promotional work for Slugs, distributing posters and flyers. That lasted up until the time that Lee Morgan was killed in the club, on February 19, 1972, which effectively ended Slugs's run.

So after I began promoting Jackie, I started promoting other artists too. And then Billy Taylor hired me in 1965 to work for Jazzmobile; I did fifty years with Jazzmobile as a talent buyer. As a result there was a whole lot of stuff that I got into; I was working with the bassist-educator Larry Ridley for eight years at Livingston College, promoting his concerts. After promoting another Jackie McLean concert in 1978, I began looking at the reviews. There was a guy named Jon Saunders who wrote for the *Amsterdam News*, and the review that he wrote was, to me, the best one, because he got into the essence of what the concert was about.

After reading Jon Saunders's review I thought to myself, "Damn, seems to me there should be more black writers dealing with this music." There were a lot of black writers around, and I tried to encourage them to form their own publication, but no one seemed to want to do it. One day I was at my printer—the guy who did my posters and fliers—and I saw him printing a newspaper, so I decided to publish the *Jazz Spotlite News*. The first issue, in 1979, was twelve pages. Blue Mitchell had just died, and Maxine Gordon presented a tribute for Blue Mitchell at the Village Vanguard toward the end of 1979; that's when the first issue came out. It was very well received. The saxophonist Frank Foster, who later led the Basie band, was the main contributor; he did a lot of writing. Gloria Ware, the wife of the bassist Wilbur Ware, did some writing on the Philadelphia scene for me, and the trombonist Benny Powell was living at that time in California, and he covered the California jazz scene. I had different people around the country that would contribute articles to the paper. Richard Henderson, for example, covered the St. Louis scene.

I started the paper to give black writers a place to write about the music. Since I was involved in the jazz business, I knew where the writers were, people that wanted to write. At that time everybody was trying to get with *DownBeat*, and the trumpeter Kenny Dorham was doing some writing for them. But when you talked to these jazz publications, they were only giving priority to their own regular writers. So that's why I tried to get the black writers to do their own thing, to create their own publication—but that never happened.

Once the *Jazz Spotlite News* came out, everybody was submitting articles. Maryjo Johnson did a lot of writing for us; Larry Ridley did some writing. It started out at twelve pages, and I published ten issues between 1979 and 1982. We started out with twelve pages and we ended up with 144 pages because I kept adding pages to it. The whole idea was to expand it as quickly as possible. The last issue came out in 1982. I stopped it in 1982 because that's when Barry Harris opened the Jazz Cultural Theatre and I partnered with him for about five years with that. At that point I was involved with my own club and I couldn't really do the newspaper anymore. I had set the tone for it, and I figured somebody else would do something similar later on. That did happen with Jo Ann Cheatham, when she published *Pure Jazz*. She took it to another level; mine was like a tabloid newspaper, and *Pure Jazz* was a magazine. Jo Ann wrote an article in *Pure Jazz* saying that African American classical music—jazz—honors Jim Harrison for publishing the *Jazz Spotlite News* for four years. She took it from there, right up until 2015. She picked up the ball and carried it for a number of years.

Black writers saw the *Jazz Spotlite News* as an opportunity to express themselves on the subject, and they did begin to submit articles. I forget how many writers we had, but we had writers in about twenty-five cities. The singer George V. Johnson Jr. did a lot of writing for us; he was heavy into Eddie Jefferson. He and Gloria Ware, Clarence Atkins; Jon Saunders actually became the editor, but then he died in 1981. So then Frank Foster became very active as the editor; he wrote that article, "In Defense of Bebop," that was very popular.

We had a lot of musicians writing for the paper; Jimmy Owens did something for us. There were some guys from Philadelphia that became very popular. It really was a very interesting experience. When it first came out, we didn't charge anything for it, we just gave it away. We did have a subscription form inside for readers to fill out. Our banner was "African American Classical Music/Jazz"—I had gotten that from Larry Ridley, because at the concerts he was doing at Livingston College he had used that as a title. Meanwhile, I was still doing promotional work for Larry.

To support *Jazz Spotlite News* we sold ads, but I underwrote most of it myself because I didn't stick to any budget. It received such a large response that I just kept adding pages because I kept getting articles from all over the place. So it was a really wonderful experience.

Many of these black writers really hadn't had opportunities to write for the other mainstream jazz magazines. The other thing that happened is that the experience they gained from the *Jazz Spotlite News* made them better qualified to get into other publications; Clarence Atkins, for example, went from the *Jazz Spotlite News* to the *Amsterdam News* and wrote there for quite some time. It was a very good experience for everybody involved.

I finally stopped publishing the paper in 1982, the year Barry Harris opened up the Jazz Cultural Theatre, because financially I couldn't afford to deal with the club and publish the paper at the same time. I had already shown that the *Jazz Spotlite News* could be done, but I had never had the experience of operating my own jazz club—and because, most of the time, Barry Harris had to travel out of town to perform, I eventually ran the club for five years, from 1982 to 1987. I still worked for Jazzmobile for over fifty years as the music coordinator, booking the artists.

More recently there have been efforts to make the *Jazz Spotlite News* available online. Larry Ridley turned it over to Rev. Ron Myers, who was trying to hook it up online; I know he had a website going on at JazzSpotliteNews.com. We published ten issues, about 25,000 copies. We started out quarterly and then ended up publishing twice a year because it got so big. At first it was strictly black-and-white, but eventually we started using color.

Haybert Houston

From his San Francisco Bay Area base, the enterprising jazz enthusiast Haybert Houston launched *Jazz Now* magazine as publisher and editor in chief, joining the thin, exclusive ranks of African American jazz magazine publishers. Later, after closing the hard copy version of *Jazz Now*, Houston introduced the online version, *Jazz Now* Interactive.

Accompanying his jazz publishing efforts, Houston hosted a broadcast version of *Jazz Now* over radio station KKUP, employing as theme music the familiar jazz standard "Stella by Starlight" as a tribute to his *Jazz Now* partner, Stella Cheung Brandt.

INSIDE THE PAGES OF *JAZZ NOW*

Reviewing *Jazz Now*'s May 1998 (vol. 8, no. 1) Seventh Anniversary Issue reveals the California-resident bassist Herbie Lewis gracing the cover, keynoting the magazine's California-centric coverage. In addition to the Lewis profile, the issue includes reviews of the 1998 International Association for Jazz Education conference, a profile of the NEA Jazz Master guitarist Kenny Burrell, and a report on a fan-instituted John Coltrane website.

Beyond reporting on the Cali jazz scene, *Jazz Now* also includes columns on New York ("Notes from the Apple," by Charles Hutchinson) and Australia ("From Down Under"), news from California's Central Coast, and Scott Yanow's Los Angeles column. Also included are book reviews and the "New Sounds" record reviews feature.

In the advertising area, there's ad space for Jazz Now Direct, the magazine's mail-order records service, plus numerous postings for new recordings from both artists and recording companies. There are ads from jazz presenters, including one from the late Pete Douglas's seaside oasis The Bach Dancing and Dynamite Society, and ads promoting KCSM's annual Jazz on the Hill festival, the Northsea Jazz Festival, the Jazz Society of Oregon, and radio stations like KKRD.

I started *Jazz Now* magazine in May of 1991. It was just Stella and me. We actually began working toward publishing the magazine in 1987, but the first print edition was published in May of 1991. In 1994 we introduced the first interactive jazz magazine on the internet. We were the first, and it ran simultaneously with the print edition until the print edition stopped in March 2000. The electronic edition continued until 2006. We were actually publishing from 1991 to 2006.

As far as my original motivation for publishing *Jazz Now*, I looked around at the jazz magazines we had, and *DownBeat* was the model because it had been around for so long. After I started investigating publishing a jazz magazine, what I found was that magazines like *JazzTimes*, and even *DownBeat*, talked about the big names all the time, talked about the names that people all over the world would recognize, the "leaders" of the jazz world. But I knew, just from being here in the San Francisco Bay Area, there were millions of jazz musicians making a contribution to the art form that were not being recognized, and some of them were older than *DownBeat*!

There was a racial disparity as well. I knew that black musicians were making major, major contributions to the art form: like, for example, a trumpeter here in the Bay Area named Robert Porter, who was a very active organizer of all kinds of musicians in general—this guy had never been recognized by anybody outside of our area. I knew his chances of getting into *DownBeat* or *JazzTimes* were almost nonexistent; it would never happen, no matter what he contributed. So the racial issue was a very strong motivator for *Jazz Now*.

I never told any of our writers to highlight black people. But as a publisher I was looking at the cultural contributions to jazz, and I wanted to remind the people that these were the people laying the groundwork, they had made the major contributions and were heads of jazz organizations throughout the country. People hadn't heard of those organizations, let alone the musicians behind them.

It was obvious to anybody you talked to that certain black musicians' contributions to jazz had been ignored. If you talked to people around the world about that—just asking them who's making jazz contributions in their area—99.9 percent of those people were black. But you had to be a Monterey Jazz Festival performer, or something along those lines, in order for you to get mentioned in the mainstream jazz publications.

Before we started *Jazz Now* we had not written anything on jazz, so we were real amateurs; that was very difficult, but we managed. When I decided to go for it, I started looking for basic ways to publish a magazine. We've got colleges and universities all over the world, but I could not find anything about how to publish a magazine. There were no instructions anywhere, nothing that said if you want to publish a magazine this is what you do. I couldn't find that information anywhere. So I had to go from scratch, to figure out how to publish. And not only that: at the time that we started in 1991, we were in a transition period—the world was moving from the precomputer stage to everything being done via desktop publishing.

We went to the College of Alameda and took a course in computer technology. After we learned how to use the computer, I told the instructor what we wanted to do. I told him we were there because I was planning on publishing a magazine. I asked him what he suggested I do, using the computer sciences and equipment available at the time. He said to start on Apple Macintosh. So I went back to Laney College here in Oakland, and I took desktop publishing on Apple Macintosh. We bought the equipment, and we were off and running. We were setting our own rules, but we got a lot of help.

I reached out to everybody I knew. My cousin lives in Chicago, and I knew that Johnson Publishing Company, the publisher of *Ebony*, was based there—we met with a woman there. I told her what I was going to do and asked for her help. She suggested that I contact *Playboy*, because *Playboy* was the master of magazine distribution. I knew that they distributed their own magazine, but they also had a network that distributed *most* magazines. So that's how I got the magazine distributed, and it was so helpful because not only did *Playboy* get the magazine out in this country but they hooked me up with Tower Records, which was worldwide. Tower got my magazine distributed in Taiwan and other places where there was no way I could have gotten the magazine distributed otherwise. So from seeking advice, asking, and begging for help, we took off.

Our publishing and distribution numbers were never where I felt they should have been, but they were sufficient to get us around the world. We had about twenty thousand subscribers; at that point the internet was taking off, and I can't remember how we tracked the internet numbers, which was also a very big issue.

To attract subscribers in the various areas that we covered, I would ask people where they purchased their magazines. For example, where did they get *DownBeat* or *JazzTimes*. To find out how those readers were connected to the jazz world, we had questionnaires inserted in the early editions of *Jazz Now* that helped a bit, but it was mostly word of mouth that helped with distributing the magazine.

When we first started *Jazz Now*, I wasn't aware that I was the only African American publishing a monthly jazz magazine. I kept hearing that, but I wasn't sure because I had no way of checking that out and I didn't want to make that claim and have somebody say, "Oh, I've been publishing my little newsletter for a hundred years!" So we never made that claim. Others made that claim for me very often, but I never made that claim because I couldn't verify it.

Recruiting writers to contribute to *Jazz Now* was not difficult. For example, I went to most of the jazz shows in the Bay Area, and there was a lady I would consistently see at every one of those events. She was a white lady who would be sitting up front, very clean, very sharp, blond hair with a bun in the back looking very conservative. But she was nodding her head with all the music, so I thought, "This lady is really into the music; she's always here." I found out who she was, I talked with her, and I found out that she had been taking photos at all these different events, so I asked her had she ever considered writing. She said, "No, I've never thought about writing about the music, this photography is just for me." I finally convinced her that she should be writing about her experiences. Then I consulted others in the jazz community and asked if they knew of anybody writing about jazz they could recommend, and some people would recommend someone, but it was just kind of a hit-and-miss, word-of-mouth thing—it was very basic, we didn't have headhunters or anything like that.

I didn't find a lot of African Americans writing about jazz, but I did find some, and some of the guys that were writing about it didn't think that *Jazz Now* would last, so they were not interested. I would have to work really hard to convince writers to contribute to the magazine. Doug Edwards, at the time a jazz radio broadcaster at KPFA, really helped me a lot; in fact, he was with the magazine right up until he died in 2010.

One of the first articles that we published was about Pearl of the Jazz at Pearl's club in San Francisco. I got a young black guy to write that article on Pearl for the first issue, and I think he charged me something like $600, which was way more than I could afford, but I had no way of determining how much people were getting paid to write until I met with that woman at *Ebony*. So the guy overcharged me and I thought, "Wow, I've gotta find a better way to do this." Doug Edwards told me to tell people that we were a poor magazine, that we would pay them $25 an article; so I did that, and people agreed because most of them just wanted to write about jazz and for them it wasn't really about the money. I paid writers from that time forward, but I just couldn't afford to pay them very much. I paid them $25 an article, and they were happy with that. I was surprised that they were happy with that because for $25 you can hardly buy a pack of cigarettes!

I was able to attract other black writers to the magazine, and I was so pleased with that. We attracted some really good writers; I think of Elizabeth Goodwin, who was writing for somebody else before I got her. She was a very conservative young woman, but very smart and articulate, and she had some good writing experience. She did a number of interviews over the history of the magazine. When I would find somebody that was a writer, I would try to convince them to write for us, and in most cases they would. Black writers were open to contributing to *Jazz Now* because of who we were, and I was happy about that. A lot of black writers even said, "I see where you're going, don't worry about trying to pay me," and that was very helpful, that made me feel good that I was getting some help.

It was very difficult to publish *Jazz Now* because, first of all, I had to pay the printer. I finally got this guy who was going to generate some revenue through advertising sales, and that lasted for a few years, but our advertising never really generated enough to cover the cost of publishing. It was really hard to get the advertising support that the magazine demanded and required, but I got a lot of help, and sometimes individuals would donate money for the magazine. These were primarily black people, but some of them were white. At the time I worked for a company called United States Leasing International. The vice president of that company gave me about $9,000 for the magazine, which was just wonderful!

Before I started publishing *Jazz Now*, I didn't know who the black jazz writers were. I knew that there had to have been black jazz writers, but I couldn't identify anybody. Black writers would be introduced to me or referred to me, but I didn't know a lot of jazz writers at that time.

I think the fact that there are so few black jazz writers has to do with the publishing industry as a whole. I think that's where the disparity arises; that's why I went to *Ebony*—because they had been publishing for years—and they helped me so much. I just chose to go where I knew there were black writers of any kind because I didn't know of any black jazz writers—or of any black publishers. The woman at *Ebony* didn't make many recommendations of writers to me, but she helped me in many other ways.

I didn't know how to find black writers unless they came to me. After the magazine came out, black writers would come to me saying they wanted to write. Most of our writers were people new to the industry who hadn't written for magazines before but wanted to make a contribution or knew something specific. Like that photographer I mentioned earlier, I would recruit them based on what I thought they could do.

Before we started publishing *Jazz Now*, I didn't think the lack of African American jazz writers contributed to how jazz was covered, because those editors decide what goes in the magazines and what does not. I knew that a lot of writers had run into reluctant editors. They would submit articles and they would get turned down unless they were writing about big names. Editors would tell writers wanting to write about Joe Blow from Wilson Creek that nobody's going to buy the magazine to read that. Writers would tell me about that!

I'm only talking about *professional* writers. Some of the professional writers, when I approached them about contributing to *Jazz Now*, they wouldn't even bother, saying, "No man, I can't tie up my energies in something that isn't going to go anywhere." That was shocking, and it made it very difficult, but that's what I was trying to overcome, to change all of that misperception. I feel that, to a degree, we did gather some recognition and we did change some of that perception. We had some black writers that started with *Jazz Now*, and they grew up with the magazine. Then they started to go over to other magazines and into radio broadcasting, but they always kept us in mind and recognized that *Jazz Now* was where they got started.

Jazz Now was absolutely an incubator for some writers. It's not just that I was told that—I could see it. We made a difference in the publishing world. I would hear that people recognized what we were trying to do, and we got a lot of support along those lines.

There is an organization in Germany, the Jazz Institute in Darmstadt, and this guy was so thrilled that I started the magazine that he helped in any way he could. I had a relationship with him, and he told me about the struggle that he had establishing the Jazz Institute, but he was very, very helpful to me. I got a lot of information from them, and I also learned a lot.

As far as mainstream black publications' indifference toward jazz, not everybody appreciates the art form for what it has contributed. A lot of black folks were church-oriented, and because of the way that jazz was originally introduced—when it was played in the brothels of New Orleans—it was looked down upon as a dirty music, as just bawdy house music. I'm not sure why we didn't have more jazz coverage in black publications.

We did achieve some rewarding acknowledgment when we would get recognition from places like the Monterey Jazz Festival. I got to know those people really well; they supported us and would give us a heads-up notice about whatever was going on, asked us to cover it and go to their shows. We were welcomed by most of the jazz community.

Publishing *Jazz Now* in California was certainly part of our original motivation. You might remember, the magazine used to say, "California *Jazz Now*, the Magazine of the West Coast Jazz World," and that was because we knew there was no other jazz magazine published out here. *DownBeat* was in Chicago, and any coverage of the guys in the West was limited.

I'm happy to say that black musicians assisted the magazine. There was a bass player here named Harley White who had an organization that recognized *Jazz Now* many times. Harley White had played bass for Earl "Fatha" Hines. His organization was called the Jazz Preservation Society, and he gave me an award. His recording secretary was Ed Kelly, one of the most admired piano players on this side of the country, who passed in 2005, and he was also a great supporter of *Jazz Now*. There was a lot of pride in the magazine from black people working in jazz; they knew what a struggle it was to publish a jazz magazine. In general, people in the jazz community tried to support *Jazz Now* as best they could.

Publishing *Jazz Now* was a very enlightening and rewarding experience—and we're not talking monetary rewards here. But it was very rewarding; I got to find out that what I'd imagined was true, that there are some truly remarkable musicians who weren't being covered. When we got somebody to cover them, they were elated to know that we were around—and I'm talking about white musicians in Sweden, or white musicians in Australia. It wasn't just black people who recognized what we were doing to highlight those musicians who had been around but had gotten no recognition. People really thought that was a great idea; it never turned around monetarily, but we got a lot of gratification.

Financial success was elusive. We never publicized this and never talked about it at all, but at one point Stella and I had to declare bankruptcy. I was going overboard in my out-of-pocket support for *Jazz Now*; I just wasn't getting the kind of return to make it viable. So it was never really a monetary success; most of the time it sustained itself, but then there was a time when it got very, very difficult.

When we first got to the twenty-thousand-subscriber level, it became much more difficult to publish hard copy. So we were the first jazz magazine that resorted to the internet issue, which we published at the same time as the hard copy *Jazz Now*; but the printed issue required a lot of time and money. I found that, no matter what medium I used, what I lacked most was a professional advertising person who knew how to generate revenue. One time my editor, Bob Tate, said, "You need to pay the advertising guys more." When he said that, I knew that he really didn't understand: the advertising guy was supposed to generate the revenue for him to get paid.

We did have advertising in our online edition, as well as subscriptions. We had a catalogue of releases there, and we would get the musicians to advertise their releases. That helped a lot but not enough to sustain the magazine. Ultimately it made me feel so good to publish *Jazz Now*, to know that I had done something positive for the art form; I would do it again at the drop of a hat.

Ron Welburn

Ron Welburn is Assateague/Gingaskin and Cherokee, descended from African Americans and from the Native peoples of the Delmarva Peninsula and eastern Virginia. A native of Berwyn, Pennsylvania, where he began school, he grew up in Philadelphia. Ron began writing poetry and fiction as an undergraduate at Lincoln University in Pennsylvania in the mid-1960s, and his poems have appeared in over a hundred literary magazines and anthologies. In 1976 he cofounded and edited the independent, black jazz–focused journal *The Grackle*, becoming one of only a handful of people of color to publish jazz periodicals.

In the mainstream jazz press, Ron has reviewed jazz recordings for *JazzTimes* magazine. His jazz historian experience includes conducting oral history interviews. In 1980 he interviewed "Big Chief" Russell Moore, the Pima trombonist, for the Jazz Oral History Project at the Institute of Jazz Studies (IJS) at Rutgers University. The following year Welburn produced a two-hour radio program for IJS, "American Indians in Jazz," an endeavor he plans to update.

Since the 1970s, Ron has been associated with the Greenfield Review Literary Center, which he has represented at book fairs and at powwows for the Native American Authors Distribution Project. Ron is an associate professor in the English department at the University of Massachusetts Amherst and is the director of the certificate program in Native American Indian Studies. Among his current projects are developing a study of Native Americans in jazz and early blues—and writing more poetry.

INSIDE THE PAGES OF *THE GRACKLE*

The Grackle was a literary journal published by Ron Welburn that featured extensive jazz record and jazz book reviews and commentary from a black perspective. See the anthology for a selection from *The Grackle*.

I was originally encouraged to write about music by what I saw as a discrepancy in jazz radio programming in Philadelphia compared to what was available in New York—that article was published in 1963. I was particularly annoyed that the commercial FM jazz DJ in Philadelphia—Sid Marks, Joel Dorn, and Del Shields—avoided playing records by Ornette Coleman and Cecil Taylor, though they did play people like Coltrane, Dolphy, Ken McIntyre, and Prince Lasha.

I expressed my concerns to the Philadelphia pianist Damon Spero, and he invited me to submit an article to the tabloid of the Jazz at Home Club organization, whose sessions I was attending. "What's Wrong with Philadelphia's Radio Jazz?" was the title of the article. Those DJ didn't like it, but Hag Ross, a jazz DJ at WXPN at the University of Pennsylvania, thought the piece was great.

Once I got to Lincoln University in my native Chester County, PA, I had a chance to review LPs for the school newspaper. After Lincoln, I really never stopped writing. Working on my MA in English and Creative Writing at Arizona, I contributed regularly to an alternative newspaper in Syracuse called *The Nickel Review*, and I placed a few album reviews in *Negro Digest/ Black World*.

After two years in Tucson I headed to Syracuse via Philadelphia because Walt Sheppard, the editor of the *Nickel Review*, suggested I could help him with the publication. Ultimately I landed a spot with the university's new Afro-American Studies program.

Later I wrote a jazz column for the alternative weekly *Syracuse New Times*. When I left in 1975 to join my then wife, who had a law gig in Brooklyn, I picked up some spot writing opportunities at *Music Journal*. The *New York Amsterdam News* published a few of my reviews. I wrote for *Rockingchair*, and in 1976 for *Radio Free Jazz*, which became *JazzTimes*, where my music writing was almost exclusive until 2001.

I first became aware of the small number of black music writers in the early 1960s. As a *DownBeat* subscriber I read Barbara Gardner's, and then LeRoi Jones's "Apple Cores," columns. Later, the trumpeter Kenny Dorham and Bill Quinn contributed to *DB*. African Americans have produced few outlets for critical music writing. I can only suppose that editors at African American newspapers and populist magazines feel that "serious" music journalism will not interest their readers, and they would rather not provide vehicles where artists might be taken to task critically.

Young white writers have chomped at the bit to write about this music, often for free. I've never fully figured out why young writers of color tend to shy away from this kind of writing, but they're in the foreground criticizing those white writers who do. Maybe it's an orientation whites have that writers of color in mainstream journalism shun.

Back when I was reading *Latin New York*, I was aware of good writing by Aurora Flores, and I met and talked with the writer Max Salazar. Hilly Saunders (at *Jazz Spotlite News*) and my Cherokee buddy Lewis MacMillan (at *New York City Jazz Gazette*) didn't promote much critical writing in their publications.

I wrote a few pieces for Ken Smikle's publication, and Ornette Coleman told me he liked the one I wrote on his harmolodic method. Today, I'm among a few Natives writing about Indians in jazz, blues, and pop; yet even for these venues, the serious writing isn't fully there. If I have a standard or model for serious jazz writing, it's probably a combination of jazz magazines like *DownBeat, JazzTimes, Coda,* the jazz magazine that was published in England, and assorted academic prose.

What I appreciate are reviews that demonstrate that the writer is informed by history; even if it's not specific in the review, it provides authority. I enjoyed reading Bob Palmer's reviews in the *New York Times*. I've never felt comfortable with hip cultural jargon, even the few times I used it. Nor do I like what I call "advertising style." They're just not my sound.

I like descriptive prose that vividly portrays the encounter between the form and the performers and that makes an impression on the audience. I feel that my amateur experiences as a musician, composer, and arranger helped me appreciate how to describe my subject. You have to give something of yourself to be a responsible music writer, to get to know musicians without patronizing them.

After thirty-six years of music writing, I stopped publishing serious music reviews in 2001 because I couldn't keep up with it—what with my teaching, the serious illnesses of an uncle and a friend, and writing a book. Second, what I've seen and studied tells me that cultural wars are a mainstay in American life, and I place the onus for them on the music industry more than on the musicians.

White musicians are just musicians wanting to perform a vibrant music that makes them part of a significant culture. Even those who don't or prefer not to perform with black musicians are just trying to make it. It's the machinery and politics of culture that exploits them as pawns, and they haven't got a clue! What I mean by their being exploited is that it's the promoters and marketers who've always been predisposed to having a "great white hope" in jazz.

Colonel Tom Parker, who recorded and promoted Elvis Presley, was on record saying that, if he could find a white boy who could sing like a black R&B singer, he could make a million dollars. I wouldn't blame Elvis for that. For the same reason, I couldn't blame Stan Getz and his bossa nova records for distracting jazz from the luminal development between hard bop and early avant-garde.

Music is a universal language; jazz is irrepressibly international. Jazz will prevail no matter who plays it, and jazz will periodically insinuate itself out of the low profile to which the market relegates the music. Jazz has been all over the world almost since its inception. And there are always going to be marketers and people who benefit from targeted marketing. Yet just about every musician I've spoken to, going all the way back to when I was in college, concurred that it's all about the music—and they were not naïve about racial issues. They have an almost spiritual bond among themselves about the importance of creating and protecting this beautiful music that transcends race and international issues—but also helps them address those issues.

People who start publications tend to call on their friends and fellow devotees to contribute. Essentially that's how it was with *The Grackle: Improvised Music in Transition*, which published five issues between 1976 and 1979. *The Grackle* was meant to be a forum of ideas for the three men of color who created it: James T. Stewart, Roger Riggins, and me. I invited Victor Manuel Rosa to write on Latin/Nuyorican music. But I turned away at least two white writers who virtually begged for opportunities to contribute. I didn't like doing that, but I told them that they had outlets not available to us and that, being in the early stages of the publication, we had ideas we wanted to work out. But it's hard trying to create our own vehicles.

The three of us started *The Grackle* on a shoestring. We went from typewriter to newsprint; then we had to distribute it ourselves—plus, one of the partners didn't turn in any money from sales! Our mail order operation was unsophisticated. I found myself doing more than my share as managing editor, and after the fifth issue I closed it down. If I had any desire to do something like that today, I'd use my relationship with a college or university the way many literary magazines make use of support from such institutions. Perhaps someone at one of the HBCUs could do something. Some measure of a jazz education program at a school would certainly help in that endeavor.

There's so much involved in self-publishing a journal. And you have to make sure you're doing business legally: a seemingly minor issue, but it involves registration of the "business" and keeping track of taxation, especially if you plan to sell magazines. I found out that I have no skills for that, but I recommend that anyone wishing to create such a vehicle should definitely get some legal advice.

Serious music journalism has an academic quality, and I see nothing wrong with that. Perhaps it could continue to loosen itself rhetorically, but if writers of color are afraid of offending their readers, white writers will always fill the void. Publishing vehicles differ according to whom they view as their readers. The late Eileen Southern, of *The Black Perspective in Music*, and Samuel Floyd, of the *Black Music Research Journal*, edited academic publications. I don't recall many serious essays about jazz in Eileen Southern's journal. Bear in mind the context that jazz was not considered serious music by a lot of academics, including by many African American academics. Attitudes by writers for the jazz magazines were what they were; but the most egregiously racist piece I ever read was a review of Albert

Murray's book *Stomping the Blues* in which the reviewer accused Murray of not knowing anything about the blues!

I've been blessed to enjoy just about all of the encounters with musicians that turned into pieces either assigned or volunteered, including with some outside the jazz field. Although the music editor for the *Syracuse New Times* didn't want me writing it, I published a remembrance in 1972 of hearing Albert Ayler for the first time in 1962; and I also covered the Newport Jazz Festival, New York edition, and the downtown Counter Festival from 1972 to 1975. As that *New Times* editor was bearing down on me and I was leaving the paper, I waved in his face my Jazz Criticism Fellowship award from the Music Critics Association and the Smithsonian seminar, which had been given to me for my writing in that paper. The music editor was sour, but the publisher was delighted.

The second, and I believe the last, of these Smithsonian seminars was in 1975. Ten journalists were invited, including Stanley Crouch—who had recently relocated to New York from Los Angeles and was writing freelance on jazz for *Players* magazine and the *Village Voice*—and Earl Caldwell of the *Chicago Defender*. We were the only writers of color. Other invited writers included Arthur Lenz of the *New Orleans Times-Picayune*, Maggie Hawthorne of the *St. Louis Post-Dispatch*, Bill Fowler, who was writing jazz music theory pieces for *DownBeat*, Peter Keepnews of the *Village Voice*, Bernard Laret of the *Cleveland Press*, and Peter Occhiogrosso of the *SoHo Weekly News*.

The jazz writer Martin Williams, an editor at the Smithsonian, was the coordinator of these seminars. Dan Morgenstern, by then a former editor at *DownBeat*, and Albert Murray made up the stellar faculty. It was a great and heady experience, coinciding with the Newport Jazz Festival in New York, and we all got tickets to most of the performances we wanted to cover at Carnegie Hall and Alice Tully Hall. The seminar went on for about ten days, and we met in the ASCAP building across Broadway from Lincoln Center. Walter Wager, a novelist who worked at ASCAP, attended some sessions. The seminar made me realize both how difficult it is to be a jazz writer and to meet the demands of being a responsible writer.

Martin took us through the paces of responsible historical knowledge; Dan focused on the craft of writing; and Albert grounded us in his theories of the blues—he was working on *Stomping the Blues* and gave the lectures constituting his book *The Hero and the Blues*. I was enormously fortunate to be a part of that seminar. We had opportunities to meet a few one-day visitors and others just hanging out, including journalists from England, Scandinavia, Italy, and Chile and Joachim Berendt from Germany. To meet so many people from all over the world that wrote about jazz was just over the top! I saw *Swing Journal* guys from Japan but didn't meet the editor until years later; the Japanese hung in a pack loaded down with cameras.

One highlight was covering a few festivals of Asian music and writing a few articles for *Music Journal* at the invitation of Guy Freedman, a wonderful individual to whom I was introduced by pianist Ran Blake. Another highlight was reviewing international music recordings for a little Philadelphia-based literary publication called *Rockingchair*. I was studying ethnomusicology at the time and wrestling with Spanish. I was also reviewing belly dance music, and Greek, Israeli, Arab North African, Bhutanese, and French Canadian music and music from the Comoro Islands.

Other career highlights included hearing John Coltrane perform live five or six times, each stronger than the one before. Another was covering the Creek/Kaw Native tenor saxophonist Jim Pepper at the South Street Seaport and reviewing his album *Comin' and Goin'*.

I haven't encountered any terribly caustic obstacles. I learned that editors of black newspapers weren't concerned about the timeliness of a review; and they were not above cutting the final paragraph or two of a relatively short review, which is what the *Amsterdam News* did, maybe twice. But I believe everything happens for a reason. The breaks I didn't get meant I probably wasn't supposed to be there.

Thanks to Glenn Siegel, the music director at the University of Massachusetts Amherst's WMUA and the creator of the Magic Triangle series and Jazz Shares, I've heard some promising new music, including CDs by Makaya McCraven and Mike Reed's People, Places, and Things. The most exciting and innovative music I've heard in the last five years, both live and on CD, includes that of the pianist Michele Rosewoman and that of the saxophonist Rudresh Mahanthappa, who is rewriting the vocabulary for playing the saxophone as part of a long arc coming out of South Asia. A development like this in jazz was bound to happen. And yet a 1997 Sonny Rollins concert at Mount Holyoke College tops just about any concert I'd heard, before or since. Astounding! I'm still speechless!

4

black dispatch contributors

ROBIN JAMES AND RON SCOTT

Those writers interviewed for this section represent the unique niche of writing on jazz subjects for publications geared specifically to the comings and goings of the African American community and to developments unique to the needs of that community. Their exceptionality strikes also to the fact that, despite jazz music's being a distinct development of the African experience and presence in the Americas, jazz has not always enjoyed a welcome, open presence within the pages of black community–oriented publications. Owing perhaps in part to the way that certain sectors of the black community have historically looked askance at jazz and its influence—notably the clergy (the old "devil's music" canard)—jazz reportage has rarely enjoyed a prominent or sustained position in black publications.

There are notable exceptions—as is illustrated by the experiences of these contributors—but for the most part research shows that jazz activity in black community–oriented publications was most often limited to incremental notes and mentions of jazz activities in the black community as part of larger "social activity" roundup notes. Another factor that has diminished jazz music's presence in black publications has been the music's historic migration from a true presence in the black community in the form of venues (history shows its presence in bars, nightclubs, ballrooms, and community centers in the black community) to the gradual gentrification of jazz, or the "downtown" migration of places of jazz performance, and thus of its musicians.

Robin James

I first met the Minneapolis-based writer Robin James at an annual conference of the now-defunct International Association for Jazz Education. Later, when my friend and colleague Clarence Atkins, the Harlem-based black jazz writer, passed, a modest fund was dedicated in his name by the Jazz Journalists Association, earmarked for mentoring aspiring black jazz writers. As the vice president of the JJA I facilitated an opportunity through that fund for several young black writers to attend an arts criticism conference in Los Angeles; Robin James was among that contingent.

Robin James has written jazz columns for several years at the *Minnesota Spokesman-Recorder*, the African American newspaper of the Twin Cities. She has continued to contribute to various prints, including contributing a rare interview with Ornette Coleman to *DownBeat* magazine.

I originally began writing about jazz out of curiosity stemming from two jazz concerts in Minneapolis. The first jazz concert I attended, in 1996, featured Joshua Redman and his band; the other was the Lincoln Center Jazz Orchestra with Wynton Marsalis in 2000. Both men and both concerts changed my thinking about jazz and what this peculiar American art form means to this country.

It's difficult to describe in words exactly the ways in which those two concerts changed my thinking about jazz. But I did experience some sort of epiphany. I went swiftly from discovering Redman on the car radio, and feeling an instant connection with his music, to having the chance to interview him on his birthday, to experiencing his music live, and then talking to him in person. After having had these experiences, I took the music much more seriously. And as I began to research the art form further, the deeper I wanted to go. I started connecting dots, and in the process discovered the rich historic tradition of the art form, a tradition that stems directly from the black community.

Even before these experiences, I had a history with jazz. My grandmother, who was a descendant of Samuel Clemens (Mark Twain), told me stories about how her husband, a Pullman porter, had developed friendships with jazzmen like Hot Lips Page, Buck Clayton, Thelonious Monk, and Dizzy Gillespie. She specifically told me about the time "Diz" called the house. It took some time before I would learn about who these musicians were and understand their importance to the creation of our music.

In the very beginning, I had heard a selection from Joshua Redman's *Spirit of the Moment: Live at the Village Vanguard* on the radio, and it pulled me in. I remember enjoying the music and then becoming curious about it. It was an inspirational moment for me. Then I found out Redman was on his way to town, so I asked for an interview and luckily secured one—on his birthday! I was a new reporter, and my interview ran over its allotted time. But he was very kind to me over the phone and in person. At the time, I knew nothing except that I was falling in love with the music. And I loved the way it made me feel.

At both the Redman and the Marsalis concerts I noticed that there were hardly any women or people of color in the audience, and that concerned me. So I wrote about those concert experiences after I was given the tremendous opportunity to write a jazz column, starting in September 2000, by the *Minnesota Spokesman-Recorder*, a historic black newspaper (established over eighty years ago) and the oldest minority-owned company in the state of Minnesota.

I had graduated from the University of Minnesota. In passing I mentioned to one of my classmates that jazz was an interest of mine. She suggested I contact her uncle Jerry Freeman, an editor at the *Minnesota Spokesman-Recorder* newspaper, about writing about jazz for the paper. I called Jerry and then met him in his backyard to discuss the possibilities. He was thrilled about the idea of having jazz featured in the paper, and Jerry was the one who suggested that I write a column.

Prior to that, as an undergrad, I needed two credits to complete one of my writing courses in college, and the only way to do that was to get published somewhere. So, with the help of my childhood friend Paul, who happened to work for the *Minnesota Spokesman-Recorder* (at the time the paper was called the *Minneapolis Spokesman, St. Paul Recorder*), I wrote a short piece on Minnesota HUD grants for the paper. I mentioned this previous experience to Jerry. When I wrote that first piece on Redman, I worked with a different editor. And for the record, that Redman article turned out to be a disaster. The final edit was atrocious. My entire piece had been rearranged. I didn't even recognize it. Needless to say, I was horrified.

Imagine my disappointment upon meeting Redman and not being able to present him with my published article featuring our interview! But all was not lost, as I made sure to give him a copy of the original article that I had written. Of course, I explained the situation and apologized. I was extremely embarrassed. I don't even have a copy of our interview. It's lost. I think I mistakenly gave Redman the original.

This unfortunate incident was not the end of the world. Later I was lucky enough to get a chance to redeem myself by writing a concert review about Redman and Derek Trucks for the *St. Paul Pioneer Press*, after having begun writing overnight jazz reviews and general jazz articles for that local daily.

The second jazz concert I attended, at Northrop Auditorium on the University of Minnesota campus, was the Lincoln Center Jazz Orchestra (LCJO) with Wynton Marsalis. I was dating someone who had spoken very highly of Wynton and the band. During my first trip to visit him in New York, I brought him Wynton's book *Sweet Swing Blues on the Road* as a Christmas gift. Beyond what he had told me about Wynton and his orchestra, and the book I had purchased, I knew nothing about them. But I was deeply curious. When the band came to town I attended and reviewed the concert. After the concert I met Wynton at the venue. I noticed he was playing a song on the piano with a student. The song was "A Dream" by Bunny DeBarge. A few moments later, someone introduced us and took our picture. That picture appeared in the newspaper along with the article.

I was immediately struck by his warm, welcoming spirit. After seeing the LCJO and Wynton in action, I began to question why more people like myself didn't seem drawn to the music. I have since come to the conclusion that some people simply don't have the luxury of exploring the worlds of art and music. They may have a desire but have bigger and more basic concerns to deal with day to day, or perhaps they've never been exposed to jazz, or not exposed to it enough to develop a strong interest. Perhaps they don't even know it exists! Or it could be that they know exactly what jazz is, yet they elect to admire it from a distance.

I feel very strongly that jazz chose me. It makes me want to share my experiences with readers. I hope that some readers out there will get curious and inspired to learn more, to explore the music more fully for themselves in much the same way that I did. I think my overall jazz learning experience is extremely rare. In recent years, I've discovered that I was exposed to jazz-related music at four or five years old. My father loved Chick Corea and played his music around the house. My uncle told me that, when he would babysit me, he would often play Sonny Rollins. I began to explore the music further because opportunities to learn kept presenting themselves.

About a year after meeting Wynton Marsalis, I was at the Book Expo America in Chicago, where I had traveled to work with book authors; I was a book publicist at the time. Wynton's book *Jazz in the Bittersweet Blues of Life* was being promoted there. He played a concert to help with promotions. It was after the concert that we were reacquainted at the book publisher's after-party.

A month later I was back in Chicago for the Ravinia Festival, where the LCJO and Wynton were performing. He read my first column aloud, where I expressed my concern about why more women and people of color were not drawn to jazz. After he read my piece, he offered me encouraging words that inspired me to keep writing about jazz. Wynton also acknowledged how difficult it is to write. Honestly, I still don't know if I'm any closer to a true understanding of why more women and people of color are not as drawn to jazz as I am.

However, there is diversity in this music and it ought to be reflected in the evaluation of it. Perhaps, if this were the case, more women and people of color could find something in the writing that resonates with them, which in turn could spark imaginations and inspire greater exploration, and even love of this music known as jazz.

In my case, for someone as accomplished as Wynton Marsalis to take an interest in me and make time to read my work, at such an early age—well, it made me want to keep striving, keep writing and learning about jazz. After that initial meeting with Wynton I got in touch with Bob Protzman, who at the time was one of the only full-time jazz writers at a major daily, the *St. Paul Pioneer Press*. He helped make it possible for me to write jazz previews and reviews for the newspaper. Plus, Protzman was hosting a radio show on our jazz station, KBEM Jazz 88 FM. I listened to him frequently and learned a lot. Eventually I became a cohost of my own KBEM show, Sweet on Jazz. I interviewed Jackie McLean, Lou Rawls, Sonny Rollins, Branford Marsalis, and Kurt Elling, among others.

I wrote for *St. Paul Pioneer Press* from 2002 to 2004 and then stopped to focus on writing opportunities with *DownBeat*. That opportunity led to my writing a piece for *EQ* featuring Grand Mixer DXT, the Bronx native credited with being the first to fuse hip-hop and jazz. He had completed the sonic restoration of the Blue Note release *Thelonious Monk Quartet with John Coltrane at Carnegie Hall*, a historic live recording discovered at the Library of Congress.

At my first Jazz Journalists Association event in New York City in 2003, I reached out to the veteran jazz writers Ashley Kahn and Gary Giddins. Both were very supportive and also helped me along the way. Due to a referral from Gary I received my first and only assignment from the *Village Voice*, an album review for Nicholas Payton's *Sonic Trance*.

My experience working with the *Village Voice* music editor Chuck Eddy left a lasting impression as well. He taught me how to say something with 250 words or less. Ashley Kahn encouraged me by teaching me how to craft pitch letters. I also reached out to Stanley Crouch; he too offered me encouraging words of wisdom and instruction. And I also got to know the late African American music writer Tom Terrell. He was one of a kind and was a huge influence for me. Still is. I marvel at the powerful enthusiasm that he was able to project in his writing.

I still had no idea there were so few African American jazz writers! But as I began to travel, meet more people from the jazz world, and attend jazz conferences, I discovered that the number of black people covering jazz was extremely low. I was naive at the time and didn't really understand why. But I suppose it comes down to power, access, and interest. Having knowledge of and access to art is powerful. But first you've got to have interest, interest in art, interest in the artist, interest in the audience. All it takes is one voice to spark something great, which in turn can inspire individuals and even a nation. That's power. But it goes deeper than that. And as far as I know, the people who've been in this business the longest, who have benefitted the most, have yet to fully explain their process. And on top of that, there seems to be—as I have come to understand—an ongoing fight over custody of this art form and over how its story unfolds, and over who gets to tell that story.

First of all, not everyone is comfortable about being in the role of evaluating art, much less jazz. Nor are they comfortable with the authority that comes with that. Then again, there are those who exercise an overdose of authority, which sometimes leads them to protect the knowledge that goes along with their process. By *process* I mean the ways in which the media goes about informing the public about jazz-related music and the artists trying to make a living on their craft. I'm also talking about the personal process of decision-making.

When it comes to the thought that goes into the creation of a given composition or solo, there's a great deal of personal vulnerability involved. The same thing applies to writers. I've had virtually no problems operating in the mostly white, male critical establishment. The one incident that comes to mind still makes me wonder about how far I can actually be permitted to go with this writing. When I hit that brick wall I thought to myself, I have the credentials, I've earned them, so now what? Having long-range, active experience writing original content for a mainstream readership and for specialized audiences isn't enough. Sometimes it comes down to relationships and to how those relationships are cultivated; it's not fair, but it's realistic. The only other thing that may help is having a genuine passion for the music. That can't be faked. But you still have to have a certain combination of skills and experience; otherwise, it's easy to get redirected.

Some editors in particular enjoy working with the same writers, assigning them the same material to cover, because I believe they think that gives them more control over the outcome. Plus, they have the satisfaction of knowing that they're helping someone establish or grow a career. But then you have to question whether we are offering the public a comprehensive look at all of jazz; and the answer would have to be no.

Considering that there is currently a major revision underway in the music's language, with a lot of jazz artists incorporating hip-hop and R&B into their original work, I believe it's even more important then ever to demand and expect greater diversity and inclusivity in the journalistic evaluation of this music. Yet can the powers that be allow themselves the discomfort of letting go of the clout that comes along with evaluating art?

Until that changes, and news of such a change is documented or talked about openly by African Americans and by all of those who know the difference, we're not going to get very far. The public deserves better. The artists deserve better. And most of all the black ancestors that helped create this music deserve better.

Very little light has been shed on this subject, for whatever reasons. Too much time is devoted to and focused upon everything but the real, important issues, which relate directly to economics. This allows people in positions of power to feel more comfortable with the same people writing the same things, and in the same way. The people in power, publishers and editors, feel more comfortable assigning people who look like them; I know this for a fact.

One of my black writer friends, who contributed to one of the local dailies, explained that, when layoffs began at the paper, he believed when it came down to it, the people in positions of power ultimately chose to continue working with people who looked like them. He said those exact words. However not all media folks in positions of power feel threatened by a diversity of talent; it seems some actually thrive on it.

I would welcome a healthy discussion by veteran jazz writers, authors, and editors from jazz publications and African American–oriented publications.

What it boils down to is that we're talking about the human condition and about humanizing that condition: the music, its sources, and its implications.

I do think that the relatively small number of African American writers contributes to how the music is reported on and criticized—absolutely! From a cultural enrichment standpoint, there's a lot that has the potential to get missed or misunderstood, which can lead to miscommunication. Certainly, there are stories and viewpoints that are best told or conveyed accurately by African American writers.

Consider the work of Zora Neale Hurston. She was a folklorist, anthropologist, and author. Only she could have conducted the kind of anthropological research that she did, and in such a successful manner. Her observations were uniquely her own and accurately reflected her community and her African ancestry.

Also, if you're a black person who was a child of the 1970s, your perception of the times, the music, and even the language are going to be different from that of others. What colored your experiences is most likely a reflection of the community you came from. If you're writing about a jazz artist covering pop songs from that era, particularly if that artist is black, chances are you will have a common understanding of what went into their vision and artistry. If that turns out to be true, perhaps that will resonate with readers. There's an undeniable authenticity that can come out of this, which only makes the story that much more revealing and interesting. Isn't that the goal? Black folks have a rich oral history, too. There comes a time when we need to document history in the making, in *our* words.

It's all about preserving the wealth and the well-being of this music. When you're documenting what's happening now, you've got to be careful about how the information is transmitted. When I'm considering future generations with respect to African American history, I know I strive to get the perspective right, because it may be my one and only shot at doing so. By shaping the now, you're shaping the future and how it gets viewed later. It's like African American folklore. When the truth doesn't get told, you have alternative stories going that can then be viewed as myths. The truth doesn't always get the forum it deserves. Some things become lost in translation. Yes, that's unfortunate, and yes, that's 100 percent preventable.

At first I used to wonder and question why and how certain musicians become elevated over others, but now I don't. I get it. Editors are the key here. How they think definitely matters, or so we've been conditioned to believe. Sure, editors get pitched by writers, which helps shape their decision-making process; but it still comes down to how editors think, which directly relates to what gets covered and who covers what. Again, that comes down to economics and relationships.

Then again, it may not have anything to do with the lack of cultural diversity among writers covering the music—unlike in the Grammy nomination process. First of all, I know that if I hadn't written album liner notes for a nationally distributed record, I would not have qualified to vote in the Grammys. Plus, you have to be a member of the Recording Academy in order to vote, which means you have to *pay* to become a member. I don't know of many black writers covering jazz that have those credentials. Not to mention women, or women of color. The bottom line is that we need more incisive and observant female voices and black voices in music writing.

A lot of critics with unearned credentials have this inflated illusion of influence floating around their heads. But what are they doing that's so influential? Ultimately, editors ought to focus more on making music writing more vibrant, and to continue to think about how to do that in ways that are more inclusive. There is no doubt that there should be a more concerted effort to listen to and value diverse voices, especially when it comes to this music.

As it relates back to what I said about economics and relationships, I don't know how much a writer's actual talent, abilities, or interests adds to the equation. I suppose all of that ought to be considered. In my case, I'm very fortunate in that, because I write a jazz column, my editors let me have free reign. My position is extremely unique; I realize this and feel very grateful to have the freedom to write about pretty much whatever I want. Of course, I'm asked to be mindful of our audience when I do make my choices.

The fact that I write my column for one of the few African American publications to pay any attention to jazz comes down to economics. I imagine that other publications have to consider their overall space, content, and advertising budgets. With the *Minnesota Spokesman-Recorder*, the publisher made a conscious choice to devote space to jazz, in both good and not-so-good economic times. We still have a long way to go in this arena. I definitely don't see a lot of coverage being devoted to jazz elsewhere, a fact that is very disappointing and troubling to me.

I continue to constantly look ahead, noting the music's potential along the way as I take my place in this ever-evolving musical landscape. I've come to accept that doing some extra legwork is necessary if I want to keep up and stay on top of the news. It's tough, but it's well worth the effort. A column might get bumped, or a front-page story may get eliminated or delayed. It all depends on developing news. I've also shifted a bit to writing online for both the *Minnesota Spokesman-Recorder* and *DownBeat*. It's my hope that *DownBeat* will welcome more coverage of what's happening here in the Twin Cities music scene because I'd also like to inform their readership about the changes taking place. This market is highly underrated, which I find to be ironic since a lot of artists choose to begin their tours here in Minneapolis. Our audiences are sophisticated music lovers.

We're living in a changing media environment. Media outlets, at least in the jazz world, appear to be changing their formats (see, e.g., *DownBeat's* Hot Box section). So the incentive and opportunity to embrace a greater diversity of voices does exist. The issue may or may not have to do with standards of talent and fit. Are editors at media outlets aware of the issues black writers face? There's an impression that black writers have been locked out of securing writing opportunities in our limited number of media outlets.

The issue needs a reset. When it comes to gender, it's common knowledge that an Old Boys pattern exists as it relates to writing opportunities and outlet coverage. And what about pay structure and distribution? So there is a whole range of related issues to address. Male privilege in jazz writing does exist. It just seems to me that a music as diverse and inclusive as jazz ought to be just as all-encompassing in its writing and coverage. If any music writing ought to be more diverse and offer more perspectives to its readers, it's jazz writing!

Ron Scott

One fact clearly established in this series of dialogues with African American music writers and their challenges at getting into print is the peculiar level of disinterest in creative black music on the part of the traditional, weekly African American print media known colloquially as the black dispatch. A general consensus seems to be that the disinterest is commercially driven; that what African American publications publish in editorial content is entirely driven by what sells. That neglect has been particularly obvious over the last five decades, roughly corresponding to the post-desegregation decades, when the so-called black dispatch has been more revenue-driven than morally obligated to featuring blacks in the creative arts.

This puzzling disparity in reportage comes despite the fact that, historically, some of the earliest black newspaper writers got their start at such essential African American community–oriented publications as the *Pittsburgh Courier*, the *Chicago*

Defender, the *Baltimore Afro-American*, the *Kansas City Star*, the *Indianapolis Recorder*, the *Cleveland Call and Post*, the *Washington Afro American*, and other black dispatches, including the glossy magazines *Ebony*, *Jet*, and *Essence*.

Ron Scott's creative music writings have been published as a happy exception to that historic neglect; his columns on jazz and other creative black music have been featured in the *Amsterdam News*, the oldest black community–oriented publication in the country. For many decades, New York City's most reliable dispatch of news in and around the black community has been this Harlem-based weekly. In addition to the *Amsterdam News*, Ron Scott has contributed to the *New York Times*, the *New York Daily News*, *Time Out New York*, *Positive Community*, *Pure Jazz*, and Johnson Publications. He served as the senior editor of the *Forever Harlem* book project.

To be honest, writing wasn't really part of my program when I was coming up, though English was my favorite subject in high school. As a senior in high school I submitted two short poems for the yearbook; unfortunately, they weren't accepted, and I was very disappointed. While in college I continued writing poems as I pursued my goal of becoming a social worker. One undergrad year I was looking for a part-time job when I noticed on the school bulletin board a freelance writing position for the Brooklyn-based soul music magazine *Soul Sounds*. I went for the interview and was immediately hired; that was the beginning of my career as a music writer.

Jazz music is a dynamic force that keeps me motivated to tell its story. At live shows the musicians and their music is so captivating I feel a spiritual connection that obligates me to share with readers what I've witnessed through my writing. I am also motivated by the history of the music; it is a story that must be told over and over again. African American young people need to understand this is their music, stemming from the shores of Africa.

When I first started writing about music, I was not aware of the scarcity of African Americans writing about serious music. I started out in music writing about rhythm and blues. Later on I met and became close friends with several writers in that genre; at that time I wasn't particularly aware of black writers in jazz. When I started reading the *Village Voice* on a regular basis, I was inspired by the contributions of Greg Tate and Stanley Crouch. They brought out the heart of the music. When they wrote you could literally feel the music in the moment and experience the history of the black aesthetic. Tate and Crouch spoke with soul, historical knowledge, and great wit.

I view jazz music like the NBA—where there's a host of black players but very little black representation as coaches, general managers, lawyers, publicists, agents, or writers. Institutional racism is alive and well in jazz.

Just look at our representation in the major jazz publications, like *DownBeat* and *JazzTimes*—including what happened to Stanley Crouch at *JazzTimes*, from which he was fired. Even a writer as great as the late Amiri Baraka, who wrote a wealth of books, including my bible *Black Music*, was not a welcomed contributor on the music at any daily newspapers, much less at the major jazz publications. He was fired as a columnist by both *DownBeat* and *JazzTimes* magazines—and was certainly not replaced by another black writer.

I do believe that the relatively small number of black music writers contributes to how the music is covered. Music is objective; it's based on emotions, life experiences, societal stimuli, and cultural background. When black writers aren't proportionately involved in sharing their insights about the music, the coverage becomes decidedly one-sided. Everyone who writes about this music is contributing something useful and valuable that benefits all of jazz. Black writers need to be writing for jazz publications, and this is simply not happening on a regular basis.

Each writer, black or white, brings their own unique perspective to the work, and we need all of those diverse viewpoints in the mix. The approach to covering the music is the same, but each of us as a writer adds our own cultural outlooks, experiences, knowledge, and the personal relationships that develop with musicians and industry people, each adding yet another level of insight to the music and the musicians. Black writers may come from a more culture-specific perspective, since at its foundation jazz is black music and since the music is a distinct part of our history in this country.

I view this disparity as parallel to Benny Goodman's being hailed as the "King of Swing." How could that be possible when he walked the earth at the same time as Fletcher Henderson, Duke Ellington, and Count Basie? Certainly the lack of cultural diversity in the music media is an obvious factor in how this music is covered.

Though I contribute to a black periodical, the indifference of African American publications toward providing regular coverage of serious music is a difficult question. Most of that neglect has to do with issues related to black history. I think if more black folks were truly aware of their history and of the role that jazz has played in society, those publications would be more apt to cover the music.

I write for the *Amsterdam News* thanks to the publisher Elinor Tatum, who, like her late father Bill Tatum, feels the music has to maintain a voice in all aspects of the black community. One of the reasons why serious music coverage has diminished in many papers—black or white—is because, back in the day, jazz was dance music; everyone from fifteen to sixty was swing dancing. Dancing was the key to the music's success, the motto being "No parking on the dance floor." But when bebop came to fruition and the music began to become more cerebral, more of a listening experience, the younger crowd moved on.

Today jazz is treated like a stepchild by the mainstream mass media—let alone by the black media—so it doesn't get prime-time play the way it should. Thankfully, the *Amsterdam News* has historically loved and respected the music, which has afforded me an opportunity to share my love of jazz with its many readers.

5

magazine freelancers

BILL BROWER, JANINE COVENEY, LOFTON EMENARI III,
EUGENE HOLLEY JR., JOHN MURPH, DON PALMER,
AND RON WYNN

The contributors to this section have operated largely as freelance writers for those publications with their bylines and not, typically, as staff contributors or columnists. Some have indeed been identified in the publication's masthead as "regular contributor," even though their contributions are often of a cyclical nature, largely governed by editor and publisher proclivities that can operate like shifting tides.

The nature of such freelance work generally requires the writer to "pitch" his or her editor various contribution ideas, themes, and topics in order to achieve an assignment to contribute to a given periodical.

Bill Brower

Call him William, W. A., or Bill Brower—the various bylines he wrote under—Brower, who joined the ancestors in 2021, was a writer who used the power of the pen to open other doors into the music. Bill's work included, notably, many years as a concerts and events producer around DC and other parts of the jazz globe, including many years stage-managing the Jazz Tent at the New Orleans Jazz and Heritage Festival. Additionally, he was a longtime producer of the annual Congressional Black Caucus jazz event.

From his high school days, the Toledo, OH, native was deeply invested in jazz and other forms of black music. That thirst became an obsession as he matriculated through Antioch College and a full-blown addiction when he entered the professional job marketplace in Washington, DC. Writing was deep in Brower's DNA, his late father having been a very active and influential newspaper journalist who always encouraged that side of his only son's interests.

After arriving in DC in the early 1970s, Bill Brower wrote about the music and served as an oral historian for the Smithsonian Institution. Encouraged by one of his college-era friends and colleagues to seriously apply his obsession with jazz to the pursuit of the written word, Bill Brower brought a wealth of insights to our dialogue, and a sense of certainty that, indeed, there "ain't but a few of us."

I think writing about music had been something that was in me, and I'd danced around it without even being clear that writing about jazz was destined. But the direct motivation came around 1974–1975. Prior to that time, I had been a community organizer working around racial discrimination issues in government, and that work concluded. Then I worked for one year as the executive director of the Conference of Minority Public Administrators. When that ended, I kept trying to use the contacts I had made to get some consultant work in government, and I even contemplated going to graduate school to study economics.

A guy named Tom Porter, whom I had known since my Antioch College days, posed a question: "When you come home at night, do you open up books on price theory and econometrics, or do you listen to John Coltrane?" I said I listen to John Coltrane and Charlie Mingus. He said, "Then you need to be writing about this music, not trying to go to graduate school to get a masters or a PhD in something that you aren't that interested in." I was amassing a significant record collection. I was always reading about the music, and I had done a few things prior to that time that were writer-oriented—interpreting, documenting, evaluating jazz. So that's what made me decide that I would pursue writing and other things around the music.

I had produced festivals when I was at school, and I'd done some writing in association with those festivals. For my high school senior paper at Western Reserve Academy, I brought my class to my dorm room and discussed recordings. By that time I had read *Blues People, The Wretched of the Earth*—I was sort of synthesizing a lot of different things, and it had given me a perspective looking closely at the music I was interested in. Tom Porter contacted the *Washington Post* columnist Dorothy Gilliam on my behalf, and that's where I made my first writing contribution on jazz.

My father was a journalist; I had grown up around newspapers and books, and I had always been a bookworm. All of that encouraged me to write about the music. Dorothy Gilliam introduced me to the Style section editor, who gave me some opportunities to be a stringer. Those first writings were reviewing shows and records.

I was aware of the scarcity of black music writers because I was reading the literature. Before I started writing, I read about jazz, but I had not been studying it in an academic environment. I'm pretty much an autodidact—I pick a subject, bury myself in it, and that's how I learn. I wasn't following any kind of curriculum, I hadn't been exposed to jazz in a classroom setting, but I had surveyed the jazz literature. It's the same thing with records, just like one book will lead you to another book . . .

I was aware of A. B. Spellman, Amiri Baraka (then LeRoi Jones), and a few other black writers. My motivation to write was part of recognizing that, in the field of jazz—serious black music, or whatever term you use—black folks were woefully absent in almost every aspect beyond the bandstand. So much of what I've done in my life has been in response to that, across the board, whether it was production or writing. Anything I've done has been in response to the fact that I always recognized the paucity of black folks' engagement in the business and documentation sides of this music.

One book that I really found very interesting was about the backstory behind the famous 1956 Duke Ellington performance at the Newport Jazz Festival, *Backstory in Blue: Ellington at Newport '56*. The book talks about how that initial generation of jazz writers were all students who knew each other from these Ivy League schools and who were avid record collectors. They created a network of jazz writers, and to a large degree I believe that network has been perpetuated over generations; it has not encouraged African Americans to do that work. For the most part, black writers that have written about the music have not been included in that network. We may have friends, we may have associations within that fraternity, but we're really not in the inner sanctums of that fraternity.

People like LeRoi Jones and A. B. Spellman were gate-crashers. One of the things I read in high school was "Apple Cores," the column that LeRoi Jones was writing in *DownBeat*, including his documentation of the "October

Revolution in Music." I was aware that what he was doing—or the occasional black musician that ventured into writing about jazz, like Bill Dixon, was doing—was exceptional. The other consideration was purely economics. Eventually I turned away from jazz writing because I couldn't feed my family.

When I got deeper into producing events and started to have a personal economy from it, I drifted away from writing about jazz. I also felt that I needed to write at a different level. The experience that I've gained over the years has given me a better grounding to write than when I started. I've been a participant-observer, and it's all conspired, I hope, to take me to another level.

Most of what people cover in music occurs in the white world; we still live in a segregated society. There are plenty of places where we commingle, but socially and culturally we're still separate. There are sort of overlapping spheres, so it's not fixed or totally black-and-white—or the lines aren't necessarily always that hard—but in my experience Betty Carter could be playing at a black-owned joint like the Pigfoot and you wouldn't see a peep about it in the *Post*; but if she were playing Blues Alley she'd get seven inches of copy.

Among the things that have really annoyed me over the years is the lack of print coverage of the annual Benny Golson Awards at Howard University; nobody covers that—it's like it doesn't happen. And so perception becomes reality; the perception about what's going on in the business of jazz, let alone in the culture of jazz, is determined by what people have access to, are interested in, what they gravitate toward—and that tends to be situations where people are comfortable.

Consequently, an editor is going to tell you to go to the Kennedy Center, or to the Historic Synagogue at 6th and I, to cover Washington Performing Arts concerts, but they're not going to send you to cover something a black presenter like Vernard Gray is producing. Perception becomes a certain reality. I absolutely think that who the editors are, who the beat writers, the columnists are, what they're comfortable with, who they know, and what they have access to absolutely determines what gets covered—and that's a problem.

I'm sensitive to the fact that which musicians are covered is determined by who's doing the writing. Joe Lovano is a good example for me. I hear people railing against why Joe Lovano gets so much play. Well that isn't Joe Lovano's fault at all, it has nothing to do with the quality of his musicianship, it has nothing to do with how he looks at the tradition, or any of that; it has to do with editorial decisions. I don't put that at the feet of the musicians, and I don't paint them with any kind of brush. I mean, what are they supposed to do, say, "Don't write about me, don't publish me, don't review me?" That's ridiculous.

But at the same time, I think once again that *who* gets covered is about taste, it's about preference, it's about what you know and whom you're comfortable with. Either in a very direct way or a subliminal way, I do believe that some of those choices and some of those emphases are conditioned by who's making the editorial decisions—and we know what that picture looks like.

As a DC correspondent for *DownBeat*, I just sent in news bits, and pretty much anything I sent they would publish. The feature assignments I got from *DB* were about African Americans, with the exception of the piece I did on NPR's *Jazz Alive* series. They had me do pieces on Stevie Wonder and on George Clinton—I think that was because they had a sense that I had a broader engagement with creative music beyond just jazz. I can't remember whether I pitched those ideas or not.

When I went to Detroit to write my George Clinton piece, that's the only press junket I took, where a record company sent me a ticket and put me in a hotel. George was doing a bunch of stuff, and I think his record company was pushing all these different projects because he had multiple labels he was involved with and multiple aggregations under different names, but it was essentially the same musicians. There was an interest in getting that story out there.

Because of how you get paid as a freelancer, you need to have contributions in the pipeline. As for black publications: my father had introduced me to the idea of writing for *Sepia* and *Bronze Thrills* magazines. I would send them jazz stuff and front-of-the-book stuff on anything that was happening in Washington. I kind of had this thing in my head that if you had enough $25 and $50 pieces all kind of stacked up with this publication and that publication—it would add up.

I was trying to feed them as many small bites as I could; we're talking about thirty-five years ago, and I don't remember any resistance to that. I had a good vibe with the editor of *Sepia* at that time, who I never met in person, but I never felt that the phone conversations we had were condescending or anything of that sort. When my relationship with the *Washington Post* ended after less than a year, I had written probably less than a dozen pieces for them; it ended with their editor basically saying, "Stop calling me." When I asked Dorothy Gilliam about that, she said, "Well, it's kind of like a date: if you keep calling a girl, leaving messages for a date, and she doesn't call you back, she's sending you a message—she doesn't want to go out with you." You can either belittle yourself by calling her or just realize it's time for you to knock on another door.

I needed to figure out whether I was going to continue writing about jazz, because I really hadn't done enough where it was some kind of crazy passion with me. I was into writing, and that's when I started a column with the *Washington Afro-American* newspaper. It was very short-form stuff; I was calling in the stories on the phone, so it's not like I was writing five-thousand-word pieces. When the *Afro-American* situation ended, I had to figure out whether writing was something I wanted to stay with—and I did.

As far as African American publications, I also wrote for the *Washington Informer* for a time, and I wrote stuff for *American Visions* magazine. I've worked with a range of African American publications that are either owned by African Americans or are—like *Sepia*—owned by other entities but are oriented toward the African American market. I don't think it would be fair to generalize about the range of attitudes or dispositions toward the music from black publications, because each situation was a bit different. What I think they all have in common is the economic factor; they're all driven to keep the publication happening. Ultimately, all publications are not about editorial content but about advertising dollars. That's where I think the answer lies to the question of the attitude of African American publications toward jazz: it isn't based on their disposition toward the music, it's fundamentally about how jazz plays out in terms of business.

When I was writing for the *Afro*, the editor was Art Carter. My father's second job as a journalist was with the *Washington Afro-American*, and Art Carter had been there when my father was there in the early 1940s. When Art first agreed to publish me—and I had come in there cold and sold him on a column—I don't know whether he liked jazz or not. I gave them some good content, and I was providing him with inches of copy on something they weren't covering. I was doing this gratis. When I sold them on the idea, I'd made the decision that, yes, I want to do this, and at the time I didn't even have a typewriter: I used to write the stuff out longhand and take it to my wife at the time—she would type it up at lunchtime on her job, and I would walk it over to the *Afro* office.

I was getting access to clubs and a load of music—we're all record collectors, and so I was happier than a pig in slop. I could go into One Step Down, Blues Alley, Club Etcetera, wherever I wanted. If McCoy Tyner came some place for six nights, I could be there six nights—I had carte blanche. I really just wanted some travel money—you know, $15, just give me *something*—and

Art Carter basically looked at me like I had lost my mind. He did that from the perspective of, "If there's no advertising revenue associated with your column, what's the point?"

I got to a point where I said to myself, "Man, this is some bullshit." My gut reaction was, "Why don't they get this, this is black music!" What caused me to think about it a bit differently were two other experiences with African American publishers. When I wrote for *Sepia* I got paid. I did some pieces for *Bronze Thrills* on Miles Davis and Betty Carter, and I did a lot of front-of-book stuff. I never really wrote on jazz for *Sepia*; I wrote a lot of front-of-book stuff on things happening in Washington, and I did some features that weren't jazz-oriented.

By this time, in the 1970s, I'm writing for *JazzTimes* and thinking I'm going to write for the *Washington Informer*, DC's African American weekly. I met with Denise Rolark Barnes, the publisher, and she found some dollars to pay me for a couple of pieces a week—and once again I had a platform.

I think the newspaper now is fairly healthy, but during those times, when Denise first took over, it was struggling. One day we met with Denise's father, Calvin Rolark. He told me, "Writers are a dime a dozen; what I need is a good advertising man." Then he told me, "You make sure the next person you write a story about commits to taking a hundred copies of the paper." So for him there was a direct relationship between editorial and commerce; and I found a similar relationship—if not so bluntly presented—with *American Visions*.

Not that I wouldn't prefer that African American publications have a broader vision. If I'd gone to Calvin Rolark's house, he might have had a living room full of Sarah Vaughan, Dave Brubeck, and Miles Davis records, but I know that as a publisher his thing was, "I gotta pay this guy that prints these newspapers, I've gotta pay the rent on the building, and my decisions about what I publish are driven by that." I think the decisions at the *Washington Post* are driven by the same elements, but they're at a different level in terms of capitalization, access to credit, and cash flow. So how those decisions present themselves to the staff is different—except that, when they say, "Oh, guess what, half the newsroom is fired," they can give people severance pay because they're in a position to make those decisions. They're making the same kinds of decisions but with a level of resourcing that none of these African American publications can even imagine.

Denise did everything she could to make it possible for me to do what I was doing, so I couldn't paint her with a brush of being some obtuse black person who doesn't care about the culture. She did, or she wouldn't have bent over backward, despite her father's point of view, to let me do the jazz writing I did for the *Informer*.

This music is of an African American provenance, and I always use that term. If you trace back the origin of its creativity, of its invention, its chain of ownership—and I believe this includes jazz, and certainly blues, spirituals, gospel, all those streams pouring into jazz, and then also its children, jump blues, rhythm and blues, rock and roll—it's all of African American provenance.

When I go to a good church where people sing and clap, I hear the sock cymbal in the congregation. If that kind of stuff is not genetically encoded, it is culturally encoded. African Americans start with a leg up, if not two legs up, as players or anything else we want to do in this jazz culture: probably even more so from the 1940s to the 1980s than now, but it's culturally encoded—it's in the DNA of our culture, which is the DNA of that music. Does that mean somebody else is incapable? No, but I do believe that to some extent it may require them to overcome certain illusions, delusions, and prejudices.

Music is both a cultural phenomenon and an art phenomenon, and on another level it is a scientific and mathematical phenomenon. It depends on what aspect of the music, or of the evaluation and criticisms of the music, you're interested in. If you're interested in music as a scientific or mathematical phenomenon, that's a different question than if you're looking at it and trying to understand it, interpret it, or document it from the cultural or artistic dimension.

I think the artistic dimension bridges the cultural and scientific dimensions of music. A good writer has all of that in their tool bag, and they may use a different mixture of those things in how they approach their work. I'm averse to generalizations, but at the same time I do believe in trends. I'm averse to generalizations because if you take two guys walking down the street, and one guy is black as tar and the other guy is white as a white sheet with a few freckles, you might say that black guy has a leg up, but it's really a lot more complex than that.

Here's another way I look at it, and now I'm speaking beyond the domain of writing about the music, but I think it applies: I'm not so concerned about every note that Bird played; I'm not so interested in reciting that "he had twenty-nine outtakes of this song and that song." I'm actually more interested in the experience of hearing the music.

I've got a lot of records, but I'm more interested in occupying the space where it's being played: I think that what's recorded is just a fraction of what has been played, and it doesn't even reflect the best of what's been played. One of my fondest experiences listening to music was seeing the McCoy Tyner band with John Blake, Joe Ford, George Adams, Guillerme Franco, and that whole crew. I don't think they made a record that even approaches what I heard live. So why am I going to valorize a recording—which is simply the commodification of culture—over the experience of the culture itself?

I know guys that don't ever go out to hear music, don't really engage it as a live phenomenon, and to me that reflects a cultural prejudice: it's not like when we express prejudice as racism; I simply mean a preference or orientation that valorizes or gives worth to one type of thing over another thing. Any question you ask me, I'm going to answer from that point of view.

The business of jazz has been mistaken for the history of jazz. Jazz is a culture, it's a way of life, and it infuses more than just performance. The value of improvisation in providing a personal voice, or the stylization of how musicians think and feel and envision things, is part of a culture that's endemic to us—at least to this point in time. It may change, but I feel I was at least fortunate enough to be born into that. What I call the academicization of the music may be taking it somewhere else, maybe toward a loss of personality.

My most important encounters with musicians happened with my oral history interviews, though I had a ball writing about George Clinton. That was a great experience; we got snowed in, and I wound up staying multiple days in Detroit. The most personally rewarding experience was coming to know Billy Taylor through writing about *Jazz Alive*. Writing, and doing oral history interviews, has allowed me to engage some of the great masters of the music in an intense way.

My oral history interviews were with Clark Terry, Jackie McLean, Slide Hampton, Philly Joe Jones, Art Blakey, Jimmy Cobb, Curtis Fuller, and Cedar Walton. The opportunity to sit with them over two or three days is where I really got my boots laced. Just to have access to them for an intensive engagement, to ask them about their lives, to ask them about who influenced them, what were high points in their careers, where they saw the music going, their appreciation of other players—and particularly of players that haven't been documented by recordings, the unsung heroes—the cities they grew up in, what drove them to be engaged with this music. Those experiences were invaluable.

When I did a story on Sam Rivers for *DownBeat*, I went to New York and hung out at Studio Rivbea for two or three days interviewing Sam, photographing his rehearsals—you can't beat that with three sticks! One thing about interviewing these gentlemen, which in some cases came as a surprise, was that in every case I got the distinct impression they were happy that a black writer was doing the interviewing.

For example, I was talking with Randy Weston and found out his father was a Garveyite. I know about Marcus Garvey, so when that comes up, even if I'm in a different camp than Garvey, I've still got a working knowledge of that history and what that would have meant to Randy—as opposed to somebody who's not conversant with the history of Pan Africanism, black nationalism, and so on. And Randy isn't the only one: when I'm talking with Art Blakey, or with Max Roach, I've got stuff in my memory bank that white writers either don't have or maybe have a jaundiced view of.

As a black man I'm just generally in a different cultural space—and even a different knowledge space—than some people for whom their engagement with jazz is their sole engagement with an African American phenomenon. They might have grown up when the civil rights movement was happening, but they weren't necessarily engaged in the movement—they likely don't know a lot of the ins and outs, the figures and different developments and trends, at least not from personal experience.

One of the challenges is understanding that I need to write for an audience that may not be acquainted with that sort of in-group language; I should assume that people don't know things and should explain them more fully; I shouldn't use language that people would perceive as coded. Editors are always concerned with whether the person reading something can make sense of it. I didn't have that perspective when I first started writing, but I recognize that in writing you shouldn't assume a great deal about readers.

If you're writing for an academic publication, you should assume that using technical language, the in-group language of the particular discipline in which you're writing, is acceptable. But even if you're writing for fanzines—like *DownBeat*, *JazzTimes*—the language is different. For the most part I've not written for academic publications, but I've studied them to enhance my understanding. My biggest obstacle is understanding how to express my ideas, how to unpack my ideas for a broader audience about whom I should not make assumptions as to what they do or don't know.

When I'm dealing with black musicians, they could be my uncle, they could be my older brother, they could be my father—I felt that kind of relationship, particularly if I sat multiple days with them. I'm confident that in your six degrees of separation you're connected with jazz musicians, just by being an African American, it's in your family orbit. My father's homestead and the Coltrane family homestead in High Point, NC, was like four houses apart. My dad never talked about Coltrane, because to him Coltrane was one extra person at the dinner table. My uncle had grown up with Coltrane. I'm saying all that to say we're back to six degrees of separation—and that's why I say jazz is our provenance.

Janine Coveney

Janine Coveney was formerly the West Coast head writer for the syndicated entertainment news service Pulse Content. She has also been a contributing writer to *JazzTimes* magazine and EURweb.com. When I first met Janine, she was covering the Rhythm and Blues Foundation's annual Pioneer Awards during her productive stint as R&B editor at *Billboard* magazine, for which she also served as the managing editor of *Billboard Airplay Monitor*. Janine has also contributed to *Gavin*, *Impact*, and *Essence Magazine*.

My career in writing about music began at *Billboard* with R&B and pop, which some people might not consider "serious" music, and my writing continues these days covering a lot of contemporary and smooth jazz, which many folks in jazz don't consider "serious." But I submit that few popular instrumentalists, of any stripe, go into a studio to create anything they *don't* take seriously, and many of them have been trained in jazz.

As a writer I'm challenged to cull and comment upon the serious elements of this work. I like the process of analyzing music *and* musician—something that many artists don't like at all. They don't want to be dissected: most feel that the music should speak for itself. But as a writer I think my job is to place a particular piece of music within historical and cultural contexts and to judge not necessarily the musician's level of skill on an instrument (which some of us writers are frankly not qualified to do) but his or her level of skill as a communicator. Does the music make us feel what the musician intended? Can we hear his or her influences and inspirations? What is the impact on the listener?

When I started my music journalism career, I was not truly aware of a scarcity of African Americans writing about serious music. It seemed to me that things were as they had been for a long time: whites in the majority, blacks employed in token positions—that seemed to be the status quo. I knew of Stanley Crouch, but when I wrote for *Billboard* the jazz editors were white.

As I've continued working in the industry, I've seen the number of African Americans writing about any kind of music at various outlets dwindle. If I was aware of a dearth of black music writers, it was that there were not more African American *women* writing about music in a serious way, because the music beat—particularly in jazz—has been primarily a male domain. This is still true. Female music writers have traditionally focused on the celebrity aspect of a musician's life and not the art and craft of the music itself.

Reasons are many for these disparities. First of all, the traditional media itself has diminished. There are fewer outlets for writers of any color to publish work about serious music, and so the African American music writer becomes even more of an anomaly. Secondly, the audience for serious music by black musicians has changed.

There is an intellectual component to "serious" jazz—straight-ahead or avant-garde—and in this age of marginalization, trivialization, instant gratification, and lack of music education, the black audience seems to have fled. With that flight went valuable media space.

Fewer African American writers are really versed enough in jazz to write on it. As one generation of jazz scholars and writers age out and die out, there is not a generation behind them broad enough to take up their mantle. But even when writers have some grounding in jazz, one must ask: can they pull steady paychecks writing about it? Doubtful.

I'm no jazz scholar; I have a basic understanding of the development of jazz music in this country and of the contributions of pivotal players, but I cannot cite you chapter and verse the personnel on a particular Miles Davis recording session. I don't write from a place of jazz scholarship but from a place of continuous discovery and appreciation. This is why I don't write theoretical essays about jazz; instead, I conduct interviews and constantly ask questions about the form and content and relationships within the jazz milieu and share my impressions of that while contributing to my own knowledge.

My career trajectory has forced me to become a bit of a jack-of-all-trades and a master of none—which has happened to many writers surviving within the confines of corporate media these days. But there aren't enough new African American writers to write with authority with a foundation in either jazz scholarship or jazz appreciation—or who have ever had any music education. Jazz is too hard for them: it's too old-school or too inscrutable. I've been fortunate to write about jazz from time to time, but the canon of jazz writing should not be left to the likes of writers like me.

That the low number of black music journalists affects how the music is covered is absolutely true. I would say that there is a race line within jazz music that no one cares to discuss in any serious, public way, one that has to do with how and where the music originated, compared with who has now studied the shit out of it and is doing it their own way and raking in the praise.

There is a cultural approach to covering the music and an academic approach. At times there may be a difference as to which jazz releases may be considered important or praiseworthy because there is not a great enough diversity of voices and viewpoints adequately to write about innovative artists. Much of the documentation of jazz, and jazz criticism, has been contributed by white writers and authors—this isn't to say that they're not qualified, but it does become curious when the leading authorities on a music founded and developed by African Americans are not themselves African American.

I am frequently astounded by what passes for the Next Big Thing in jazz and other genres of popular music. But I do respect artists who have perfected their approach and their sound and marketed it to a specific audience. And while their music may not be to my personal taste, as a writer I have to be able to understand the economic, artistic, and cultural conditions that support their popularity. While my surprise at what is promoted as the Next Big Thing is often a product of the lack of cultural diversity in the reporting, more often I find it's a function of age. I'm over fifty, and I remember the music of the 1960s and 1970s, and I heard and know much of the music of my parents' generation: the music of the 1930s, 1940s, and 1950s. Sometimes younger writers will hail some musician doing something they think is novel, and I think, "That ain't hardly new, children . . ."

Reasons for the apathy toward jazz by African American–oriented publications are twofold: first, serious music is considered too "hard" for the average reader to relate to; and secondly, most black-targeted magazines are in a thankless struggle for circulation and readership and therefore have to appeal to the widest possible number of readers. Whose face on the cover will sell more magazines—Dee Dee Bridgewater or Beyoncé? David Sanchez or Jamie Foxx? Also, because the internet has grown at such a rapid rate and celebrity can be conferred on just about anyone who has appeared on television, the gossip and scandal element is what sells these days—the more drama the better.

In covering smooth jazz news, I always tell people how difficult it is to develop regular "news" items because jazz people generally only do two things: release recordings and go on tour. They don't do many of the things that artists do in other genres to grab headlines: they don't record "diss" tracks, they don't have public "beefs" with fellow artists, they don't have posses that deliver beatdowns to other artists, they don't pose nude in *Playboy*, they aren't on reality TV shows, they don't marry movie stars, and so on. If jazz artists have domestic drama or substance abuse issues—or even if they do serious charity work—they tend to keep it under wraps. Jazz folks are low on public drama. And black-targeted media these days—indeed, most general interest media—seems to be more interested in perpetuating drama than providing a forum for intelligent discourse about the arts.

I would say that there would definitely be a difference in how the music is covered based on who is writing about it and in what outlet that writing would appear (i.e., the target market). If you are reviewing a new album by a jazz trumpeter, your point of view will be different if your only reference points are Wynton Marsalis, Chris Botti, and Arturo Sandoval. If you've never heard recordings by or know little about Louis Armstrong, Miles Davis, King Oliver, or even Jon Faddis, Chet Baker, Hugh Masekela, or Nicholas Payton, you may be able to write about the music's appeal but not about its roots.

Most of my encounters with jazz musicians have been pleasant and upbeat because I approach them from the standpoint that they are creative artists, and I have a healthy respect for how art is created. Also because, in most of my interviews, I let them know that I represent the fans—lay people who love their work and want a peek inside how they do what they do. Usually my encounters go well, because the artists understand that I am somewhat informed about them and want to have a conversation. More memorable are those experiences when I've met an artist and the discussion did not go well or the vibe was somehow off. And of course the most rewarding encounter is when a reader says, "I read your piece on (whatever), and it was amazing."

Unfortunately a lot of what I've written over the years has been tied to a record sales—or airplay chart–driven aesthetic. Many of the more interesting, innovative, and genre-flouting serious musicians make records that don't get within spitting distance of any sales or airplay chart. This means that those who don't currently get airplay can't get column inches either, which is a catch-22 circle of hell both for them and for me.

Another issue that I recall vividly and bitterly from my days at *Billboard* under the late Timothy White is that, even though I was the "Black Music" columnist, if an African American artist "crossed over" to the pop side enough to warrant front-page coverage, I was deemed unqualified to write the story.

It was taken from me and assigned to a white writer, someone equipped with no better understanding of that artist—or superior writing skills—to mine. Though I also appreciated artists like Elton John or the Police, I would never get an opportunity to write about them.

Though I was raised in a Caribbean family, and I knew a good bit about reggae, soca, and Latin and roots music, White—who had written the "definitive" Bob Marley biography, *Catch a Fire*—forbade me from ever covering any sort of island music in my column. He literally would take my proofs and scratch out any lines about a reggae release or festival. There was no other place for reggae coverage in the magazine in the 1990s, so artists and publicists were counting on me to give them some column inches. I never denied White's level of expertise on the Marley family legacy, but for him to deny my cultural knowledge was insulting. If there were other motives for him to exclude reggae coverage, he never explained them to me.

I also got my grounding in those days writing about contemporary jazz because *Billboard*'s jazz columnists did not write about anything but the strictest straight-ahead jazz releases by a small circle of artists. That's how I first met Nnenna Freelon, Cassandra Wilson, Christian McBride, Terence Blanchard, Nicholas Payton, Branford Marsalis, Greg Osby, and T. S. Monk, among other jazz innovators and artists.

There is definitely a shortage of black writers in the music space. And since I originally contributed to the *Ain't But a Few of Us* series, the world of jazz coverage—indeed, music coverage in general—has continued to change dramatically due to advances in technology and shifts in culture. The issue of access is impacted by these facts: there is a limited pool of old-school media outlets that pay for work; you have to have impeccable, long-standing credentials or know somebody there to get your work accepted; your perspective on the music may not be appreciated or thought to be in line with the majority of the outlet's readers; those outlets are struggling to stay afloat financially; even the new-school media outlets won't pay what your work is worth; and you're competing in a sphere with self-appointed experts whose free content receives thousands, if not millions, of "likes" and followers.

What many of us viewed as the official publications of the jazz world have shrunk or disappeared from newsstands, maintaining more staggered publication schedules, fewer pages, or an online-only presence—if they continue at all. The staff writers and contributors at those magazines are clinging for dear life to their posts, and there is little room or money to take on newcomers. That has meant limited access for all writers to have their work exposed in those titles.

Instead, the internet has expanded. There are more online culture mags. More blogs. More podcasts. More YouTube channels. Any writer with an opinion about jazz can share their views, review projects, interview artists, and create whatever content they like and put it out there without a middleman. They are creating their own media platforms, becoming less reliant on editors at established media sites to rubber-stamp their pitches. Whereas once black writers may have complained about access, about having a seat at the table at major magazines to write about music being made by black artists in this genre, today I think the issue among writers and those they write about is the *quality* and *credibility* of coverage.

Many people writing today for the blogs, podcasts, and so on, are music fans, not trained journalists; or they are internet geeks building a brand to push other ideas or products; or they are in fact decent writers who lack a deep foundation in music education or jazz history and cannot convey the import of what they're covering. Many of the artists and producers themselves have become chroniclers of the jazz experience on their own websites. The person best able to promote their content via social media is viewed as the prevailing expert. So accomplished writers now have to change up how they create their coverage in order to be competitive. Another issue for writers in all genres is the ability to get paid for their work. The pay available for writers at those outlets that do pay freelancers is minuscule, driving out better writers in favor of novices.

So the coverage of jazz may, in fact, be broader, but the problem is that what's there isn't necessarily deeper. And many of today's readers have lost their taste for the long read and don't know what they don't know. They want to be entertained, not educated, by what they read.

Lofton Emenari III

Lofton Emenari III's music writing has appeared in *DownBeat*, *Cadence*, the *Chicago Citizen*, *eJazzNews Online*, the *Chicago Observer*, the *African Spectrum*, *Jazz Online*, *Black Scholar*, *All about Jazz*, and other publications. He is a longtime jazz radio programmer at WHPK-FM, the radio voice of the University of Chicago.

Many years ago I learned that being a so-called "black" writer on jazz music would be an enriching but harrowing journey. I was a child of the civil rights movement, with parents that instilled a love of kith and kin, past and present, ever cognizant of the social realities abounding. It was from this fertile nest that I became a writer and journalist—initially seeking, altruistically, to address seeming wrongs and to speak for the unheard and unseen.

Jazz was a part of my household—played every day either on the record player or via radio. As a child I was exposed to *DownBeat* magazine and became an avid reader in high school. Back then I had no real working knowledge of black writers in the music field—yet. Once out of high school I joined various writers' collectives in Chicago. That alone gave me more intellectual power and measurement. The first black jazz writers I learned of were LeRoi Jones and A. B. Spellman. And while Baraka would leave the jazz arena for a moment, it took years for me to break his spell, not only on my thinking but on my writing style as well. He was that influential as a motivator.

Later on I would be influenced by the writings of Albert Murray, Ralph Ellison, Richard Wright, Ted Joans, and ultimately Stanley Crouch. These icons set the bar high. They collectively told *our* story as no others dared to or could. It was because of them that I diligently studied the history of this music. It was, as the title of Val Wilmer's classic tome indicated, *As Serious as Your Life*. The study of this music, the very research, began in the venues and in the lives of the musicians themselves. Everywhere the music was, I went to hear and feel it.

At the same time I became a broadcast journalist, with a weekly jazz radio show on WHPK-FM at the University of Chicago. It was there that I met Ted Pankin, who remains one of the most knowledgeable and interesting writers on jazz—black or white. Ted followed the exploits of the avant-garde, and in particular the Chicago-based Association for the Advancement of Creative Musicians (AACM).

I would also form some lasting friendships with some of the music's most glorious practitioners. At this point, by my count, I've interviewed over a thousand musicians. I first became a published writer on jazz through the initial impact of reading "underground" magazines like *The Grackle*, which was published in New York by a loose coterie of black writers—Roger Riggins, Ron Welburn, and James Stewart—in the mid- to late 1970s.

I later found out there were even more black music writers out there when copies of the *Jazz Spotlite News* made their way to Chicago from the magazine's New York base. Here in Chicago there were perhaps two black writers on jazz: Brent Staples, and Salim Muwakkil, the onetime editor of *Muhammad Speaks* and the current columnist of *In These Times*. They would become invaluable mentors and significant friends.

My first article in a major jazz publication was for *DownBeat* in 1979, thanks to the then-editor Howard Mandel, and subsequently I've voted in the annual *DownBeat* International Critics Poll. I began writing about jazz for various community newspapers and journals, including a ten-year column in the *Chicago Defender* and twenty-eight years writing in the *Chicago Citizen Newspaper Group*.

At one point, due to the apathy I felt was prevalent in jazz journalism, I published a journal, *The Creative Arts Review*, soliciting articles from writers on the music. I solicited those articles regardless of gender or race. It was a one-issue wonder that included the writing of voices such as Hakim Sulieman (an unrecognized jazz historian and archivist), Brent Staples, Larry Queen (an accomplished black art critic), Keith Boseman, and a few others. But it was mainly a platform for my own theories on the music.

Over the years I've found the niche of writing album liner notes to be an almost closed circle of contributors. This was particularly prevalent with the so-called major jazz labels. In the late 1970s and early 1980s I began to query some of the musicians I knew on a personal basis about writing their liner notes. I asked Bobby Watson, David Murray, Joe Henderson, Arthur Blythe, Terence Blanchard and Donald Harrison, Wallace Roney, Javon Jackson, and many others. Only Blanchard and Harrison, Jackson, and Roney granted my wish. This was for Columbia-Sony, a major label, and at the time, those artists were major voices, in the wake of the Marsalis phenomenon. Of that wave of artists, Wallace Roney recorded for Muse Records, a mid-level label. Later on I secured liner note gigs for Donald Brown, Billy Pierce, and Stephen Scott recordings.

Yet there was something missing from the average liner notes; most often I dreaded reading liner notes, for there seemed to be the same contributing writers on regular rotation. I called it the Bob Blumenthal Syndrome of liner note writing, since his byline seemed predominant. What I experienced from the average liner notes was patronizingly dull, mundane, almost pedestrian writing, basic ABC writing that catered to "new" jazz listening. I recognized that most liner notes were either: (1) biographical, a recounting of the biographical background of the featured artist; or (2) musically detailed. Which prompts a discussion of the whole issue of liner note writing as genre (which some awards, like the Grammys, deem an awardable category for recognition).

An incident with the producer of a Javon Jackson record was most trying. Prior to that point I had the honor of penning liners for Jackson's first recording as a leader on the Criss Cross label. Jackson asked me to write some liners for his second release, his debut on the heralded Blue Note label. After dutifully submitting the notes, the producer phoned me in a very matter-of-fact way to inform me that my writing was way too "Amiri Baraka–ish" and my language "too hip"! Needless to say, I was floored when she said that she couldn't use my notes due to deadline constraints—blah, blah, blah.

My mind was in a tizzy. How can liner notes be "too hip"? At worst, sounding too "Amiri Baraka–ish" was a flag-waving signal. Yet I was at a loss. Javon Jackson, whom I considered a close friend, apologized, and I understood his position; he was powerless against the might of the corporate Blue Note. I didn't blame Javon; I blamed the Bob Blumenthal Syndrome. I got similar remarks from the producer of the Stephen Scott disc as well, although Verve went with my notes.

The first Chicago artist to offer me liner note assignments was the late trumpeter Malachi Thompson. I wrote the notes for his first domestic debut for Delmark, a great Chicago indie label. However, because of a remark I had made in an article about the beloved white jazz DJ Dick Buckley, the (late) Delmark label owner Bob Koester considered me an outcast—even to the extent of unofficially banning me from his store, the Jazz Record Mart. We patched up the rift and moved on, and he then offered me liner note assignments for Delmark.

Herein lies the situation for black musicians and artists. Who owns the labels from which they are afforded the opportunity to record? The Black Jazz label of the early 1970s sought to rectify or balance the artistic outlets available, as did countless other independent efforts. The Black Jazz label died due to economics, lack of media exposure, and so on, ad nauseam. Yusef Lateef's own YAL label was for a time perhaps the only self-produced, black musician–owned and –operated label.

Eugene Holley Jr.

Eugene Holley Jr. is a Delaware-based writer and essayist. He has written on jazz and other music, and on books, from a variety of perspectives in such publications as *Philadelphia Weekly*, *Publishers Weekly*, *NewMusicBox*, and *Waxpoetics*. His work has also appeared in the *New York Times Book Review*, *Ebony*, the *Village Voice*, Amazon .com, *Vibe*, *DownBeat*, and *JazzTimes*.

Holley's work is featured in the anthologies *Best Music Writing: 2010* and *Albert Murray and the Aesthetic Imagination of a Nation*. He served as the music and program director for WCLK in Atlanta, GA, and worked as a producer for the documentaries *Dizzy's Diamond* (for NPR) and the Duke Ellington Radio Project. Eugene has also written on politics at *AlterNet*.

In the early 1990s, Holley joined our staff at the former National Jazz Service Organization (NJSO) in Washington. In those days, the DC area offered not one but two radio outlets primarily devoted to jazz music, WDCU and WPFW, the latter of which (the station for "jazz and justice") continues to carry the torch today. WDCU ("Jazz 90") was a potent jazz resource until, beset with municipal money woes, the District of Columbia government sold the frequency—which had been the radio voice of the University of the District of Columbia—to C-SPAN Radio. Though he was largely a pinch-hitting substitute programmer, whenever Eugene Holley Jr. showed up on WDCU's airways you could count on committed, informative jazz radio.

Not long after, as his tenure at NJSO progressed, Eugene began expanding his jazz writing skills by contributing to *DownBeat* and *JazzTimes* magazines, as well as to a number of general interest publications. His perspectives have always been literate, informative, and geared not only to the cognoscenti but also to those who may be new to the music. Eugene Holley Jr. has always recognized the need to relate to a broad spectrum of readers.

I started writing about jazz in 1987, when I worked as a DJ at WDCU-FM in Washington, DC, by writing a couple of record reviews for the station's program guide. Then I wrote for the quarterly *NJSO Journal*, and I began contributing to *DownBeat*, *JazzTimes*, and *Tower Pulse* magazines. My radio work began years before I started writing. Radio gave me a good grounding in how people respond to jazz recordings in real time: with listener phone requests—pro or con. The radio experience provided me with a visceral portrait of the real jazz audience, as did my experience as a jazz record buyer at Tower Records. So when I started writing, I had a real awareness of the readers I was writing for.

When I first began writing about jazz, I wasn't really mindful of the scarcity of African Americans writing about the music. That's primarily because my jazz mentors included three black men writing about the music—Willard Jenkins, A. B. Spellman, and Bill Brower—and they were very visible on the scene and in print. It wasn't until a few years later that I noticed the scarcity of black jazz writers on a national and international scale.

As I became more aware of how few African Americans were writing about jazz, it affected me in an oddly positive way, I'd say in retrospect. And that's because I was so committed to the music—I was a jazz zealot. Because of the scarcity of black writers, I saw it as my mission to dedicate myself solely to the music by writing only about jazz. But in retrospect, that was a mistake. I could have and should have written about other music genres, as long as the quality was on a high level.

Given the nature of jazz music—emanating from the African experience in America, with significant numbers of African American musicians still making this music—the answer as to why there have been so few African American writers on jazz is complex. First, there's the lack of exposure of jazz in American media—radio, TV, film, and so on; and it's worse in the black-oriented media. Then there's the nature of the music itself; jazz is a listener's music, not easily accessible to those of a pop sensibility—although there are a significant number of jazz musicians for whose music that doesn't always apply.

The arts are not supported in public schools where most black folks matriculate. Another oft-overlooked factor, but a key generational observation, is how few African American parents born after 1970 have a jazz record collection to pass on to their children, the way earlier generations of African American parents did. So many of us first heard the music from our parent's record collections; back then, any African American parents with good taste had some jazz in their record collection. Couple that with the fact that most jazz clubs of note are not located in black communities, whereas in the past—particularly in the 1950s and 1960s—you had live jazz opportunities in black neighborhoods. Let's not forget that black community organ joint tradition of jazz organ groups' frequent presence in black-owned establishments.

It wasn't until I moved to Harlem in the mid-1990s that I had the pleasure of walking to a neighborhood jazz club—St. Nick's Pub, which by then was rare even for the Harlem community. All of those factors contribute to this disparity. Having a black-owned jazz club within walking distance from my apartment provided me with a level of familiarity and comfort that was on a more intimate level than I would experience at the major downtown clubs. Consequently, that sense of intimacy became a benchmark for how I would later write about live jazz performances.

Whether the fact that we have so few African Americans writing about jazz ultimately affects the way the music is covered in the media depends upon the location: if it's the big urban markets like New York, DC, or Chicago—then probably so. If you're talking about anywhere other than such markets, probably not. I say that because jazz is an urban art form, and the largest African American populations cluster around major cities in the Southeast, the South, some cities in the Midwest, the Bay Area, and southern California. All of those areas have more media outlets that feature jazz and jazz performances, if not regularly then at least on occasion.

Several of those big urban areas still have black publications. But as for the African American–oriented publications and their lack of jazz coverage, no question that's about the bottom line: money! Although jazz lovers are economically diverse, that diversity does not translate into the kind of economics black publications find feasible enough to warrant providing regular jazz coverage. There's also the perception that jazz is too deep for their readers. I've had several editors of well-known black publications tell me that verbatim! Talk about underselling their readership! But I've reached a point where my attitude now is to work with any publication that is dedicated to jazz, regardless of race. Before, I would get upset at the kind of attitude I've faced from some publications regarding jazz and their narrow perception of their readers, but in the end that's counterproductive to my ongoing desire to write about this music.

As far as the treatment of artists by the press, I used to feel that it was mostly due to race that certain artists were hyped over others. After being in the business for a minute, now I think that other variables, like marketing, demographics, and a strong artist management and publicity team, are also considerable factors determining who gets the coverage. That's not to dismiss race as a factor in who gets the ink; race still dictates too many factors in modern life. But I've seen white musicians who can play yet never got signed to a label and black musicians who are mediocre by comparison but still achieve reams of publicity. Frankly, those factors are more important than the diversity, or lack thereof, of the writers.

I do think, however, that there is something to be said about how this music is too often covered according to *who* is writing about it. We jazz writers are basically advocates for the music. Sometimes that advocacy—mixed with the jazz writer jargon (which is too often so much inside baseball)—coupled with the unavoidable bitterness of knowing that the music you love is ignored, is off-putting to jazz neophytes, who are already intimidated by jazz in the first place. Here's an example of what I mean by that kind of off-putting, inside-baseball approach to jazz writing: "The pianist's modal improvisations clustered around a circle of fourths and concluded with spiraling arpeggios." When what might work better for the less thoroughly jazz-immersed reader might be: "The pianist built a suspenseful solo that went from a whisper to a scream with great verve and vigor."

An effective writer has to find a happy medium, a way to incorporate those two approaches—an ability to speak authoritatively on the music without shooting over the head of the average reader—into something holistic that can speak to both the seasoned listener and the neophyte. Certain writers, including Gary Giddins, Robert O'Meally, and the late Ralph Ellison and Stanley Crouch, were great at doing that.

Are black writers constrained by ancestry or access? The answer is complex. Of course, black writers—writing in any idiom—are going to come up against the Racial Mountain of prejudice and exclusion. That said, well after the changes of the twenty-first century, a black writer is less limited by access to the media than ever before. In the days when print was the only game in town, the access to writing for publications was harder to come by. But with the explosion of the internet and social media, black writers, even those writing in the hyperspecialized field of jazz, have an intriguing set of literary options to choose from.

For example, there are writers, like Gene Seymour, Michael Gonzales, Ericka Blount Danois, and Herb Boyd, who write for a multitude of publications and websites on a regular basis. And that doesn't include books, blogs, Facebook, Twitter, and Instagram accounts. This also extends into areas where writers also supplement their literary works with different kinds of side hustles, including writing press releases, artist bios, liner notes, and doing audio scripting for documentaries and feature films—as is evidenced by Nelson George's vivid and varied career.

There's also another important aspect of access that we must consider, and that is the access of choice. Because of changes brought by the internet and social media—along with the collapse of the record industry's dominance in defining who hears what (and by extension, the declining number of jazz radio stations)—black jazz writers now write in an abundance of other literary music idioms.

There was a time, perhaps twenty years ago, where there was an unspoken impulse to "stay true to the music" and restrict oneself to writing only in the major jazz outlets, the *DownBeat*, *JazzTimes*, and *Jazzwise* venues of the world. This imperative paralleled the blood libel of "selling out" that would be applied to jazz musicians who chose to work and record with pop musicians. Personally speaking, one of the biggest mistakes I made in my early writing career was not to pursue writing about other genres of music when I was contributing to *Vibe* and the *Village Voice*. I restricted myself from doing so because I worried whether my writing would be taken "seriously" by my jazz peers. Thankfully, by the time I contributed to Amazon.com as a writer and black nonfiction editor from 1998 to 2008, those inhibitions became casualties on the road to truth.

So given the multiplicity of avenues and opportunities a black jazz writer can traverse today, that aforementioned Racial Mountain may be "too high to get over" and "too low to get under," but it is easier today to go around, thanks to the kaleidoscope of outlets we have at our disposal.

Writing about jazz is not without its rewards; this pursuit is very much a yin and yang experience. Some of my most fulfilling opportunities writing about this music have included traveling to cover festivals, or meeting Herbie Hancock, Mario Bauza, the late, great writer Albert Murray, and countless musicians. Some of my most disappointing experiences have included not getting paid for my work, and writing for publications only to see them unaccountably fold. I've been very fortunate to be published for over twenty-five years.

As Billy Strayhorn would say, "Upward and Onward." I'm still astonished and delighted by the inclusion of my interview with bandleader-arranger Maria Schneider in the book *Best Music Writing: 2010* and the presence of my essay "My Travels through Cosmos Murray" in the anthology *Albert Murray and the Literary Imagination of a Nation.*

My work has appeared more recently in *Ebony,* the *Crisis,* and *Philadelphia Weekly.* I've contributed to NPR's jazz web presence and to *Publishers Weekly.* In 2013, I wrote an essay for the online publication *NewMusicBox* that dealt in part with the complexities of race and jazz, titled "My Bill Evans Problem: Jaded Visions of Jazz and Race," which generated hundreds of hits and lots of reader feedback, and which was subsequently published in the anthology *Writing Music: A Bedford Spotlight Reader.* And that's encouraging, because it was admittedly the most autobiographical piece I'd written.

John Murph

John Murph has successfully channeled his voracious appetite for modern music into a keenly social outlook that takes into account more than just the music or musicians themselves. As an African American music writer who also happens to proudly self-identify as gay, John Murph has often written from those two unique perspectives and against the dual challenge he's faced in securing bylines; consequently, he is that rare writer who has covered music for both African American and gay community publications.

Murph is blessed with an encyclopedic appetite when it comes to modern jazz, the leading edge of hip-hop, trip hop, drum and bass, electronica, house, broken beat, and assorted other jazz-informed hybrids and flavors—including classic R&B and funk—often in various combinations of the above. A devoted "crate digger," it's not unusual to find Murph elbow-deep in assorted vinyl record bins wherever he can find an outlet for his voracious need to hear music.

In over two decades of writing about music, Murph has coupled his diverse music interests with a writing skill and style that translates to both scholars and novices. In the process, he has become one of the more astute modern music observers of his generation. He has written for publications and online sites such as the *Washington Post*, NPR, *The Root*, *Atlantic Monthly*, AARP, the *Washington City Paper*, the *Washington Blade*, *JazzTimes*, *DownBeat*, *Jazzwise*, and *Vibe* magazine.

In the early 1990s, when Suzan Jenkins, then the CEO of the Rhythm and Blues Foundation, sent a tall, slim, bespectacled young Mississippi State University grad to the former National Jazz Service Organization offices for an exploratory chat, the young man from Pass Christian, MS, was quite earnest in expressing his intent to write about music. Murph soon joined the NJSO staff. Given that Murph followed the late Wayne Self and Eugene Holley Jr. in that position, I suppose the NJSO executive director exhibited a soft spot for aspiring jazz writers.

From his NJSO days, Murph went on to develop web content for NPR and then for Black Entertainment Television. All the while, he was growing his keen jazz and modern music writing craft as well as a prodigious appetite for the music. In addition to being a sharp commentator in print, Murph was also a programmer at WPFW-FM in DC, where he was just as likely to spin some newly minted young Brits, Germans, or Norwegians who use jazz as a launching pad toward new expressions as he was the growing crew of new-jack American stalwarts or edgy explorers like guitarist Jean-Paul Bourelly.

I think access is a huge issue. As in most areas of employment in the United States, black writers and writers of color and women may face assignment or employment discrimination at major media outlets by comparison with their white male counterparts. Of course, I have no statistics to back up my claims. But from clear observations, I don't see black writers at such outlets as *DownBeat*, *JazzTimes*, NPR, or the *Washington Post* making the same rapid inroads in jazz journalism as our white male counterparts.

Networking plays a huge part in getting assignments in the jazz community, and it probably plays a bigger role in who gets hired for permanent editorial positions. Some months back, when Brian Zimmerman left his editorial post at *DownBeat*, I bet that job announcement didn't reach any black and brown writers in the same manner as it did our white counterparts. I could be wrong, and I hope that I am.

I started writing about music in college at Mississippi State University for the school newspaper, *The Reflector*. When I was growing up, a lot of my family members either listened to music or read about it. The music seemed ever-present, and in several varieties.

During my second year in college I was still an accounting major, but it was music and writing that I really loved and that eventually captured my true spirit. Still, back in college I didn't see music journalism as a viable career option because there weren't that many role models at the magazines, particularly African Americans from my generation. And writers for, say, *Rolling Stone*, *Spin*, and *Musician* magazines seemed galaxies away.

Fortunately, I landed a paid internship at the Smithsonian, working with the Duke Ellington Collection in the American History Museum's Archives Center, which is where I first encountered the influential Reuben Jackson, an African American poet and historian who has also written about music. I did two consecutive summer internships there, which served to open the doors wider for me to pursue music journalism.

When I began contributing on music to various publications, in the beginning I wasn't really conscious of the relatively small numbers of African Americans writing about music. When I arrived in Washington, DC—first interning at the Smithsonian, and later working in arts administration at the National Jazz Service Organization and the Rhythm and Blues Foundation—I had African American mentors, such as Willard Jenkins, Dr. Anthony Brown, and Reuben Jackson. I also befriended other African American writers such as Eugene Holley Jr., Wayne Self, Bill Brower, and the late Tom Terrell. And I was reading a lot of stuff by Greg Tate, Stanley Crouch, and Nelson George.

Perhaps the first thing I noticed when I started writing nationally about serious music was the age gap. I always felt like a kid in the company of other jazz journalists. It wasn't until I started writing for the *Washington City Paper*, the *Washington Blade*, *JazzTimes*, and *DownBeat*, and attending events like the International Association of Jazz Educators conferences that I began realizing that I was indeed a "flyboy in the buttermilk." It *really* hit me, when I worked at National Public Radio, just how few black writers there were and how few on the business side of music.

When you look at the field of music writers and you stop and consider the relative scarcity of black music writers, you come up with so many answers and perspectives that it could very well serve as a collegiate sociology course. When it comes to African American music and culture, it always seemed as if our community was much better at creating than documenting, especially after the civil rights era. For some reason, anything vaguely related to the past seems too passé for many African Americans to devote the level of attention that is required to document the music on a regular basis. So when it comes to serious music with a long legacy (e.g., jazz, blues, and increasingly R&B), a lot of that gets ignored for what's currently popular (e.g., hip-hop), and that attitude is far too prevalent in the black media.

You cannot ignore the paucity of coverage of serious music in black media—*Ebony*, *Jet*, *O*, *Essence*—all of which have the potential of not only giving black music journalists more writing opportunities but also of cultivating a more erudite audience for serious music.

For anyone breaking into music journalism, the task can prove daunting—especially when it becomes more about "why you know" than "what you know." For writers of color, this can prove even more challenging if white editors and publishers see little value in having a multicultural writing staff beyond tokenism.

I do indeed think the scarcity of black writers covering the music ultimately contributes to how music is covered. Take for instance the coverage of jazz singers. If you examined retail outlets such as Amazon.com and Starbucks, your impression would be that the epitome of a jazz singer now is a white female. How the media (print, film, radio, internet) covers jazz and, more importantly, whom they choose to cover feeds into that perception.

I've got nothing against Diana Krall, Jane Monheit, Madeleine Peyroux, or Norah Jones—but it seems incredibly difficult for both emerging and established black American singers to make the same rapid inroads in terms of achieving coverage not only from mainstream glossy magazines but also in the traditional jazz publications, such as *JazzTimes* and *DownBeat* magazines. Just to cite one example, I find it incredible that Carla Cook, who has often been cited as one of the best and most natural jazz singers of our generation, has yet to land a major feature story in *JazzTimes* or *DownBeat* (that she has also not been afforded many opportunities to record as a leader is also duly noted).

When the singer José James released his splendid debut release *The Dreamer*, it was somewhat sad that I had to make special note of his race and the fact that it's been a while since a young African American male singer had emerged—compared to, say, Jamie Cullum or Peter Cincotti.[1] In my opinion, despite critical (albeit underground) acclaim, José James has yet to receive the same, timely, amount of ink as his white counterparts.

You could also argue the same with regard to some instrumentalists. When the Bad Plus and, again, Jamie Cullum first hit, they graced the covers of *JazzTimes* and *DownBeat*. Stefon Harris, J. D. Allen—not so much. A decade ago, heavy hitters such as the pianist Rodney Kendrick and the guitarist Jean-Paul Bourelly hardly got any ink in comparison to, say, Brad Mehldau and Bill Frisell. I remember a rumor circulating that Rodney Kendricks's personality was "too urban"—or some words to that effect—to achieve a major feature story.

Then there's the whole idea of what is deemed more artistically valid when it comes to jazz artists incorporating contemporary pop music. I notice a certain journalistic disdain or dismissal when some black jazz artists channel R&B, funk, and hip-hop, while their white contemporaries get kudos for giving makeovers to the likes of Radiohead, Nick Drake, and Björk.

I think there's a tendency, of which writers of all creeds are guilty, to try to make "serious music" appear "smarter" than it needs to be. Brad McKee of the *Washington City Paper*, one of my all-time best editors, told me this: "Jazz is already smart. You don't need to make it sound any smarter. Just *be* smart." It took me a while to really get to that. But the main takeaway I gathered from that is that oftentimes we forget to insert that human element and a bona fide narrative arc when writing feature stories on "serious musicians," especially if their music is deemed "avant-garde."

When I was writing about Andrew Hill, the late pianist and composer who had a slight hitch in his speech, one of the clichés I always tried to avoid was, "He talks the same way he plays the piano," equating a speech impediment with his distinctive approach to improvisation. Indeed, the ploy is great when trying to portray a distinctive musician as more "artistically exotic" than he or she needs to be, but those clichés can marginalize the artist as well.

I think it's always beneficial for journalists who write a lot for niche magazines, such as *JazzTimes*, *DownBeat*, and *Jazzwise*, to challenge him or herself to write for a mainstream, less informed audience without sacrificing what makes the musician great but also portraying that artist as a

1. *Editor's note:* Since then we've also witnessed the rise of another African American male jazz singer, Gregory Porter.

well-rounded person—and doing so in a manner that is more easily digested by the average, less deeply immersed reader.

I see intersections occurring in the music I cover—including jazz, hip-hop, drum and bass, house, classical—in terms of "points of reference" from both the musicians' and the music consumers' standpoints. From checking out electronica (house, broken beat, drum and bass) and hip-hop, I've noticed a number of jazz artists (e.g., Marc Cary, Robert Mitchell, Tarus Mateen, Kurt Rosenwinkel, Roy Ayers, Roy Hargrove, Robert Glasper, and Derrick Hodge) playing on those tracks. Some would argue that they are doing it for the money (which is a valid point). But oftentimes these musicians see something of artistic value that attracted them to play those non-jazz genres.

Also, many people listen to a variety of music. I grew up in the 1970s with a healthy diet of R&B and funk, but I also heard country, blues, and jazz. So hearing Willie Nelson, Z. Z. Hill, and Return to Forever was hardly any different from hearing Bill Withers, Parliament Funkadelic, and Millie Jackson. It was only when I was in college that I realized that Santana was considered rock, then later Latin-rock. Since Santana was on Columbia Records, as were Earth, Wind & Fire and Weather Report, and the music of all three had a distinctive Afro-Latin tinge, I associated them together, thinking they were all black music—for better or worse.

Then you can link the improvisational nature—particularly when it comes to rhythm—between jazz and hip-hop, drum and bass, and broken beat, in addition to them all being rooted in the African musical diaspora.

Among the musicians I hear most successfully addressing those intersections in their music, from a hip-hop perspective, I would look at how the late J Dilla had a profound influence on jazz-identified artists such as Robert Glasper, Stacy Dillard, Jaleel Shaw, Nicholas Payton, Roy Hargrove, and Jeremy Pelt—but he's not the only influential hip-hop artist on jazz: there's the Wu Tang Clan, Q-Tip, the Roots, A Tribe Called Quest, De La Soul, Dr. Dre, Madlib, Pete Rock, Jazzy Jeff, Mos Def. These hip-hop legends, and many more, have had a significant influence on many post-Motown jazz artists. And we can talk for eons about how many jazz samples filtered through hip-hop during the golden period of that genre.

West London's broken beat scene (e.g., I. G. Culture, Mark de-Clive Lowe, Kaidi Latham, 4hero) is also of note, especially when you hear how its sonic imprint is rooted in electric jazz-funk (i.e., Roy Ayers, Herbie Hancock, Patrice Rushen, Chick Corea, Fela, Tom Browne, Donald Byrd, Sun Ra, the Mizell Brothers, Charles Stephney, and Eddie Henderson) and how that broken beat scene influences the music of today's British jazz renegades such as Leo Tardin, Soweto Kinch, and Robert Mitchell. From a house music perspective, you can look at the works of Jazzanova, Masters at Work, Carl Craig, King Britt, and Moodymann and immediately hear the jazz influences in their work. So these complementary, cross-genre influences are evident from many perspectives.

Don Palmer

Don Palmer's byline, which I first encountered in *DownBeat* magazine, was consistently the assurance of an approach that was a bit beyond the usual musicians-tunes-performances-chords approach to whatever music or musicians he was covering. One never got the sense that his reportage was about what he knew that you didn't—not the "I know the science of music and you don't" approach so prevalent in jazz writing—and more about delivering a sense of enlightenment from a broader, sociocultural perspective.

It later became clear, when we met, that he was a bit of a kindred spirit, perhaps because he also came from a background of arts administration work: Don retired from the New York State Council on the Arts. He was one of the writers who traveled to Chicago for our 1987 Arts Midwest jazz media conference at University of Illinois Chicago, the conference that marked the birthplace of the Jazz Journalists Association.

I grew up in Toledo, OH, and actually as a six-year-old kid I was forced to take piano lessons from Abel Shealy, who had apparently played with Art Tatum back in the day in Toledo and who was also Stanley Cowell's piano teacher. We were a middle-class family who'd migrated from the South, and we had a piano in the house. I had a teacher in second grade named Dr. Carroll who taught us the history of music; we had to learn who the great composers were, and when he would quiz us on that, if you weren't paying attention he'd throw an eraser at you.

My dad was the choir director in church—he wanted to be a musician in college, but it didn't really work out for him. He used to go and see jazz performances and would take me. We would also go to the opera; between the ages of six and nine I saw nine full operas, so I was exposed to music as a kid.

As I got older and started buying records—stuff like *Snoopy vs. the Red Baron*, the Dave Clark Five, and so on, Dad would say to me, "If you're serious about music you'll listen to jazz." As I got into my teens I started listening to blues because I wanted to know whom these blues-playing rock bands from England were listening to. My father had Ornette Coleman, some Monk albums and stuff, so I had music around me, available to me just to listen to at my own leisure. My parents took me to see fellow Toledo native Stanley Cowell when he was playing "The Viet Cong Blues" and playing the electric piano. They would take me to concerts—James Brown, Sly Stone, Funkadelic—going to hear music was part of my childhood.

As for writing about music, that was probably something I wrote for my high school newspaper, or something like that. I went to a school where you had to write, you had a vocabulary quiz every week, you had to write in complete sentences, you'd have pop quizzes on a quotation on the blackboard—it could be historical, it could be cultural—you had twenty minutes to write an essay, so you had to write. I probably wrote about music and various things just because I had to. That was part of my upbringing.

I went to the University of Wisconsin and probably started to write seriously about music when I was a twenty-two-year-old in Madison, Wisconsin, because I was working at the radio station WORT as a DJ. I once read a guy who wrote an article about Wardell Gray, reviewing the *Central Avenue* gatefold album on Prestige, and he asked why we didn't hear more from Wardell Gray. And I thought, maybe that's because he was found dead in the desert with a broken neck—it's kind of hard to record after that! The way he wrote, it seemed he was unaware of this stuff.

He said, "I don't really like to write about this stuff, but someone needs to do it, so why don't you do it instead of me." So that's when I started writing for a biweekly newspaper in Madison called *Free for All*, which was a feminist-socialist, hippie paper. But before that, my senior thesis was on jazz in Kansas City, the cultural history of Kansas City and jazz. That was my first stab at long-form writing, in 1977.

As far as black writers on jazz, I knew about Baraka, I knew about A. B. Spellman—they wrote the books I used in writing my senior thesis. I knew about Ralph Ellison's "Shadow and Act" and that stuff. Then I moved to Madison, and I didn't really think about it that much because—well, I moved there to go to graduate school, which I never did. My girlfriend was there too, so I was following her.

It wasn't until I moved to New York, in 1981, that I became aware of the small number of black jazz writers. When you travel in the circle of jazz writers, you realize that. You meet these guys, they mean well, they listen to a lot of music, they're smart, and they're stuffy white guys—if you scratch them, they've either got trust funds or grandma's money. So then you start thinking, "Okay, so that's how they can afford to not have a job and do whatever it is." Then you meet other writers and you see who's out there, and you also find out from various things that there are not many black people writing about this music.

Rafi Zabor hired me to write at *Musician* just because I was new in town; he knew there weren't many black people writing about jazz. Greg Tate was around, he was writing for the *Voice*, but he didn't necessarily write strictly about jazz. I was writing for the *Voice*, and I knew Stanley Crouch—he was one of my teachers in college, so I knew he was a writer. And then you look at people's names and you figure Dan Morgenstern is probably not a man of color. You see the circles you travel, and then, also, once you're familiar with lots of black musicians, they tell you there are not too many brothers writing about his music, so you learn who's who.

Because I was black, some musicians were more forthcoming; some were not, it really was personal and individual. The reality was dependent a lot upon what a musician's career trajectory was: whether they had management, a press person, and stuff. Ultimately what they really wanted was press—they could care less if a black or a white writer was writing it.

When I did an interview with one musician, who shall remain nameless, I didn't have a tape recorder and I made a statement in the piece paraphrasing them. And of course I wouldn't make it up, but I got a letter written to the publication, a call from the publicist and management people saying, "He would never say anything like that, why would you . . ." My response was, "Why would I make up that quote?"—it made no sense to me. But it turned out that the real issue was that this musician was up for a feature in *Esquire* magazine and my paraphrasing or quoting him that way might endanger that piece because it might make him look like a black militant. The musician was cool with me about it, but the management people—who were white—were concerned about how it appeared.

Also, I chose to write about social context and the cultural context of the music; I wasn't necessarily writing about the technical aspects of music. It wasn't about "how they read charts" and stuff like that. I wrote about the cultural and social context of the music or musician. That was a bit different than others writing about jazz, because most of the music writers had little interaction with the black community, except for intellectually or because they were writing about jazz.

That was just what I wrote about: I was a social historian, that's what I did, that's what I studied. I was a historical materialist in college. I was brought up doing that before it had a fancy name. So I read Marvin Harrison, the anthropologist, and Franz Boas.

A social approach takes a greater depth of knowledge of the black community; the publicists, the record labels, and often the musicians themselves don't really care about that approach because what they want is fawning, good press promoting their product. Bob Christgau, the *Voice* music editor at the time I wrote there, once said to me, "Your writing is fine, you described this just fine, but why do these jazz critics get a record, play it, start with side one, song A, write about every song, and flip it over and repeat that. Who cares? What's the record mean? Does it have any greater value than a bunch of notes on plastic?" That was him saying, "Don't fall into that trap." And he would say, "You don't need to write something in a review or profile that's entirely biographical. The readers think they know more than they really know, but don't insult them by talking down to them by giving them a blow-by-blow; interpret it, reference their past, but you don't have to say it liberally." So I thought, "Yeah, you're right, but that's what jazz critics do."

Once I started pitching articles to publications, I would say there was some resistance to that approach, more than receptiveness in any case—not that many editors were interested. There's an age issue too, because at some point your editors are younger than you are, and they're not interested in that because they don't really know anything about that. I was once told, "You've got like seven ideas in the first three sentences; maybe just do one or two." I was like, "Okay, I can see that . . ." But being told by the *New York Times* that I need to dumb down my language—I said, "Well, they can use a dictionary." But to be told that talking about something using real language, not me making up stuff to be poetic or something, to be told that it was too smart? Sometimes I could get touchy and say, "So you don't like Negroes being smart? Or is it just that you want it simplified?"

Many writers hadn't developed and maybe still haven't developed the sensitivity, but it's the marketplace: you want to churn out copy, and frankly you can sell stories based upon what kind of reed they use, what their tour is like—people read that personal interest, but there's not a lot of complexity to that kind of writing. As a musician said to me, there's music reportage, but there's no critical writing about the music; there's what's available, what the new releases are, but there's not any critical writing. And that's the state of cultural, pop journalism, mainly. I never said I was a great critic, but I tried.

I had some editors who reached out to me when I hadn't been writing for a while to get me back in the game because they wanted to hear my voice.

I've had people say, "You need to write more, you have a different perspective; it's not just about the recording, it's about larger issues." So there were some receptive editors.

About the time jazz achieved that status of serious music, like classical music—I have issues with trying to equate the two in that way—but by the time jazz did reach that status, classical music was crashing and it kind of took jazz down with it, the commercial aspect of jazz. I think jazz has come back, in a way, but that's because you've got jazz guys playing with hip-hop guys, there's a different generation, and I think that helped. When there was a downswing in the music industry in general, it hurt classical and jazz, but that's a market issue.

I would be writing for one publication, and my editor would leave, and then the next editor would ask me what I was referring to here, could I explain that there. And I would say, "Well, what is it you don't understand?" And they would say, "You referred to this place—well, where is it?" I said "Kenya, it's in East Africa!" Like *really*? I have to actually say Kenya is in East Africa? That takes up more space. They'd say, "Well, you have to take that out." I'm saying, "They can look it up!"

I grappled with that, depending on who the new editor was. I had a *New York Times* editor who, when I referred to a musician wearing wire rims when describing their attire, called me and asked what was I talking about. I said, "Wire rim glasses!" He said, "Well, they could have been car tires." I said, "Not wearing them," and in any case, not really, because that would mean a Model T, but in the end I did have to say "wire rim glasses." That fucks up the flow from an aesthetic standpoint.

Certain things bothered me, but in the end I had a day job at the New York State Council on the Arts, where I had to make a living. That was my parents' rule when you finished college: get a job or come home, but we're not paying for you. So I wrote on the side. I was also one who wouldn't take an assignment I didn't want to do, so I wasn't a shill, I didn't necessarily write for the money. I didn't get freelance writing jobs, because who's going to give you work if they know that it isn't critical to you—but that's a different issue, that's the marketplace and the writing brotherhood. I say *brotherhood* because there weren't that many women working in it.

There weren't very many black music journalists. It's analogous to that joke about the anthropologists that go into a culture, or collectors, for instance, who say, "You people don't know what you're doing with that art; we know what to do with this art." Take Native American art: they move it into a museum to preserve it, but the Native Americans might say it's not meant to be preserved like that; the purpose is to make it from organic matter and then it goes back to organic matter—it's not meant to be preserved in that way. There's the European codification, so it's got to be top-to-bottom according to those standards; and of course the white patriarchy understands things better than you other people do. So there's that tradition, and then casual racism: like the notion of women's music, that only women could write about it—or being asked by a white woman in a job interview at the *New York Times* if I can write about white people.

Since I'd been sort of forewarned that I was going to get some sort of question like that, I was semi-prepared, but I was just flabbergasted by who asked me! Of all people, I didn't expect this particular white woman to ask me that. I have a difficult time reading anything she's written ever since.

I told her, first of all, I've been writing for your paper in the Sunday Arts & Leisure section; I'd written about Carla Bley. I was the first Negro in an all-white school in first grade; I went to the opera; I grew up seeing Alice Cooper, Brownsville Station, and whatever else—but instead what I really should have said was, "Can you write about men? And for that matter—why do you white people write about black people?" I really should have asked that, but I didn't care about the job. I tried to explain to her—but I can only tell you when she asked me that question, she didn't really say what she actually meant, but it's like that's the casual racism white people engage when writing about black people. To actually ask a black person if they can write about white people . . . I mean, I'm a doctor's son, my mother's a schoolteacher, listen to me talk, do I sound like I came out from under a rock in some really pisshole city ghetto like Donald Trump characterized? So to me, that's casual racism, just like the way white men—mainly in the past—were encouraged to write all about black people and their serious music, whereas we were not considered literate enough to do that.

I don't know what the purpose of the question was. I didn't get the job, and they hired Jon Pareles, who hadn't even applied yet. They had called me as an affirmative action interview. The job was with the cultural desk of the *New York Times*, and they called me and asked me to apply. I would have followed Robert Palmer after he left the *New York Times*.

Too many times I've read things and seen things where people want to be special and lord that over the musicians—they want to be kingmakers. They don't want to admit that they don't know something, and that's what I meant by blind spots. They should say, "Wow, I've never heard anything like that, I never perceived that previously—this person just turned me on to a new way of hearing things, a new way of looking at the world." It's difficult to have people admit to that; it's a human thing.

The demographic issue is just that there's not that many people in America who really dig serious jazz, pop jazz, or smooth jazz—and there are even fewer people who want to write about it and try to make a living writing about it. So the demographics of the black community versus the white community—it's just the numbers. There are only a certain number of bohemian types in the world, and even fewer black bohemian types.

I once interviewed for an editorial job at *Tiger Beat* magazine, but I wasn't very serious about it. I thought, what the hell, it's something to do. You can't really go into an interview and explain how you would restructure the magazine because you think it's pretty crappy. I didn't care because I didn't really want to write about Michael Jackson's bathroom colors and toiletries.

As far as black publications, now *Ebony* apparently has some sort of online jazz coverage by Eugene Holley Jr., but back when I was writing, *Ebony* wasn't covering jazz. Name me an African American publication that actually has some sort of regular jazz coverage, unless it's something special—they might cover Kamasi Washington. I did write for *City Sun* in Brooklyn, when they wanted to have jazz, they wanted to be highfalutin. They gave me free rein.

Black publications' indifference toward jazz coverage is all about ads, and probably not enough record labels are going to be buying ads in African American newspapers to make it seem worthwhile for them to cover jazz. You might see an African American newspaper in a major American city with a major jazz club that buys ads to appeal to the black community, but that's not a big arena.

I was once trying to pitch a story, maybe even at the *New York Times*, about Ornette Coleman playing opera houses in Europe for an anniversary tour or something, and the editor said "What's the hook?" I said, "Ornette Coleman playing opera houses in Italy, celebrating something—this is special." "But the twentieth anniversary of the first Sugar Hill record, do you want to write about that?" "No, sorry, I don't want to write about that."

I wrote a liner note for Joe Fields at Muse Records; he liked me for some reason, maybe it was because I was a young brother and he wanted to be helpful. He called me up and said, "I'll send you a copy of the record; let me know if you can do something with this." I wrote something and he ran it. A friend read it and said, "I have no idea why they printed your liner notes and paid you for them, because you said, 'He's not just another derivative guitar player' in your lede." He said, "It really doesn't sound good, because you basically said, 'He's derivative, but he's better than the other ones.'" I said, "That's true!" I generally told the truth, and if it was really lukewarm, it wasn't because I was distracted—it was because it was an assignment and I just did it.

I had a Tony Bennett interview, and the publicist wanted me to run the questions by him in advance. I said no, and they told me there were things I couldn't ask. That was not even what this was about. Basically I called my editor and said, "You know what, these are things I've been asked, and I told them no." He said, "Well they may just cancel the interview," and I said, "But I don't work that way," and he said, "Well, we'll find someone else." But the paper itself said, "We're not comfortable, we won't do this."

When a publicist pressured me, questioned my integrity, I said, "You can call my editor and tell them this, and you won't get a story, because they trust me to do it. Either you trust me or you don't, but he's not assigning someone to reprint your press release—he's assigning someone to do a story." So those were things I wouldn't do when I felt it was meant to be a puff piece. I wasn't able to do that.

In general, if an editor called me for a reason, and I asked, "Why me?," and they were able to give me a reason, then I might do it. But I never pitched something that didn't move me, didn't stimulate me in some way. It had to get my attention, say, if I was listening to it on a subway and I said, "Holy shit, there's something different here!"

I didn't get that many assignments. They would have to explain why they wanted me for something that I didn't have an intrinsic interest in. They would have to give me the music first—let me hear it, and I'll get back to you. I usually didn't take anything sight unseen. I could afford to be that way because I had a day job at NYSCA. I was a grants officer for twenty-four years. My day job at NYSCA encouraged a certain amount of brain exercise; though I can't say that it encouraged my writing, because of conflicts of interest when I couldn't be writing about projects, organizations, or artists that applied for money.

My work at NYSCA made me think about certain issues and elements in the arts as they related to my writing, but I was often too busy to really pursue a real fundamental writing career. However, when I did write, yes, these things would come into play. I might hear something and go, "Oh, this is similar to something else." I did have access to more information, more stimulus.

When I moved to New York, I thought there would be soirees and conversations about music among writers—and there weren't. Usually, conversations among writers would be about who got what assignment and, "He shouldn't have that assignment; I should have that assignment." And usually it was folks talking about what assignments they had coming up. People are scuffling for money, so I got that part, but I found it kind of boring.

In Paris, there were dancers and poets and musicians sitting, talking, exchanging information, Ishmael Reed and those folks; there was a variety of different kinds of aesthetics in acting. So I felt like, concerning jazz, the conversation became very narrow, and that bothered me. I think there should be a more holistic view of cultural activity, but that's me. I wrote about film, I wrote about theater, so I had to know a lot about different kinds of artistic output in order for me to function at my job—and for me to function, period.

I hitchhiked across West Africa; I hitchhiked all around Kenya, and I would just go into villages and meet people and get along, that's my nature. I wrote about James Carter and compared his work to the music of Madagascar, in terms of the music of memory and place—I would write things like that. Editors thought I was crazy sometimes because they didn't know what I was talking about and they weren't willing to go there.

Working at NYSCA curtailed my ability to write things, because the stuff I really wanted to write about was part of the nonprofit arts world and I couldn't really write about that because I was a grants officer. For example, within the individual artist category, I definitely couldn't write about Uri Caine because Uri Caine was applying for a commission, so that was inappropriate—it was things like that. September 11th took me out of the game for a while; first of all, publications weren't doing stuff, and also I wasn't in the right mental space because I was pretty emotionally raw. I just got tired of dealing with shit, didn't need the money. And also when people call you and ask your advice or your assistance, or pick your brain about a story they're doing because they don't know the information, I'd think, "Why didn't the publication just call me? You're calling me to ask me to refer you to books and recordings so *you* can write a story—why didn't you tell them to call me since you're calling me?" I got tired of that stuff; I moved on.

I could be open to writing on music again. I write on Facebook, but that doesn't count, really. Actually I find out when people tell me they read stuff I post, but they never comment because they "don't want to be out there." I'm retired; I do stuff as a consultant for the Maryland Arts Council, but I'm retired. I got offered early retirement. The pension goes a lot farther in Baltimore, and I was burnt out in New York; I needed a break, and relocating to Baltimore was the best thing I ever did as an older person. And I also asked, "Can I reinvent myself one more time?" I don't find New York that interesting anymore—it's difficult.

Ron Wynn

Ron Wynn is an arts columnist and a critic for the Nashville *City Paper*. Ron has been a frequent contributor to *JazzTimes* magazine. He also contributes regularly to *BookPage*, *eMusic*, *American Songwriter*, and *Positively Green*. On the social media front, Ron Wynn is an always thoughtful presence on Facebook, where he has often posted on matters related to jazz music.

For *JazzTimes*, Ron wrote on a variety of subjects, including a penetrating piece on the issue of race in jazz, an article about which he cautions that his perceptions have since evolved and deepened in many respects. Ron is also a radio programmer, cohosting the arts and politics talk show *Freestyle* since 2002 at WFSK 88.1 FM, the Fisk University radio station.

I was introduced to jazz through piano lessons as a youngster. There was also a police officer in Knoxville, TN, who used to host a Sunday afternoon jazz show on the AM station that James Brown owned. I've forgotten his name, but I remember that he was a big fan of Eddie Harris and Les Mc-Cann, and he was constantly playing things from their catalog, including "Cold Duck Time" from their *Swiss Movement* album. Later, after reading Amiri Baraka's *Blues People* and A. B. Spellman's *Four Lives in the Bebop Business*, plus Langston Hughes's essays, I was really interested in learning more about jazz and, indeed, all forms of music.

I really didn't realize for a long time just how little interest there was in jazz generally and even less among African Americans my age, until I went to college. There, thanks to the five-college program in the University of Massachusetts Amherst area, I got a chance to take classes taught by Max Roach, Archie Shepp, and Ken McIntyre. And I also got to hear a ton of great concerts over that four-year period (1970–1974).

These concerts were reasonably well-attended by black students, but they didn't attract many African American community residents from the surrounding area. But when talking with friends, visiting, and seeing what was in their record collections, there weren't that many jazz albums, nor much interest in the music. So eventually I decided to try and see if I could generate some response and drum up some interest in the music by writing about it. I've been trying to do that ever since, and I have encountered countless problems over the years from different media outlets.

I was incredibly naïve in the beginning. I remember walking into the *Boston Phoenix* office in 1978 and asking to see Joe C, aka Joe McEwen, the great soul music writer. They let me go upstairs, and I looked around the newsroom and didn't see anything except white people, so I just assumed Joe C wasn't in. I subsequently found out that I'd been looking right at him for fifteen minutes and didn't know it, because he was a tall white guy! Joe turned out to be a great guy and is still a friend of mine, along with many other successful music writers, like the authors Peter Guralnick and Chet Flippo. But the point is, I can count on both hands the number of black jazz writers I've met over the last thirty-plus years, and sadly, half of them are dead, retired, or inactive.

The late Phyl Garland was one of the first black music writers I used to read all the time in what was then *Stereo Review*. I met the former *DownBeat* writer Bill Cole while attending Amherst College. Ron Welburn used to publish what I guess you'd call a fanzine called *The Grackle*. I also used to read Vernon Gibbs's reviews on black pop in various magazines.

Almost all the new young African American music writers, like Touré in the *New Yorker*, are into either hip-hop or R&B. I love soul, blues, and gospel music as well—plus, my son plays guitar in Public Enemy's backing band—but it does pain me that there seems to be so little interest in jazz or serious music among younger African Americans. That makes an enormous difference, because there are many blacks of all ages that truly don't think there are any black jazz musicians around today under the age of fifty, other than smooth jazz types.

I think the lack of black media commentators on the music reflects the general lack of diversity within the print media, something that's maybe worse today than it was when I started. Between the demise of hard copy print newspapers, the cutbacks in arts coverage everywhere, and the seeming lack of interest in the music, the dismal state of affairs regarding black interest in jazz doesn't seem to be getting any better.

Unquestionably the disparity and lack of black writers has contributed to this situation. That doesn't mean that every white person covering jazz is some type of racist or is insensitive, but it means that, on the whole, many publications and editors simply don't see this lack of black writers as that important of an issue.

In some cases I do wonder whether the absence of black writers affects which musicians achieve a higher profile than others, and I do think there's a cultural reason for it. I very much enjoy certain white jazz bands and artists. But I have seen far more coverage for some of them than their records merit, particularly in the mainstream press.

I must say that one other problem, at least on my end, concerns the inability to get press copies of releases from small labels. I once did a cover story on David Murray playing Bonnaroo and had to jump through hoops to justify it. I'd love to write more about those types of artists, but many times I don't get the records that I see reviewed in places like *Cadence* and other small publications, and I'd really love a chance to publicize those players.

My sense of African American–oriented publications is that they—take *Ebony* and *Jet*, for example—are so strapped for advertising and so close to perishing that they just can't afford to take a shot at writing about and publicizing musicians whose work isn't getting played in their target markets and whose audiences for the most part haven't heard of those musicians and aren't supporting serious music. That's a sad and ugly reality, but it seems to be the case, at least in places like Nashville.

I don't think there's any question that the tone with which serious music is written about has quite a bit to do with who is covering the music. I don't necessarily think that's good or bad—it's just the nature of the process—but the results can certainly be negative.

I would also add that the impact of demographics (or as they now call it in the newspaper business, "analytics") has a ton to do with it as well. Far too much of what anyone who writes arts coverage gets assigned is determined on that basis, and the degree of interest by many magazines and newspapers in jazz dips even further when the research department trots out the demographic breakdowns. The coverage often gets based on that.

Some of my greatest experiences have been the opportunity to interview black musicians like David Murray, Sonny Rollins, Art Blakey, Max Roach, Ornette Coleman, and Wynton Marsalis, and to put these stories in newspapers or magazines that don't ordinarily cover this type of musician or music. Those experiences have been without a doubt among the most rewarding things that have happened to me over the years.

The opportunity to talk about issues of race in *JazzTimes*, and also in the *Independent Ear*, has been another thrill. I've been fortunate to do some other noteworthy things with the music. These include the opportunity to host, on my radio show in Connecticut in the 1980s, the critic Gary Giddins and both Charlie Lourie and Michael Cuscuna, of Mosaic and Blue Note Records fame, in the studio for interviews.

I didn't get to write about it, but the opportunity to see Duke Ellington before he died, and to see premier concerts by the Art Ensemble of Chicago, Alice Coltrane with Pharoah Sanders, Herbie Hancock and his electric ensemble, Sun Ra, and the last great Charles Mingus group, with George Adams and Don Pullen, were also great encounters, things that still influence me to this day. Meeting Sam Rivers as a college student had a major impact. He talked about the concept of black music being a river with all different types of streams, and he was very interested in many idioms, even though he was considered an "avant-garde" jazz musician.

The biggest obstacle I've faced writing about the music has probably been the inability to get regular servicing on non–major label jazz records since returning to the South full time in 1988. Except for the two years, I worked in Michigan, I've been working in Memphis and Nashville, and the small labels just don't seem to feel there's anyone around these parts interested in writing about their music.

There was a time when I would do all types of buying, particularly mail order, back in the day. But today, with the recession in full tilt and money tight all around, I just can't do that much buying anymore. It's too bad, because every time I pick up a copy of the publications *Signal to Noise* or the *Wire*, I see all types of great records that I can't afford to buy.

One thing that I hope happens in my lifetime is the establishment of a full-time magazine devoted to jazz, with both print and online editions, that's published, owned, and operated by African Americans. That was once a dream of mine, but financial realities indicate that it won't be coming from me unless something drastic happens. Before he became a right-wing convert, Stanley Crouch used to do some great jazz columns in *Players Magazine*. A magazine that could provide full-service jazz coverage, with reviews, interviews, features, and so on—but with a focus and emphasis on the black community—would be fantastic.

6

newspaper writers and columnists

MARTIN JOHNSON, GREG THOMAS, AND HOLLIE WEST

In this section we share insights from several writers who have at points in their writing career held staff reporter or columnist status at publications, which is less of a hang-fly or precarious position than that of their freelance writer associates and colleagues. The writers in this section have by and large—at least at some point in their career—been privileged to operate with reporting or columnar mandates that provided them with a modicum of "guaranteed" publishing opportunities and with a prescribed venue.

"Regular" contributing jazz columnists or reporters at newspapers have for many years been a modest lot, generally based in major markets in the United States, and the number of African American writers who have held such positions has traditionally been smaller still.

Martin Johnson

Martin Johnson got his start writing about jazz for the *Amsterdam News* in 1984. In that respect, he joins such other contributors to this book as Ron

Scott and Herb Boyd as veterans of that long-standing chronicle of the African American community pulse, the black dispatch. Within a year of joining the *Amsterdam News* contributing staff, Martin was also writing regularly for *Newsday* and the *City Sun*. After diversifying into pop music and film criticism, he wrote for a wide variety of publications and websites, including *Essence*, *Vogue*, and *Elle*; the *Village Voice*, *New York Times*, *Washington Post*, *Chicago Tribune*, *New York Sun*, *Los Angeles New Times*, and *SF Weekly*; and *Rolling Stone*, *Vibe*, *Tower Records Pulse*, *DownBeat*, *JazzTimes*, *Paste*, Amazon.com, BN.com, and numerous other outlets.

As his career progressed, music journalism retreated from a primary revenue source into a sidebar income for Johnson as he began writing critical analysis of sports for the *New York Sun* and *The Root*. Later, he launched an information service called *The Joy of Cheese*, conducting public and private tastings in New York City. He presently writes about music for the *Wall Street Journal*.

I loved to write, and I loved music. In the third grade my dad encouraged me to write a book report on Miles Davis's classic *Milestones* record, which I had always enjoyed mostly because I had the same type of shirt that Miles Davis wore on that album cover. I was especially thrilled that the album *Milestones* included "Billy Boy," a song I knew, but I was really blown away by the catchy rhythms of his version of "Straight No Chaser." Writing about that record was a blast, and thereafter, whenever I could, I would turn a school assignment into writing about music. It wasn't until well afterward that I began thinking that particular paper was a special moment.

I went through a difficult adolescence as my family moved from the Hyde Park–Kenwood area of Chicago to Dallas right before I entered ninth grade. In school I was frequently called an Uncle Tom and beaten by other African Americans because (1) I lived in the white neighborhood; (2) I was the new kid; (3) I didn't speak with a "black" accent; and (4) my musical tastes were deemed "white." I think today my tastes would be called eclectic; I liked all the things that my black classmates at the time liked (War, the Isley Brothers, P-Funk) but I also liked Steely Dan, Bob Dylan, and Joni Mitchell and—gasp—Miles Davis, Duke, and Coltrane! I try not to dwell too much on that era of my life, which was not a happy time.

I figured that getting far away from there to go to college would solve that situation, but I was wrong. I worked at WKCR-FM in college at Columbia University, both as the jazz director and as a member of the executive board. When I was the jazz director at WKCR, I was called on the carpet by the Black Students Organization and asked to explain why the station didn't play any "black music." I enthusiastically explained about the annual day-long on-air festivals devoted to Thelonious Monk, Billie Holiday, Duke Ellington, and Coleman Hawkins, among others, and that the station was at that moment doing a two-hundred-hour-plus marathon broadcast devoted to the music of Max Roach. I remember one woman student bellowing at me, "No, I mean *real* black music!" By that time, I was accustomed to the fact that my personal concept of blackness might not match other African Americans' concepts of blackness, and I could mostly deal with that. But if I had to defend the blackness—err, the "real" blackness—of Billie, Duke, Monk, and Coleman Hawkins, then I knew I was dealing with people I shouldn't be in with, and I left.

My senior year I coproduced the "Interpretations of Monk" concert, which later became a live recording. I had won journalism awards in high school, so this seemed like a natural synthesis. After graduating I spent a couple of years spinning my wheels in an unproductive job, so I quit. I took unemployment and marched into the office of the *Amsterdam News* and told the editor Mel Tapley that I would write about jazz for him. Fortunately he interpreted my declaration as a request rather than some rash demand and said, "Sure young man, what would you like to write about?"

So I started writing, and one of the first people I met was Don Palmer, another African American writer with, ahem, eclectic tastes. Then I met Greg Tate, then Stanley Crouch—I didn't know if these cats had written about Miles Davis in the third grade like I had, but it felt like they had. I was thrilled and proud to be part of this contingent; I felt like I'd found the crowd I'd been looking for all my life. My relationship with these fellow writers was collegial.

On the other hand, from the way that musicians treated me, after a while I soon realized that these particular writing colleagues might not be the norm. All jazz musicians in general, but African American musicians in particular, went out of their way to look out for me; sometimes they'd come to my home for interviews. They'd call me to praise the pieces I wrote. I wasn't getting paid much money for my work, but it was richly rewarding. With the skills that it takes to be a great cultural commentator, you could do a lot of things that would make a lot more money.

I assume that most African Americans with options choose not to starve and worry endlessly about the rent. The scarcity of African American writers does contribute to how the music is covered, but that's one of the breaks of the game. At the level I work at, in terms of why and how musicians are elevated over others, so much of this stuff is just timing and luck. If I wrote for music magazines with some regularity, I might be compelled to wonder.

But I've never written regularly for music magazines, so I have no idea what my perspective on that aspect might be.

As far as the scarcity of jazz coverage in the traditional African American press, in some ways I'm the wrong person to answer that question; remember, I grew up among African Americans who thought that listening to Duke was "acting white." On the other hand, you sell more issues with Beyoncé on the cover than with Cassandra Wilson. Overall though, I think most African American publications dropped the ball on critical analysis of life—cultural and otherwise—a long time ago, so it should come as no surprise that jazz falls through their cracks.

I have been writing for over twenty-five years. In 1985 I was invited to Max Roach's house to watch a ball game. He was checking me out before agreeing to an interview. Max tested me on my knowledge of Negro League stars. Satchel Paige? Of course! Josh Gibson? Hit a home run out of Yankee Stadium! Oscar Charleston? Ummm . . . Max leaned back on his sofa and smiled, looked at me, and said, "You don't know as much as you think you know." That was true about baseball and is good advice in general. When I asked him about his insatiable appetite for experimentation, he offered another resonant piece of advice: "You can't win today's ball games with yesterday's home runs."

A few weeks later the phone rang one morning when I was sleeping late. I rushed to answer it (no voicemail in those days), and the man on the other end was Sonny Rollins; he heard I wanted to interview him, likely from Max. I thought I must have been dreaming! Rollins asked if he should call me later (are you kidding, how often is Sonny Rollins just going to ring me up!). I did the interview on the spot, and he spoke at great length about everything.

I had two memorable encounters with Don Cherry. In the mid-1980s he and his son Eagle-Eye met me at the radio station, and we walked the two miles down the Upper West Side to Gray's Papaya so his son could get a hot dog. And then, with the traffic whizzing by us on Broadway, we sat on one of the benches in the median in between lanes on the busy street and did an interview. Then, a few years later, I was to meet him in an East Village bar for an interview. He arrived on roller skates! He beseeched the bartender to put on a certain CD he brought with him. The bartender agreed; it was his daughter Neneh's debut disc, and Don danced on his roller skates to "Buffalo Stance" before settling in for our interview.

Lunch with Betty Carter in 1992 ahead of the *Vogue* piece I wrote on her was great. For the first time in my life I had an expense account, a rather large one at that. But Carter insisted on going somewhere fairly modest. We ate at a Union Square restaurant with outdoor seating, and while we were talking, Jimmy Heath walked up and the two of them traded great war stories about the 1950s and 1960s. Then afterward Betty and I shopped together at the farmer's market and she wouldn't even let me send her home in a limo, though she seemed genuinely flattered that I wanted to!

Walking through Tompkins Square Park in 1984 with Butch Morris was an education on how he hears the world around him. Sometime in the mid-1990s, *DownBeat* assigned me to do an equipment piece on the keyboardist Adam Holtzman. We met on Avenue A, got massive pastrami sandwiches at Katz's Delicatessen, and then went to his studio in a basement on the Lower East Side. Then for the next four hours he pulled out rig after rig and played me lines, if not entire songs, that he had performed with Miles Davis and with Chaka Khan. It was like a private concert.

My editors have been great . . . all of them—seriously! Okay, maybe one or two exceptions, but in over twenty-five years, that means all of them. I got lucky, I got into the biz at a good time, made some great connections, lucked into a few others, never expected this stuff to be easy, and I've had a great time. It saddens me a little that you can't make a living writing about this music; but you can't make a living writing about sculpture either.

Greg Thomas

Like many of the participants in this dialogue with black music writers, Gregory Thomas, who grew up in Staten Island, NY, has a diverse jazz activist portfolio. Greg's byline has been featured in numerous publications, including *Salon*, *The Root*, the *Guardian*, the *Observer*, *American Legacy*, Africana.com, BlackAmericans.com, the *New York Daily News* (as a jazz columnist), and others. In addition, he is the founding editor in chief of *Harlem World Magazine*.

Greg Thomas has taught jazz education at the Brooklyn Academy of Music, the Thurgood Marshall Academy, and the Frederick Douglass Academy. He serves as a consultant and educator for the National Jazz Museum in Harlem and for Jazz at Lincoln Center, and for both he has also served as a facilitator and moderator of humanities programming.

In his electronic media life, Greg has hosted a weekly jazz radio program at wvox in Westchester, NY. Additionally he has produced radio specials for wbai (99.5 fm in New York City), where he also hosted a regular monthly jazz show. Greg has also produced and hosted his own web-based television show, *Jazz It Up!*

In partnership with his wife Jewel, Greg has presented and produced jazz performances on stages in the New York metro area. These have included such venues as Ginny's Supper Club, MIST in Harlem, the Friar's Club, and Alvin and Friends restaurant in New Rochelle, NY.

My motivation to write about music came from home. The foundation was the music my parents listened to, which included jazz, and my deep study and enjoyment of the giants of jazz that I'd been listening to very intently since high school. Inspired by a high school stage band concert, I began to play the alto saxophone at fifteen years old. I took lessons from the Staten Island sax legend Caesar DiMauro, studied music theory and saxophone method books, played in various classical and jazz ensembles, tuned in regularly to jazz radio, first WRVR and then WBGO, and minored in music at Hamilton College, where I also hosted a jazz radio show for three years. During a master class that Clark Terry gave at Hamilton on April 17, 1984, I had an opportunity to share a melody line with the trumpet icon. It was an epiphany, a mystical experience of musical ecstasy!

A few years after graduating from Hamilton College, I met Keith Clinkscales and Leonard Burnett—later of *Vibe* and *Savoy* magazines—who launched their first publication, *Urban Profiles*, in the late 1980s. I was more troubled, frankly, by how relatively few black folk attended live jazz performances than I was by the dearth of black writers covering jazz. So Keith and Len published my very first professional piece dealing with that burning issue, titled, "Why Black Folks Should Listen to Jazz." A few years later I became a staff writer for the African American community news–focused, Brooklyn-based *City Sun*, writing about jazz and other subjects. Since then I've freelanced for a variety of publications, including writing frequently about jazz music.

I still believe that not only black folks should listen to and appreciate jazz—*everyone* should. Yet black Americans are the creators and innovators of the jazz idiom, one of the most powerful art forms we have created. Ancestral pride and recognition of historical value are reasons enough, but today I propose that black folk in particular check out jazz, not because of nostalgia but because it can point to answers about the puzzles of personal and cultural identity in a postmodern age.

Jazz can lead those curious enough to some of the greatest music ever made. Not only that, the music will point to ingenious writers and thinkers who've addressed the music, such as Ralph Ellison, Albert Murray, and George Lewis, who is also a composer, trombonist, and creator of a software program that improvises with human beings. Stephon Alexander wrote a book called *The Jazz of Physics* in which he relates the music and John Coltrane's search to cutting-edge physics, at both small-scale quantum and universe-scale cosmological levels.

If black folks really want a source of affirmation in spite of a history of injustice, and in the face of the folklore of white supremacy and the fakelore of black pathology, and to understand themselves in cultural *and* cosmic terms, jazz is here, patient, like Penelope waiting for Odysseus to come back home.

As far as the number of black writers covering the music, it wasn't as bad when I started reading about jazz as it seems to me now, when there are even fewer black writers at mainstream outlets covering jazz. Back when I started writing about the music, I'd read pieces on jazz by Stanley Crouch and Greg Tate in the *Village Voice*, Gene Seymour in the *Nation* and *New York Newsday*, and jazz writings by the Harlemite Herb Boyd and a contemporary of mine, Eugene Holley Jr., in various publications. All of these guys were in New York in my early years as a writer, as were the elder grand masters, Ralph Ellison and Albert Murray.

These days there are fewer print outlets than ever covering jazz. The few that do consider jazz worthy of coverage hardly have any writers of color. Martin Johnson, who writes for the *Wall Street Journal*, was an exception, but even he doesn't write about jazz for the wsj with the frequency of some of their white contributors, like Will Friedwald and Marc Myers.

I suppose that most black commentators who focus on music generally deal with more popular genres because pop music is more likely to have a larger audience and readership, and therefore publications willing to pay for their writing. There are fewer and fewer publications that even cover "serious music" anymore.

With respect to the auspicious African American history of jazz, the glaring disparity has to do with black musicians being acculturated early on to the cultural power and appeal of jazz expression, particularly since their ancestors founded and innovated the blues idiom vernacular called jazz—versus black media commentators who privilege popular music forms (and the career benefits that coverage might bring) over jazz, a fine art they may not even like or feel qualified to write about.

Pop and youth culture hold a powerful sway, whereas you have to go deep in the woodshed to write about jazz with substance. Most black commentators, even those in the academy, apparently are not ready, willing, or able to go that deep in the shed about this musical form at the very pinnacle of their culture.

In terms of the black intelligentsia's and academics' seeming ignorance of jazz, with some noble exceptions, the neglect of jazz by black intellectuals has been the case throughout the entire history of the music. So-called black public intellectuals feel more comfortable discussing hip-hop for reasons similar to those I suggested earlier about other black journalists. Some of this is generational, since jazz's popularity in the United States dates back to at least the mid-twentieth century. Some black public intellectuals are fine with making passing references to jazz in their rhetoric (i.e., Cornel West), because of the deep structural value of jazz in both American culture writ large and in black American culture. But such references are superficial and a disservice to folks who read their work and hear their speeches. If they would go deeper, perhaps more black folks would be willing to pursue listening to and learning about the jazz idiom themselves. But on the other hand, perhaps writing about the fine arts, about "serious music," considering our difficult history in this land, has aptly been viewed as a luxury until more recent times.

Ultimately that lack of diversity among those who write about jazz contributes to how the music is covered. But I think we can only take that point so far. Most writers covering jazz readily acknowledge the black American roots of the music, so that's a commonality. But there are different viewpoints on the value of certain styles or subgenres, and as a result different emphases arise based on stylistic preferences. I don't think there is an underlying racial motivation in those different views. These and other motivating factors play a role in how the music is covered just as much as or more than race considerations.

As in politics, where race doesn't necessarily determine whether one is liberal or conservative, African American writers don't share the same opinions about the music based solely on their cultural identification. Neither is this the case with white writers. Some black writers appreciate and write about what's called "mainstream" blues and swinging jazz, while others prefer the offshoots of what in the 1960s was called "free" (or avant-garde) jazz. These are questions of taste, not race. Also, white writers and others who don't identify as "black" still share in the values and expressive content of black American culture by a sort of cultural osmosis, because that blues idiom is in the very fabric of American society and culture writ large. If you consider yourself American, you're part black too!

I have at times questioned why some musicians may be elevated over others in the coverage of jazz. And though the backstory is usually more complicated than a simple "race" analysis, race being an ever-present cancer in the body politic does play a role in which musicians are elevated over others. Some white jazz artists still have more market value than black jazz artists on the same instrument who are just as talented. But in the marketplace, many factors tie into why various artists are paid at a certain level versus others. Race factors in, but not as prominently as it did in the first decades of jazz development.

It's important to note that race and cultural diversity are actually two different things—the confusion between race and culture has been deadly—but I think it better to confront race in jazz so that we might better move beyond such considerations. The concept of race is ultimately trivial and stupid, but to transcend race we must face the illusion/delusion of race squarely.

Record label and public relations campaigns factor in to the seemingly unwarranted or hasty elevations of certain artists, as does the need among some writers to find the "next hot artist." But race is a tricky rubric with which to assess "next hot artist" designations. For instance, Esperanza Spalding was championed by many writers; since then, the same has been true with Kamasi Washington, both African American. So many good jazz artists labor in relative obscurity that when they do get some attention, I usually don't have a problem with it. Cultural diversity among writers will generate more diverse perspectives but not a consensus on which artists deserve to be elevated over others.

However, I don't agree with certain musicians being labeled "jazz" artists when they themselves will acknowledge that what they play is more "instrumental rhythm and blues." The way the term *jazz* has been marketed is problematic, especially by festival promoters and the radio industry (e.g., "smooth jazz"). They endeavor to profit from the veneer and sophisticated brand of jazz, while pulling in other genres to make more money than they might with jazz proper.

That's part of the economic reality and challenges of presenting jazz qua jazz. Kenny G is a popular instrumentalist, but when he is elevated by the mainstream press as a "jazz" artist, due to his level of record sales and radio play, over someone like Kenny Garrett—the most influential jazz alto saxophonist of his generation—that's pure hype, not an accurate evaluation of genre or of artistic weight and authority.

Furthermore, I think there is an undercurrent of race in why other white artists, such as Diana Krall, Chris Botti, and Norah Jones, have become popular performing a mellow, soothing, less experimental style of music. They fill a niche in the music and radio industries and for certain market segments. But I don't criticize those artists for that; it isn't their fault as individuals, but the dumb idea of race is so entrenched that they benefit from white privilege as well as from their musical style and talent as artists.

Neglect of the music by black publications is also a fact. Jazz is a fine art, and most black publications focus on popular music. As Albert Murray said, the quality and range of aesthetic statement can be grouped into folk, pop, and fine art categories for pedagogical purposes. Our celebrity-worshipping, short-term-memory, profit-driven society overall doesn't value fine art's intrinsic or long-term worth. If art doesn't have a big audience, then it won't be considered relevant to most black publications, because they compete in a media field where popularity and celebrity trump all.

This is especially sad and tragic because elder jazz masters such as Roy Haynes, Wayne Shorter, Sonny Rollins, Charles McPherson, Reggie Workman, Louis Hayes, Jimmy Cobb, Ben Riley, Benny Golson, Buster Williams, Melba Joyce, and Ahmad Jamal are still on the scene. I could easily name twenty more living legends unknown to a wider black audience or to the general public.

The audiences consuming black publications are aware of Quincy Jones and Herbie Hancock, even Wynton Marsalis, but they usually aren't hip to these senior giants. To rephrase Carter G. Woodson, this is the miseducation of the black American. These jazz masters should be revered and honored by black publications and media outlets as a cultural and ancestral imperative.

American Legacy magazine, a publication to which I've contributed features on Ralph Ellison and Albert Murray, was one of the few African American periodicals I can point to that delved into the historical and cultural depths beyond pop culture and contemporary hype. *American Legacy* had a history of covering jazz, but not just jazz: they covered the legacy of black American music as a powerhouse cultural form. But alas, they are no longer around.

Oprah Winfrey's fame and worldwide celebrity far exceeds the black audience. She could reach that demographic and beyond. I wrote an open letter to Oprah in *All about Jazz* in hopes of inspiring her to have more jazz musicians on her original show, not just as performers but also as commentators. Jazz musicians are some of the worldliest, sophisticated, and smart people I know. Exposing wider audiences to jazz musicians as artists and as thinkers is one way to address the low cultural moment in which we find ourselves, especially low as regards most pop music.

The public education system and the music industry are largely at fault for the current state of affairs, where a vicious cycle of mediocrity predominates. It's incumbent upon those of us who love and value this music's contribution to the world to be more entrepreneurial. The *Independent Ear* [where this interview first appeared] is an example of this. *Jazz It Up!*, my online jazz news and entertainment series was another.

How serious music is reported is a matter of individual taste, depth of historical aesthetic, literary and musical knowledge, native talent, and the disciplined application of all of the above. These factors fluctuate, of course, among writers of varying backgrounds. How the music is covered also has to do with how the writer views his or her social and cultural function.

I produced and moderated a panel discussion at the National Jazz Museum in Harlem a few years ago that brought together the jazz critics and scholars Gary Giddins, Howard Mandel, and John Gennari and the jazz musicians Steve Coleman, Lewis Nash, Jon Gordon, and Vijay Iyer for a dialogue. I ventured a definition of the role of jazz criticism: to function as a bridge between the artists, the art form, and the public for the sake of publicity, education, and aesthetic evaluation. That's how I see my role, so that orientation grounds the tone and approach I take when I write about the music.

Some of my colleagues bristle at the notion of the publicity aspect of criticism, because publicity work is considered to be for hacks. But when jazz is so low on the public radar, I don't think it's wise to have our noses in the air like that. Yes, journalism and public relations are not and should not be considered the same. Yet jazz journalists know well that they serve the function of publicizing the music. And that ain't nothin' to be ashamed of!

Some of my most rewarding moments covering this music have come from opportunities to meet, interview, and even become friends with musicians who play the music that moves my soul. Of course, hearing great music live that I otherwise may not have been able to afford is another. When a reader says to me, "I felt like I was there," I say to myself, "Mission accomplished!"

There is also a community of academics and scholars with whom I've interacted as a member of the Jazz Study Group at Columbia University. I'm grateful to Robert O'Meally for asking me to join in 1999 as I worked toward a doctorate in American Studies at NYU. (I decided not to pursue academia as a career.) Last, but far from least, are the friendships and mentoring relationships I've nurtured over the years, which stem from jazz and an abiding appreciation for black American culture at the root.

On the other hand, the main obstacle I've run into in this pursuit, other than difficult editors and indifferent publications, is making a living covering jazz. So, like many others, I've had to supplement coverage of jazz with other work to support my family. Another obstacle has been getting due recognition in the jazz press about my online show *Jazz It Up!* Though we had a little coverage in *DownBeat* and *JazzTimes* magazines when we launched in 2007, since then the coverage hasn't been commensurate with what we've accomplished. *Jazz it Up!* was the only online TV series at the time devoted to this music, and over the course of eighteen half-hour episodes we garnered close to three million viewers online. That's jazz news that warrants coverage.

Ironically, the organization that produces and presents the Emmy Awards has recognized *Jazz It Up!* In fall 2008, the National Academy of Recording Arts and Sciences nominated *Jazz It Up!* for a Global Media Award in the Long-Form Entertainment category. Not one jazz publication—online or otherwise—reported this achievement!

More recently I had interesting experiences writing about jazz for the *New York Daily News*. I had excellent editors there, but when the former fashion editor took over the features section, I knew my days were numbered. The page formerly devoted to my jazz column now displays clothing for the younger demographic of that paper. I had support systems there, people who subsequently either retired, died, or were fired. I could tell it was only a matter of time, especially because columnists who had been there much longer than I were being dismissed. That paper has been bleeding staff for a while in this harsh environment for print journalism. Fortunately, my work as a consultant, curator, producer, lecturer—and, coming soon, a book author—has sustained me.

Frankly, I think that the access issue is moot in our current time. Why? Because there are fewer and fewer media outlets for *everyone*. At the same time, we all can write freely—and for *free*—for many online venues and even for personal blogs. How many jazz magazines still exist? Those that still remain don't have the influence they used to in decades past. Access was a major issue then, especially at places such as the *New York Times*, which now has only one jazz writer. As you know, I was the *New York Daily News* jazz columnist from 2011 to 2013. I'm proud of the work I did there; more everyday folks were exposed to jazz happenings in New York, featuring everyone from elder masters to young artists. But little jazz had been covered there either before my tenure or after. Whether in print publications or on network or cable television, jazz is virtually invisible.

I honor the relatively few of us black writers focusing on jazz in such a time of massive media and technological change. The music will survive with or without us. Let's hope that it's with us.

Hollie West

Hollie West for many years achieved the rather unique status of being a regular contributing jazz writer and columnist for a major daily newspaper. While a lifestyle reporter for the *Washington Post*, West got assignments for profiles on Duke Ellington, Dizzy Gillespie, Miles Davis, Ralph Ellison, and James Baldwin.

West's initial daily newspaper writing opportunity came for the *Oakland Tribune*. Following that stint, he wrote for the San Francisco and Sacramento bureaus of the Associated Press before moving east to launch the AP's Harlem bureau during the Black Arts Movement of the 1960s. Later he wrote on jazz for the *New York Daily News* and the *Detroit Free Press*.

My interests in music started with listening to my sister's records. When she left to attend Wilberforce College in 1943 and I was about to enter the first grade, she left her records behind, including Coleman Hawkins's classic rendition of *Body and Soul*, and Erskine Hawkins, Harry James, and Woody Herman records. I would listen to Hawkins's *Body and Soul* over and over again; even at six years old, there was something that intrigued me about that. Then I started playing trumpet in the seventh grade and I was gung ho! I didn't play jazz so much, but I took part in statewide competitions and I played Herbert L. Clark solos and solos written by other people and competed with people from Oklahoma City and Tulsa. I was intending to major in music in college.

I started writing, not about music, but for the local paper where I grew up, in a segregated Oklahoma town about sixty miles east of Oklahoma City called Wewoka, the seat of Seminole County. Our local paper did not cover our football and basketball games at Douglas High School, so they would always ask a student to do so. In my junior year I was asked by a teacher to provide that coverage, and I jumped at the opportunity. I was an avid sports fan and I read sports articles in the newspaper, so I patterned my game accounts after what I read in the papers.

After graduation I went off to Ohio State and majored in journalism. I started writing about music in the spring of 1957 when I took over a record review column at the student daily. My first column was on the album *The John Lewis Piano* on Atlantic Records. I wasn't given any records; I bought my own records, and I tried to write about a variety of music, not just jazz but also folk music, some R&B, and some pop music.

When Duke Ellington's Orchestra played the ROTC Ball on Ohio State's campus, they played a concert the afternoon before the ball at St. John Arena, and I went there to review it. I took one of my fellow students, Theodora Robinson, to that concert and to the ball. She wanted Ellington's autograph, so I went backstage and talked with his longtime baritone saxophonist Harry Carney, and then we got the autograph.

When I finished college I went into the army because it was a peacetime draft that I couldn't avoid. I graduated in December 1959 and applied to different places but couldn't get a job. I had been the campus stringer for the *Cleveland Plain Dealer* and I couldn't get a job there because my draft classification was 1-A, which meant I could be drafted at any time. So I went into the army and most of the time I was a specialist, with two summer tours in Greenland with a research and development outfit. We didn't have weapons or field gear; we were strictly a support outfit for civilian and military scientists. After the army my first job was at the *Oakland Tribune*.

My wife Barbara and I had met in Dallas and had been waiting to decide what we were going to do about this relationship, so—this is how youth are—I went out to Oakland without a job in sight and without any promise of a job. Barbara was working as a medical technologist at Mt. Zion Hospital in San Francisco. I looked for a job for several months. I went to the *Chronicle*, and Abe Mellinkoff said, "Well, Hollie, we want a Negro reporter but we want one with five years of daily newspaper experience. " I said, "Well, you want Carl Rowan, and he's not coming out here." By that time, Kennedy had appointed Rowan head of the USIA.

The *Tribune* had offered me a job as a copy boy with the possibility of being promoted. At first I turned it down; then I crawled back to them after not being able to find a job anywhere else and took the job as a copy aid. Within eight weeks I was promoted to reporter, but I didn't do any music writing there at all. Russ Wilson was the jazz critic there, and I used to talk with Russ a lot. He was on a contract basis and was not a staff person. Russ was quite a character: he came into the office late at night to write his reviews, usually of people playing in San Francisco. He used a cigarette holder so he had his cigarettes dangling, and he wore a monocle and sometimes a beret; he was quite a personality and I enjoyed talking with him.

I was very committed to writing about music, but it was not anything I was ever hired to do. I was hired primarily in the latter part of my career as a feature writer to do news features. That's why I was hired at the *New York Daily News* and at the *Detroit Free Press*, and I had carved out that niche at the *Washington Post*. I wrote about jazz probably once every week or two in the *Daily News*, but it was rare for me to write about jazz in the *Detroit Free Press*.

At the *Daily News* I wrote a piece about panhandlers. I hung out with panhandlers on the streets of New York for a week. I didn't panhandle myself; I just talked with them and saw how they operated. I did the same thing with the phenomenon of telephone party lines. I listened, then I interviewed some of the people and went to some of their gatherings, and I wrote a long piece about telephone party lines. It was a little different feature writing for the *Daily News* because I was writing for a tabloid and the demands were different. Before I worked at the *Daily News*—between 1987 and 1993—I was at the *Detroit Free Press* and I wrote features there.

I started writing about music professionally for the *Washington Post* in 1967. My friend Chuck Stone's wife Louise's uncle Arthur P. Davis taught literature at Howard University, and her father taught at Hampton. When I got there, Louise was writing a record review column on a contractual basis for the *Post*'s old entertainment section; there was no Style section at the time. They had people covering classical music but no one was writing about jazz or other American music—the food editor Bill Rice sometimes wrote about some club activity, but it was nothing regular—so I saw an opportunity. Frankly, I didn't think Louise was doing a good job writing that record column.

Several months after I started at the *Post* in April of 1967, I wrote the editor Ben Bradlee and proposed that I write the record review column because I was a full-time staffer and Louise was not (she was a freelancer). I included some sample columns, and I wrote a critique of her columns. I got the job writing the record column, but back then no one was interviewing musicians. Leo Sullivan was the entertainment editor at the time, and I suggested covering blues singer Bobby Blue Bland at the Howard Theatre. I interviewed him, which I later turned into a piece for *Rolling Stone* back when it was still in tabloid form. They had approached me about doing a piece for them.

Later I wrote a piece on Bill Evans, who was appearing at the old Bohemian Caverns. I had a very interesting conversation with him that I wish I had taped, but I wasn't taping interviews at that time. There were other music pieces I wrote between 1967 and 1969. The Style section started in January of 1969, and I was brought in as a charter member of that section, which is when I started writing about jazz regularly.

I wasn't writing features; I was covering DC politics and the city council up until they started the Style section. When I first got there I was doing general assignment reporting and very few features. Then, later, when President Lyndon Johnson appointed Walter Washington mayor and appointed the city council—back when DC citizens didn't vote on those positions—Bob Kaiser covered the mayor's office, and I covered the city council, starting in early 1968.

My music writing was largely adjunct at that point. I got permission from the city editor to do that adjunct work, and it amounted to a large percentage of my work because if I did one feature every couple of weeks or so that didn't take up a lot of time. The first record column I wrote was on John Coltrane, because he died in June 1967 and I'd written a column about an album of his that came out that fall. People around town were saying, "Who is this Hollie West?" because the *Post* hadn't been featuring jazz in a prominent way. There was a photograph of Coltrane and my commentary about the album. I had free rein to write what I chose to.

Once I started that record column, it appeared every Sunday, originally in the entertainment and then later the Style section. I even had a logo for the column, which was called "The Rhythm Mode." I took a cue from Ralph Gleason, who had his "Rhythm Section" in the *San Francisco Chronicle*. I never met Gleason, but I wrote him a couple of angry letters because I thought he was shifting to too much coverage of pop music.

When I started contributing to the Style section, I wasn't covering just African American or jazz musicians. I was writing a lot about pop, because the *Post* at the time didn't have anybody to do that. So I wrote about Janis Joplin, about Big Brother and the Holding Company appearing at the Alexandria Roller Rink; I went over and did a review of the concert, but I didn't have any sympathy for that music.

When the Style section began, they were spending money and I was sent to New York to review Janis Joplin at the Fillmore East. And whom did I find sitting next to me? Benny Goodman and one of his daughters; she had persuaded him to take her to hear Janis Joplin. I interviewed him on the spot, so I had a sidebar about Benny Goodman.

After a year or so they hired Tom Zino, who had an interest in rock music. They wanted to cover youth culture and I wasn't the person to do that, so he was hired. I was still young at the time but he was just out of college in 1970. Two of my first pieces, outside of record reviews, were on the Modern Jazz Quartet, who were appearing at Blues Alley. I interviewed their pianist John Lewis, beginning a relationship that continued until his death. I interviewed Oscar Brown Jr., who was appearing with his wife Jean Pace at the Cellar Door; that was a piece with several photographs, so they made a pretty good layout on that. This was all while I was still covering the city council. That was the first of several interviews I did with Oscar over the years.

When I started covering music, I was definitely aware of the absence of African Americans writing about music just from my reading. I was a voracious reader, starting with *DownBeat* magazine when I was in high school. I discovered *DownBeat* on a summer trip to Cleveland to see my late sister. I would walk up to 105th Street to the drugstore, and I saw *DownBeat* magazine there. I bought a copy and soon subscribed, in 1950 to '51. So I knew who was writing and who was not writing.

One of the first pieces that made a deep impression on me was Alan Morrison's piece about Bud Powell in *Ebony* magazine in 1953. I knew he was a brother because it was a black magazine and I read that piece over and over. What struck me was the penetrating quality of the piece, because it was about Bud's mental condition, his deterioration. It was about his music too, but how his condition intertwined with his music. I wasn't thoroughly familiar with Bud Powell at that point. Living in Oklahoma, I had more access to George Shearing and Dave Brubeck; I knew their work better than I knew Bud Powell's music.

Back then I had to order records on the jazz labels. I could get records on Columbia and RCA by ordering them at the local music store, but they couldn't get Prestige, Blue Note, Dial, or other jazz labels. I saw an ad in *DownBeat* for the Modern Music Shop in St. Louis and started ordering records when I was in high school.

It was always exciting when I got a package of records in the mail, and that's how I got *A Night at Birdland* when it was a 10-inch, or Clifford Brown's *New Star on the Horizon*, or Miles Davis's *Walkin'*—all of those were 10-inch records. I didn't have anybody in high school to talk with about these things, except one guy named Otis Funches, who was a trumpet player. He would come down to my home and we would stay up all night listening to records.

I knew there were some black writers covering the music, because when I started writing about music I knew about Barbara Gardner in Chicago, who was the associate editor of *DownBeat*. I knew about Marc Crawford; in fact, I knew him, and we used to joke about Marc because he tried to appear like Hemingway so much that he wore a safari jacket. But he was an interesting brother and I was very much aware of his writing—he wrote for *DownBeat* too. But I knew there wasn't a lot of interest among black writers in covering jazz. Among my fellow reporters, I knew all the black guys in New York; we were all pioneers to a degree—Earl Caldwell, Tom Johnson,

Gil Scott, Austin Scott—none of those guys had any interest in writing about music, art, or literature.

Another black writer on jazz that I was aware of was Frank London Brown, because I spent a lot of time in the library. Frank London Brown's primary work was in fiction, but I think I might have read him first in *Down-Beat* back in the 1950s. But I wasn't going to let the dearth of black writers on jazz stop me. Even before Barbara Gardner, the only two black writers on jazz that I was aware of were Alan Morrison and Frank London Brown.

I've thought a lot about the fact that there were so few black writers on jazz, because I was so frustrated in trying to recruit people to write about the music. I've felt that many of my journalist friends were not interested in music in the first place, or if they were interested, it was in R&B. When Dick Prince started working at the *Post* I tried to interest him in writing about the music, but he had no interest. I did get Bill Brower in there for a while as a freelancer, but I don't know if he liked that routine or that discipline so much, so he didn't stay long. I think the brothers and sisters who are writing, most of them are just not interested in writing about music, and maybe they just consider it a pastime.

I do think the lack of black writers contributes to how the music is portrayed. I hesitate to be personal about this, but I think of the people who wrote about jazz before I got to the *Post*, and they seemed to concentrate more on white musicians. The people who would write about the music occasionally, their interests were white musicians.

I remember Ken Ringgold having some very negative things to say about Charles Mingus in my presence, but he was very fond of Brubeck. Maybe their music was simpler and more accessible to these guys. They have the power, they have the inroads and the influence, and it was only my tenacity that got me in the position to write about music at newspapers.

I knew there were white guys, constantly nipping at my heels, who wanted to replace me. I had very good relations with most editors, but this one editor said my pieces would be better suited to *DownBeat* than to the *Post*. I guess that was specifically because of the way I was writing about music. But I had a lot of encouragement from editors. Lon Tuck was the deputy editor of the Style section, and sometimes my pieces would *grow* in length under Lon's editing. He was very interested in music—though not so much in jazz, where he had a passing interest—but in classical music, especially piano.

I think white writers bring a different perspective to the music as a general rule, though there are some white writers who are very much aware of the differences. When I attended a screening of the Clint Eastwood movie

Bird, about Charlie Parker, I was outside discussing it afterward with fellow critic Gary Giddins, and I mentioned some racial aspect of the film—and it had never occurred to Gary to even think of that.

Martin Williams was very much aware, though; in fact, he had some guilt about his position in writing about music. During my Nieman Fellowship year in 1973 to 1974, Nat Hentoff was one of the people I brought up to Harvard. We were allowed to bring two writers up, and I brought in Nat and Albert Murray. The other Nieman Fellows in my cohort knew nothing about either of them; they were complete revelations. I grew up reading Nat when I was in high school, because he was writing the "Counterpoint" column for *DownBeat* then. His writing was a big influence on me.

The indifference of the African American press has been a question that has puzzled me for years. They're more interested in readership, and they think their readers aren't attuned to serious music. I wrote a piece for *Ebony* magazine, on a topic that they had suggested to me, which they subsequently titled "Can Whites Sing the Blues?" I wrote a second piece for them, titled "Love in Blues Lyrics," but they never published it. They paid me, but I was told that the chief editor, Lerone Bennett, killed that piece because he didn't think it had enough depth. The editor who commissioned it, Charles Sanders, thought it was fine, but it was not in his power to run it if Lerone didn't like it.

Ebony doesn't run pieces about musicians, because they think their readers don't want them. In talking with my fellow writers and reporters at newspapers, I just gleaned the fact that the black press doesn't have anything more than a passing interest in music. It's tough being a writer of this music because it requires a lot of sacrifice in both time and monetary resources.

I think the way this music is covered has the world to do with who is writing about it, black or white. Remember that most of the people in mainstream journalism—that is, in white-dominated publications—have been white, and they have set themselves up as authorities for whatever they've written about. If I had any differences with editors, I was able to win because I could cite something very specific to white editors who generally didn't know much about music. I never had any showdowns with editors.

I encountered very few obstacles in my writing. As I mentioned earlier, there was the assignment editor who said I should be writing for *DownBeat*, but he didn't present an obstacle because there were so many people of greater authority than he who liked what I wrote. A writer once suggested to one of the editors at the *Washington Post* that I do a piece on Wild Bill Davison, who was appearing at Blues Alley or Mr. Henry's. The routine was that I would suggest whom I wanted to write about. But I did that Davison interview and wrote a short, respectable piece; I wouldn't consider that an obstacle, just a minor roadblock. I was basically placating the editor's interests.

There have certainly been some rewarding encounters along the way. Interviewing Ellington was one of the high points; I spent an hour and forty-five minutes with him when his orchestra was playing at a hotel in Indianapolis. It was a high point just to see the orchestra in action in a ballroom setting.

The *Washington Post* Style section thought nothing of sending me up to New York to review a concert, despite the fact that there'd be no Washington people there. I asked for the assignment to go up one night to the Guggenheim Museum; they had several musicians performing unaccompanied solos: Cecil Taylor, Sonny Rollins, a string quartet playing a piece by Ornette Coleman—that was one of the grand experiences.

The first interview I did with Sonny Rollins in 1975 led to an extended piece. I did interviews of two or three hours; that was nothing. On one occasion, Dave Brubeck had written an oratorio, so he and I met at Kennedy Airport and took a plane together to Cincinnati, where he was conducting the oratorio. I interviewed him on the plane, then he took a car into Cincinnati and I caught a plane back to Washington.

One artist response that stood out was a Chicago interview I did with Muddy Waters in 1971, prior to a festival at the Kennedy Center where he was on the program. We sat down, and Muddy said to me, "If I'd known you were going to be a brother I would have had some pork chops waiting!" We sat there and talked, and his wife Geneva fixed some breakfast for us; he opened a bottle of sparkling wine and said, "I always drink a bottle of champagne with my meals."

Most of the black musicians I interviewed, I suppose, might have inquired about me with other musicians. Sometimes I know they did, because they knew who was coming, though sometimes they thought I'd be a woman with the name Hollie. Usually people were extremely open. A lot depends on how well informed the writer is—and not on the writer's ethnic background. I think it's more about that. One more anecdote about that comfort factor: when I interviewed Art Pepper, he was so comfortable that he talked about how he wished that he had been black!

Personally, I never had any question of access to media outlets for my writing, because during most of the time I wrote about music I was a staff writer at a newspaper. Moreover, music was never my full-time focus. I wrote about music while I worked at the *Washington Post* (1967–1981) and the

New York Daily News (1987–1993), and the outlet was at arm's reach. At other newspapers, I either wrote little about music or none at all. Early in my career, before the *Post*, I was trying to learn the news business.

Only a handful of times did I do any outside writing while working full-time for a newspaper. In the early days of *Rolling Stone* magazine, I was asked to write a couple of pieces. In later years I approached *DownBeat* about an idea, which was welcomed and published.

The bottom line is that I was focused on my main duties and had little time to freelance. One of the fortunate things about working at the *Washington Post* was that I was given the chance to write about music in a way I never could have as a freelancer because I got a lot of space, received a regular salary, and got my research trips subsidized.

Between the time I left the *Post* in 1981 and returned to newspapering in 1986, I wrote several pieces for *JazzTimes*, including interviews of Wynton Marsalis, Cecil McBee, and Benny Bailey. The ideas were mine, and I had no problem getting the pieces published.

7

the new breed (online)

BRIDGET ARNWINE, ANGELIKA BEENER,
AND ANTHONY DEAN-HARRIS

The writers interviewed for this section include some of the younger generation of black jazz writers. In our evolving publishing paradigm, where print media has steadily eroded in prominence and supremacy with regard to where the public derives its news and information, online publishing has continued its upward arc as younger generations' information gathering medium of choice.

Rather than pitch their ideas to traditional jazz magazine publishers and await the typical thumbs-up or thumbs-down pronouncement, the contributors in this section have answered to no one—neither editors nor publishers—regarding what they choose to write about the art form or their individual mode of expression. Monetizing their online efforts is another consideration for another forum, but what this brave new world of publishing has afforded these writers is the freedom to choose their own topics and issues to explore at whatever length and breadth they choose. This is the new breed of jazz writers, whose ranks will persist as online publishing continues to grow its market share to dominant proportions.

Bridget Arnwine

Bridget Arnwine is an example of a person inquisitive about expressing a desire to write about jazz as a young person, who has subsequently worked her way into various bylines. She first communicated her desire to write about jazz in the late 1990s, and after reading her prose I arranged for her to write program notes for the annual Tri-C JazzFest, back when she lived in Cleveland. In 2005 Bridget took advantage of a one-time fellowship that was established by the Jazz Journalists Association in the name of the late Harlem-based jazz writer Clarence Atkins. That fellowship, awarded to a small group of deserving and aspiring African American jazz writers, enabled Bridget to attend the National Critics Conference in Los Angeles in the summer of 2005.

Since then Bridget has continued to develop her writing craft and her jazz chops, writing about jazz weekly for Examiner.com, AXS.com, and occasionally JazzPolice .com since moving to the Baltimore-Washington area. Additionally she has developed her own jazz apparel business, Jazzheads. In 2018 she contributed the chapter "The Beautiful Struggle: A Look at Women Who Have Helped Shape the DC Jazz Scene" for the acclaimed book *DC Jazz*. Additionally, she has contributed to the *Encyclopedia of Hip Hop Literature* and writes about the music for her own blog at bridgetsjazzplanet .wordpress.com.

Some of my interest in writing about jazz was a result of meeting Wynton Marsalis in August of 1995. I was a volunteer intern in the office of Congresswoman Cynthia McKinney from Georgia. One of the other interns approached me about driving down to Augusta, GA, to set up a voter registration drive at a Wynton Marsalis concert slated for that night. I didn't want to go, but she said that Congresswoman McKinney might look on us favorably if we did go. Then she told me that everything had already been set up: she knew Wynton, she'd gotten permission to set up at the concert, and we'd be staying with one of the Congresswoman's staffers. I packed my bag, and she picked me up.

Turns out she hadn't quite told me the truth—we really didn't have permission to register voters at Wynton's concert, and we didn't have a place to stay—but she had met Wynton before. We happened to arrive at the venue while the band was in sound check. She was able to get the person at the venue's box office to interrupt sound check to deliver a "Hello, I'm the girl you met . . ." note. To my surprise, we were told that one of the guys responded. We were told that if we met the band in the hotel lobby by 6 p.m., we could walk to the performance venue together. That's when my colleague revealed that we didn't actually have a place to stay, so we rushed over to the hotel, and, by some miracle, I was able to reserve the last room in the hotel for the night (I soon realized that I was actually only invited along to fund the trip). We met the band in the lobby as instructed, and we ended up spending the entire weekend shadowing them and attending the concerts.

The band for that event was Wynton, Eric Reed, Victor Goines, Herlin Riley, Wycliffe Gordon, and Wess Anderson. They played like they really, really enjoyed the music. I'd never experienced anything like that—ever! None of those guys would be able to pick me out of a lineup if I were standing in front of them today, but I'll never forget them because meeting them changed my life. It was a long time coming, but when I finally did fall for jazz, I fell pretty hard.

Up to that point, all I knew about jazz was Kenny G. I was more intrigued by hip-hop, R&B, and rock music than anything else; in my mind, jazz was something for other people to enjoy. I don't sing, I don't play an instrument, and my dancing is wild and unstructured at best. Years ago I began to feel an urgent need to express my love in writing for this music. I came up with the "brilliant" idea to write a book comprised of interviews with jazz musicians. I began to contact musicians and publicists requesting interviews. The only person to say yes was Wynton, but I didn't have a book if my book of interviews consisted of interviews with only one person!

As a last resort I contacted Wynton's personal assistant and asked for guidance—and she gave it to me! She suggested that I take time to first build my writing resume, so I joined the Jazz Journalists Association (JJA), and I started writing reviews. I'm a bit shy and overanalytical, so in actuality the review and bio writing was a better fit for my personality. When I first started writing about jazz, I wasn't aware that there were so few black jazz writers. When I first started writing, my motives were purely selfish, so I had no idea. I figured it out pretty quickly though.

Reading the jazz publications over the years and looking at who contributed which articles was very revealing. Attending JJA events and discovering that most of the black people in the room weren't the writers but the musicians was another revelation. It didn't take a rocket scientist to figure out that there weren't many African Americans writing about this African American art form. That said, I know how many times I've pitched some of those jazz publications, so it made me wonder if the reality was actually that African American writers simply weren't being included. Whichever reality is true, pick up a jazz publication and the names you won't see will be glaring.

In my opinion, black writers are going where the money is—and that certainly is not in jazz writing. I write about jazz because I've come to love it, but it's hard. A lot of the work that I've had to do in my years as a writer has been for free. Who can afford to do that? I don't want to work a nine-to-five, but I have to in order to sustain myself. That's not to say that every black writer covering this music has the same experience, but starting out can be tough. Couple that with the fact that black audiences for jazz are typically small. When you look at it that way, then the small number of black jazz writers makes sense.

The lack of black writers definitely contributes to how the music is covered. I write with a bit of emotion, because I have to rely more on describing how the music makes me feel than does a writer with a musical background. I don't think a musical background is necessary to write effectively. It definitely helps, but it's not necessary. The people I know the best who love music as much as I do aren't musicians. Music has been the safe place for many of them. You don't need to read a note of music to connect with it on that level. That said, having a musical background adds an element to the review that "legitimizes" your opinion in the mind of the musician. If you're a writer who's ever tried to connect with musicians, you can't dismiss that.

Some of the people who have worked as editors for my writing usually don't get the gist of my work because of the emotional element, so I'm always struggling to preserve the uniqueness of my voice so that my writing doesn't sound like everyone else's. It's a challenge, particularly when you have to adhere to someone else's writing guidelines.

A funny example of that for me involved my time writing for a heavy metal webzine. I always discussed the music and my thoughts on the band and I always threw in a few funny little extras, but my reviews were heavily edited because to them my writing was "too professional" sounding! I've yet to have a jazz editor tell me that about my writing!

I do sometimes wonder how it is that certain musicians are elevated over other, more deserving musicians. I was thinking recently about the negative press that some of our African American jazz icons received during their lifetimes. Before I really got into the music I had heard that Miles Davis was a jerk and that Charlie Parker was an addict. I'd not heard a lick of music from either of them, but those statements were discussed around me more than their music, and that's unfortunate.

On the other hand, about a year ago I read something about Stan Getz, and there was mention of his drug abuse and the extent of his physically abusive behavior toward his second wife. I remember being shocked because I'd never heard anyone mention that when talking about Mr. Getz. Clearly someone covered it because I did read it, but I wondered why that aspect of his personality wasn't discussed on the same level that Miles's and Bird's issues were. Was it because of the lack of diversity among the writers covering this music and its artists? At the time I couldn't help but think so. To that end, however, I do think Miles and Bird were celebrated for their musical achievements more than Stan Getz was, so I don't know how to process that. How was it that Miles and Bird were so highly regarded and so commonly persecuted while Getz was an awesome talent who often acted outside of himself? In my mind, it's all in how the picture is painted.

The lack of jazz coverage in African American publications goes back to my thoughts about money; jazz music—and serious music of all genres—is largely not popular. Popular music is what sells, so that's what you find discussed in those pages. I would think that the African American–oriented publications would be a place where jazz musicians, as well as less popular but equally talented musicians from other genres, would have a home, but I guess money is money.

On the whole, when more writers of color start covering jazz, I think things will change. Going back to the example of Miles, Bird, and Getz, I've often wondered whether or not, in a perfect world, having a majority of writers covering jazz being African American and a majority of jazz publications being run by and owned by African Americans would have changed Miles's and Bird's stories. Would the stories have been more about their gift for the music? What about Miles's love of boxing? What about the impact Bird's relationship with his mother may or may not have had on his music? I may have idealized things, but I imagine that coverage of their talents would have been much broader had more black writers been writing about them.

Some of my own most rewarding encounters writing about jazz involve just seeing people's faces when I'm introduced as a jazz writer. Sometimes people are really surprised to discover that I'm Bridget Arnwine. Other times people really want to talk to me and keep in touch. I'm a very brown woman, but I'm 100 percent certain that I turn red when that happens! It's an awesome feeling!

One obstacle that I've faced is being unknown *and* being a woman of color. That's definitely a double whammy. There was a time recently where I'd written a book review that wasn't received very well. I liked the idea of the book, but I thought it was poorly written and poorly edited. I struggled with that, because the author of the book was a woman and she's been around for a long time. I contacted the publication's editor about how torn I felt over wanting to write an honest review without being offensive and he advised me just to be honest. I had the misfortune of making a mistake in my review (I incorrectly noted the wrong college when referencing the author's alma mater) and I really, really beat myself up over that mistake. Here I was critiquing someone else's book (a book that people would have to purchase to see the errors I'd pointed out), and I made my mistake in a free publication!

When my review was published, the editor I worked with was bombarded with emails from the author, and he happened to share some of those emails with me. He wanted me to be prepared in case the author decided to reach out to me personally. The emails turned into an official Letter to the Editor! I was advised not to respond, and, even though I really wanted to, I followed the advice and did not respond. Surprisingly the author only mentioned my mistake once and in passing. What really seemed to set the author off was the fact that I didn't like the book. What stung most about those emails and that letter was that, when referring to me, she said, "At least she's not one of us."

Just like there are few writers of color covering jazz, there are also only a few women. I'd never met this woman, so I don't know whether she surmised that I was black, but I was left with a bad taste in my mouth over that "not one of us" comment. To read those comments coming from a woman really hurt, particularly when I'd gone out of my way not to be negative in my review of her work. I'd never felt like more of an outsider than I did after I read her words. I ended up taking another hiatus from writing, and I'm only now starting to feel like I want to write again.

I saw a popular blog make the argument that (and I'm paraphrasing), by the numbers, there are actually quite a few black music writers. That blog post came out as the dialogue with black writers was developing. Not to attempt to paraphrase the entire blog post or to attack the writer (because I honestly cannot remember every point made and I don't think his points were coming from a malicious place), I do remember feeling as if some of the points made in the blog post were dismissive at best.

In my mind, the issue at the root of the discussion was about representation and access. It's not been about how many people considered themselves black writers. If a person opens a magazine or logs onto a website dedicated to discussions about music, black music, how many of the writers who were given an opportunity to share their viewpoint were black? How many were women? Even if the numbers suggest that there are a large number of black writers or women writers, how are those voices included? What about black photographers?

If I, as a black woman, contact a publication to pitch a story and they tell me that they aren't accepting content from new writers, but then a few months later I pick up that publication and see a "welcome to our new writers" section, what am I to think? What should I do? If I pitch a story to a magazine about dedicating an issue to female musicians and they tell me that they're not interested, but then a few months later I see an issue dedicated to women and *not one* of the writers is a woman, and maybe one of the writers is black, again, what am I to do and what am I to think? If I ask about submitting a photo to a publication and they don't respond, is it a volume thing? Should I say, "Well at least I can say that I'm a black writer," or, "Maybe they're just busy?" When do I decide to find or create other vehicles for my voice to be heard?

I applaud every black person who has or has had an opportunity to regularly contribute to jazz publications. I absolutely love reading John Murph's and Angelika Beener's stuff. They are two of my favorites. I used to purchase magazines simply because I saw that Murph contributed an article (not just a CD review), and I followed Angelika's blog religiously for a time because I was such a fan of her work. I've never met or communicated with Eugene Holley Jr., but I remember reading some of his stuff in either *Ebony* or *Jet*. I thought that was super cool, especially since I hadn't seen many discussions about jazz in those publications in the past. But what about the other black writers?

Sure, any writer of any race could probably make the same argument, but it's glaring when the music in question is the baby of black culture. If I hadn't injected myself into this world and I were on the outside looking in, I'd think, if the majority of the writers about a black art form aren't black, something's wrong. At the very least there should be more than two of their stories included at a time per publication. And that's not sour grapes.

I still dream of a time when I can say, "Look mama, my article about Dr. Lonnie Smith is featured in jazz publication *x*!," but I feel as if I've got one foot out of the proverbial door. After almost fifteen years of writing about jazz, I've grown tired of asking to be included. I recently made a commitment to paving my own lane, and I have been super focused on trying to make that work—so this isn't only about me per se. That said, honestly speaking, I don't see a lot of us represented in these publications, and that desperately needs to change.

Today, I definitely don't take things so personally. I also take a lot more time to inspect and interpret email communications. Misunderstanding someone's words is just as uncomfortable as actually being insulted. I make sure that I'm certain before I react. I'm a lot more chill these days, so no one's scaring me away from anything. That said, my home is so far away from everything that I really have to be inspired to write these days. I'm getting back out there though. I really miss the scene.

Angelika Beener

Angelika Beener represents the twenty-first-century generation of jazz and music writers. Characteristic of the online new media paradigm, Ms. Beener arrived on the jazz media radar through a series of thoughtful posts via her *Alternate Takes* online journal. She quickly parlayed those writings into print and online media opportunities at *DownBeat* magazine, *A Blog Supreme* (National Public Radio's informative former jazz-oriented blog), and other venues. Her latest vehicle is the online journal *Kultured Child*. She and her son Riley live in Brooklyn.

I think I was always writing. When I attended public school in the Bronx I won writing competitions as a little kid. I always loved to write, short stories and essays, things like that. When I started working for Blue Note Records in marketing and publicity in 2005, it was mostly about marketing, but writing press releases and marketing copy for albums sparked the creative side of my writing again. Then, when I started working at WBGO in 2007, I would write for their *Up Beat* magazine, and that's when I started doing more interviews and writing more editorial pieces. When I left WBGO, I knew I wanted to write full-time.

That compulsion was about a combination of things. I think working for the record label was a bit of a conflict in a way. My great-uncle was Thelonious Monk, so after hearing the stories from family about how Blue Note kind of screwed him over in those early years, my working for Blue Note was interesting. Before that I'd worked at American Society of Composers, Authors, and Publishers (ASCAP), and my Aunt Nellie Monk would tell me all these stories about how ASCAP wouldn't sign black composers. ASCAP actually confirmed that when I got the job, in a sort of full disclosure meeting.

At ASCAP, they called me and another intern into an office; we thought we were in trouble for something! An associate sat us down and she said,

"We have a dark history that you have to know about if you're going to work here." It was pretty straightforward, and I thought that was kind of great, actually, for them to put it all out on the table that way.

A similar conflict arose when I started at Blue Note; not that my family hasn't continued to work with Blue Note in a certain capacity, but you just kind of know vaguely that some stuff went down that wasn't cool. I think, in general, my constant advocating for artists was a conflict for them. They said, "We're trying to sell records." But I worked there, so I had an obligation.

It was just business practices that weren't cool: signing an artist reluctantly that you don't want to sign, selling them a pipe dream, making them think they will record more albums with the label when the label actually has no intention of doing that. They're toying with people's lives. The percussionist Ignacio Berroa was one example. I was working in the international department when Bruce Lundvall signed Ignacio, and my boss at the time gave me these paper-thin envelopes to insert Berroa's CDs for mailing—no padding, no nothing. So I said to her, "Why would we put a CD in a paper envelope when it's going to be broken by the time it gets to Germany or wherever?" She picked up that CD and said, "Do you really think anybody cares about this project?"

Maybe I was naïve going in. It's funny that, when I told my mentor at ASCAP, "I really think I want to pursue a career in the music business," he replied, "You love music too much to pursue the music business." I was nineteen when he said it, and I never forgot that, but I didn't know what that really meant until later.

At Blue Note it was almost like *jazz* was a dirty word; my focus was too much on jazz. At WBGO it was like a weight had been lifted off me, because they're all about jazz and I was encouraged to advocate for the artist. That's where I was able to write what I preferred to write and put whomever on the cover I wanted to and just be freer and write more. When I left WBGO, that's when I said, "I really want to write full time. I don't want to do marketing, I don't want to sell the station, I don't want to round up members at pledge drives, and all that kind of stuff. I want to write, and I want to write about music, with a social-political slant."

I think my first taste of wanting to do that specifically was when I pitched an idea to General Manager Cephus Bowles and my higher-ups at WBGO around Black History Month. I asked if we could, for the month of February, pick a different, politically aware jazz album and just talk about that album, how the music and the history are so entwined. And they said, "Um, I don't know about that because we don't want to turn off our members, we don't want to offend anyone, and we don't want it to be too racially charged." I thought, "Hmm . . . and this station is in *Newark*?"

So I pitched the idea to the news department. I thought, "I'll just go around this mountain." And they loved it! David Crews, who is the host of *Newark Today* at WBGO, produced it; I conceptualized it and hosted it. We did a four-part series that included Randy Weston, and we won an award. The series was called "We Insist: Jazz Speaks Out." I interviewed the writer Robin D. G. Kelley about Max Roach's album *We Insist*. The second part was Terence Blanchard on the Miles Davis *Jack Johnson* record; the third was on Randy Weston and his African-centric musical pursuits; and the fourth was on the perspectives of a younger-generation musician, saxophonist Marcus Strickland. It won an award from the New York Association of Black Journalists.

I conceptualized the series, I picked the four artists, I picked the four albums, and David Crews and I worked on it together. I got an award for "hosting," but it was my project—lesson learned there. But I think that was when everything came together. I was still trying to figure out where I wanted to go under this huge umbrella of music: what exactly is my lane?

I think that my experiences with racism, sexism, and even generation-ism (if that's a word) sort of burned me out from wanting to work for an-other company. And I told myself that I was going to do this writing on my own; that way, I wouldn't have to censor, I could say what I wanted to say, I could interview who I wanted to interview, I could do what I wanted to do. So I started a blog, but I treated it as if I was reporting to a nine-to-five job. I dedicated anywhere from eight to twelve hours a day to writing. I knew what the angle was, I knew I wanted to write about music and social issues, I knew the platform; I was very focused and strategic.

The first couple of pieces I wrote weren't interviews; they were just ran-dom thoughts that people enjoyed. Then I interviewed Ambrose Akinmusire about his Blue Note record, where he played a song for [the police violence victim] Oscar Grant III, and I interviewed Nicholas Payton, Orrin Evans . . . people who had something to say that would lend to the theme of what I was writing about. I started *Alternate Takes* in April 2011, and it seemed to really fill a void; it was so well received, and people paid attention.

Then I was approached by the online publication *Nextbop*—they're young, and they love the music. They asked me if I would post my *Alternate Takes* pieces with them, or rather if I would allow them to repost my blog posts, and I said "sure," because it's sort of branching out to their audience—they're a little more established, they'd been around a little longer, and they were young and interested, so I thought that would be cool. And then *DownBeat* approached me to write a book review on Gil Scott-Heron's memoirs. I think that was my first published hard copy piece, outside of my work for wbgo, with my own byline. From there came npr's *A Blog Supreme*; I did a few stories for them. One I really enjoyed was writing about the drummer Marcus Gilmore and his relationship with his grandfather Roy Haynes.

Nate Chinen, who was then writing on jazz for the *New York Times* and later shifted to editorial director at wbgo and became a regular contributor to npr Music and its *Jazz Night in America* program, tweeted some variation on "Where are the women writing about jazz?" Some people responded to Nate by tweeting different names, and a woman by the name of Kyla Marshall asked, "What about Angelika Beener and *Alternate Takes*?" Nate did an end-of-year roundup where he invited four different folks to talk about what they were into that year, what were their highlights, and he invited me to contribute. I think that was the first thing, and then from there *DownBeat*, npr, and Jazz at Lincoln Center approached me.

I just find it so interesting that the value of black women is so marginalized when it comes to this music, and yet the most important people in my life—when it comes to understanding this music, having a love for it, being exposed to it—were black women! My mom, for sure; my dad was the jazz trumpet player Oliver Beener. He and my mother were separated by the time I was really small, so although we share dna and some of my love for this music probably is an innate thing, when it comes to who was playing records and who was telling me about the music, it was my mother. She had an amazing record collection, and from growing up with Nellie and Thelonious Monk, she had so much knowledge and so many experiences—and she passed all that down to me. I did have Nellie until 2002, when she passed, and I sure wish I had her now.

I wasn't really aware of the small number of black music writers. Robin Kelley hipped me to Farah Griffin. Later, when I interviewed Geri Allen for her Christmas album she likewise asked, "Do you know Farah Jasmine Griffin?" I said no, I don't, and I subsequently met Farah once or twice. Then I got invited by Professor Guthrie Ramsey to lecture at the University of Pennsylvania when I wrote the liner notes for Robert Glasper's *Black Radio* album. Professor Ramsey and Solomisha Tillet cotaught a class. I came and spoke to their class, and that's when I met Solomisha. I remembered that I had seen her on the Melissa Harris Perry show a couple of times, but I didn't really know she was at Penn. I started finding inspiration from other women of color and finding that a lot of other black women were reading my blog about jazz; they would leave comments on the blog. What I try to do is write from a perspective where you don't have to know a whole lot about jazz to enjoy the pieces.

I absolutely do think that a lot of jazz writing is preaching to the choir. My son Riley told me about an invisible string. He said, "You and I have an invisible string." I said, "What's that?" He said, "Even if we're not in the same room or together there's a string from my heart to your heart." I love that, and I think that there's something where that string is not connecting in jazz journalism overall. I think there's a disconnect between the jazz writers and who they're trying to reach. In other genres it's very apparent what the writer is going for and whom they're hoping will listen, and I don't find that to be the case in jazz journalism. I don't know if it's ego, jealousy, racism, sexism—I don't know what it is.

Even in their so-called dissecting of the music from a theory perspective, jazz writers don't even know how to do that right. And I don't think anybody cares about "a clave at this part of the song"; I mean, who cares anyway? I know what a major ninth sounds like, but most people don't, and it doesn't matter to their readers. I think it's that string that Riley was talking about: they're not writing from the heart to the heart—and this music is all about heart. I think one part is writers trying to impress their peers, and the other part is laziness. These jazz writers are writing in a very cookie-cutter, traditional mold, and I think it's comfortable for them, but it's not effective; I find their writing disrespectful.

I haven't talked to many black writers about this. But I have talked to a lot of musicians, and I've had musicians say to me, "I want *you* to write about whatever project I'm working on because you *get* it, or you can express verbally what I'm trying to do; I'm just trying to do my music, I'm not a writer, so I need someone who can sort of translate what I'm trying to do in a way that is not what these other folks are doing. They don't get it, they're missing the point, all that kind of stuff." So musicians are very frustrated with jazz journalism, and I don't think it's necessarily about "so-and-so gave me a bad review"; I think the musicians themselves are frustrated and feel misunderstood at times.

I wrote about Ambrose Akinmusire's composition dedicated to the transit police shooting victim Oscar Grant. I'm a black woman raising a black, male child in America, so I think—just by default—I'm going to understand that. I have brothers who I worry about. And I think that's sort of the elephant in the room when it comes to this music: Why would a predominantly

African American art form be examined through a predominantly white lens? How does that make sense? How's that effective? I think that's kind of the bottom line.

I don't allow people to say, "Oh, well, they want to talk to you because you're the niece of so-and-so, or because you're cute, or because you're . . . whatever." I don't allow those excuses, because that's what they are, excuses, and I was very careful when I started out.

People on the inside know about my relationship to Monk, and I did that on purpose because it was important to me that people see that this is my voice, this is me standing on my own two feet with my own thoughts. I'm relating to people who look like me who created this music; that just makes sense.

The opportunities for African American music writers are not there. When I started doing this, I felt like an anomaly. It still happens to me every day. I'll hop in a cab and I'll say, "Oh, can you put the radio on 88.3 (WBGO)," and cab drivers are reluctant because they think it's gonna be something that they don't want to hear. Then they hear that it's jazz, and they hear Rhonda Hamilton's voice, and they hear this whole public radio vibe, and they're like, "You listen to this, you like this?" And I say, "Yeah," and they say, "Oh, I thought you would want to hear KISS 97." I think people don't expect the interest in jazz from me. I didn't meet a lot of people who were of similar interests until I started the blog, and then I said, "Oh, there are some folks out there"—not a lot of us, or, like you say, "ain't but a few of us"—but we're out there.

I have a few observations about how certain musicians are elevated above other deserving musicians in the media. One is that rocking the boat or being too vocal about things that make people uncomfortable will never help your career, but I think that's across the board and that includes this music. You don't see that Amiri Baraka kind of fearlessness as much. But I think that having too much to say that's uncomfortable doesn't help, and I also see how toeing a certain line when it comes to the music itself plays a role as well. But then there are so many unsung musicians, and you say, "What happened? Why . . . ?" and those remain mysteries to me.

At WBGO I experienced a lot of that sort of old school versus new school generational stuff. I remember when I put Lionel Loueke on the cover of *Up Beat*, and everybody was pissed off at me. "Who is that, nobody knows who he is?" I said, "If no one knows who he is, then as a leader in jazz radio aren't we supposed to be ahead of the curve, aren't we supposed to know what's hip?" But there was a whole lot of generational stuff.

Ted Gioia's piece on *Black Radio 2* was just so hateful and so vile, but I was reacting to the ignorance that keeps people thinking that jazz and the people involved in it are stuck up and pretentious, that this is not the people's music, that you have to have something other than what you already have to enjoy the music. I said, "You know, it's idiots like you that are perpetuating the stereotype, as opposed to someone like Robert Glasper who is trying to bridge the gap." Why is this record such a betrayal? Why do you feel so betrayed because somebody did an R&B album? Robert never said *Black Radio 2* was a jazz album.

Then, when I started reading Art Taylor's book *Notes and Tones*, and I read what Carmen McRae said when she was asked, "Are you a jazz singer?," she said, "I'm a singer." Once I started seeing what was happening with Glasper, and just the public media lashing out against what he was doing, I realized from reading *Notes and Tones* that this is nothing new. The people that writers are holding up as the Holy Grail of jazz—have you ever read what they had to say about pushing forward? They were on the same path. I've read what Charlie Parker said: basically, "screw it, do your thing, your voice."

I feel like this sort of judgmental media attitude and this reluctance for things to progress and keep evolving is old and it's really tired at this point. A lot of the younger jazz musicians don't come from jazz per se; they come from the church. So should the church, the gospel community, say, "Oh, you abandoned us to play jazz?" Where does that begin to make sense?

There have certainly been some rewards writing about jazz. Interviewing Geri Allen was quite rewarding: she was so smart and gracious, she had a lot of really great opinions, and they could be intimidating, but her manner was disarming because it was just real. I think I learned a lot from people like Geri, people who are not so much about shooting from the hip.

When I spoke to Professors Ramsey and Tillet's class at Penn, I talked to them about the *Black Radio* liner notes—which, I would have to say, was another rewarding experience for me. Robert Glasper has said, "I can't do an interview without them talking about those notes. That's the first thing they want to ask me about is the liner notes." It allowed me to describe with words what was happening on the album, because that record was a game changer.

It was a mixed class at Penn, but a lot of young African American women were asking me about how I prepare and those kinds of things. I really don't know, I don't have an answer for that kind of question, there is no approach that I can articulate. Right now I'm just writing from the heart, and it may not always make sense or be particularly scholarly, but what I do have is the tremendous gift of growing up the way I grew up, around the people I grew up around, having the experiences that I've had. That's truly invaluable, and I think that's a unique perspective to write from—being a jazz kid, and a black woman who's still very much involved. When I write about music, it's not just my job—it's my life. I think that's what I bring.

I would tell students who are interested in writing about music that you have to love it because it doesn't pay well. But if you wake up in the morning and you're writing in your head, this is what you're supposed to be doing. If concepts and ideas and themes are brewing in your head; if you're waking up like, "Oh, that's a great idea," I think you're meant to do this. I know it's not the most lucrative business, but in jazz, when Louis Armstrong said, "People have died for this music," that's true. This is still very much a labor of love. There's still a great sacrifice that comes with playing jazz, writing about it, and so I think that you're chosen—because I don't think you choose it.

Anthony Dean-Harris

Anthony Dean-Harris's initial contributions on the music arrived via web-based media. He has established his viewpoints via the very active jazz-based *Nextbop* blog. Dean-Harris has also freelanced with the Art of Cool festival in Durham, NC. Like Bridget Arnwine and Angelika Beener, Anthony Dean-Harris is representative of jazz writers and contributors to the *Ain't But a Few of Us* dialogues who've arrived on the jazz writing scene in the twenty-first century.

I've always loved jazz, grew up around it, and I've known I wanted to be a writer since high school. I wanted to go to Trinity University in my hometown of San Antonio, TX, for college because of its jazz station, KRTU. However, I didn't get a scholarship to Trinity; I got one to Morehouse College. So I ended up going there, and my family soon followed me to support me and to experience Atlanta, the American black mecca, for themselves.

When I graduated from Morehouse in 2008, the recession had just hit and my family decided that since I was done with school, we'd all head back from Atlanta to San Antonio. Once home, I volunteered for a city council race and met the late Kathy Clay-Little, a columnist for the *San Antonio Express-News* and the publisher of the community newspaper *African-American Expressions*.

We were talking at the campaign office one day about her plans to put on a small jazz festival on Father's Day and about which artists she should try to book. When she learned of my love of jazz, she asked if I'd like to cover concerts for her paper. I gladly said yes, and one of my first assignments was to attend the annual KRTU spring concert with her, including the opening VIP reception. It was there, before the evening's performer Ramsey Lewis played, that I met many of the folks who ran KRTU, particularly Aaron Prado, who went on to get a doctorate in music from UT Austin and still plays throughout San Antonio, and Matt Fleeger, who went on to run KMHD Portland. Those folks said I should have a show at KRTU, especially since one of their hosts would be leaving soon. Over the next few months, I ended up taking over a show called "The Line-Up" and subsequently posting the playlists to my personal blog.

It was around this time that I ran across sites like *Nextbop* and NPR's jazz blog, *A Blog Supreme*. The former editor of *ABS*, Patrick Jarenwattananon, posed a question to a few folks on the jazz scene: which ten albums of jazz music from the last twenty years would they share with a newcomer to the genre. *Nextbop*'s founders, Sebastien Helary and Justin Wee, submitted a great list. That's when I became impressed with the *Nextbop* site and its potential. I also put together a list and, unsolicited, sent it to Jarenwattananon, who graciously posted it to the site. Conversely, that's how Sebastien ran across my blog, those playlists from my radio show, and my writing from college, back when I was on the student newspaper staff as the opinions editor.

Seb contacted me about writing for *Nextbop*. As time went by and we developed our rapport, and as he learned that my college journalism background had been perfect training for managing and growing the site, I eventually ended up as *Nextbop*'s editor, and my role writing about jazz music there was pretty much cemented. I can see God's hand in a lot of this, leading me from one role to another, which made me incredibly happy, though still pretty poor. But I get plenty of new music and see a lot of shows in support of this community, so it all works out.

I can't say I was initially really aware of the dearth of black writers on jazz music, but I can't say I was too surprised either. The genre has been growing and changing a lot over the century of its existence, but as it goes with pretty much anything, it's all too common for blacks to be shut out or limited from telling our own stories, framing our own narratives, or just giving our own perspective built from our backgrounds. Fortunately, it's now a bit easier for us to alter this, as the internet has democratized our access and ability to do so—but our work continues. I don't like to think there are so many countervailing forces out there oppressing black journalists in this regard; there might be some who are indeed doing so maliciously, but I don't want to cut wide swaths like that. I do think that it could mostly be the public's lack of familiarity with black voices on the music.

Much of my writing focuses on contextualization—we are what we see and experience every day. We cannot know what we have not been exposed to, and we're experts on those things that surround us. There may very well be newspaper, magazine, and web editors who simply don't encounter writers of color who are aware of black jazz (and R&B/hip-hop/soul) music and have no recognition of that ignorance. In an increasingly niche-based music landscape, where people tend to read only the coverage they want to read, it may be getting easier to get our voices out there, but it's difficult in entirely different ways to get our work read by disparate eyes.

I definitely think the relatively low number of black writers focused on music contributes to how the music is covered, largely because of contextualization. Take, for example, a Kanye West appearance on *Late Night with Jimmy Fallon*. The following day there were many posts on music blogs linking to the performance—the standard web aggregate coverage of the day without much substance added to it other than, "Watch this video!" It may have been noted that Charlie Wilson was on the set singing on the same show, but a black voice well-versed in Wilson's body of work could have noted how many of Wilson's trademark "shabba-dabba-tweet-tweet-tweets" (and one or two "ooh-weeEEs") he ad-libbed. Of course, white writers who aren't exposed to the back catalog of the Gap Band, where that phrasing came from, may not have even noticed that this merited mention, because they don't know what they don't know. This is how that added black perspective affects the discourse. For black music to be, as it has always been, a crucial part of the culture, informed people must also be part of the discourse about the music's impact.

Since I've been writing about jazz, especially as I've run my own web publication, I've come to realize how the attention given to some artists over others can occur naturally, not necessarily governed by who's doing the writing. I've realized some of the seemingly ephemeral elements, like when appealing album art determines whether or not I'll devote attention to an album, or when an email hits my inbox at just the right time for me to care, or how having a good press release and readily accessible songs to stream makes spreading the word a more appealing prospect to me.

Witnessing the inner workings of music journalism like this has helped me understand how the whole industry functions like this to some degree.

This doesn't even take into consideration how it all works in other genres or at larger publications that may pay more attention to optimization than to merely discussing quality music and informing the masses about talent that deserves to be publicized. The inner workings of the music industry machine, and its sense of how we as people pay attention to things, does explain so much about why music journalism is what it is. Adding diversity into this consideration adjusts things a bit, because it's easy to assume people of different cultural backgrounds would have their respective attention drawn to different works. It's the nature of the beast.

When it comes to how black publications cover serious music, I don't like to think of it much differently from how mainstream white publications cover mainstream pop music in comparison to other more sophisticated music. I've been so immersed in the world of jazz since listening to it as a child, but especially since I've been involved in *Nextbop* and radio hosting at KRTU, that I have overlooked how some jazz music is indeed somewhat inaccessible to the average person. I listen to music for its musicality, dynamism, quick decisions made on the spot, communalism among musicians, and other aspects that don't bore me like simplicity does; and that is distinctly different from how many others listen to music, searching for that quick, visceral connection.

Every culture has this sort of dichotomy in its art, and I'm loath to say black art may have this problem more than other cultures. Black culture's influence on the culture at large does shine a different sort of spotlight on the matter that is at times distressing.

I'd agree that how music is covered has much to do with who is covering it, but in much the same way that writing about essentially anything is affected in that way. I'm a writer who loves not only music but also television and film. As a result I'm one of those writers who uses the word *showrunner* a lot and who cares about Aaron Sorkin's oeuvre and things of that sort. When people ask me why I care about these sorts of things and how I remember details about television like I do, I tell them it's all part of being a storyteller.

In one's family or circle of friends, there's always some person at dinner—a guy from back at college, that crazy uncle, a fellow bar patron—who tells stories in a way that makes people listen. Perhaps that person describes things ornately, maybe they use wild hand gestures, perhaps they have a great speaking voice. Whatever the particulars, the storyteller has attributes that make his or her stories appealing. A person tells a story in his or her own way that people remember, that causes them to come back for more.

Whether a storyteller has a tendency to talk about interoffice relationships, uses a camera to illustrate the story, or uses the internet to talk about what happened at a jazz club in New York—these are all different ways of telling a story. I always try to understand that each medium lends itself to different strategies and means of performing the same function: there are people out there who want to hear what the storyteller has to say.

A very rewarding experience I had since taking over the editorship of the *Nextbop* site was putting together our first unofficial party during the South by Southwest festival in Austin, Texas, one year. It was the first performance event I had ever organized, and we had Texas-based bands and bands of world renown agree to play a little burger place built from a transformed auto garage. It was humbling that such talented people as Australia's Hiatus Kaiyote and Canada's BADBADNOTGOOD would agree to play at the request of a clear novice like myself, and even more gratifying that it was attended as well as it was.

After the dust cleared and everyone there had a great time, I could step back and marvel at what had just happened. Writing is such a solitary act, and writers, like many artists, are often very critical of themselves to the point of self-loathing. So to throw an event, where people actually show up and enjoy what you produced and are happy to say so, was extremely gratifying.

Lately, I've really enjoyed the editing work for *Nextbop*. I've enjoyed editing essays like Jon Wertheim's critique of the trumpeter Nicholas Payton's contentious nature or Ben Gray's series looking at original versions of jazz songs and comparing them to cover versions, or posting anything Angelika Beener writes. I'm immensely proud of *Nextbop* and what it has grown to be over these last few years.

Since I've mostly been working as my own editor and manager since taking up music journalism, the most difficult part of all this has been learning the ropes on my own: arranging interviews, obtaining press credentials for events, maintaining contact with publicists, and things of that sort; I'm constantly developing my process. Another part of that, though, has been figuring out how to make all of this a viable business. The *Nextbop* site has largely been a labor of love and has yet to make money. I've been working on selling ad space to change that, but this, too, is one of those new roles in the business for me. Running this whole business and learning the trade has been a lot, and though it's been slow going, it's sometimes a comfort to realize how much I've picked up along the way.

8

anthology

Classics

Jazz and the White Critic
LEROI JONES (*DownBeat*, 1963)

Most jazz critics have been white Americans, but most important jazz musicians have not been.

This might seem a simple enough reality, or at least a reality that can be readily explained in terms of the social and cultural history of U.S. society. And it is obvious why there are only two or three fingers worth of Negro critics or writers on jazz if one understands, say, that until relatively recently those Negroes who *could* become critics, who would largely have had to come from the black middle class, have simply not been interested in the music. Or at least, jazz, for the black middle class, has only comparatively recently lost some of its stigma, though by no means is it yet as popular among them as any vapid musical product that comes sanctioned by the white majority's taste.

Jazz was collected among the numerous skeletons the middle-class black man kept locked in the closet of his psyche—along with watermelons and gin—and whose rattling caused him no end of misery and self-hatred. As one Howard University philosophy professor said to me when I was an undergraduate, "It's fantastic how much bad taste the blues contain."

But it is just this "bad taste" that this man spoke of that has been the one factor that has kept the best of Negro music from slipping sterilely into the echo chambers of middle-brow U.S. culture. And to a great extent such "bad taste" was kept extant in the music—blues or jazz—because the Negroes who were responsible for the best of the music were always aware of their identities as black Americans and really did not, themselves, desire to become vague, featureless Americans, as is usually the aim of the Negro middle class. (This is certainly not to say that there have not been very important Negro musicians from the middle class. Since Fletcher Henderson, their number has increased enormously in jazz.)

Negroes played jazz, as they had sung blues—or even earlier, as they had shouted and hollered in those anonymous fields—because it was one of the few areas of human expression available to them.

Negroes who felt the blues impulse, as a specific means of expression, went naturally into the music itself since there existed fewer social or extra-expressive considerations that could disqualify any prospective Negro jazz musician then, say, existed for a Negro who thought he might like to become a writer (or even an elevator operator). And any Negro who had ambitions in literature, in the earlier part of the century, was likely to have developed so powerful an allegiance to the sacraments of middle-class U.S. culture that he would be horrified with the very idea of writing about jazz.

There were few "jazz critics" in the United States at all, until the middle '30s, and then they were influenced to a large extent by what writer Richard B. Hadlock has called "the carefully documented gee-whiz attitude" of the first serious European jazz critics. They were also, as a matter of course, influenced more deeply by the social and cultural mores of their own society. And it is only natural that their criticism, whatever its intention, should be a product of that society or should reflect, at least, some of the attitudes and thinking of that society, even if such attitudes were not directly related to the subject they were writing about, i.e. Negro music.

Jazz, as a Negro music, existed, until the time of the big bands, on the same socio-cultural level as the subculture from which it issued. The music, and its sources, were *secret* so far as the rest of the country was concerned, in much the same sense that the actual life of the black man in America was secret to the white American.

The first white critics were men who sought, consciously or not, to understand this secret, just as the first serious white jazz musicians sought not only to understand the phenomenon of Negro music but also to appropriate it as a means of expression that they themselves might utilize. The success of this "appropriation" signaled the existence of an American music, where before there was a Negro music.

But the white jazz musician had an advantage the white critic seldom had. The dedicated white musician's commitment to jazz, as an *ultimate concern*, proposed that the subcultural attitudes that produced the music as a profound expression of human feelings could be *learned* and need not be passed on as a secret blood rite. Negro music is essentially the expression of an attitude, or a collection of attitudes, about the world and only secondarily an attitude about the way music is made. The dedicated white jazz musician came to understand this attitude as a way of making music, and the intensity of his understanding produced the great white jazz musicians and is producing them now.

Usually the critic's commitment was first to his *appreciation* of the music rather than to his understanding of the attitude that produced the music.

This difference meant that the potential critic of jazz had only to appreciate the music—or what he thought was the music—and that he did not need to understand, or even be concerned with, the attitudes that produced it, except perhaps as a purely sociological consideration. This last idea is certainly what produced the white patronization that is an early form of Crow Jim. The stereotype "all you folks got rhythm" is no less disparaging simply because it is proposed as a positive trait.

But this Crow Jim attitude has not been as menacing or as evident a flaw in critical writing about jazz as has another manifestation of the white critic's failure to concentrate on the blues and jazz attitude rather than his own conditioned appreciation of music. The major flaw in this approach to Negro music is that it strips the music too ingenuously of its social and cultural intent. It seeks to define jazz as an art (or a folk art) that has come out of no intelligent body of sociocultural philosophy.

We take for granted the social and cultural milieu and philosophy that produced Mozart; the socio-cultural thinking of 18th-century Europe comes to us as a historical legacy that is a continuous and organic part of the 20th-century West. The socio-cultural thinking of the Negro in the United States (as a continuous historical phenomenon) is no less specific and no less important for any intelligent critical speculation about the music that came out of it. And, again, this is not a plea for narrow sociological analysis of jazz but only that this music cannot be completely understood (in critical terms) without some attention to the attitudes that produced it. It is the philosophy of Negro music that is most important, and this philosophy is only partially the result of the sociological disposition of Negroes in America. There is, of course, much more to it than that.

Strict musicological analysis of jazz, which has come into favor recently, is also as limited as a means of jazz criticism as a strict sociological approach. The notator of any jazz solo, or blues and blues lyric, has no chance of capturing what, in effect, are the most important elements of the music. A printed musical example of a Louis Armstrong solo or a Thelonious Monk solo tells almost nothing, except the futility of formal musicology when dealing with jazz. Not only are the various jazz effects almost impossible to notate, but each note also *means something* quite in addition to musical notation.

The notes of a jazz solo exist in a notation strictly for musical reasons. The notes of a jazz solo, as they are coming into existence, exist as they do for reasons that are only concomitantly musical.

Coltrane's cries are not "musical," in the academic sense—but they *are* music and quite moving music. Ornette Coleman's screams and rants are only "musical" once one understands the music his emotional attitude seeks to create. This attitude is real and perhaps the most singularly important aspect of his music. Mississippi Joe Williams, Snooks Eaglin, Lightnin' Hopkins have emotional attitudes different from Ornette Coleman's, but all these attitudes are continuous parts of the historical and cultural biography of the Negro as it has existed and developed since there was a Negro in the United States and a music which could be associated with him that did not exist anywhere else in the world.

The notes *mean something*; the something is—regardless of its stylistic considerations—part of the black psyche, as it dictates the various forms of Negro culture.

Another hopeless flaw in a great deal of the writing about jazz that has been done over the years is that in most cases the writers, the jazz critics, have been anything but intellectuals (in the complete sense of that word).

Most jazz critics began as hobbyists or boyishly brash members of the U.S. petit bourgeoisie, whose only claim to any understanding about the music was that they knew it was *different*; or else they had once been brave enough to make a trip into a Negro slum to hear their favorite instrumentalist defame

Western musical tradition. Most jazz critics were (and are) not only white middle-class Americans but middle-brows as well.

The irony here is that because the majority of jazz critics are white middle-brows, most jazz criticism tends to enforce white middle-brow standards of excellence as some criterion for performance of a music that in its most profound manifestations is completely antithetical to such standards—in fact, quite often is in direct reaction against them. (As an analogy suppose the great majority of the critics of Western formal music were poor, uneducated Negroes?)

A man can speak of the "heresy of bebop," for instance, only if he is unaware of the psychological catalysts that made that music the exact registration of the social and cultural thinking of a whole generation of black Americans. The blues and jazz esthetic, to be fully understood, must be seen in as nearly its complete human context as possible. People made bebop; the question the critic must ask first is *why?* But it is just this "why" of Negro music that has been consistently ignored or misunderstood; and it is a question that cannot be adequately answered without first understanding the necessity of asking it.

Contemporary jazz during the last few years has begun to take on again some of the anarchy and excitement of the bebop years. The cool and hard-bop-funk movements since the '40s seem pitifully tame, even decadent, when compared with the music men like Ornette Coleman, Sonny Rollins, John Coltrane, Cecil Taylor, and some others have been making recently. Of the bop pioneers, only Monk has managed to maintain without question the vicious creativity with which he entered the jazz scene in the '40s.

The music has changed again for many of the same basic reasons it changed 20 years ago. Bop was, at a certain level of consideration, a reaction by young musicians against the sterility and formality of swing as it moved to become a formal part of the mid-stream U.S. culture.

The "new thing," as recent jazz has been called, is to a large degree a reaction to the hard-bop-funk-groove-soul camp, which itself seemed to come into being in protest against the squelching of most blues elements in cool and "progressive" jazz. Funk, groove, soul has become as formal and cliched as cool or swing, and opportunities for imaginative expression within that form have dwindled almost to nothing.

The attitudes and emotional philosophy contained in "the new music" must be isolated and understood by critics before any consideration of the *worth* of the music can be legitimately broached. Later on, of course, it becomes relatively easy to characterize the emotional penchants that informed earlier esthetic statements.

After the fact is a much simpler way to work and think. For example, a writer who wrote liner notes for a recent John Coltrane record mentioned how difficult it had been for him to appreciate Coltrane earlier, just as it had been difficult for him to appreciate Charlie Parker when Bird first appeared. To quote: "I wish I were one of those sages who can say, 'Man, I dug Bird the first time I heard him.' I didn't; the first time I heard Charlie Parker, I thought he was ridiculous. . . ."

That's a noble confession and all. But it was the writer's responsibility to understand the music and in no way involved Charlie Parker or what he was trying to do. When that writer first heard Parker, he did not understand *why* Bird should play the way he did, nor could the "why" have been very important to him. But now, of course, it becomes almost a form of reverse snobbery to say that one did not think Parker's music was worth much at first hearing, etc. The point is that if the music is worth something now, it must have been worth something then. Critics are supposed to be people in a position to tell what is of value and what is not, and, hopefully, at the time it first appears. If they are so almost consistently mistaken, what is their value?

Jazz criticism, certainly as it has existed in the United States, has served in a great many instances merely to obfuscate what has actually been happening with the music itself.

The woeful harangues that raged during the '40s between two schools of critics as to which was the "real jazz," the new or the traditional, was one very ugly example. A critic who praises Bunk Johnson at Dizzy Gillespie's expense is not critic at all; but then, neither is a man who turns it around and knocks Bunk to swell Dizzy. If such critics would (or could) reorganize their thinking so that they began their concern for these musicians and their music by trying to understand why each played the way he did, and in terms of the constantly evolving and redefined philosophy that has informed the most profound examples of Negro music, then exclusivist thinking would be impossible.

It has never ceased to be amazing and infuriating to recall that in the '40s a European critic, Hughes Panassie, could be arrogant and unthinking enough to inform serious U.S. jazz musicians that what they were feeling (something that exists before, and without, the music) was false.

What had happened was that even though the white middle-brow critic had known about Negro music for only about three decades, he was already trying to formalize and finally institutionalize it. It is a hideous idea. The music was already in danger of being forced into that pile of admirable objects and data the West knows as Culture.

Recently, the same attitudes have become more apparent in the face of a fresh redefinition of the form and content of Negro music. Such phrases as "antijazz" have been used to describe musicians who many consider are making the most exciting music produced in this country. But what does antijazz mean? What is the definition of jazz? And who was authorized to make one or the other?

Reading a great deal of old jazz criticism is usually like boning up on the social and cultural malaise that characterizes and delineates the bourgeois philistine in the United States. Even re-reading someone as intelligent as Roger Pryor Dodge in a 1955 issue of *The Record Changer* can make a person either angry or nearly hysterical.

An example: ". . . let us say flatly that there is no future in preparation for jazz through bop. . . ."; or "the boppists, cools, and progressives are surely stimulating a dissolution within the vagaries of a nonjazz world. The revivalists, on the other hand, have made a start in the right direction."

It sounds almost like political theory.

Here is Don C. Haynes in the April 22, 1946, issue of *Down Beat* reviewing Charlie Parker's *Billie's Bounce* and *Now's the Time:* "These two sides are in bad taste and ill-advised fanaticism. . . ." And "this is the sort of stuff that has thrown innumerable impressionable young musicians out of stride, that has harmed many of them irreparably. This can be as harmful to jazz as Sammy Kaye." It makes one blush.

There were few—very few—jazz writers of the '40s who understood the importance of bebop or who supported it in their writings.

Of course, there have been some fine writers on jazz, even as there are today. Most of them have been historians. But the majority of popular jazz criticism has been on about the same level as the quoted examples.

Nostalgia, lack of understanding, or failure to see the validity of redefined emotional attitudes that reflect the changing psyche of the Negro—in opposition to what the critic may *think* the Negro ought to feel—all these failures have been built many times into a kind of critical stance or esthetic, an esthetic whose standards and measure are connected irrevocably to the continuous gloss most white Americans have always made over Negro life in the United States.

Failure to understand, for instance, that Paul Desmond and John Coltrane represent not only two divergent ways of thinking about music but, more importantly, two different ways of viewing the world is at the seat of most of the established misconceptions that are daily palmed off as intelligent commentary on jazz or as jazz criticism. The catalysts and necessities of Coltrane's music must be understood as they exist even before they are expressed as music. The music is the result of the attitude, the stance—just as Negroes made what everyone recognizes as the blues and other people did not—because of the Negroes' peculiar way of looking at the world.

Once this attitude is delineated as a continuous, though constantly evolving, social philosophy, directly attributable to the way the Negro responds to the psychological landscape that is his Western environment, criticism of Negro music will move closer to developing as consistent and valid an esthetic as criticism has in other fields of Western art.

There have been so far only two U.S. playwrights, Eugene O'Neill and Tennessee Williams, who are as profound or as important to the history of ideas as Louis Armstrong, Bessie Smith, Duke Ellington, Charlie Parker, or Ornette Coleman, yet there is a more valid and consistent body of drama criticism written in the United States than there is a body of criticism about Negro music.

This is simply because there is an intelligent tradition and body of drama criticism, though it has largely come from Europe, that any drama critic can draw on. In jazz criticism, no reliance on European tradition or theory will help at all. Negro music, like the Negro himself, is strictly a phenomenon of this country, and we have got to set up standards of judgment and esthetic excellence that depend on our native knowledge and understanding of the underlying philosophies and local cultural references that produced blues and jazz in order to produce valid critical writing or commentary about it.

It might be that there is still time to start.

note

Originally published in *DownBeat*, August 15, 1963.

Requiem for a Heavyweight

MARC CRAWFORD (*Transition*, 1966)

The unpressed suit looked Brooklyn pawnshop, and the frayed collar and cuffs of that once white shirt, and the shine-hungry shoes, had enjoyed better seasons. Thinning hair was turning gray with his years, and the tell-tale pink of his dark lips said something about a lot of great gigs on a lot of great bandstands, all of them in the gone times. Now he stood there in the mortuary, waiting for the rosary service to begin, stood there stooped over the coffin, his tears staining dark the white silk framing the corpse.

"In the bars along Kingston Street," the black man told the black corpse, "they said I shouldn't bought you all them drinks. You know I had to, don't you? They didn't understand, Bud. They didn't know who Bud Powell really was. Now we don't have to worry about that no more. You safe now, Bud. Baby you safe."

HAIL MARY FULL OF GRACE THE LORD IS WITH THEE

"I further certify," wrote Dr. H. Eisenberg on Bud's death certificate at Kings County Hospital, "that death was not caused directly or indirectly by accident, homicide, suicide, acute or chronic poisoning, or any suspicious or unusual manner and that it was due to natural causes."

BLESSED ART THOU AMONG WOMEN

PARIS—sometimes in the season of the sun he'd sit alone by the hour, there in the churchyard beneath the towering spires of St. Germaine de Pres. Not a muscle would he move nor sound make and his fingers laced in the fashion of men grown old. It was then he seemed most at peace with himself. He'd watch the passerby at that corner which is the crossroad of the Western world, and then it would hit him like a whiplash, first the terrible pain in those big bulging eyes, then the fear, the awful fright in those eyes before they went out like a light, and then the kind hand of priest Abbe DuPree on his shoulder massaging away the menace of all those years.

And then in the early hours of morning, after his gig at the Bluenote Club was finished, Bud walking back to the Right Bank so that he could buy red wine with the money that was his taxi fare. Walking, as he had many times before, down the Champs Elysee, and marveling:

"That's the Eiffel Tower ain't it?"

"Yes, Bud. That's the Eiffel Tower."

"You see that in pictures sometimes."

"Yes, Bud. You see that in pictures sometimes."

Now at the Cafe L'Eschaude, his money gone, his red wine finished, calling out to the waiter who loved him like a brother, worshipped him like a god, and made it his business always to take the cigarette butt from between Bud's fingers, just before the tender place that held it began to burn.

"Robert, give me a red wine please. I'll pay you tomorrow, hear? Honest, I'll pay you tomorrow."

"Oui, M. Powell," he'd say, knowing tomorrow for Bud would be like all his yesterdays.

And the young French pianist, sitting across the room, fixing Bud in his stare, eyes glazed, getting out of his chair, charging across the room, confronting Bud and shouting at the top of his lungs: "I do not care, Bud Powell. To me you are still the greatest in the world." And Bud, looking at him for a long minute, his glass suspended in the air, a feeble awareness of forgotten things fighting for a place in his eyes, then wordlessly putting the wine down untouched, pushing the table away, and shuffling out into the streets—into that no man's time, which neither fully belongs to the night nor the morning, and home to Buttercup, and their son Johnny.

Porkchops and soul food at Gaby and Haynes restaurant, and more wine, despite doctor's orders against fried foods and drink. Bad liver, you know? And Buttercup taking him to the mountains and sea places of Europe, trying to help Bud find the peace that eluded him from his beginning. Bud turning from a magnificent sunset, and in a rare moment of lucidness, softly asking: "Buttercup, why are you always trying to save me when you know how bad I want to die?"

And Buttercup with no other reason than: "I love you, Bud."

AND BLESSED IS THE FRUIT OF THY WOMB, JESUS.

NEW YORK—Bud coming home after five years having to face the lie he'd told himself so many times. He had not gone home when his mother died. Why should he? "She isn't dead," he told himself. Then home and the terrible truth of it. Bud tired, sick of music and the stale taste of music in his life. Blaming music for the death of kid brother Ritchie, who died with Clifford Brown in a 1956 auto crash, when both of them stood on the threshold of greatness. Bud sick of music because it imprisoned him from his earliest recollection.

"Heh, heh, heh," William Powell laughed remembering. "I tell you when Bud was seven the musicians would come and actually steal him, take him from place to place playing music. Nobody had ever seen a jazz musician that young or heard one play like Bud. He was a li'l old chubby fellow, and by the time he was ten he could play everything he'd heard by Fats Waller and Art Tatum. Music just come natural in this family. My daddy was a guitar player. He went to Cuba during the Spanish American War and when he came back, he was one of the greatest Flamenco guitarists in the country. I played piano. I taught Bud on that old upright Play-o-Tone there, I couldn't go on the road and have a family too. So I stayed home. But Bud was a genius. When he was just a little fellow, they'd come and steal him and make him play sometimes to 2 or 3 o'clock in the morning. When he was just a little fellow."

Bud in the last years of his life, his place in the history of jazz secure, begging his father to teach him a trade besides music just as he'd done for Ritchie. Bud trapped because he didn't know how to do a single thing other than play piano.

Bud in his early years, in his most sensitive years, living in the most primitive of societies for all its riches and chrome plating. Bud, a part in the creation of an art form which shall echo down the corridors of human existence so long as men inhabit this earth, being told that his skin colour made him less than a man, being forced to look in the distorted mirror of American life for definition. Bud, rejecting the reflection, fighting it, hurling himself against it again and again until he was bent, busted and broken by it, driven beyond the limits of his sanity by it on at least four different occasions.

That is why Bud did not even care, even as he lay dying, that the Congress of his country was still debating whether or not Bud Powell should have a legal right to live in American suburbs with American people—the white-skinned kind. Long ago he had given up on his country. Though he carried a strange love for it. In his own way, it was a little like loving a woman whom he knew would never love him.

So Bud dying slowly and knowing it and not caring because nearly all of his old friends were gone—Bird, Prez, Fat Girl, Lady, Waddel, Oscar— nearly all of them. "He wanted to be where they were," Buttercup said. And that is what she thinks he had in mind when he uttered his last words: "I'll be alright." He was going to be with them.

In some far off times, men not yet born will say, "Once there lived a great jazz pianist named Bud Powell." But perhaps only those of us whose lives he touched will ever have an inkling of the high price Bud Powell was forced to pay for his greatness,

HOLY MARY, MOTHER OF GOD, PRAY FOR US SINNERS NOW AND AT THE HOUR OF OUR DEATH. AMEN.

note
Originally published in *Transition*, no. 27, 1966.

Inside the Horace Silver Quintet

BARBARA GARDNER (*DownBeat*, 1963)

Nice guys just don't make it in this business. Everybody knows that. The sweet cat finishes last. The world is just waiting to shoot him through the grease. Sure, everybody knows that. Everybody, that is, except a 34-year-old pianist named Horace Ward Martin Tavares Silver, who seems to be holding onto the merry-go-round's gold ring.

It isn't as if he hasn't been told. And certainly experience should have taught him something.

When he was a youngster of 12, back home in Norwalk, Conn., he fell in love with an older woman of 14 who liked to play the piano. So, being a nice guy, he began taking lessons to create a mutual interest.

Not only did he never get the girl but when he got to high school he also discovered that piano lessons weren't offered as part of the curriculum, so he had to take tenor saxophone lessons in order to get in the school band. He didn't protest but studied the saxophone diligently in music class and used his gym periods and lunch hours to sneak into the auditorium to practice piano.

That bit of co-operation netted him less than two years in the tenor chair, and when the baritone saxophonist graduated during Silver's sophomore year, the band director prevailed on the band's nicest guy to play baritone—by taking away his tenor altogether.

While in high school, Silver also was playing piano on weekends with a trio at the Sundown Club in Hartford, Conn. Following his graduation from high school, he continued playing dates near Hartford. In 1951 Stan Getz was guest star at a session at which Silver led the rhythm section, and the tenorist hired all three of them.

"I certainly am glad that happened," Silver said. "I might have still had cold feet and still been in Hartford. Competition was so rough in New York, and I was scared."

After a year on the road with Getz, a very nervous, insecure Silver settled in New York City to wait out his Local 802 card. During this period, Silver, still awestruck by the proximity of his jazz idols, went from club to club on weekends listening to the giants and playing their 78-rpm records at home on his windup phonograph.

After a few months, the big break came. Tenor saxophonist Bo McCann, playing in a small club, heard the unknown pianist and recommended him to Art Blakey, who hired him as soon as he heard him play. Silver not only got a chance to play with the drummer's band, but Blakey allowed him to write for the group too.

"This was really the first chance I had to write for a bigger group," Silver remembered. "I was scared to death and came in with my two little arrangements. I had no idea Art would use them."

But Blakey used his material, and soon New York jazzmen were aware of the 23-year-old musician, who looked like he should be in school but who was playing funky piano and writing soulful tunes.

A Cannonball Adderley remark succinctly categorizes the New York opinion of Silver at that time:

"How can a cat look one way and then play so funky?"

Silver was not robust looking—5 feet 10 inches tall, he didn't weigh more than 150 pounds. His small-boned features and slight stoop added to his appearance of fragility. But his handshake was firm, and strength twinkled in his eye. He was a man whose strength ran deep.

The pianist worked with the Blakey organization until mid-1952, at which time he left to work as pianist with several jazz titans, such as Coleman Hawkins, Oscar Pettiford, and Lester Young.

In 1955 the first Horace Silver Quintet was formed. If there still remained any doubts about his motivating power, a session of listening to his hard-driving, breathtaking quintet quickly dispelled them. For the group was merely an extension of Horace Silver—and like the good guy, it was a good group.

Just as the character and personality of an individual is formed through interaction with other people, the mood and tone of the Silver group was formed through interaction of the five individual members.

The major problem in the beginning was stabilizing the group; but the pianist reflected on the situation philosophically:

"Well, it taught me one thing—that nobody is indispensable. It was rough, but I made it. And there was never any hard feelings when the cats split. I just couldn't pay much bread in the beginning."

This attitude contributed even more to the widely spreading opinion that Brother Horace was a "beautiful cat." For almost two years the quintet escaped heavy-weight critical analysis. By 1958, however, his reputation was well established among the musicians and listeners who were becoming enamoured of a new "school of music," soon to be known as Soul music.

Jazz writers began looking through their thesauri for new ways of saying "he's a nice guy and what he's playing is exciting and all, but I'm not sure it is really creative and original."

For a time, there was a furor raging as to what was really "soul" and what was just plain "stole." Groups sprung up under the soul banner, flourished briefly, and faded away. By the end of 1961, it was evident that "soul" as a movement had been corrupted, suffocated, and killed. When the dust had settled, one group stood as sound and firm as the good earth—the one belonging to the nice guy, dubbed the "father-apparent" of the style—the Horace Silver Quintet.

But Silver was being damned with faint praise.

Barry Ulanov categorized him as an "individualist of skill in constructing figures of his own devising as well as those of other musicians; one of the most distinguished of the post-boppers."

In describing the funky style as a regression, Martin Williams, in 1958, credited Silver with directing the movement and went on to say, "Piano styles, including Silver's, soon tended to degenerate into disconnected interpolative four-bar fragments."

"Limited," suggested some writers; "sameness," others maintained.

Nor was criticism his only hindrance: Silver has had his share of frightening physical ailments.

Upon being examined for the Army, he was found to have a curved spine. Until then he had dismissed an occasional troublesome backache as merely a nuisance. Even though he was classified 4F because of the ailment, he attached little significance to it until about 18 months later when pain and loss of nerve control struck with alarming severity. This condition was treated and temporarily brought under control. Subsequently, a sprained wrist and rheumatism almost spelled the loss of the use of his hands.

Throughout his career, rumors of some hovering, disabling ailment have buzzed 'round Silver. He has adopted a tolerant attitude about it, however.

"No, I don't mind talking about it," he said. "Actually, it's a bore that people are interested. And when I had that problem with my hands in 1960, well, it was pretty frightening, even to me. Fortunately I found a doctor who could cool me out, and I'm straight now."

And so rumors of illness notwithstanding, Silver continues to work 46 to 50 weeks a year, making two albums a year, maintaining a group with few changes of personnel, apparently unaware that, according to most good-guy-bad-guy theories, he absolutely should not be making it. In this period of a shrinking jazz market, the Horace Silver Quintet is working steadily in this country and preparing for a European tour in September.

Since its inception in 1955, the Silver quintet has never substantially altered its style or concept. While it is accurate to state that the Silver approach is blues-based and is made up of surging, driving undertones best described as "funky," it would be erroneous to suggest that Silver is a limited musician.

As a composer, he has demonstrated that he can be melodic, tender, polyrhythmic—and, even, exotic. As a pianist, he has a proclivity toward the blues, and this underscores all his playing. But he is, at the same time, a two-fisted pianist and attacks his instrument with a vigor tempered with thorough musical knowledge.

There is no mistaking the ownership of the group. It is a Horace Silver unit from first to last note. It reflects the leader's driving, smoking intensity, but each member contributes to that unit-feel.

This is neither an incidental nor accidental factor. The many empty hours on the road are spent in band rehearsals and practice. It is here that a group democracy operates.

"Usually I bring in the new material—something I've written," Silver said. "Or sometimes one of the guys will bring in something, and I tell them primarily what I want. I always give them the freedom to elaborate on the basic idea. We try all the ideas and suggestions and finally come up with something that we all dig—you know, something where everybody can say something musically and still keep the same feeling."

Seldom is a tune put into the book as it is first written—or for that matter, as it was originally conceived.

"Writing is strange," Silver suggested. "When you're really trying to sit down and do something, nothing happens most of the time, but you can be just fooling around and hit a chord, and it'll start something that can turn out to be pretty nice."

Rehearsals are not haphazard, run-through occurrences. The quintet members are expected to attend regularly, to arrive promptly, and to settle down to work immediately. Rehearsals are as exacting as a classroom theory hour. Each member, including Silver, is like a student-teacher; they all try experiments with and instruct each other. But it does become the task of the leader to tie the lesson together for the benefit of the group.

In performance, the group is a supreme example of disciplined abandonment in music. While each soloist is permitted blowing room, he is constantly aware of the full, fast-paced arrangement moving with him, and usually he works effectively within it. As with any creative art, however, this technique is not 100 percent guaranteed.

"Some nights we just don't have it," Silver admitted. "Looks like no matter what we do, it just won't come out the way we know it should. Then on other nights, seems like everything we try comes out solid. Maybe the people—the audience—has something to do with it. You know, I like soulful joints; the people seem to let go and enjoy the music. And you can kind of get a groove going."

If the group members learn the material well enough and if luck is with them, they are able to reproduce this groove on a record.

Silver plans far ahead for his recording sessions. He cuts two albums of original material a year. He said he feels that two is enough:

"If I'm lucky, we're busy working and traveling, so I really don't have time to write any more than that. And when you stop and think that what you put on records is *it*, you want to be sure it's the best you can do."

Whether this best occurs as a result of deliberate planning by Silver or by instinctive and unconscious kinship of spirit among the members is debatable. It is true that the bulk of the raw material that makes up the group's repertory consists of original Silver tunes; but the leader does not believe he deserves all the credit.

"No, this is the best band I've ever had," he said of his present group. "The cats all have a similar feeling toward music, and they're versatile. That's really the secret. You have to have versatile cats to play the kind of music we play."

The average age of the musicians is 30, and they have a combined group tenure of 27 years. Each man leads his own private life, but there is an overall guiding principle.

"Everybody in my band is a clean liver," Silver explained. "And this is necessary to make it in this band."

The only other necessary qualification, Silver said, is the ability to feel and contribute to the togetherness that is representative of the unit.

In a recent interview the members say there is a mutual educational benefit derived by working together. Though each is reluctant to talk about his own particular contribution, he is eager to relate his musical growth since working with Silver.

Tenor saxophonist Junior Cook, 28, said he has become proficient with several reed instruments, including the flute and clarinet.

One of the least-appreciated trumpet players in jazz is Blue Mitchell, 33, who has been the brass section of the Silver unit for more than four years, having replaced Donald Byrd, who had taken over from Art Farmer.

Mitchell writes as well as plays. An indication of the compatibility of the Silver group is the philosophical attitude Mitchell takes concerning his tunes: "I don't write, as such, for our group. Horace writes almost everything for the group; but I have written some things for my own date on another label. Working with Horace has been very valuable to me in both my writing and playing."

Drummer Roy Brooks, 24, came to the group when Louis Hayes left to join Cannonball Adderley in 1959.

Silver at first was reluctant to hire Brooks, who had just come to New York from Detroit, but Hayes recommended him so strongly that Silver relented—without even hearing him play. Brooks quickly dispelled any qualms by pushing the unit with fiery playing. With the exception of about seven months in 1962, when he was ill (John Harris Jr. replaced him), Brooks has been with the band 3½ years.

A small, reserved man, Brooks does not boast but is justifiably aware of his contribution to the group.

"I guess I help to contribute to the togetherness we have," he said. "And we do have a togetherness that few groups have. We have been playing together for a long time now."

Like the other members of the group, Brooks composes. His tenure with the Silver unit, he said, has broadened his musical scope.

"I feel that musically I have grown a lot since I came with the group," the drummer stated. "I am learning more each day about putting *my* ideas across musically to the public. That's not always easy for a drummer—especially if you have to worry about helping to keep everything else moving along."

One musical characteristic each member talked about was the growing ability each has to play meaningful passages within an arrangement and its confines.

"Junior and Blue work so tight," Silver commented, "they sometimes sound like one instrument, and that's the close feeling you need . . . and Gene [Taylor, bassist, who was not present at the interview] is right in the music with us with that beat. Of course, Roy is kicking all of us right in the behind and we got to move to stay in front of him, so we just keep together and go."

There is nothing obvious or contrived about the group's togetherness. The members do not work at maintaining it; there is simply an esprit de corps that welds individual to group. Each musician is considered an excellent technician and a driving expressionist in his own right—yet the group has no real star. In a sense, not even Silver can be so considered: the sound and feeling that have come to be identified with him are the result of writing, instrumentation, and performance.

His impact on the musical taste of the world jazz population is felt most keenly in Japan, where he has toured twice, building a bridge of communication directly to the people, despite the differences in languages.

"I would like to spend more time playing in places throughout the world where we have never been before," Silver said. "I am not sure that I deserve the worldwide public acceptance which I am enjoying currently. I do know that all of us in the group try hard. It is co-operation that means the difference, and I am very lucky to have these cats with me."

As to why his group has survived and prospered after the passing of the funk era, it might be because Silver recognizes allegiance to no school or movement. His music survives because he survives. And his music is his personal expression stated as honestly and artfully as he is able to state it.

To deny the best efforts of Horace Silver is, in essence, to deny the expression of musical truth.

So, you see, nice guys do not necessarily finish last. Often, when they are talented nice guys, they simply last and last and last.

note

Originally published in *DownBeat*, June 20, 1963.

Trane + 7 = a Wild Night at the Gate

A. B. SPELLMAN (*DownBeat*, 1965)

John Coltrane

Village Gate, New York City

Personnel: Coltrane, soprano and tenor saxophones; Archie Shepp, Pharoah Sanders, tenor saxophones; Carlos Ward, alto saxophone; McCoy Tyner, piano; Jimmy Garrison, bass; Rashid Ali, Elvin Jones, drums.

The band John Coltrane showed at the Gate Nov. 10 might be called "J. C. & After." Coltrane, who put the kinetic field back into the tenor saxophone after it had been lost when the Illinois Jacquets disappeared from Respectability (a small, affluent suburb of New York), assembled an aggregation of reed men who were learning their fingering when he was cutting *Blue Trane*; their harmony when he was cutting *Milestones*; their selves when he was cutting *Coltrane's Music*.

Trane, with his *Ascension* record date and with the augmented quartet he uses in the clubs, is not only creating a band with more power than Con Ed but is also introducing some of the best of the New Jazz musicians to the World of the Living Wage and, thereby, performing a double service. Shepp and Sanders, by virtue of the discomforting weight of their music, get precious few gigs, and Coltrane, by presenting their music in its proper musicological context, is performing a great service to their generation. Both these men have highly distinctive styles. They really sound nothing like Coltrane, but it is clear that they have benefited from Coltrane's line, harmonics, and dissection of a song's melody.

On this night, the two sets consisted of long interpretations of one tune each: *Afro Blue* and *Out of This World*. The difference between the two sets was that Jones didn't show for the first. And the first was, to my ear, far better.

Coltrane played the theme on soprano, and Shepp, in very good voice, took it from there. Shepp's style is reiterative—a kind of supercharged theme and variations. He stated a motif, broke it down to its elements, and returned to it every few bars. After carrying one idea through innumerable permutations he would start another. Shepp is a bluesy player who roars his masculinity. He plays at both ends of the horn, and he may spot his intensities at any part of the register. He makes heavy inflections on the notes he wants to emphasize. His opening solo, about 10 minutes long, was a strong one, as it had to be, for this is deep water.

This was the first time I'd heard Panamanian altoist Ward. He seemed to be neither a screamer nor a singer, but a talker. He seemed to be engaged in some kind of a dialog with himself, playing a rapid series of terse, self-contained, but related phrases. I liked Ward; his ear is different. I couldn't sort out his influences in this cauldron, however, and I look forward to hearing him in a smaller group.

Sanders followed Ward, and he is the damnest tenor player in the English language. He went on for minute after minute in a register that I didn't know the tenor had (actually, I did—I've heard Sanders before). Those special effects that most tenor men use only in moments of high orgiastic excitement are the basic premises of his presentation. His use of overtones, including a cultivated squeak that parallels his line, is constantly startling. He plays way above the upper register; long slurred lines and squeaky monosyllabic staccatos, and then closes with some kind of Bushman's nursery rhyme. Pharoah is ready, and you'll all be hearing from him soon. Or should.

Trane soloed on soprano which, as usual, seemed a few months behind his tenor. Here, in this reed chorus, it had the effect of stretching out the sonic boom.

The orchestral composition of the group had been expanding all along. No one was ever idle—a man would finish his solo and pick up a rattle, tambourine, or some other rhythm instrument and start shaking away. The reeds also were free to provide filler or comment for the soloist, and the effect was of an active, highly charged environment. With the constantly shifting rhythms of Rashid on drums this was free large-group improvisation at its best. Rashid's playing is an ever flowing patter that defies time signature. He once said he was after a drone effect that flowed with the horns. At the Gate, he showed how well he achieves this effect.

Garrison's bass was strong and witty, and Tyner's chords are necessarily more dissonant than before

The difference in the second set was, to me, the unnecessary addition of Jones. It was interesting to hear this band with Rashid, who, unlike Jones, disperses the rhythm centers. It has always been an aweful, pleasurable experience to have Elvin tear up my nervous system for me. I have also heard two drummers used with laudable results, e.g., the intimate communication of Billy Higgins and Ed Blackwell in Ornette Coleman's monumental *Free Jazz* LP and some work Rashid did with another drummer in a Sun Ra concert.

I think I see what Coltrane wants—an ever evolving groundswell of energy that will make the musical environment so dangerous that he and the others will have to improvise new weapons constantly to beat back all the Brontosaurs. However, if Jones is to be one of the two drummers, then Lincoln Center at least is needed to contain and separate all that sound. One simply couldn't hear anything but drums on *Out of This World*. I had no idea what the soloists were saying, and I doubt that the players could hear each other. Garrison (who played a truly virtuoso solo to open the second set) was completely swallowed up. At one point, I saw Coltrane break out a bagpipe (another demon in the forest) and blow into it, but damned if I heard a note of what he played.

Note: Coltrane played bass clarinet in some ensemble sections. I was told that the instrument had belonged to Eric Dolphy and had been given to Coltrane by Dolphy's mother.

note

Originally published in *DownBeat*, December 30, 1965.

The Testimony: An Interview with Alto Saxophonist Bunky Green

BILL QUINN (*DownBeat*, 1966)

"Keep up the intensity, keep up the intensity!" urged the diminutive alto saxophonist. He was talking to his new group in the midst of a recording session, but he could just as well have been talking aloud to himself. For most of his life, 30-year-old Bunky Green has been keeping up the intensity of the one thing with which he is most familiar—making music.

Watching the dapper altoist at work brought to mind a statement he had made, though at the time he said it, he had shied a little at the possibly corny overtones: "I think many times while I'm playing that it might be my last moment on earth, and I want to feel that my passing through has meant something to somebody. At one point or another, I feel like I'm in an attitude of prayer."

Music, Green said, was a way to affirm his existence, adding, "No musician plays for himself alone. You play, not just for self-satisfaction, but so that people will recognize your ability. We all exist through others; without people to recognize your ability—the crowd that says, 'You're making it'— you wouldn't have a reason to do any of it."

"I've heard many musicians say that they wipe out the people when they play, but basically they're playing for someone else all the time. Subconsciously they build a shield around themselves to keep from being hurt. They say, 'I don't care whether you dig my playing or not—this is where it is!' And maybe it is where it is, but all of that talking is just like that toothpaste ad: an invisible shield."

Green is as avid a communicant verbally as he is musically. While discussing his career, he injected notes of comedy or drama as freely as he does on his horn.

When Green was a junior high school student in Milwaukee, Wis., he had a friend who played alto saxophone. After petitioning his father, Green as well became the owner of an alto—nickel plated. He took lessons at school, along with "a thousand other guys in the same room," and began listening to the latest waxed word from the jazz heroes of the day.

He soon found that the attention of musicians and listeners alike was focused on tenor saxophone players, not altoists. Dexter Gordon, Wardell Gray, and Lester Young were the vanguard for those who influenced Green's thinking in those days. He decided that tenor was to be his instrument, and he traded in his practically new alto for the larger horn.

Then, as fate would have it, he began hearing talk of a sensational altoist named Charlie Parker. Green listened but initially felt that he was hearing "too much being played at once"—he didn't like it. The local hipsters' acclaim for Parker's innovations persisted, however, stimulating Green's curiosity, and the more he listened the more he liked. Shortly, Green, now a high school freshman, was back at the music store, trading his tenor in on another alto.

During his high school years, Green played local gigs with schoolmates. After graduation, he decided to go to New York City, where he had been told that musicians abounded and that there were many even younger than he who would fall in clubs with their instruments and blow the walls down.

He found that he had been put on about the youngsters, but what he'd heard about the grown men was right.

"I heard Lou Donaldson for the first time, and that down-home feeling of his was a gas," Green said. "I saw and heard much more—but Lou was enough to send me back home to tighten up my thing."

After playing and practicing around Milwaukee a while longer, the young altoist returned, in 1958, to the big city. This time things began to happen for him. Another Milwaukeean, pianist Billy Wallace, told Donaldson about his gifted homeboy, and, sound unheard, Donaldson referred Green to a bass-player friend who was looking hard for a reed man to augment his group.

"I got this phone call from Charlie Mingus," Green said. "He told me to be at his house within the hour because he was taking the group to West Virginia that night."

If it hadn't been for his Milwaukee friend, Green reflected, he would have stayed home that night. But he went—and he worked out. From there it was back to New York, then Philadelphia, and out to the West Coast. The year was 1958, and California bristled with various musical influences.

"A funny thing happened to me out there," Green recalled. "Some guy came up to me after one of the sets and asked me if I'd ever thought of 'playing free.' Of course, I didn't understand what he meant. He explained that he was talking about dropping any reliance on chord structures, wiping out the bar lines, letting the emphasis be on structure. Well, it left a big question mark in my mind at the time, and about a year later I found out who the cat was and what he was talking about: everyone was saying Ornette Coleman, Ornette Coleman."

Green felt his store of musical knowledge growing as he continued to play with Mingus. One night at the hungry i in San Francisco, a young music student, carrying an alto, asked to sit in with the group.

"Mingus liked this cat, and I thought he sounded great," Green said. "Little did I know that this cat, John Handy, was soon to replace me with Mingus."

Because of personal commitments in Milwaukee, Green had to return home. He had been with Mingus for eight highly instructive months, met many musicians, heard and played much music, and acquired healthy new perspectives regarding the way jazz was being played around the country.

"I thought when I left Mingus," Green said, "that I'd clear up my business in a short time and return to the group, but, as it turned out, I was never able to get back."

Instead, Green set about reconsolidating his forces in a rather uncharacteristic way for a former Mingus sideman: "I picked up a job in Milwaukee fronting a group in a strip show—and I doubled as emcee. We'd play tunes like *Fever, Tequila,* and *Night Train*—the kind of thing the girls could bump and grind to."

But the gig paid money, some of which Green was able to save with the intention of going back on the jazz circuit. Meanwhile, Chicago jazz entrepreneur Joe Segal had heard about the altoist, and he sent word that he'd like Green to come to town for one of his sessions. Green arrived at the old Gate of Horn and found himself in the company of tenor saxophonist Johnny Griffin and a host of other well-known jazz lights, such as the late tenorist Nicky Hill.

Inspired anew, Green returned to Milwaukee, determined to resettle in Chicago at his earliest opportunity. When it came, he found himself welcomed on the scene and was soon playing around the Midwest with trumpeter Paul Serrano. It was with Serrano that he cut his first record, *Blues Holiday*, which was supervised by Cannonball Adderley for the Riverside label.

Then, Green recalled, he had a rather sobering experience in the record business.

"I cut some 'free' things with Vee Jay records—rather like what some people call avant-garde today. The company shelved them at the time. There were some great musicians on those sides, too, like bassist Donald Garrett and pianist Willie Pickens. One of the albums, *My Babe*, with [pianist] Wynton Kelly, [trumpeter] Donald Byrd, [bassist] Larry Ridley, [tenorist] Jimmy Heath, and [drummer] Jimmy Cobb, was just released a few months ago on the Exodus label. I wonder what the influence on my career would have been if those things had been heard then, five years ago."

Reflecting further on this point, Green says that the time has passed when he can concentrate solely on experimentation, even though he would like to.

"I can't afford to satisfy my ego to that extent anymore; I have a wife and kids dependent on me now," he said. "If I played exactly what I feel all the time, I know I wouldn't get my message across to more than a handful of people around the country—and that's not enough to make it."

Though conscious of his responsibilities, Green still has his inner drive. In the next breath he was talking about the requisites of greatness:

"I don't just mean playing jazz, you know. I mean Einstein, Napoleon.... They all had to be selfish to be great—it's an occupational hazard. I even yelled at my wife this morning when she interrupted my practicing.... I was apologizing later, of course."

A clause in Green's 1960 contract with Vee Jay required that he play weekends at a Chicago jazz club called the Bird House, in which a Vee Jay official held a financial interest. Things went well there for a time, but the ill-fated aviary had to close its doors, as did many other clubs at this point, for lack of audiences, leaving Green nearly broke.

Faced with having to look outside his customary arena for employment, he was on the verge of hiring out to the first bidder. Then he heard that the big-band business was the most profitable thing going on in Chicago especially the band headed by drummer Red Saunders, which was the house band at the Regal Theater on the south side. Hastily Green sharpened his reading, packed his alto, and headed for Saunders' house, auditioned successfully, and remained with Saunders for nearly 18 months.

But the cost of living was rising and salaries paid sidemen were not keeping pace; so Green was in search of more lucrative employment once again. He found it—and a new love—with the Latin band of Manny Garcia.

"Outside of pure jazz," Green said, "I love Latin best because the rhythm is so strong I can play anything from bop to 'free'—anything I want. When I first joined Manny, I asked him what kind of things he wanted me to play, and he said, 'Play anything, man—we've got a beat for it.' On top of this, I began learning Spanish."

In the fall of 1963, Green enrolled in Wright Junior College, majoring in sociology. Jumping into things there musically, he became a fast friend of the school's band director, John DeRoule. One spring afternoon, DeRoule told him the band was going to Notre Dame University the next day to play, and he wanted the altoist to come along. That night Green packed his toothbrush, expecting nothing extraordinary.

Only after finding a large audience in front of him, he said, did he realize that something special was in the offing. As it turned out, Green was judged the best saxophonist at the 1964 Collegiate Jazz Festival. Seated in the audience were representatives of the U.S. State Department. They teamed Green with a group from the West Virginia State College for a summer tour of North Africa.

Later, Green said, he had to endure good-natured ribbing from the Chicago jazz fraternity for "taking advantage of those kids."

But Green, no older than some of "those kids," was as eligible to participate as any of them—and hadn't even known it was a contest beforehand.

While in North Africa, sightseer Green wandered into the Algerian Casbah. Along one of the narrow streets he saw a group of musicians seated in a circle, playing strange instruments, one of them a curious bagpipe.

"The instrument had only one pipe," Green recalled, "and the guy kept squeezing the bag under his armpit, filling it with air. It was the first time I had heard this music played in person, and I was intrigued by the way he played so many figures around a single tonal center.

"As soon as I left there I damned near got lost, wandering down Casbah streets I know I shouldn't have been on, trying in vain to find one of those bagpipes."

Green says that his experience with the tonally centered music he heard in Algeria led to the introduction he played on *Green Dolphin Street* on a subsequent album, *Testifying Time*.

While Green was in Algiers, Eric Dolphy died in Europe. But the altoist, who had known and played with Dolphy on many occasions since his days with Mingus, did not hear of the tragedy until he reached Paris, on his way back to the United States.

"Buttercup [Bud Powell's wife] told me about Eric," he said. "I had met her some years back when I was playing with Mingus in Philadelphia on a bill with Bud, Lester Young, Wade Legge, and a bunch of other great cats. It was kind of a sad scene because we talked about Eric's death and Bud and all the changes he was going through. Then I saw Bud, and heard him play, and I knew he wasn't himself anymore."

When he returned to Chicago, Green searched for new outlets for his music. Though he had been recorded with the Serrano group, he had never headed his own date, and bassist Connie Milano felt that this oversight should be corrected immediately. Milano pounded the pavement for Green's cause until he reached A&R man Esmond Edwards. Thanks to Milano and Edwards, Green said, he began a series of dates with Cadet records that has so far produced three albums.

Then Green joined the Latin group with which he is presently associated, that of singer-percussionist Vitin Santiago.

"I'm really knocked out playing with these guys," he said. "I speak some Spanish and the other guys speak some English, but I wouldn't have been able to convey the finer points of the musical ideas without Vitin—he's my translator. Besides, this cat has a photographic memory—if you can call it that—for music. All I've got to do is ask him how such and such a tune goes, and he can riff a little bit of it; he remembers them all!

"Another thing, for a jazz musician like me, there is a tendency to get involved with waltzes and all kinds of different harmonies. In spite of everything, I was still getting wrapped up in complex theme structures, and I found that with a Latin group this doesn't always have the impact that it has in straight jazz. Now, with Vitin, all the heads are simplified; the focus is on the solos, and I can really put Bunky in it."

Green has just recorded his first album with the Latin group for Cadet, and, in addition, the soon-to-be-released album features the altoist on the new electronic saxophone. One of the first to record on the instrument, Green said that, though the device is, in his estimation, not quite perfected, it has merit for some players.

"We had trouble recording it, and the alto needs more work done on it," he said. "But it's going to get better as it goes along. It's a boon to a person who doesn't have a strong, dynamic tone.

"The biggest feature is the double octave, but when I blew forcefully into the horn, the sub-base line was lost. I would recommend using a different amplifier for the alto than the one used for the tenor, since I've heard that the tenor works better than the alto."

Until recently, in addition to other commitments, Green worked the Monday night sessions at Mother Blues in Chicago's Old Town, and many of the musicians who came were avant-gardists. Though grounded in the canons of harmonic structure, Green is receptive to influences taken from the divergent concepts of big-band men, boppers, and "free" and Latin players; he found the new musicians a welcome addition to proceedings. At the Mother Blues sessions, however, many patrons would leave in a huff, having heard sounds past their understanding. This sometimes caused more than a little confusion in the club.

"What Chicago, and a lot of other cities, need," Green said, "are a few more places to play and a few tolerant listeners. Sometimes, at Blues I would just have to step out front and say 'come on and blow, man,' because I remember how I felt when I was trying to get together with the bop thing.

"Some of the new musicians in Chicago have a good thing going. Richard Abrams, in particular, has a deep insight and a well-thought-out process.

Other cats are not so well schooled, but they seem to have a natural talent for the new thing.

"People are going to have to try and understand the new music, as they try to understand the times. The new music is so connected to the times; there is an urgency in cats, because we all realize that we don't have 10 more years to study. We all have to say what we have to say, *now.*"

Green says that one of the first signs of old age, particularly for a musician, is the rejection of new things.

"When you start canceling things out simply because you don't understand them, or they're something other than what everybody else is playing," he said, "then chalk up a mark against yourself because you've begun to get slow—you might have let something of value slip by you."

Green referred to Sonny Stitt as a model of the ecumenical spirit: "I look at cats like Stitt, blending the Bird things with things that came before and after. Yet, when you hear Stitt—even though he is a blend of many styles—he doesn't sound like Bird or anybody else but Stitt! I try to do as Sonny does, because I love the good—what I think is good—in all of it, and I try to syphon off the best."

Things appear to be brighter than ever for Green, and it shows in everything he says and does. He talks with little regret about past adversities and much enthusiasm about the future:

"I'm going to Europe again this coming spring. If I have some bookings arranged before I leave, fine; but I'm mainly going to hear what's being played over there . . . mainly to relax and absorb the atmosphere. I'd like to get down to Algiers again and deepen my insight on that scene; I'm really interested in hearing more of that tonally centered music.

"When I return to this country, I intend to start a program of study, spend time working the jazz circuit across the country, and—most of all—to keep an open mind, to keep on digging. The thing with me is to get knowledge together, because with knowledge comes freedom."

That's Bunky Green: sincere and intense, so much so that he may sound square to the jaded. But the odd thing is that he means it.

note

Originally published in *DownBeat*, December 15, 1966.

On Jazz and Race

Putting the White Man in Charge

STANLEY CROUCH (*JazzTimes*, 2003)

Because Negroes invented jazz, and because the very best players have so often been Negroes, the art has always been a junction for color trouble in the world of evaluation and promotion. By the end of the '20s, Duke Ellington was trying to get his buddies to call their art "Negro music," possibly because Paul Whiteman had been dubbed "King of Jazz." Variations on this phenomenon have risen and fallen throughout the history of the art.

Since the '60s, however, certain Negroes who cannot play will claim to be of aesthetic significance on the basis of sociology and some irrelevant ancestral connection to Africa—which provided only part of the mix that became jazz. That had an ironic impact because we are now back to the Paul Whiteman phenomenon, as if all of those white people who had to put up with black nonsense now have their chance to express their rage. This time white musicians who can play are too frequently elevated far beyond their abilities in order to allow white writers to make themselves feel more comfortable about being in the role of evaluating an art from which they feel substantially alienated. Now, having long been devoted to creating an establishment based on "rebellion," or what Rimbaud called the "love of sacrilege," they have achieved a moment long desired: Now certain kinds of white men can focus their rebellion on the Negro. Oh, happy day.

In his essential *Blues Up and Down* (St. Martin's), Tom Piazza pulled the covers off of these men when he wrote, "Many jazz reviewers—especially among the generation that grew up in the 1960s and '70s—suffer from intense inferiority feelings in front of the musicians they write about. This results in a vacillation between an exaggerated heroworship of musicians and an exaggerated sense of betrayal when the musicians don't meet their needs." Piazza surely knew what he was talking about, especially since he was a white man who had been among these jazz writers when nobody dark was around, which allowed him to understand them and their various insecurities and their various resentments close up.

In Francis Davis' *Like Young: Jazz, Pop, Youth, and Middle Age* (DaCapo), one can get a good deal of insight into Piazza's thesis. It is a classic of its kind. Davis unintentionally makes it clear that he is intimidated by Negroes and also quite jealous of them. The intimidation arrives because of the troubles and the fun he imagines Negroes having when he is not around. The resentment flares if these Negroes have any power to define themselves and what they are doing or if they have reputations independent of Davis' permission or if they cannot be conventionally condescended to from the abolitionist's perspective that so many jazz writers have in common. Their job, they believe, is to speak up for the exotic Negro or use that Negro as a weapon against their own middle-class backgrounds or make that Negro into a symbol of their desire to do something bold, wild and outside of convention. Even being in the presence of such stuff will do, since Davis points out that rap now allows the young white person to come in contact with the Negro most removed from the white world, which used to be the role of jazz. Is that so? Since the rap Negro is nothing, at his most "street," than a theatrical version of Zip Coon, a character from the minstrel shows, how is he removed from the white world? Every Negro inferior to a middle-brow white man like Davis fits comfortably in the white world, where black refinement is never expected or is dismissed as pompous.

Disturbed by the way things have gone over the last couple of decades, Davis' answer to his Negro problem is to create an alternative order of significance. He sees, as do so many of these men, jazz that is based on swing and blues as the enemy and, therefore, lifts up someone like, say, Dave Douglas as an antidote to too much authority from the dark side of the tracks. Douglas, a graduate of Exeter and a dropout from the New Jersey upper middle class, is the perfect white man to lead the music "forward." Unlike these misled uptown Negroes who spend too much time messing around with stuff like the blues and swinging, Downtown Dave brings truly new stuff into jazz, like Balkan folk material that surely predates the 20th century in which blues and jazz were born.

There is nothing wrong with Douglas, who can play what he can play and who should continue to do whatever he wants to do, but there is something pernicious about Davis and all of those other white guys who want so badly to put white men in charge—American and European—and put Negroes in the background. Douglas, whom I have heard since he worked as a sideman years ago with Vincent Herring, is far from being a bad musician, but he also knows that he should keep as much distance as possible between himself and trumpet players like Wallace Roney, Terence Blanchard and Nicholas Payton, to name but three, any one of whom on any kind of material—chordal, nonchordal, modal, free, whatever—would turn him into a puddle on the bandstand. Unlike the great white players of the past, such as Jack

Teagarden, Bobby Hackett, Benny Goodman, Stan Getz, Lee Konitz—or, now, Joe Lovano—Douglas will never be seen standing up next to black masters of the idiom. The white critical establishment couldn't help him then.

But the deepest part of this is that it, finally, is not so much about color as it is about the destruction of the Negro aesthetic, which is why Negroes like Don Byron and Mark Turner are embraced. They accept an imposed aesthetic of "pushing the envelope" in ways that have nothing to do with blues and swing. Above all, they help these writers to bring things disguised as bulls into the middle-class china shops in which these critics themselves were born.

note

Originally published in *JazzTimes*, April 2003. Used by permission of Madavor Media.

My Bill Evans Problem—Jaded Visions of Jazz and Race
EUGENE HOLLEY JR. (*New Music Box*, 2013)

I never experienced any racial barriers in jazz other than from some members of the audience.—BILL EVANS

In the early '80s, I was working in a Washington, D.C., record store when I heard *Kind of Blue*, Miles Davis's midtempo, modal masterpiece of an album that for me, and many others, was an initiation into the colors, cadences, and complexities of jazz. Transfixed by the many aural shades of the LP's blue moods, I made it a point to get every recording the musicians on the album had ever made. But it was the poetic and profound pianism of Bill Evans that haunted me the most. When I listened to Evans's studio LP *Explorations*—with drummer Paul Motian and bassist Scott LaFaro—my Evans-induced hypnotic trance deepened; and so did my problem.

What was the problem? Bill Evans was white. And I am black.

When I got into jazz, I was in my twenties. As a child growing up in the '60s and '70s, I was a beneficiary of the Civil Rights Movement, and, more importantly, I grew up in a period of American history when, thankfully, black pride was taken for granted. I had black history courses beginning in the first grade and continuing through middle school, and black contributions to world music were a natural extension of that education. I attended Howard University (the so-called Mecca of historically black colleges and universities). Throughout my life, it had been drilled into me that jazz was created by blacks and represented the apex of African-American musical civilization. I learned about the great jazz heroes—from Louis Armstrong and Duke Ellington to Dizzy Gillespie to Charlie Parker—and of America's refusal to give these Olympian musicians their proper due as the revolutionary artists the world knows them to be. I came to know something deeper: in many cases, white jazz musicians achieved more fame and were given more credit for the creation of the music.

There are enough examples of this in jazz history. Paul Whiteman was the King of Jazz. Benny Goodman was the King of Swing. Duke Ellington knocked on Dave Brubeck's hotel door, to show the white pianist that he made the cover of *Time* magazine in 1954 before he did. (Brubeck, for the record, was hurt and embarrassed.) Then there was the 1965 Pulitzer Prize snub of Ellington. In the '70s, President Carter presented jazz on the White House lawn, with Dizzy Gillespie and Stan Getz as featured artists. President Carter asked Getz about how bebop was created, with Gillespie standing right there.

Against that historical backdrop, I also practiced a form of racial profiling of musicians. Though I was wrong about the racial identities of the Righteous Brothers, Average White Band, and Teena Marie, I knew what black musicians "sounded like" via Motown, Stax, and Philadelphia International records. Though no one stated it specifically, there was a "black sound" and a "white sound." To like a "white sound," or worse, a white musician who "sounded black," was cultural treason. Without realizing it at the time, this inhibited me on many levels, especially as a clarinetist and pianist in high school. When I was studying classical music, and I allowed myself to be moved by it, I feared that some of my black peers would see me as an Uncle Tom.

It was Bill Evans's love of, and application of, European classical styles, approaches, and motifs into jazz that was so attractive to my ears, as evidenced by the azure impressionism of "Blue in Green" on *Kind of Blue*, the intoxicating melodicism of "Israel" from *Explorations*, the lyrical logic of "Peace Piece" from *Portraits in Jazz*, and the chamber timbre of "Time Remembered" from the 1966 album *Bill Evans Trio with Symphony Orchestra*.

So it was in that hot-house atmosphere of well-meaning—but ultimately immature and xenophobic attitudes about music and race—that my Bill Evans problem existed. The problem manifested itself in many ways. I would often hide Bill Evans albums when talking about jazz musicians with fellow black jazz fans for fear of being "outed" as a sellout, given a look of disapproval, or asked, "Why are you listening to that white boy?" The fact that Evans was lauded by white critics because he was white and his classical pedigree didn't help.

Slowly but surely, my perceptions about jazz and race began to evolve and change. As my jazz historical studies deepened, I learned that music is a cultural, not a racial phenomenon. Black Americans at the turn of the 20th century created jazz by combining elements of European classical instruments, harmonies, and song forms with African, Afro-Caribbean, and American rhythms and melodic structures. As Ralph Ellison noted, "blood and skin don't think." Or to put it a different way: jazz didn't come into existence because black people were simply black. Its creation was the result of history, geography, social conditions, and, most importantly, the will to create something of artistic human value. To believe anything else plummets us into the foul abyss of pseudo-racist demagoguery that still plagues us on so many levels today.

Specifically, I asked myself, "Why would Miles Davis, a proud, strong black man, hire someone who was white like Evans?" The answer was simple: the artistry of the musician mattered more to him; not his or her color. Davis hired and collaborated with many white musicians throughout his career, from Gerry Mulligan and Lee Konitz in the historic *Birth of the Cool* sessions of the late '40s and his extremely popular mid-1950s recordings arranged by Gil Evans to his later fusion bands which included Keith Jarrett, Joe Zawinul, Chick Corea, and even British guitarist John McLaughlin. So Davis chose Bill Evans because (in his own words, as recounted in Peter Pettinger's biography *Bill Evans: How My Heart Sings*): "He can play his ass off." Davis was more specific in his autobiography (*Miles: The Autobiography*, co-written by Quincy Troupe): "Bill brought a great knowledge of classical music, people like Rachmaninoff and Ravel. He was the one who told me to listen to the Italian pianist Arturo Michelangeli, so I did and fell in love with his playing. Bill had this quiet fire that I loved on piano."

In addition to Davis, other black jazz superstars hired Evans. He recorded on bassist Charles Mingus's *East Coasting*, a superb and elegant recording from the '50s, and on alto saxophonist Oliver Nelson's '60s masterpiece *Blues and the Abstract Truth*, which also featured Eric Dolphy and Freddie Hubbard. Evans was the featured soloist on arranger/composer George Russell's arrangement of "All About Rosie," and on his third stream-meets-bop *Jazz Workshop* album. He also worked with bassist Ortiz Walton, the author of the book *Music: Black, White and Blue*. My further explorations revealed that Evans was not the lily-white suburban racial recluse I stereotyped him to be. He was heavily indebted to Nat "King" Cole and Bud Powell (Evans described Powell as "the most comprehensive talent of any jazz player I have ever heard presented on the jazz scene"). So much for being the "great white devil" or the "white hope" black and white critics made him out to be.

So what does my former Bill Evans problem say about jazz and race today? For one thing, it is firmly and correctly established in music education, and in society in general, that jazz is an African-American art form: blacks have gotten their due as the art form's primary creators. No credible critic, musician, or music curriculum would state otherwise. At the same time, it is equally true that white musicians have made and continue to make great contributions to jazz. While the role Evans and other whites have played should not be exaggerated to move the music's black known and unknown bards to the back of the bus, giving Caucasians appropriate acknowledgment does not threaten the African-American creation of the music.

If anything, jazz at the beginning of the 21st century is appropriately black, brown, and beige; with every global musical/cultural ingredient embellishing, extending, and enriching it. This is a good thing. More importantly, youth around the world—white youth included—want to play it, despite the fact that in the United States you barely see jazz on TV, radio stations that play it are shrinking, and print coverage of it is dwindling.

The declining significance of jazz in the media and marketplace has, in my opinion, increased the unfortunate crabs-in-a-bucket mentality that plagues the jazz infrastructure, which by default can cause the racial aspect to become more prominent. I see this in two distinctly different, but related aspects. The first is the notion of the "Crow-Jimmed" white musician who has been racially discriminated against by blacks, the record industry, and white critics who are guilt-tripped into adopting an "exclusionary" black agenda to support a kind of affirmative action for black musicians. This was the primary gist behind the 2010 publication of trumpeter Randy Sandke's controversial book, *Where the Dark and Light Folks Meet: Race and the Mythology, Politics, and Business of Jazz*. Sandke, a New York–based musician whom I first met when we shared a panel on Louis Armstrong at Hofstra University in 2001, sees today's jazz scene as a retreat into a cult of racial exclusionism that betrays the integration of black and white musicians who played together in the same groups going back to the 1930s. It was a phenomenon which lessened in the '60s and which was largely forgotten during the so-called "Young Lions" era of the '80s when young, African-American musicians such as the Marsalis brothers rose to prominence.

"Having once been in the vanguard, jazz has fallen prey to the same racial divisions that have plagued the rest of American society," Sandke writes. "The overwhelming racialization of jazz has not only denied outside musical influences, stifled creativity, and pitted group against group: it has also overlooked the crucial role that white audiences and presenters have played in disseminating and promoting the music."

I think, with all due respect, Sandke overdramatizes the plight of the white jazz musician. Yes, the Young Lions phenomenon was overwhelmingly black and young, and Sandke is partially right about the market-driven motives of record executives who wanted to hype black musicians to an extent, but their actions pale in comparison to how whites have promoted musicians of a paler shade for centuries. In the end, there is a big difference between the jazz intelligentsia's attempt to right an historical wrong and the willful promotion of a reverse apartheid for white musicians. Sandke's views are ironic, because many black jazz musicians and writers complain that African Americans—who, according to the 2010 CENSUS, are 12% of the population—do not frequent jazz venues in sizable numbers.

On the other end of the spectrum, there is Nicholas Payton: a New Orleans–born trumpet player and son of bassist Walton Payton. Payton has enjoyed a critically acclaimed career, earning a Grammy for his 1997 collaboration with the great Doc Cheatman. In the past decade, he has recorded two challenging and creative CDs: *Sonic Trance* and *Into the Blue*. Now Payton feels straight-jacketed as a jazz musician, and he has created #BAM—Black American Music—in response, a movement that is "about setting straight what has been knocked out of alignment by mislabeling and marketing strategies," according to his website. What started out as a provocative essay from Payton entitled "On Why Jazz Isn't Cool Anymore" has degenerated in some posts and tweets into finger pointing and name calling that advances nothing. To be fair to Payton, he is not saying that you have to be black to appreciate or play #BAM. "Black American Music just acknowledges the culture from which it sprung forth. You don't have to be Black to appreciate and play it any more than you have to be Chinese to cook and eat noodles," he writes on his website.

While, as an African American I have some sympathy for Payton's views, I have the same reservations about his conclusions as I do Sandke's views. Payton suggests that black jazz musicians cannot change the status quo of their current stature if they call their music jazz. Payton also ignores or diminishes the fact that, as I stated earlier, everyone in the jazz infrastructure acknowledges blacks as the creators of jazz. Yes, jazz artists are hampered by market-driven definitions, but that is nothing special to them. Every musician regardless of genre complains about this.

Just as my Bill Evans problem obscured my early development in my appreciation of the music, adopting verbatim the thoughts and opinions of musicians like Sandke and Payton could do the same for young people just getting into the music, whether as musicians or as fans. It would be quite Pollyannaish of me to tell someone to "simply ignore race." I (and we) live in a racialized world, and jazz is a part of that world. But if the music teaches us anything, it teaches us that we can keep racial distinctions and distortions at bay.

note
Originally published in *New Music Box*, June 26, 2013.

Where's the Black Audience?
RON WYNN (*JazzTimes*, 2003)

Everyone who's followed jazz for more than 10 years has witnessed this scenario firsthand. A great musician (Sonny Rollins or McCoy Tyner, for example) comes to town with an equally excellent band for a one-night engagement in a major city's biggest jazz club. A faithful audience gathers, and what eventually occurs is a great concert given by a mostly African-American band before a largely white audience. It's a situation that has become so customary it seldom gets questioned, even if the concerts are being given during Black History Month. While critics continue to argue whether white or black artists get preferential treatment in the jazz media, a better question might be, Where's the black audience for jazz?

Now before the polemicists fire up their word processors, let's stipulate to a few things, as they say in court. This is not an implicit bid to exclude whites, Latinos, Asians or anyone else who treasures jazz from participating in either playing or appreciating it.

Unfortunately, it has become impossible to even attempt an objective discussion of any issue involving culture and color without including this type of preamble, but nonetheless jazz is such a vital, exciting and delightful music that it belongs to the world, something that makes the continuing ambivalence toward the music among many blacks even more troubling.

Yes, there are African-Americans across the nation who've been longtime, faithful fans of jazz, who continue to buy the records and support the few stations in the country still playing it. You can hear outstanding specialty programs on African-American college radio stations in places like Atlanta, Nashville or Washington, D.C., and BET's Jazz Channel has done its best (within certain parameters) to raise awareness within the African-American community. Also, festivals in New Orleans and Atlanta and Los Angeles and Chicago do attract African-American fans among their constituencies. In addition, many distinguished black academics and critics have fought the good fight to expand the audience for jazz in Black America. Such landmark books as Amiri Baraka's *Blues People* or A. B. Spellman's *Four Lives* were integral works that awakened and enriched the lives of many young African-Americans, showing us that jazz certainly had deep and considerable black roots. Bill Cosby's efforts with both situation and dramatic television, as well as Dr. Billy Taylor's longtime national-television journalist gigs have been equally invaluable.

In addition, there has long been the thesis advanced that the avant-garde killed jazz in the black community by finally and forever divorcing the music from all semblance of soul, structure, etc. Personally, I never heard any outside or avant-garde music live until attending college in Massachusetts in the '70s, but there are those convinced that one evening's exposure to Ornette Coleman or Albert Ayler in the '60s forever ended the lure of jazz among vast numbers of African-Americans. Personally, I'd argue that the demise of many major clubs in black communities, due to ill-timed urban renewal initiatives, probably had a lot more to do with generations not experiencing or enjoying jazz than a mass recoil from hearing Ascension, but that's another issue. Whatever the case, except for brief periods of popularity during the early '70s thanks to Miles Davis and the CTI label, the black audience for jazz has ranged from small to meager, and there aren't any visible signs of major improvement. Without lapsing into pseudo-political territory, let me suggest a few reasons for that situation as well as some potential remedies. These are not listed in order of importance.

The regular presence in African-American media.

Whether they've tried in the past and failed or not, jazz labels must either continue or begin to advertise in African-American periodicals. Such magazines as *Ebony, Jet, Essence*, even *Savoy*, have sizable constituencies and represent potential untapped fans. The same holds true for African-American newspapers, which continue to have a healthy readership, even if journalism surveys and consultants ignore them. These publications and magazines also usually have critics and writers looking for stories. A couple of articles about Dianne Reeves or James Carter in a few more local African-American newspapers will do far more for their profile in the black community than more *New York Times* or National Public Radio profiles, though these also certainly have their share of African-American fans. Anyone who goes back through the archives of such great black newspapers as the *Pittsburgh Courier, Baltimore Afro-American* or *Chicago Defender* will see regular, distinguished coverage of the arts in general and jazz specifically, a reality that obliterates the myth that African-Americans don't have their own critical tradition. Record labels might also think about servicing critics who write for black publications. There are quite a few who would love to review jazz titles if they could get them.

The establishment of a jazz equivalent of *Vibe* or *The Source*.

This one's trickier, and I can already hear the cries of reverse racism coming from the more conservative end of the jazz press. But there should have been a black-owned and operated jazz magazine a long time ago. The long defunct, sorely missed *Black Sports* magazine (once edited by Bryant Gumbel) as well as the edition of *Players* magazine that featured Donald Bogle doing television and *JazzTimes'* own Stanley Crouch reviewing jazz represented two examples of popular magazines with a black viewpoint that were incisive, often controversial and far more diversified in coverage and approach than anything currently on the market. Also, it is no slight on anyone to say that the perspectives of black writers on jazz might be a bit different than those of their white counterparts. It is unfortunate, but until the society reaches that mystical point in time like the Star Trek bunch, there are segments of various communities that will respond more favorably to a publication reflecting what they feel is their experience and sensibility than those they feel don't.

The return of jazz to mainstream black radio.

Here, we're probably looking at the impossible, but in the '50s and early '60s, there were some jazz types such as Cannonball Adderley, Lee Morgan and (dare I say it) Ramsey Lewis whose songs were regularly aired on R&B and soul stations. There were a number of African-American owned and operated outlets that also had extensive jazz and blues specialty programs on the weekend, and there was at least a presence on the airwaves that's completely missing today. Given the conglomerate grip on broadcasting that's now extended into the urban arena, we're not likely to hear much jazz on urban stations, but if jazz artists really want to reach more African-American listeners, this is another area that needs much work. Artists might also again begin to think about cutting single versions of tunes, and maybe even, in appropriate situations, remixing cuts for radio. Just to cite two potential examples, there are songs on the recent releases by John Scofield (*Überjam*) and Pat Metheny (*Speaking of Now*) that rhythmically and musically would work on urban radio stations in a remixed format. The same holds true for tracks from past releases by Olu Dara or Russell Gunn. If those labels already tried that tack and failed, my apologies, but if they didn't, they missed the boat. Having someone like Olu Dara on a program such as *The Tom Joyner Morning Show* (assuming it would book him) would not just bolster him, it would help the cause for jazz artists everywhere.

Less emphasis on history, hipness, etc.

Too many young African-Americans, including my own 16-year-old, view jazz as either antiquated, esoteric or both. Certainly it is important to know about the music's innovators, heroes and great figures, but there's nothing wrong with beginning someone's immersion into jazz with less intense, more pop-influenced material, or using vintage jazz-rock or soul-jazz as an introductory vehicle. It's also a little silly to get upset because there are large groups of people unaware of Lester Young, John Coltrane, etc. Rather than submitting them to a verbal beatdown, engage them and gradually introduce them to the beauty of their music. The problem is that few people are willing to listen, much less consider, the rantings of elitist snobs who hector them, dismiss their musical preferences or otherwise infer they're less culturally aware because they don't own 100 Duke Ellington albums or haven't spent their entire lifetime patrolling used-record stores. On the other hand, showing the undeniable links between various idioms, or the influence of jazz on other more familiar styles, can often work wonders. There's a sizable number of jazz converts who have been swayed by the rapper Guru in hip-hop publications. He's one of the many hip-hop figures who need to be engaged and recruited rather than ridiculed or attacked.

More outreach to the African-American community by jazz performers.

Yes, there are plenty of great black jazz players who've spent lifetimes in the black community, and they are hardly the target of this missive. But for every Randy Weston or Max Roach, there are many others who for whatever reason don't play black clubs, appear at community functions or otherwise interact among African-Americans as a whole. Black club promoters should be a priority-one outlet for jazz labels and performers. For all those who continue to dog Wynton Marsalis, he is one of the very few jazz musicians of any color that is well known and admired throughout the black community, even by people who don't care about anything other than the 20 pop songs being endlessly recycled on urban radio.

Lobbying to increase availability of BET's Jazz Channel.

BET on Jazz: The Jazz Channel is available here in Nashville only via digital cable. I recently bought a Dish Network satellite system, which not only doesn't have the Jazz Channel, it has no current plans to add it. Every phone call inquiring about it only brings the response, "We'll add it to our list of potential stations we're considering getting." While some of the channel's featured artists may lack jazz pedigree, the outlet's overall importance and visibility as an advocate for the music deserves bolstering. Call your cable or satellite operator today and demand the Jazz Channel.

More publicity for jazz's online sites.

As someone who frequently uses the Internet professionally, I know there's a host of great sites that might hook the younger computer junkies. But unless you're a subscriber to jazz periodicals, or can actually get the Jazz Channel in your town, these young eyes are among the least likely persons to know these jazz Web sites exist. Jazz Web sites are much better recruiters of youthful ears than aged critics or older musicians, and they can also help get newer listeners up to speed faster.

Enhanced jazz presence in black retail record stores.

The record store in my neighborhood stocks only a small amount of highly commercial jazz titles, mostly of the smooth variety. Some of that is undoubtedly due to demand, because it also recently stopped carrying gospel, but some of it is also because distributors who handle jazz product have never contacted the shop. If the titles aren't even in black community stores, who could expect those fans that do live there to know about them? Only music junkies and players exhaust their disposable incomes buying every rag in sight and scouring the reviews and new-release lists. Far more people will peruse what's available in a store, perhaps ponder it and then make their selections. It's also not possible for jazz to be played in stores that don't get the records in the first places.

Jazz performances at venues other than those in white neighborhoods.

The loss of so many small black-owned clubs dealt a major blow to jazz and the music's identification within the community. Now the bulk of tiny mom-and-pop clubs either play records or book only R&B/soul/pop cover bands. There may not be much money in it, and that's an old story for jazz musicians, but some of the finest shows you'd ever hear were done at places like the Paradise in Memphis or even Elks Lounges. No one is trying to glamorize the chitlin' circuit, but many African-Americans saw lots of great music in similar places. Black colleges should also be utilized more often as locales for jazz concerts.

Highlight notable young black jazz stars.

The aforementioned Reeves, Carter, Gunn, Dara and many others like Cassandra Wilson, Mark Turner and Joshua Redman are bright, photogenic, and could certainly be persuasive and eloquent jazz champions in the black community. Again, some of these people have already done some of that, but they could certainly do more of it. Here's where some efforts could be combined, like campaigns in black publications and ads that use these individuals in principal roles. Big posters of Wilson, Gunn or Carter in black record stores, just like the huge ones of country stars in Nashville's or R&B greats in New Orleans' Tower Records, only enhance and expand their visibility.

These are only a handful of suggestions designed to heighten the popularity of jazz and black jazz artists in the black community. As someone who loves a host of idioms, jazz included, I've long found it a mystifying proposition that so much energy and rhetoric is expended on cultural racism, but so little time and attention is devoted to ensuring that the black audience for jazz isn't restricted to journalists, musicians and record collectors.

note

Originally published in *JazzTimes*, January/February 2003. Used by permission of Madavor Media.

Whither the Black Voices

ANTHONY DEAN-HARRIS (*Nextbop*, 2013)

About a year and a half ago, some time after he challenged a fledgling jazz blogosphere to put together their Jazz Now lists, Patrick Jarenwattananon emailed me asking my input on why I was one of the few, if not the only black guy who contributed to the project and possibly in the jazz internet at large. Naturally, I put together my thoughts on the matter (back when my personal blog served more of a purpose than the initial depository for Line-Up playlists. A little while after that, I joined the ranks of Nextbop and have since pressed on with championing jazz on the internet whenever I could. Fast forward to last week, journalist and blogger Harry Allen made a keen observation on his Twitter, noting that the music writing staff of the *New York Times* is all white, even when they take the time to praise all black artists. He later noted that "Both The @VillageVoice's and @TheNYTimes's music sections seem to be composed completely of white guys." Since I've touched on this subject before, and I being Negro, I'd like to delve into this topic once more.

This is not to say that I have any doubt in the music staffs of the *New York Times* and the *Village Voice*. I can talk all day about how I love the work Nate Chinen does and his importance to jazz discourse. I also relish the writings of Jon Caramanica and Jon Pareles when their insights reach my computer screen. Still, while I take great joy in their words, I know that culturally, there are certain insights that could better paint the music pages of their publication. (How often do you have a Hawaiian on such a major publication, though? That's pretty cool.) Add to that Stanley Crouch's scattershot, sometimes contentious words (which while still a black voice on the page, may not be altogether helpful to the forward movement of black musical discourse).

Please note that I'm not making the blanket statement that there aren't black music journalists. Obviously, they run rampant throughout hip hop and I certainly don't have the patience to hyperlink the myriad blogs covering that genre. Also, as I've noted before in my aforementioned post on the absence of blacks in jazz journalism, we can all look to Willard Jenkins' *The Independent Ear* for his insights. Also, this past year saw the christening of OkayPlayer's The Revivalist which is constantly putting together fantastic content covering the crossroads of jazz and hip hop while giving credence to classic fusion sounds (and has managed to snatch our own much heralded contributing writer Kyla Marshell from us from time to time). Even here on

Nextbop's pages, we have trumpeter Jared Bailey and relative jazz newcomer Alexander Brown to give insights. The level of black voices in the interest of jazz writing are not nearly as comparable to our white counterparts on the internet nor to the black musicians in the genre, but there certainly isn't a shortage of them like there was just a mere year ago.

In this era of major publications scrambling to survive, it does seem a little odd to ask why blacks and other minorities aren't more present in journalism, but we still beg the question nonetheless. It's hard to get a job in journalism today, black, white or otherwise (I can assure you, I know). Making smaller endeavors or striking out on one's own, typically for little or no money, is just the way things are right now. Yet, when there is so much diversity in music today, why is there so little diversity in music's criticism?

This is the same rationale that spurred Spike Lee (c/o 1979) to start my alma mater, Morehouse College's, sports and journalism program. The primary focus of the program is sports journalism and was spurred as a direct address to the fact that there are so many black athletes yet very few blacks covering these athletes. While the stories are lived, we had little control over the narrative. This is the very same thing that's happening in jazz today. We can praise the diversity of the music but think little on the general whitewashing of its commentary.

So to note as Allen has that the *New York Times* nor the *Village Voice* has any black writers even as it praises black musicians is not negligible. There's a certain degree of cultural insight lacking on very public forums because of this. We're making great strides right now. PJ's original question posed to me for black voices not only found answers but subsequent solutions (and the contributions I made and my twisting the arms of those who've written on these pages were not for their blackness but because I think they're awesome writers who happen to be black, although we did all go to black colleges so there is naturally a skewed sample there). Yet there is still much more to do. There is a need for diversity far and wide, not just on the internet but also in print. I still remain hopeful. We've all made some great steps in the last year and we're certainly showing no signs of slowing.

note

Originally published in *Nextbop*, August 28, 2013.

Brooklyn's Jazz Renaissance

ROBIN D. G. KELLEY (*ISAM Newsletter*, 2004)

In March 2003, Jazz at Lincoln Center hosted a forum titled "Jazz and Social Protest" that drew a predominantly black, standing-room-only crowd. Moderated by Robert O'Meally, director of the Center for Jazz Studies at Columbia University, the panel consisted of poets Sonia Sanchez and Amiri Baraka, and trumpeter Cecil Bridgewater. All three artists made explicit statements against the war in Iraq. Coincidentally, three days later the *Los Angeles Times* ran an article by critic Don Heckman arguing that there were few jazz musicians out front against the war.[1] From this, he concluded that despite some historic exceptions, the jazz world simply is not that political.

Of course, critics like Heckman who look for "politics" in song titles, explicit references to world events, or musicians' commentary, invariably reduce politics to *protest*. But during the forum, Baraka insisted that the language of "social protest" obscures the real political meaning of the music. Indeed, the entire panel discussed jazz in terms of building community and sustaining African American culture, mentoring new generations in the tradition, recognizing the democratic, communal, even spiritual nature of jazz performance, and reclaiming and preserving this great African American art form.

If these issues really lie at the heart of the politics of jazz, then a revolution is taking place in Brooklyn. While predominantly white "downtown" audiences squeeze into the Blue Note or the Vanguard to be entertained by the hip, across the bridge Brooklyn's black activists and artists are reclaiming the music's roots and employing it for the political, social and spiritual uplift of the community. Jazz is everywhere in Central Brooklyn—at intimate nightclubs like Up Over Jazz Cafe, Pumpkins, and The Jazz Spot; at local coffeehouses like Sistas' Place; in community centers; even in the house of the Lord. Brooklyn has its own black-oriented jazz magazine, *Pure Jazz*, edited by the tireless JoAnn Cheatham. And as anyone who has attended the annual Central Brooklyn Jazz Festival can tell you, the audiences for the music are predominantly black, representing all classes and ages. Quiet as it seems, reaffirming the music's links to black community struggles and social transformation marks a radical challenge to jazz's current trajectory, which has become deeply commercialized, rendered colorblind and apolitical, and promoted as American high culture.

The key force behind the Brooklyn revolution is the Central Brooklyn Jazz Consortium. Founded about five years ago by a group of black artists, activists, and entrepreneurs, including the late singer Torrie McCartney, trumpeter and composer Ahmed Abdullah, and veteran black community activists Viola Plummer and Jitu Weusi, the CBJC set out to promote "African American classical music" as a collective, community project. The CBJC is made up of several club owners, nearly half a dozen churches, and a variety of community centers. More than a business venture, the CBJC was created to spread positive cultural values through the music. Bob Myers, owner of Up Over Jazz Cafe and original CBJC member, explained, "This is the African way, to promote the culture through the music and arts, and to do so not in competition but in cooperation."[2]

What the CBJC is attempting to do has deep roots in Brooklyn's history and its rich jazz heritage. Back in the day, Miles Davis, John Coltrane, Thelonious Monk, Lee Morgan, and others played at Brooklyn venues like Putnam Central, the Blue Coronet, the Baby Grand, Club La Marchal, or Tony's Club Grandean. Trumpeters Freddie Hubbard and Lee Morgan helped put Brooklyn on the global jazz map in 1965 with the release of *Night of the Cookers, vols. 1 and 2*, recorded live at the Club La Marchal on Nostrand Avenue and President Street. Brooklynites enjoyed occasional concerts at the Paramount Theater, and many danced to big bands at the Elks or Sonia ballrooms. But this barely scratches the surface, for as longtime Brooklyn resident and former musician Freddie Robinson told me, "The music was everywhere. Every little corner bar had jazz." Some of the better-known joints were the Pleasant Lounge, Club 78, Kingston Lounge, and Club Continental.[3]

Brooklyn jazz musicians have also been working cooperatively for at least a half-century. Indeed, one of Myers's models for the CBJC was Club Jest Us, a group of jazz musicians' wives living in Brooklyn during the 1960s who worked collectively in order to secure gigs for their husbands. A decade earlier, Brooklyn-born pianist and composer Randy Weston recalled working with his neighborhood pals, including drummer Max Roach, to organize musicians' collectives. Weston and other musicians learned a great deal about cooperation and self-reliance from his father, Frank Weston, who inspired young musicians at his restaurant with stories of Marcus Garvey, Africa, and the continuing struggle to uplift the black community.[4]

During the 1960s and early 1970s, the late Cal Massey, an extraordinary composer and trumpeter, turned his Brooklyn home into a veritable community center. Besides writing explicitly revolutionary pieces like "The Black Liberation Suite," Massey organized benefit concerts for the Black Panther Party that encouraged the full participation of the community, especially youth, by banning alcohol and providing free childcare. Around the same time, Jitu Weusi, founder and current chairman of the CBJC, promoted jazz as a cultural and political force to mobilize Brooklyn's black community when he founded The East in 1969. Located in the heart of Bedford-Stuyvesant, The East was a black cultural center where artists such as bassist Reggie Workman performed and held workshops for youth.[5]

During the 1970s and 1980s, in the wake of the borough's decline due to high unemployment, federal cutbacks, and drugs, black activists who sought to revitalize Brooklyn once again turned to jazz. The Bed-Stuy Restoration Corporation was one of those institutions that helped pave the way for the current Brooklyn renaissance. The Center for Arts and Culture at Bed-Stuy Restoration Corp, for example, trains young people in the art of jazz and runs the Skylight Gallery where musicians frequently perform. Myers's Up Over Jazz Cafe is also a space for community building. Neighborhood musicians work out ideas through open jam sessions, and Myers has even hosted several nights of "Hip Hop Meets Jazz," where singing sensation Bilal jammed with friends, including the equally sensational pianist Jason Moran.

Perhaps the best-known and most politicized community space for jazz is Sistas' Place on Nostrand and Jefferson Avenues. Run by a collective whose members have ties to political organizations such as the December 12th Movement and the Harriet Tubman/Fannie Lou Hamer Collective, Sistas' Place hosts a wide range of cultural activities. Any given week one might hear the Sun Ra Arkestra or saxophonist René McLean, or check out a Sunday afternoon panel discussion on reparations for slavery or police brutality.[6]

The jazz revolution in Brooklyn has not led to a distinctive "Brooklyn aesthetic," largely because virtually all genres are represented—from bebop to avant-garde. Nevertheless, some general characteristics of the music and artists deserve comment.

The CBJC encourages young artists by hosting frequent open jam sessions and promoting conversations between jazz and other musical genres. During the 2003 festival, for example, BRIC Studio on Rockwell Place hosted DJ Logic performing with jazz musicians, and The Jazz Spot committed its entire March calendar to young women instrumentalists. The most important characteristic of the CBJC's artistic vision is its reverence for black music and musicians throughout the African Diaspora and on the continent. Following in the footsteps of native son Randy Weston, a pioneer in the movement to reconnect Africa with African American musical traditions, several of the festival performers incorporate African instruments, Afro-Latin and Caribbean rhythms, as well as various forms of black sacred music. Ultimately, if there is any essential principle behind the movement, it is to celebrate and reclaim black music for Brooklyn's black community.

For CBJC co-founder Ahmed Abdullah, the very existence of black, community-based spaces for jazz is "regenerating."[7] Abdullah himself has helped to create these spaces by working closely with schools and churches. In February 2003, Concord Baptist Church held a well-attended tribute to Gigi Gryce and Randy Weston, at which elementary school kids sang Gryce's "Social Call" and a teenaged band known as Friends and Strangers struggled valiantly with Weston's best-known compositions. The predominantly black crowd embraced this music with the enthusiasm of a Sunday morning revival. For the last two springs, Concord hosted "100 Golden Fingers in Praise," a concert of sacred music led by pianist Barry Harris and at least nine other pianists, including Bertha Hope, Gil Coggins, and Valerie Capers. Besides Concord Baptist Church, several other religious institutions including St. Philips Episcopal Church, Our Lady of Victory Roman Catholic Church, Jane's United Methodist, First Presbyterian Church, and Hanson Place Central United Methodist Church have hosted performances as part of the Central Brooklyn Jazz Festival. Last year, Brooklyn's 651 ARTS and musical director Akua Dixon brought together a jazz ensemble, featuring trombonist Craig Harris with the Total Praise Choir and rocked Emmanuel Baptist Church.

For many of the ministers involved with the CBJC, as well as for activists like Abdullah, bringing the music back to its roots in black communities is necessary, both for the music's survival as well as for the community's resurrection. No one is saying jazz ought to be the exclusive property of black folk; it never was. Instead, the music needs to be "allowed to grow in the atmosphere that nurtures its creative juices," Abdullah explained. This is not a tale of protest but a story of social and spiritual liberation. And for Abdullah, and presumably most of the folks behind the Brooklyn revolution, thinking of jazz as a spiritually liberating force for a community in struggle can serve as a model for the rest of the world: "That's what the music is about anyway. That's why it's loved around the world. That's why I say in its true essence Jazz is a music of the spirit."[8]

notes

Originally published in *ISAM Newsletter* 33, no. 2 (Spring 2004). Courtesy of the H. Wiley Hitchcock Institute for Studies in American Music.

1. Don Heckman, "Music (and Musicians) as a Force for Change," *Los Angeles Times*, March 21, 2003, E19.

2. Bob Myers, interview with author, February 21, 2003.

3. K. Leander Williams, "Brooklyn, New York," in *Lost Jazz Shrines (The Lost Shrines Project, 1998)*, 12–16; Bilal Abdurahman, *In the Key of Me: The Bedford Stuyvesant Renaissance, 1940s–60s Revisited* (Contemporary Visions, 1993); Randy Weston, interview with author, August 20, 2001; Bob Meyers, interview with author, February 21, 2003.

4. Myers, interview with author; Weston, interview with author; Ira Gitler, "Randy Weston," *DownBeat* (February 1964): 16–17; Arthur Taylor, *Notes and Tones: Musician-to-Musician Interviews* (Da Capo Press, 1993), 20–21; Valerie Wilmer, *Jazz People* (Da Capo Press, 1977), 79.

5. Fred Ho, "'The Damned Don't Cry': The Life and Music of Calvin Massey" (unpublished paper in author's possession); Eric Porter, *What Is This Thing Called Jazz? African American Musicians as Artists, Critics, and Activists* (University of California Press, 2002), 216; Ahmed Abdullah, email message to author, March 17, 2003.

6. Abdullah, email message to author; www.millionsforreparations.com.

7. Abdullah, email message to author.

8. Abdullah, email message to author.

Additional *Ain't But a Few of Us* Contributors

Wynton Is the Greatest!

PLAYTHELL BENJAMIN (*Commentaries on the Times*, 2016)

The great composer, arranger, bandleader and trumpeter Gerald Wilson once told me emphatically during an interview: "Wynton Marsalis is the greatest trumpeter in the world!" And as a failed trumpeter who retained a passionate love for the instrument, as well as an acute appreciation for the formidable obstacles and treacherous pitfalls which confronted the aspiring artist that attempted to master it, I wholeheartedly agreed.

As a serious lover of complex instrumental music I had listened to many great trumpeters in Jazz and European concert music—the former a New World invention, a 20th century art that expressed the Afro-American love of freedom as well as the quintessential American ideals of Democracy, Personal Liberty and Innovation; the latter a great art music from the Old World of Europe that was already centuries old, and reflected the hierarchal and highly formalized character of the societies that produced it. And although both musical idioms employ the same instruments, and the music they make is based on the same system of melody and harmony—a European invention that produced sublime sounds by their great master composers—the two musical forms were profoundly different in instrumental technique, compositional structure and artistic philosophy.

In the classical music of Europe the instrumentalist is a vehicle for the ideas of the composer. And if they perform in symphony orchestras, operas or chorales they are also subjected to the dictates of tyrannical composers. Hence in European concert music the creativity of the instrumentalist is severely circumscribed. Everything from tempo, intonation and interpretation of the music is dictated by the composer and enforced by the conductor with an iron fist. Hence conformity to tradition and achieving excellence based upon well-established standards of performance is the objective to which the successful artists must aspire.

Conversely, the art of Jazz performance demands that the performer seek their own voice, follow their personal muse, and create something new under the sun. Furthermore the music must swing to the clockwork rhythms of the unique machine-age milieu in which it was born . . . the most modern civilization the world had ever seen. Hence all Jazz is modern music. That's why visual artists from American Abstract Expressionists Jackson Pollock and Willem de Kooning, to European masters of Modernism such as Pablo Picasso and Salvador Dalí lionized their music.

The difficulty of mastering both musical idioms is self-evident in the fact that of all the great musicians that have lived in the world, there are so few that have achieved virtuosity in both that we can count them on our fingers and toes. Flautist Hubert Laws, trumpeter Arturo Sandoval, pianists Chucho Valdez and Herbie Hancock, bassists Ron Carter, Carlos del Pino, Richard Davis and Ortiz Walton first among them. However Mr. Marsalis is the only musician on any instrument who has won the coveted Grammy for performances in both genres. And he has achieved this impossible feat nine times! Four were for "Best Classical Performance" and five for "Best Jazz Performance."

For this presentation I have chosen one of the most difficult instrumental pieces from each genre where Wynton is featured as a soloist. Added to this are two performances with Wynton as accompanist to a singer . . . a fine art unto itself. For the instrumental Classical repertoire I have selected *The Carnival of Venice*, and for the Jazz performance I have chosen *Cherokee*. As to the difficulties posed by the first piece, suffice it to say that when trumpeters auditioned for the great United States Marine Band, billed as "The Greatest Brass Band in the World"—under the direction of its founder and premiere composer Maestro John Phillip Sousa—who wrote such enduring works as *El Capitan, Semper Fidelis, Anchors Away!* and the immortal *Stars and Stripes Forever—The Carnival of Venice* was the piece that they were required to play.

This is because Arbans' *Carnival* presents the trumpeter with a series of obstacles that requires mastery of all the technical problems posed by trumpet performance: legato and staccato phrasing; triple tonguing, circular breathing, fingering the keys, exquisite timing, embouchure and intonation. Clearly Wynton masters them all . . . and with ease! This is a heroic achievement, because a trumpet after all is just some twisted brass pipes with a hard metal mouthpiece and only three keys! Yet it is capable of playing all the notes in the musical lexicon.

This amazing feat is achieved by manipulating sound from the way one blows into the instrument, which is to say mastering embouchure. It is such a marvelous feat, the only reason that great athletes such as Michael Jordon and Russell Wilson attract more fans than Wynton is because more people understand the greatness of what they do. Everybody has had some experience playing sports—if only because physical education is a required component of every school curriculum . . . and sadly instrumental music is not. However to grasp the brilliance of Wynton's performance on *Carnival*, one need only read the comments of trumpet players from all over the world under the video and note their astonishment—one even said that "suicide would be easier and a lot less painful than the epic failure one would experience trying to duplicate this performance!"

Cherokee, the Jazz selection, was the piece that the hep cats at Minton's Playhouse threw on Charlie "Yardbird" Parker to prove his mettle when he showed up at Minton's Playhouse from Kansas City "looking country" totin his alto-sax in a cardboard case. But when he took out his axe and begin to "cut heads" with his complex, erudite and original musical statements, Bird astonished everybody who witnessed it. Dizzy Gillespie, a key figure in the aggregation of musical rebels who congregated in Minton's and experimented with new ideas, said when he heard Bird he thought: "There it is, this is the sound we have been searching for." He said that they had bits and pieces of the music that would become world famous as Be-bop, and Bird filled in the gaps and brought the whole thing together.

From that musical communion came a genre of Jazz that would change the way musicians heard and played music all over the world. The artistic challenges Bop presented intrigued musicians from the great to near great to apprentices. If I had to sum up Bird's achievement I would say that he did for the world of music what Einstein did for theoretical physics: change the relationship between time and space forever.

The great writer Ralph Ellison, a well-schooled trumpet player competent in both the classical repertoire—he was a music major at Tuskegee, where he studied with the outstanding Afro-American composer in the classical European style but with an Afro-American voice, William Dawson—and was also grounded in the hard swinging blues style of the "Stomp" that was popular among the "Territorial Bands" that played in his native Oklahoma City—Bird hailed from nearby Kansas City.

Ellison was so astonished and overwhelmed by what he heard in Minton's that he wrote, "They were playing be-bops . . . I mean re-bopped be-bops." The drummers had abandoned the steady bass drum pulse that was so essential to the dancers who got down to the Stomp, that Ellison was horrified by the seemingly free form complexity of their rhythms and described them as "frozen faced introverts dedicated to chaos!"

The experience of hearing this new music called "Be-Bop" invented in Harlem's Minton's Playhouse by players like trumpeter Dizzy Gillespie, pianist Thelonious Monk, bassist Oscar Pettiford, drummer Kenny "Klook" Clarke and others [so affected Ellison] that he gave up playing the trumpet and became one of the great writers. So music's loss was literature's gain.

When listening to *Cherokee*, remember that essential to the genius of Jazz is not only the requirement of virtuosity on the part of each instrumentalist . . . but one must be able to compose complex music while swinging the blues over chord changes at the SPEED OF THOUGHT!!! Hence the speed at which Wynton is playing adds to the magic of it all! So kick back and check out the marvelous vibes from the horn of Maestro Marsalis . . . THE GREATEST TRUMPETER IN THE WORLD!!!

note

Originally published in *Commentaries on the Times*, August 2, 2016.

Jazz Is . . . Free . . . ?

RON WELBURN (*The Grackle*, 1976)

Jazz Is, by Nat Hentoff (Random House/Ridge Press, 1976)

Free Jazz, by Ekkehard Jost (Beitrage zur jazzforschung/Studies in jazz research, Universal Edition, No. 4)

Jazz Meets the World (MPS/BASF Stereo 29 22520-8, double album)

Karuna Supreme, John Handy/Ali Akbar Khan (MPS/BASF Stereo DC 227913)

Jazz, the American classical music, continues to be appreciated internationally as an aesthetic experience. It has long been respected in Europe and in Japan. It has no respect in America because the racial group that initiated it is not respected as human beings. In some quarters, jazz sympathizers feel that the end of the Afro-American contribution and direction for jazz has come, despite the reality that the black musician, his/her community and sensibility continue as the main spiritual, rhythmic, and developmental force and inspirant of all contemporary music.

Both enthusiasm and concern should greet the widening international jazz community. On the one hand, although idolized American stylists in the African continuum are being xeroxed, some composers and conceptualists abroad no longer display strict reliance on American jazz idioms or structures. Promising work in recent years is evident when the various nationals bring their indigenous music cultures to bear on the jazz spirit. On the other hand, Americans know precious little about these developments, and what is recognized is often misconstrued. The Afro-American community, furthermore, is economically out of position to have any political impact or direction in this regard.

Meanwhile, there is much to be done. The business of listening, research, performing, analysis, and commentary goes on. The items noted indicate some sort of crossroads in our apprehension and appreciation of improvised music and should encourage outlines for an eventual stage.

Hentoff's *Jazz Is* offers a surprising disappointment for readers familiar with *The Jazz Life* (1962) and other writings of his from that and previous periods. An overpriced compilation of journalistic tidbits, it provides few insights not already raised in the liner notes, book and article quotes by either himself or others as they vamp through his personal notes and re-writings since the mid-sixties when he all but left active jazz commentary. A writer with Hentoff's experience and ability offering us such a book at this time makes us query the state of jazz writing in America at this time.

Enough writers young and established have created their own myths, and Hentoff ranks among the few who've avoided this. But the casuality of this book is disturbing. The young convert to the music might gain something from its being such a handy compilation of other material; but that merit is overshadowed by what it lacks in terms of what aficionados and scholars alike might be seeking at this time.

American jazz writing tends toward the journalistic for entertainment purposes more than it does the critically analytical. Journalism is not to be negated; but jazz needs to be taken seriously as a study area. Music by Joplin, Jelly Roll, Tatum, and Coltrane has been transcribed for performance and study, thus creating a body of classical works conservatories will not be able to morally ignore much longer. Jazz writing must continue where a few pioneers have left off.

Jazz criticism should be encouraged, or at least stimulated, by Ekkehard Jost's *Free Jazz*, the first definitive investigation of the so-called avant-garde. By impact of its fairly accurate transcriptive illustrations and analyses, this book has a different stripe from the strict prose of Philippe Carles and Jean-Louis Comolli's essays in *Free Jazz/Black Power* (Editions Champ Libre, 1971), Willy Roggeman's *Free En Andere Jazz-Essays* (Nijgh + van ditmar, 1969), and Frank Kofsky's *Black Nationalism and the Revolution in Music* (Pathfinder, 1969). American writers may think Jost too pedantic, but his book happens to be one that is significant now when some of us seek (and are working on) this kind of methodological approach. We should also note that European (and Canadian) critics over the years demonstrated an almost inescapably analytical prose style in writing about the music that makes much American jazz writing pale by comparison as entertainment journalism. Sadly enough, so much of the critiques of recordings and concerts in the Black press fits this description perfectly.

The reader might be interested to know that Jost wrote *Free Jazz* while not being able to visit America during or soon after his period of focus. He relied on recordings and tapes, attended concerts and club dates mostly in Germany and spoke with visiting musicians, and he consulted the jazz press. His treatment thus recalls the endeavor of the late German literary ethnologist, Janheinz Jahn, who synthesized a spectrum of scholarly and creative writings to write his *Muntu: An Outline of the Neo-African Culture*, once considered a bible by Black cultural nationalists here after its 1964 English translation.

Jost at least goes one better than Jahn with his illustrated analyses. He seems to understand much of what went down in purely musical terms. His socio-political realizations inform his insights without pervading them—one will find little political exposition in *Free Jazz* at all. He accepts black nationalism as a major force behind this music, and seems to know what he is dealing with regarding the Afro-American continuum, and the music to which contemporary improvising musicians feel at least intellectually responsive, European art music. But Jost concentrates on the style, identity, and posture of "Free Jazz" through its major architects: Taylor, Cherry, Shepp, Ayler, Sun Ra, the AACM, Coleman, even Mingus, have one chapter each, and Coltrane has two. Each chapter demonstrates its points as Gunther Schuller did in *Early Jazz*—doubtful that any other critical discussion of jazz utilizes such extensive transcription (we are not talking about books by Mahegan, Coker, Dankworth, Russell, or Baker, which are valuable as *work books* in this context, not scholarly treatises).

Recorded music serves as text material, and a few areas in sound defying transcription are shown by a graph (Shepp) and an "electro-acoustic registration" (an Ayler solo). Jost does not intend to be cute or way out by doing this but merely uses them for purposes of calling our attention to possible aids for analyses. He pinpoints changes in style, rhythmic and melodic emphases as pertinent to an important recorded solo, and he is concerned about matters of form and sound, deliberately premeditated as well as spontaneous. Must reading. *Free Jazz* will have to be ordered from Beitrage zur jazzforschung for the time being (ask about their jazz periodical, too).

Of the two albums, *Jazz Meets the World*, to be distributed by Audio-fidelity, has historical importance. A fellow German, Joachim Berendt, the writer-impresario (*The Jazz Book*), compiled this anthology from a dozen albums he produced in the sixties with this theme. The Handy-Akbar Khan album extends that project. The original albums from the first set were scarce here; an Allentown, Pennsylvania, distributor serviced alert collectors, and a few showed up in shops.

Jazz has been meeting the world for decades—France during World War I, Japan via records after Red Cross volunteers went there after the earthquake of the mid-1920s, Moscow and South America via Sam Wooding around the same time. The endeavors of Tony Scott, Don Cherry, and Berendt abroad, and Yusef Lateef here, are noble experiments not always successful. Berendt's visits and studies in the early sixties (viz *Down Beat*, November, 1963) resulted in this project.

Eleven of the dozen sessions are represented—Alexander von Schlippenbach's *Globe Unity* is missing. Included are *Noon in Tunisia*, with Bedouin musicians meeting Belgian pianist George Gruntz, American expatriot Sahib

Shihab, and others; *Flamenco Jazz*, with saxophonist Pedro Iturralde; *Wild Goose*, with a British husband and wife folksinging team meeting an Ayler-esque Heinz Sauer and the Mangelsdorfs; Baden Powell's *Folklore e Bossa Nova do Brasil*; *From Sticksland with Love*, with Gruntz, Nathan Davis, and Franco Ambrosetti meeting the Basel (Swiss) Tambours; Manfred Schoof and Barney Wilen with indigenous musicians for *Jazz Meets India*: Tony Scott's *Indonesian All-Stars*, featuring "Asia's Art Tatum," Bubi Chan; Wilen's *Auto Jazz*, a collage with a tape from Lorenzo Bandini's fatal crash at the 1964 Grand Prix (!); Don Cherry's Indonesia-conscious *Eternal Rhythm*; the late drummer Hideo Shiraki's quintet, with Terumasa Hino plus koto players for *Jazz Meets Japan*; and *El Babaku*, Chango cult music from Cuba.

The Handy date, from late 1975, Berendt considers one of the best ex-amples of jazz playing with an indigenous music, and with Indian musicians particularly. The altoist and sarodist interact like old friends, putting the strengths of their respective traditions into each performance. Compare Handy's boppish and modal *jazz* articulations and improvisory technique with those on *Paul Horn in India*, a Blue Note reissue (BN LA529-H2). Horn was a "guest" in an Indian situation and improvised within that sys-tem. Handy does not, and is less a "guest" than a sharer of ideas, creating something close to defying Horn's annotator Bob Palmer's doubt that such meetings could "produce anything like a jazz/raga fusion." John Mayer and the late Joe Harriott had their moments (*Indo-Jazz Fusions*, Atlantic) but Horn makes little jazz, despite his attention to ascending and descending scales and modal sections in the form. Such a portrait of a jazz musician! It hardly seems that he is playing at all; better to suggest that he is playing along in a situation in which he is outclassed. His experience in India in 1966 led to his recordings with whales for Columbia. The Handy record-ing offers us a meeting of an Indian music with the basic improvisational tradition of Afro-American music; Akbar Khan's trio and Handy exert their independence of each other while pulling it all together.

True, these meetings are forced and self-consciously assembled. Only the sessions involving the Japanese, the Spaniards, the Latin Americans, and perhaps the Indonesians (why Berendt used such a stereotyped example is unknown, and that session is one I never encountered) indicate truly indig-enous jazz where the Brazilians and Japanese have made the greatest strides in conceptualizing their jazz or jazz-inspired musics. The other meetings one suspects Berendt attempted as experiments between jazz players from Europe and Black Americans who happened to be in Europe at the time meeting indigenous musicians whose music already possesses a rudimentary rhythmic or rhytho-melodic affinity to jazz; as brilliant as the entire Tunisian set is, for example, one would be hard-pressed to hear anything like it anywhere except on record. "Meetings" like that, and like Shepp's performing on the streets of Algiers with Taureg and Berber musicians, do not happen but once in a blue moon. Only when jazz performers emerge from these cultures will their jazz, and their meetings with Western jazz performers, have any validity as examples showing us the true international performance scope of jazz or Afro-Western improvised music.

Informed critical analyses and jazz musicology will have to recognize international jazz for what it is worth. Miles Davis and Coltrane exploring modal improvising recognized the importance of harmonic shifts (modulations) built into the AABA structure (e.g., "So What?" "Milestones," "Impressions"). Current jazz-rock and disco use "modality" suspiciously as a means toward improvisational ease and some kind of feigned psychological buoyancy. But the modes common to much indigenous music have only been superficially explored in the jazz context by either Western or Eastern musicians. Handy's album is surprisingly significant because the length of Indian music performance permits *harmonic* modulation fundamentally similar to the late-fifties' modality, escaping the insipid noodling and scalular exercises the idiom superficially encourages.

Part of the jazz commentator's job will be recognizing the relative merits of jazz from abroad, as well as from outside its indigenous American community. Some cultures are strong in trombonists and bassists; a country weak in drumming may develop its own percussion characteristics (Japan, e.g.); India promises improvisational length. Africa and its children are melorhythmic, and the Afro-Asian world's strength is rhythm. Right now; all this is an iceberg we must sooner or later encounter while never forgetting that the source for all this expressive vitality is here, in the Miles Davises, Yusef Lateefs, and Cecil Taylors whose diverse experiences celebrate their places in the African continuum of a major spiritual and music force.

note

Originally published in *The Grackle*, Fall 1976.

Why Jazz Will Always Be Relevant

GREG TATE (*The Fader*, 2016)

Quiet as it's kept, the music we call jazz began life as an experimental remix of dance grooves from Africa and Europe that got chopped and screwed by high-stepping bluesicians of New Orleans over a century ago. From the git-go, the jazz thing has been as much about alchemy as flashy chops.

Everything we love about modern song, noise, and dance sprang from swing and bebop roots: R&B, rock, Motown, funk, disco, hip-hop, Detroit techno, Chicago house, drum & bass, et al. are all extensions of a movement-inciting continuum that started in antebellum New Orleans' Congo Square—breakbeat culture's ground zero. It was the explosive site where enslaved Africans were permitted to get their ya-yas out to the beat of the drum—well, at least until the human traffickers of that time figured out rebellion was also being plotted in the Square under the cover of a funky good time. Same as it ever was.

Early New Orleans jazz connected those rebel riddims to funereal and carnivalesque marching band stomps; Jelly Roll Morton decided ragtime piano was needed to further excite the cipher of tubas, trumpets, clarinets, bass drums, and tambourines. Duke Ellington brought a rich palette of colors to big band swing that was adopted from the spirituals, Debussy, and Stravinsky. Louis Armstrong made a trumpet emulate a man laughing to keep from crying his eyes out and transformed his singing voice into a sardonic freestyle horn. *What did I do to be so black and blue?* Armstrong inquired in 1925, and his existential query has yet to stop worrying the minds, bodies, and souls of African-Americans to this day.

The flavors that Armstrong's triumphant horn shot out so perplexed the French manufacturers of his instrument that they sent engineers to his first Paris concerts to find out what modifications he'd made to his trumpet. *Sacre bleu* could have been the only response when the builders realized Satchmo's ancestral African lips and tongue were the only technological innovations at play.

By the 1970s, Sun Ra had already pioneered the introduction of electric pianos and Moog synths into serious freedom jazz: Miles Davis had strapped a wah-wah pedal to his horn and was in the studio making vicious break-beats with tape loops, tabla players, and live handclaps on electronic jazz masterpieces like *On the Corner* and *Get Up With It*. Students of Miles—like Herbie Hancock, Chick Corea, and Weather Report—soon followed, with sublime composition, improv chops, and grooves steady enough to yank in hardcore disciples of James Brown, Sly Stone, and Funkadelic. Meanwhile, Maurice White's Earth, Wind & Fire so wickedly blurred the line between avant-garde soul and electronic jazz as to render distinctions between the genres patently absurd.

In a nutshell, the pioneers of '80s and '90s breakbeat dance culture were following precedents set by jazz musicians of the 1920s, '40s, '60s, and '70s—even if some didn't know it. Not entirely their fault: serious jazz got a lot less concerned with the dance floor from the mid-'40s on, thanks to Charlie Parker and Thelonious Monk, who were more concerned if their virtuosic flights made *them* happy than if they did everyday people; all the serious hoofers, toe-tappers, and lindy-hoppers got the message and moved on. Where they moved to was a hot, newfangled conflagration of gospel beats and vocalizing gone blasphemously secular, jazz harmonies and gutbucket blues forms—all that mess being pioneered by one Ray Charles. This kitchen-sink template set the stage for everything that's come down the pike since, from mojo-handed talents as diverse as Little Richard, Nina Simone, Jimi Hendrix, The Isley Brothers, Larry Levan, Ron Hardy, A Tribe Called Quest, and Lauryn Hill. Collage, cut-and-paste, sampling, remixing, and genre contamination has been a preferred mode in African-American music since the 1800s.

Guru and DJ Premier of Gang Starr did much to assert the common humanity and creative urges of rappers and beboppers in their collaborations with Donald Byrd and others on their epochal *Jazzmatazz* series of albums of the late '90s and aughts. They sparked a breakbeat-jazz hybrid scene on both sides of the Atlantic that yielded much musical fruit for a brief time but never cracked the blinged-out materialist hip-hop mainstream of the late Clinton and early Bush years. The Soulquarian Movement rallied by the Roots to assemble D'Angelo, OutKast, Jill Scott, Common, Bilal, Black Star, and Erykah Badu under one roof, and all threw hints and flashes of their own jazz genes into the conversation for those who knew the codes.

On the contemporary set, cats like Christian Scott, Jason Moran, Flying Lotus, Thundercat, Marc Cary, Vijay Iyer, and Robert Glasper are reuniting the urge to cunningly improvise with the urge to move the crowd. So of late we're seeing a revival within the jazz world of electro-acoustic forays that refuse any opposition between software-driven sonic modernity and a good old-fashioned bebop-infested blowing session—both in the studio or on the stage. Ironically enough, as DJing has evolved into a stand-alone art form, it's become much akin to '60s freedom jazz, drawing crowds who don't feel weird about gathering to hear turntablists experiment in public with their craft.

The ever-ambitious Flying Lotus—grand-nephew of Alice Coltrane and her husband John, a far-flung composer of dream-dusted cosmic music in his own right—has done much to surgically conjoin the beatmeisters and jazzers of now through his Brainfeeder label. It's an enterprise which in a relatively short while has normalized the curious drift of instrumental improvisers to the dark side of hiss-and-glitch clouded boom-bap, and vice-versa.

Political upheaval and jazz revivals tend to go hand in hand for African-Americans, and this Black Lives Matter–defined moment is no different in that regard. The jazz-damaged hip-hop artist of now who has made the convergence of ambient sonics, beats, and sexy improv seem inevitable, a seamless *fait accompli*, has been Kendrick Lamar—especially given how fluidly and fluently he deployed Glasper, Thundercat, and other bi-coastal jazz pros in the composing process that produced *To Pimp a Butterfly*. Because critics were so quick to label the album a black protest psalm, *Butterfly* hasn't yet been fully recognized as the *Bitches Brew* of our time— an artist's nuclear meltdown of this era's dominant musical tropes into a definitive abstract-expressionist statement—one that We The People can feel, call and respond, rally around, freely quote, space out, get our wiggle on to, etc., etc.

Butterfly is a bedazzling combo of beats, rhymes, and live in-the-studio experimentation. Jazz heads have no choice but to flip over "For Free," a straight-up freedom swing where Kendrick turns rapping into scatting and what author Jack Kerouac called bebop prosody, while string and drum breaks pop like bomb bursts around his head. It's a ballsy declaration of jazz-funk allegiance from an MC not afraid to play a game of virtuoso chicken with players who routinely eat knotty changes for brunch. There's as much Isley Brothers and P-Funk influence as Coltrane and Mingus, but in the '70s it was never unusual to hear funk bands sharing stages and tours with Miles acolytes like Hancock and Corea. A musical rapport and mutual language was shared, one bonded by the warm-blooded tones of the Fender Rhodes piano—the universal solvent of '70s black music across the rhythmic spectrum. Ya gotta love that Kendrick recognized having Glasper on *Butterfly*—with his sumptuous touch on the Rhodes—gives more life to the sonic beds his rhymes flowed over. Ditto Terrace Martin's yearning-burning alto sax on "Alright," which establishes a stellar emotional plateau for jazz and hip-hop hybrids.

That Lamar is a multidirectional rapper—able to supershift his cadences, character-acting, and melodic caches on a dime—is what unveils him as a jazzer in hip-hop guise. He's not alone in these mutant abilities: the members of Freestyle Fellowship, The Pharcyde, Snoop Dogg, and Del Tha Funky Homosapien all inject that gene into a loosey-goosey California rap skill set. Lamar's just the first artist to make it so fearlessly explicit at breakneck tempos when many of his generational peers are still drawling lockstep to gothic trap beats. It's hard to imagine Drake, Young Thug, or even Chance The Rapper so viciously and fluently going toe-to-toe with a stomp in 9/8 like Kendrick does at the midway point on "Momma." Fortunately, the race toward the dreamy side of the jazz-ecstatic aesthetic continued on K-Dot's surprise March release, *untitled unmastered*—a spooky revisitation of the trans-dimensional realm of loops and live-riffing in modern rap that he and his cohorts have made their privileged wheelhouse.

The most immediate beneficiary of this perfect storm, though, has been Kamasi Washington and his comrades in the West Coast Get Down crew. Washington's May 2015 release, *The Epic*, signals how modern acoustic jazz could go down to the breakbeat and improv, harvesting a global flow of heads ready once again to embrace 15-minute tenor saxophone solos with as much ardor and attention as they'll bestow on their favorite MC's next 64 bars.

Washington's rapid ascent to world-stage prominence has been linked to both exceptional good fortune and family ties within jazz, but the striking thing about *The Epic* is that there's nothing overtly hip-hop-friendly about it. It's as pure a sonic throwback to the '70s freedom-cum-cosmic swing of his dad's youth as has been heard in acoustic jazz since that era, when Alice Coltrane, Pharoah Sanders, and McCoy Tyner extended the range of Sun Ra's intergalactic inventions into forms that found traction among a post–Black Power generation of listeners on historically black college campuses. Also woven in are nods to the smoother funk-jazz of the ear, purveyed by Grover Washington Jr. and The Crusaders. The twain rarely met up and played nice back then due to political divisions in jazz over spiritual purity and pop ambitions. But as frequently happens when the gems of our parents' eras undergo rediscovery, old rhetorical baggage fades and the glorious innocence of crate-digging for soul gold remains. Even more remarkable, though, is how Washington has made those open-ended modal jazz forms relevant, rabidly followed by the musically intrepid and curious collegiate crowds of now—the Black Power flower children of the Black Lives Matter era. Many of us jazz lifers got lifted seeing more twentysomethings at Washington's February coming-out gig in New York City than we'd witnessed at a Gotham jazz club since the Marsalis brothers and Steve Coleman's confederates stormed their youth movement onto the scene in the 1980s.

As always, jazz never went away; it just kept vibrating in its batcave, laying in stealthy wait for a shaken-and-stirred world to get hip and revolutionary-minded again, between wars and between the ears.

note

Originally published in *The Fader*, May 5, 2016.

Rhapsody in Rainbow: Jazz and the Queer Aesthetic

JOHN MURPH (*JazzTimes*, 2010)

Evangeline Harris is piquing the curiosity of some pedestrians outside of Mova Lounge, an upscale gay bar in Washington, D.C.'s Logan Circle neighborhood. It's a gorgeous Sunday evening in late April, and Harris and her four-piece E & Me band are entertaining a sparse group of patrons. As some people chat and clink martini glasses in the rectangular-shaped bar, the musicians stand behind three large open panels, allowing the music to seep outside.

People hear music blaring inside Mova every day, but this time it's different. Harris is not a drag or disco queen; she's a jazz singer. Tonight's set includes admirable renditions of Nat "King" Cole's "Straighten Up and Fly Right," Herbie Hancock's "Watermelon Man" and Norah Jones' "Don't Know Why."

As a mere five bargoers sit close to the players and listen intently, the performance turns ironic during Bonnie Raitt's "I Can't Make You Love Me," which is given a mid-century torch-ballad treatment. Harris' anodyne soprano nearly goes unnoticed as she embodies the song's angst-ridden protagonist. Given jazz's status in mainstream gay culture, the disinterest seems apropos. Harris could have been personifying jazz itself, desperately seeking affirmation from the patrons, most of whom appear ambivalent about its presence.

When discussing the soundtrack to contemporary mainstream gay life, jazz is often treated as an allergen on a musical landscape more devoted to vocal pop, club hits and electronica. At the risk of stereotyping, gay culture feels more allegiance toward Lady Gaga than Lady Day. As someone who frequents gay bars with almost the same regularity as jazz clubs, I often sense a great divide between the two worlds. "It is extremely polarized," argues saxophonist and clarinetist Andrew D'Angelo, "so much so that when my ex-boyfriend came to one of my gigs, some of his gay friends were so disproportionately removed from my [jazz] scene. If they come to one of my shows it feels like a huge statement."

It would seem that there'd be more overlap between the jazz and gay communities in relationship to mainstream society. After all, both foster communities that cut many strata, including those dealing with race, ethnicity, gender, economic status and age; both have been historically scrutinized; both advocate collective and individual freedom; and both are constantly fighting for greater acceptance. "I find myself far more inspired by the struggles of someone like Chet Baker or Eric Dolphy than some glamorous Hollywood actress," says the openly gay vocalist and composer Theo Bleckmann. "Just by Eric and Baker's constant fight for acceptance and their battles with inner demons, I wonder why more gay people wouldn't look up to people like them than someone like Judy Garland, who was already accepted by the Hollywood establishment."

Jazz has, however, produced its fair share of gay luminaries, among them Billy Strayhorn, Cecil Taylor, Gary Burton, Andy Bey, Ian Shaw, Fred Hersch, Lea DeLaria, Patricia Barber and Allison Miller. And support for the gay community within jazz as a whole has mirrored the growing acceptance found in mainstream American culture. In other words, it is by no means necessary to identify oneself as gay (e.g., Rufus Wainwright, George Michael and Melissa Etheridge). Sometimes it's a matter of showing ardent support and respect for the gay community (Barbra Streisand, Madonna and Beyoncé).

Expressing the concerns and issues facing the gay community is not, of course, the first time jazz has been involved with potentially controversial identity politics. Often trumpeted as a constantly evolving, democratic art form that advocates freedom, the music has explicitly illustrated the plight of black Americans with such classics as Duke Ellington's *Black, Brown & Beige Suite*, Sonny Rollins' *Freedom Suite* and Max Roach's *Freedom Now Suite*; examined that plight through the prism of womanhood with Nina Simone's immortal "Four Women"; and offered gateways for numerous other ethnicities and nationalities to forge their cultural identity through music. So where are the jazz works that unapologetically give voice to the queer community?

As stigmas associated with gay and bisexual culture continue to fall by the wayside, jazz songs that explicitly rhapsodize or, at the very least, acknowledge the queer community are surfacing at a fair pace. Among the most engaging entries in this canon are works by openly gay artists: say, Barber's "Narcissus," which explores a Sapphic love affair, and Hersch's "Out Someplace (Blues for Matthew Shepard)," a moving piece dedicated to the 21-year-old Wyoming gay man who was murdered because of his sexual orientation.

But gay-themed work isn't exclusively solemn or serious-minded, either; rather, queer-oriented themes are being brought to the fore in ways alternately bold, brash, prankish, clever or cute. "I think there are undertones that are now coming to the surface," argues D'Angelo, who leads a band called Gay Disco, and who has given some compositions such provocative titles as "My Prostate" and "Cheek Spread." "Every time I go to a jazz gig with my band, we're like, 'Yeah, we're here, we're queer!' It doesn't seem like there is that huge battle that we used to fight."

On Dave Koz's latest disc, *Hello Tomorrow* (Concord), the saxophonist uses Burt Bacharach's "This Guy Is in Love With You" to advocate same-sex marriage. "I've refashioned that as a wedding song in support of gay marriage," Koz says. "It's an interesting way to re-listen to a classic. That's one of the reasons why I choose to sing it as opposed to playing it. It was important that I sing because of what I was trying to get across. When people listen to it, I hope they listen to it in that framework."

That's not Koz's first gay-centered musical statement. He calls his 2007 disc, *At the Movies*, his "gayest album" yet. "It starts out with a Judy Garland classic ['Over the Rainbow'] and ends with Donna Summer singing. C'mon—you want to talk about bookends?" he laughs. "I don't have a shrine to Barbra Streisand, I don't listen to disco or worship Judy Garland, but I am gay and I do love all of those songs. I wanted to pay tribute [in a way] that felt the most authentic for me."

Indeed, authenticity plays a vital role in how some gay jazz artists deal with interpreting standards. "I just don't feel like I'm being true to myself if I sing a love song or a standard and I use the word 'he,'" says pianist and singer Dena DeRose. "I remember a critic making note that on one of my early recordings I would either sing some songs in third person or sing 'she' when I'm singing directly about the affairs of the heart."

In discussing *At the Movies*, Koz also brings up the immense popularity of musical theater among gay people. It's not uncommon to find gay bars that dedicate at least one night a week to show tunes. But singing show tunes with theatrical dazzle can tip some jazz artists unwillingly into the realm of cabaret, which many jazz fans disdain or ignore. Such is the case with New

York–based vocalist and performer Raven O. More than any other genre, he considers himself a jazz singer, and he's performed with elite jazz musicians such as pianist Frank Kimbrough and saxophonists Michael Blake and Ted Nash. He's also collaborated with bassist Ben Allison for over two decades.

In summer 2010, for a limited run at New York's Bleecker Theatre, Allison supported Raven O in a one-man autobiographical show, *One Night with You*. Despite Allison's acclaim as a bassist and composer, if you mention Raven O's name in most jazz circles you're bound to hear crickets. "I don't even think [the jazz world] knows who I am," Raven O says. "It doesn't even acknowledge what I do. I've never played at any of the jazz clubs, or thought that I could even get into jazz clubs, because I'm such an underground artist."

Allison has contributed to the emerging queer canon with "Dragzilla," an homage to Raven O and Joey Arias, both cross-dressing performers, and with the stunning makeover of the theme song from *Philadelphia* that he and Arias performed last January at Winter Jazzfest in Manhattan. And the bassist isn't the only straight jazz artist who is participating in the expansion of queer expression. This year Christian Scott gave us "The Last Broken Heart (Prop 8)," a sonic interpretation of the situation around California's 2008 state amendment that banned same-sex marriages; and Sunny Jain opened his latest disc, *Taboo* (BJU), with "Jack and Jill," which featured a wry spoken-word performance that considered the fluidity of sexuality. "Sex, particularly homo- and bisexuality, is so taboo in my [Indian] culture," says drummer Jain. "So I wanted to touch upon those types of issues, because even though they're rarely spoken of, they affect us all. I wanted to bring stuff like that to the surface with my music. Through music, I feel like I do have a platform to address certain issues."

Gay themes have even found their way into jazz's most mainstream corridors. In Dianne Reeves' live monologue that precedes her take on the Temptations classic "Just My Imagination," she tells a story about a childhood crush she had on a debonair classmate. Years later, after wondering about his whereabouts, she runs into him and his *boyfriend*. In less sensitive hands, it would have come off as typical "down low" drama, but Reeves relays the story with humor and humanity. "That was based upon a composite of many gay people I knew in class," Reeves says. "I tell that story in a live-and-let-live manner, and I've had many gay people come up to me after the concert introducing me to their partners. So it's been good. In fact, I was told that my song 'Endangered Species' is a gay anthem."

Of course, identifying gay touchstones in modern jazz proves easier through lyrics and song titles than it does with instrumental music. How would one identify a purely instrumental, improvised piece as having gay overtones? Some academics have pondered that question with varying degrees of persuasiveness. Sherrie Tucker, associate professor of American studies at the University of Kansas, wrote a provocative thesis, "When Did Jazz Go Straight? A Queer Question for Jazz Studies," in which she argued that jazz was once a hotbed for gay expression until the music moved into the mainstream. She also theorized that jazz became overly masculine with the arrival of bebop.

At a 2007 conference, "Comin' Out Swingin': Sexualities in Improvisation," Kevin McNeilly, an associate producer in the department of English at the University of British Columbia, gave an introductory talk called "Connective Tissues," wherein he examined a 2005 live performance of Thelonious Monk's "Evidence" by Fred Hersch. McNeilly traced the Monk composition to the harmonic structures of Raymond Klages and Jesse Greer's sensual pop song "Just You, Just Me." In Hersch's performance, McNeilly argued, Hersch's deconstructive introduction—during which he quotes "Just You, Just Me"—suggests a queer approach because of its difference from the myriad other interpretations of the tune. "If we claim that Hersch's performance is queer, we may be cued by his disclosure of his sexual identity, but we're not asserting that he plays in a 'gay' way," McNeilly explains. "Rather, sexuality comes to consist in the temporary connective tissues: the play between sameness and difference, which his music encounters."

When this scholarly observation is brought to Hersch's attention, he quickly dismisses it. "That's just over-sensationalizing my sexuality and my approach to music," he insists.

"What I try to do is find within the musical performance itself some ways in which you can talk in a convincing way about this deconstructive potential—that sexuality can be taken apart," McNeilly explains. "My sense is that when Fred Hersch played 'Evidence,' he did some really interesting things to take apart a music that's already a deconstructive compositional practice. In some ways, it invites a listener to rethink or to re-experience what they might understand as normative."

Even though Fred Hersch became one of the first openly gay artists of our time, he hesitates to identify a decidedly gay aesthetic in his music or in jazz as a whole. "There's no real movement that musically ties me to other gay jazz musicians," he says. He also explains that his "Out Someplace" was written for a Bill T. Jones dance score, and that his 2005 disc, *Leaves of Grass*, was an exploration of Walt Whitman the poet, not Walt Whitman the gay icon.

Hersch isn't the only openly gay artist who doesn't see any noticeable gay aesthetic in modern jazz. "For me, I don't see it as much," says saxophonist and composer Charlie Kohlhase. "If you're talking about the pop culture, then I would say that there is a gay aesthetic everywhere."

"Whether you can say in terms of the musical language that there are markers of queerness, I find that a bit more problematic because I think musical language comes from cultures more broadly," adds Ingrid Monson, the Quincy Jones Professor of African-American Music at Harvard. "They've had that debate in classical music. It was a big deal in the '90s when some people wondered if Schubert was gay. Some people said that certain kinds of cadences were more feminine. I think you end up *essentializing* some characteristics of the music."

"Essentializing" might be more easily termed "prejudice," and, indeed, it's nearly impossible to discuss being gay in jazz without addressing homophobia. In 2001, James Gavin wrote a galvanizing article in this magazine that examined that very issue. Shortly after, writer Francis Davis moderated a panel discussion on homosexuality in jazz at the Village Vanguard. That conversation included Hersch, Kohlhase, Gary Burton, Andy Bey and writer Grover Sales, and was soon after summarized in a September 2002 *New York Times* article titled "In the Macho World of Jazz, Don't Ask, Don't Tell." In both articles, the jazz world was portrayed as a scary place for gay people.

"I can't speak for the whole [jazz] audience. But it's like any community: People's rhetoric is always more idealistic than what they do in practice," says Monson. "I think the rally cry around jazz has always been about racial equality. It's not just gay people; women have not always been welcomed. There's always been an investment in the sort of masculine presentation of jazz. Many authors have pondered this in many different ways. They point to the fact that African-American men in the early 20th century wanted to earn a living with dignity and respect. . . . [And that with a career as a jazz musician], you can be a man. But it's not like the white American community was very open to homosexuality during that time, either."

"Some jazz musicians give more of a homophobic front than they actually are," adds drummer Terri Lyne Carrington. "People have a greater fear of backlash based upon their need to make a living. Most jazz artists don't have that economic freedom to come out. A lot of the jazz culture has been defined by African-Americans. I don't think that African-Americans are more homophobic, but I think that it's a matter of not feeling as free [in comparison to white Americans], which still relates back to our history."

In the end it comes down to the essentiality of personal freedom, in and out of jazz. "The more you can be who you are in every aspect of your life," says Dave Koz, "the more you can say something of value with your music. I'm not just talking about being gay; it's about showing up in your life as who you are and being happy."

note

Originally published in *JazzTimes*, December 2010. Used by permission of Madavor Media.

Black Musician-Writers

Billy Taylor Replies to Art Tatum Critic

BILLY TAYLOR (*DownBeat*, 1955)

(Ed. Note: In the Aug. 10 issue of Down Beat *appeared an analysis of Art Tatum by Andre Hodeir, the European jazz critic who writes for* Jazz Hot. *Among the protests received was one from Billy Taylor, eminent jazz pianist, who was offered rebuttal space. His article follows.)*

ANDRE HODEIR may be "one of Europe's best known and most respected jazz critics but his analysis (?) of Art Tatum is nothing short of ridiculous. A "provocative piece" indeed!

How could anyone be so presumptuous as to try to evaluate the talent of *any* great jazz artist *solely* on the basis of *one group* of his recordings? Creativity cannot be turned on and off like a light in a recording studio, and as extensive as the five 12″ LP Clef records are, they do not present every facet of the Art Tatum I know.

Anyone who has ever heard Tatum play after hours in a setting of his own choosing will bear out the fact that this is a completely different Art Tatum from the one who plays either in clubs, jazz concerts, or on records. When he plays for a select audience of his own choosing, even his "arrangements" take on a new dimension. The fabulous technical facility is then used as it should be used, to present and exploit the creative power which sets Tatum apart from other jazz pianists.

According to Messers Funk and Wagnall:—

Genius: 1—Extraordinary intellectual gifts, evidenced in original creation, expression or achievement.

2—Remarkable aptitude for some special pursuit; a distinguishing natural capacity or tendency . . .

3—A person of phenomenal and original powers for productivity in art, science, statesmanship, etc. . . .

4—The dominant influence or essential animating principle of anything . . .

Considering these definitions one by one, I think Norman Granz was correct in calling Art Tatum a genius.

Hodeir admits that in his opinion, Tatum is:

1—Extraordinarily gifted.

2—A man able to conceive and then execute things which others, sometimes able to conceive, simply cannot execute.

3—More of a pianiste d'orchestre than any other great jazz pianist.

Even among the avant-garde modernists, Hodeir admits, it would be hard to find a jazz pianist for whom Tatum is not the greatest of them all . . . (Tatum) seems to have cast a spell over the younger generation of pianists.

As Hodeir admits, the European critic is definitely handicapped by not being able to hear a particular jazzman in person. If he had heard Art Tatum at almost anytime between 1941 and 1951, I think he would be less prone to "consider these albums as a panoramic picture which the celebrated pianist at the high point of his career, has drawn of his own work."

ART TATUM is one of the few name artists who throughout his entire recording career has always been allowed to choose his own material. *Obviously* he picked the music from his repertoire which he liked best for this series of recordings, but since the *entire set* consists of at least *five more* 12″ LP albums, there is much in the way of repertoire which had not been heard by Mr. Hodeir at the time he wrote his article. Also, more often than not, it is the record company that *arranges the order* in which the musical selections are presented.

I, too, would like to hear the Tatum interpretation of *Boplicity*, but in all fairness, although many musicians agree that it is a great jazz tune, I have never heard it played *anywhere* by *anyone* other than on the Miles Davis record. I am sure that many musicians must know it, but I cannot recall *even one* other record of it by a jazz great.

In his criticism of Tatum's selection of tunes, Hodeir says "these albums deliberately sacrifice beautiful melody for sentimental ballads and authentic jazz pieces for popular hits." Yet he has nothing to say about Benny Carter's

Blues in My Heart, Ellington's *Sittin' and Rocking* or *In a Sentimental Mood,* Will Marion Cook's *I'm Coming, Virginia,* or Edgar Sampson's *Stompin' at the Savoy,* and I suppose that because of their popularity, *Over the Rainbow, Embraceable You,* and *Can't We Be Friends?* cannot be considered beautiful melodies.

WHEN HODEIR compares the approaches used by Charlie Parker, Louis Armstrong, and Lester Young to a melody with that of Tatum, he is on very shaky ground. With all due respect to their individual talents, they are still only concerned with playing *one note at a time.* It is therefore absurd to try to draw comparisons between their approach and Tatum's. Compare him with another pianist if you will. Fats Waller was one of the swingingest pianists who ever lived, but he had neither the technical facility nor the imagination required to use the Tatum approach and Fats was the first to admit it.

The fact that "every jazz pianist, even a fourth-rate saloon pianist, ornaments a theme as he plays it" does not negate that kind of approach nor does it necessarily indicate a lack of ambition. Tatum has certainly developed jazz solo piano playing to its highest point of virtuosity to date, but again I must insist, records, even the extensive Granz set, have not presented the complete Art Tatum.

note

Originally published in *DownBeat,* September 21, 1955.

Creativity and Change

WAYNE SHORTER (*DownBeat,* 1968)

Art. Art as a competitive thing among artists. I've been wondering how it has come about that art *is,* in fact, a competitive thing among artists. I wonder if artists choose to compete among themselves, or are they goaded, pushed, or lured into it as a result of the makeup of this particular society? I wonder if a young musician, hearing another musician, has an instinctive desire to compete with this other musician or instead to join forces and compare notes? I wonder if the two of them were to get together and compare notes, and their notes were appraised by a third party, the critic, would these two artists be so influenced by what the third party says that they would strive to compete with one another to please the critic? In addition, the critic speaks to a fourth party, the public, and in pleasing the critic do you please the public?

I wonder if a poll or a contest is valid to give artists an incentive to create, to go on, or to run the mile in less than a minute. Is art an art or a sport? I think polls, awards and Oscars come right out of the school system—the star you get on your paper, the A B C D mark. If we could get rid of the stigma that grading over such a long period of time has produced, I think we might have a clearer idea of what a person does when he is creating something. For instance, if a person wins first place in a category in the arts through a voting system, and he feels good about it, is he actually going to create or merely perpetuate the poll system?

It's hard to get away from voting or polls all the way, because, if you're going to play for an audience, the applause is the same thing in miniature size. Some people even consider applause as greater than a citation or trophy. Applause *is* gratifying to me and a lot of other musicians. Some musicians would deny it, but I know how they feel inside. I cannot say truthfully that lack of applause is *not* gratifying for me, because I can't say that lack of applause means lack of recognition. That has happened to me quite a bit, especially when I first started out. Even now it happens sometimes, but then when I come down from the bandstand, someone will come up and say something profound about the whole set, not just about me. This one person sounds like he's speaking for the whole audience, and he might say, "That was a deep set—a lot of thought going on." I think in that sense he was trying to say that there was no room for applause—they didn't want to disturb the essence of the moment.

Does a person create because of recognition by a large body, and, if he is recognized, does he stop creating? I wonder if any artist can grade himself, using himself as his own ruler? Maybe that has to be taught. I've rarely had a teacher who said, "I'm going to teach you to grade yourself against yourself, use yourself as your own incentive force." You can draw power, drive, from yourself, from nature and not necessarily from another person. It's hard to do, but once you know what it is and you start to reach for it, it's really something. If anyone has seen *2001*, it's like reaching for that black monolith, that symbol of Why and What and Where. If you're curious enough about yourself, you don't have too much time to be curious about what the next person is doing. You don't try to compete with something superficial and exterior, a "keeping up with the Joneses" idea. I think that if artists learned to use themselves as their own ruler, then audiences would have to learn to do this too. When they go to see Broadway plays they won't have to read what the critic says.

Who decides what is good art? It's a highly individual thing, with or without a body of people calling themselves critics or an audience calling themselves critics. A lot of people do not want to be individual thinkers and analyze something by themselves, so they turn to polls and awards to make up their minds. If enough people make up their minds that way, they might miss a lot of creative people who have something to give, without asking for something in return. When an artist creates he can feed the soul, heal the soul, make the soul well, but a lot of people in an audience listen not with their souls, but with computerized minds, assembled and conditioned by the system which includes polls and awards.

I wonder if those who believe in polls and awards believe that they are building a bridge across a body of water for someone who can't swim? The polls may be like water wings, but there'll come a time when you have to take those water wings off. What I'm worried about is the perpetuation of water wings and bridges. I don't believe that the designer, the critic, really perpetuates it, although he has an advantageous perch. The only one who can perpetuate it is the person who needs it. As I write now, I'm trying not to sit in judgment, because everything is en route, everything is in the interim. If I were to judge, I might as well try to get a great big pencil about the size of the sun, and put a period on this earth. That would be supreme judgment.

If a critic has the job of criticizing and rating records, and he is torn between giving record A a high rating and giving record B a lower rating, and the reason he is torn is that the musicians on record B, while not as good, are trying very hard, and he doesn't want to step on the toes of the musicians on record A, that's a hard thing to be confronted with, especially if that's your job. His job and his conscience . . . his conscience is a job too. If he made up his mind to give record A a higher rating and record B a lower rating, and the musicians on record B were very honest, I think that, though they may be hurt, along with honesty comes a kind of strength. But would their efforts to get a higher rating bypass real creativity? I suppose it's up to the musicians to rely on their strength to know which way to go, no matter what who says.

Is creativity good, in the sense of originality? How can you be *so* original, when you walk a little bit like your mother or father, or have the color of your father's eyes, or you make a gesture and someone says, "You did that just like your father used to do." Charlie Parker, for example, said that when he was young, his idols on the alto saxophone were Rudy Vallee and

Jimmy Dorsey. If you've heard Bird, and if you've heard Rudy Vallee and Jimmy Dorsey, I think you'd have to dig very deep, tear off many layers of wallpaper before you could find any similarity in sound, approach, or technique. I would say that the only thing which would confirm what Bird said about his admiration would be the sophistication of his approach. It's the sophistication of Westernized music, Western scales. But let's go back even further. Western scales came from around Greece, Jerusalem and Arabia. They're *world* scales, really. People are taught music history this way, separating Western music from Eastern music, but I think it's one big circle. It's hard to keep from using labels. For instance, when I said that Bird idolized Rudy Vallee and Dorsey, some people's minds would *stop* and they'd say, "Ooo, *that's* who he dug!" But I tend to use those names as a springboard into history, going all the way back to the great explosion that started this planet. You can't just go on what Mr. X said, you've got to do a little thinking of your own.

We hear a lot of the word "freedom," and if you're going to have freedom, a critic has to have freedom too. A lot of critics don't consider criticism a job. With some, it's a very esthetic thing. When they put their thoughts on paper about something they've seen or heard, they've more than seen or heard it. They get involved in it. I'm not saying that they get so involved that they're "swayed," because a *great* critic can retain a helluva sense of balance. When reading his words on paper you can feel that, actually, he's not criticizing something—his words turn into a poetic thing, become an extension of the art experience. At the same time he's not putting anyone or anything up on a pedestal. Art comes first—the Baby, save the Baby!

I'd like to return to the other side of competition—the joining, the getting together, comparing notes. When I was 16 I used to get a copy of a magazine that had articles about a musician who was playing a new music called bebop, and I heard Charlie Parker and Bud Powell on the radio. I had to get to New York . . . because of reading about how things had started at Minton's, where a lot of getting together and comparing of notes had been going on. A number of musicians then were thrown together out of poverty. They lived together, cooked together . . . they even helped bury each other. Today, the ones out of the '40s who have made it, the ones who have their own groups now, can always remember the togetherness they had then, but through their fame they have to travel their separate roads. There's some resurgence of that now among the younger musicians—the wanting to get together. They want to get together in large numbers—the big band thing, the studio thing. A few musicians have studios where they can teach students and at the same time get together, but the jam session thing is gone. That was the other way of getting together . . . just jamming.

I hear all across the country, "Where can I go to play, where can I go to be heard, what is it like in New York?" It's the same old question, but New York is not the same old New York, as far as being the center of almost anything. When I finally did go to New York in the days when I was commuting from New Jersey with my horn, I remember just before I was drafted into the Army, I went to a place called Cafe Bohemia. Charlie Parker had just died, and I walked in with my horn. There was a drummer there who now lives in Europe; there was an organ player who just got in town (he's very big today), and an alto saxophone player who's very big today had just arrived. They were all on the bandstand with Oscar Pettiford. I had a chance to sit in with them. Everyone was together, liking each other. When we got down from the bandstand we were shaking hands and talking, and you could see the light in all these people's eyes as if they were making plans for getting groups together out of the people who were there. I was feeling kind of bad because I was going into the Army and I didn't know whether I was going to be included in those plans. When I went into the Army, I felt, "That's the last of the jam session thing," but when I got out it was still perpetuating a little bit. There were enough jam sessions going on so that well-known musicians could get around to know people and see who they would like to hire.

Getting started means getting confidence, putting yourself in a context. Being around musicians who are playing, meeting them, talking to them, you're getting conditioned. You're watching how a musician walks up to the microphone and plays, or how another one may shy away from the spotlight. You make up your mind how you want to be, because the way you are does affect what comes out of the horn. You can produce barriers of shyness, barriers of lack of confidence, or barriers of over-confidence. You have to get your own balance together.

I guess I was pretty lucky, because even when I was in the Army, I had a chance to work with one of the well-known groups. I was stationed in the East, Ft. Dix, so I was not far from the Blue Note in Philadelphia, and not far from New York and Washington, D.C. I was there the night when I *really* heard Coltrane. (I had heard him before in New York but I *really heard* him this night. He was breaking away from something.) I would be in New York on a weekend pass, playing, and Coltrane would come out of nowhere and we'd talk. As a result, when I got out of the Army, Trane and I spent a lot of time together in his apartment in New York. We spent a lot of time at the piano, and he was telling me what he was doing, which way he was going, and what he was trying to work on. We'd stay all day and all night. I would play the piano and he would play his horn, then he would play the piano and I would play my horn. That kind of getting together is not going on too much now. Maybe in certain areas of New York, musicians who live in the Village who have lofts can get together. I'd like to see more of it. I'd like to branch out and help this get going. On my next record date I'd like to do a large thing, maybe 19 or 22 pieces, and call on those musicians to help perform this work. While recording, I'd like to create the atmosphere that we're not just at a recording session. I've written something down but we'll have a jam session spirit.

The term "musician" can become a hard shell. You can become callous and impersonal, but there's still a human thing there. For example, two musicians will meet in Europe (it always happens in a way-out place somewhere), and they belong to two different schools of music, but they will be glad to see each other, shaking hands and talking. I had a long talk with a very well-known saxophonist in Switzerland—some people call him the father of the jazz saxophone. We were just sitting there and I asked him how he was doing, and before he said he was doing all right, he started talking about economics. It was as if I were at home talking to an uncle. In the back of my mind I was thinking of people who admire people; a young fan of 17 for instance. If he could see a young musician that he knows and an older musician he would feel, "Wow, there they are *together*." I used to feel the same way.

In Paris in 1961 (I went to Paris with a well-known group), the bandleader walked into my room along with Bud Powell. We all sat around and then everyone left except Bud Powell. He looked at me, my horn was on the bed, and he said, "Can you play something for me?" I said okay, and I was thinking about when I was 17 and had to sneak into Birdland and sit way in the back and watch Bud play. I picked up my horn and tried to play one of the things he wrote named after his daughter, *Celia*, and then I tried something else of his, just playing the melody. When I finished he looked at me and smiled, didn't say anything else, got up, kept smiling and walked out.

At this point in my life, when I see people who are famous and great, I don't want to ever lose the memory of the awe I had when I was younger. I don't want to become so sophisticated and confident that I can say "We're all in this together"—a sort of smug "thing." Now, when I am in the company of a large number of great musicians, I feel very comfortable and I can see them as human beings, see myself as a human being among them, and respect and dig whatever they have produced through the years.

Where is the new music going? I don't know if that's as important as where did it come from, because if you know where it came from, it's going anyway. I don't like labels, but I'll say "new music" anyway—total involvement. When you're playing, the music is not just you and the horn—the music is the microphone, the chair, the door opening, the spotlight, something rattling. From soul to universe.

I saw something on television where they had total involvement. Two men were discussing what was about to happen. Then there was a little ballet. It started and the camera went from the dancers to the two men talking, and they were a part of the ballet, still talking about it. I liked that, as a start.

I think this is a very exciting time to live in. Some people are concerned with an end of things. Then, all of a sudden you hear a small voice say, "this is a renaissance." Things are happening now that have never happened in history and art will reflect this. Everything is speeded up so you can see the change and feel yourself changing. Those who don't change, who refuse to change, can feel themselves not changing, and some of them don't like it.

Every time we go to California, I always make it a point to go to Berkeley. I've visited the homes of students out there. Some of them are 14 years younger than I am, and everything was very communicative. I found it easy just to be *me*, not to be young. We were all together. No one asked me my age. They want change.

About certain people being reluctant to change for the betterment of all concerned—I find that the people who find it easiest to change and keep evolving, who don't want a status quo, are able to move around. A person who is stationary finds it difficult to change. In the business I'm in, we move around and travel like troubadours. We are not bound to any city government or neighborhood government. The students I met out in California live in Berkeley and go to school there, but I noticed that they kept moving around. They'd go to San Francisco, then to L.A. and up to Seattle, then all the way to New York, and then back to school.

I saw evidence of a great change when we played two concerts at Berkeley. One change was this—the concert was given by a 21-year old Chinese girl, a jazz impresario. She told me she had been listening to jazz since she was 8. She put on the concert with a lot of opposition from the school staff about allotting money and other things, but she worked and did it. She had some of the most well-known names in jazz. At the last concert she gave, there were over 20,000 people at the Greek Theater in Berkeley. The audience was rock 'n' roll oriented and most of the people had never seen these artists before and had rarely heard them. I saw them turning their ears to jazz, something they had never really heard. They focused their attention and they listened with a lot of respect and at one point they kind of went wild with applause.

When I hear a jazz musician say, "Well the young people—rock 'n' roll is their thing—they're not going to even listen to jazz"—I think that they'll change and grow up. Rock 'n' roll is changing with them. I'm hearing a whole lot of things from them. The "labels" are being taken off the bottles. As I said about the different scales, Western and Greek, it's all one big thing. I saw kids with long hair, beards and sandals, sitting right down in front of the bandstand and they were part of a thing called jazz. The same thing happened in New York at the Village Gate. I met a lot of young people there, and I spoke to one person who had long hair and everything. I'll describe the way the person looked and then you'll have to piece together how he looked and what he does. He had long hair, beard and moustache, and he had on beads, a buckskin jacket, and an Apache head wrapping. He writes opera! He came to listen to the music labeled jazz, and he's meshing and welding what he knows about sound with what he hears everywhere. He said, "I have to be here. It's part of the thing."

East and West I saw evidence of a meeting of minds. The change I like is always that getting together. The person who has been labeled hippie and rock is breaking out and taking his own label off. The younger people will tend to look at the artists who are really doing something and use them as guides, so there's nothing really to worry about.

I'm saying all these things because I myself don't like to stand still. Art Blakey told me once, "Music is like a river. It must flow." When someone would ask, "Why does it have to flow?" he would say, "If a body of water has no inlet or outlet, it's bound to get stagnant." I doubt if you'd find anything living in it. He who drinks from it will have an awful stomachache—or start digging six feet. Any person knows when he's stagnant. If he doesn't know, there's a whole lot of "camouflage" going on. You can be taught to know things, and you can be taught *not to know* things. If you think you're not stagnant, check yourself out.

When we played at Berkeley with a 19-piece orchestra, I looked out in the audience, I looked at Miles, I looked at Gil Evans, I looked at a 19-year-old girl who was playing the harp, then in the French horn section there was an elderly man whose hair was stone white, there was a middle-aged lady playing French horn next to him, then I looked at Howard Johnson on tuba, and I said, "All ages, all ages here, and we're having a ball with sound." No one questioned "What is this—it's not normal." The young female harpist would only ask a few technical questions and that was all. That's what goes on in music, the interplay between ages. I saw life come to *life* that night. I'd like to see that with young people and the elders throughout the world. The youth can't get their hands on the *tanks*, they can't get their hands on the plans at the Pentagon and the Kremlin, they can't get their hands on the buttons, they don't have access to the material power, but if the elders are so nervous about the youngsters and they aren't getting nervous about the power *they* have in *their* hands, evidently the youngsters' *mental* power is upsetting someone.

Just recently I've been looking at clothes, and I found one place in New York where a lot of young people hang out. One thing caught me as soon as I walked in—they were playing records in the store. Everybody was looking at clothes and some people were kind of swinging and swaying to the music. I went back to the store another time—no one was buying, everyone was dancing, and the owner was dancing, too. He said, "Well, the main thing is to have some fun, as long as I can survive." He's not afraid if someone comes in the store and doesn't buy. They'll buy or trade something eventually and at the same time they're trading a little happiness. I like that approach. The same spirit—breaking up something that's stiff—happens on the bandstand sometimes. When there is an obviously straight up and down audience, sometimes I know that the musicians feel compelled to throw themselves into the music and break up the ice.

Life to me is like an art, because life has been created by an artist, the Chief Architect. Some people can only relate their soul to God. It seems as if they can only do it when it's time to go to church, or when times are hard. They think that the soul in relation to the universe has to do with religion all the time. I think part of the stiffness we see is due to that, because they cannot relate their soul to a table, for example. They can't see any practical use in relating their soul to a table, to a bug on a windowsill, to musicians on a bandstand, or a picture hanging on a wall, or salt and pepper. You can say that's going from the sublime to the ridiculous, but is it? It's like saying, "A bird does not fly because it has wings. It has wings because it flys."

People who are hung up in stiffness think in issues, broad issues, the issue of making a living, the issue of crime in the streets. The issue turns out to be a hangup—the issue of asking someone to come over to your house to have dinner. What is an attitude and how can you change an attitude? They say how can you legislate attitudes, but when you get down to the nitty gritty, you say, "Come over to my house and have dinner." Some people say, "I don't want to associate with 'outside' music, I don't want anything to do with it." What I hear from younger people is who needs that hangup, everything is everything, let it be, let's do it whenever, if I can't get you tomorrow, whenever. . . .

Among these young people there's no room for jealousy as a force, jealousy between men and women, jealousy about things. I like to call jealousy an emotional rage, and it exists very much among the older age bracket. In the last few years I haven't heard the word "jealousy" used among the young people. When I look at some of the soap operas, I see in their conflicts that they're still perpetuating those things that the young people have almost completely eliminated.

I can't talk about music at this stage of my life without putting it in a wider context. I can't talk about social ills or goods without trying to sneak in something about art. Many musicians who came up about my time are taking care of business when they're not performing, taking care of paperwork, legal things. For a long time I used to hear, "All you've got to do is play your horn and the business will take care of itself, you'll have people to take care of business for you." I think musicians today should try to read about business and copyright laws, etc. They should know what certain words mean when they're confronted with a contract and not just look at the number of zeros attached to a digit and a dollar sign. I wonder how many musicians today have thought of drawing up wills.

Music has always played a great part in inventions. I think there may be something coming along that would be an extension of the TV set and I believe that music will play a part in it. Along with these inventions there comes a new amendment in your business mind. I've written to Washington to get the juke box bill passed, and I know Stan Kenton's working on it. That, and royalties for the way an artist interprets a certain piece of music. No one's getting any royalties from juke boxes. The copyright law says that royalties should be distributed to the artists in the event of any mechanical reproduction of musical sound. If they can't get the juke box bill passed, anyone who invents something to reproduce music may look at the juke box as a loophole, since it would be advantageous for him not to pay the people whose music is being reproduced.

I mentioned the idea of "total involvement." Everything I've said about art, about youth, about business, indicates that the music and musician of tomorrow will be totally involved. Neither he nor his art will be confined to the stage.

note
Originally published in *DownBeat*, December 12, 1968.

An Artist Speaks Bluntly

ARCHIE SHEPP (*DownBeat*, 1965)

I address myself to bigots—those who are so inadvertently, those who are cold and premeditated with it. I address myself to those "in" white hipsters who think niggers never had it so good (Crow Jim) and that it's time something was done about restoring the traditional privileges that have always accrued to the whites exclusively (Jim Crow). I address myself to sensitive chauvinists—the greater part of the white intelligentsia—and the insensitive, with whom the former have this in common: the uneasy awareness that "Jass" is an ofay's word for a nigger's music (viz Duke and Pulitzer).

I address myself to George Russell, a man whose work I have always respected and admired, who in an inopportune moment with an ill-chosen phrase threw himself squarely into the enemy camp. I address myself to Leonard Feather, who was quick to exploit that phrase and a few others, and who has asked me to be in his *Encyclopedia of Jazz* (I prefer to be in *Who's Who*; they at least know that reference works are about men and not the reverse). I address myself to Buck Walmsley, to Don DeMicheal and Dan Morgenstern, in short, to that entire "critical community" that has had far more access to this and other media of communication than I and fellows of my sort.

Allow me to say that I am—with men of other complexions, dispositions, etc.—about Art. I have about 15 years of dues-paying—others have spent more—which permits me to speak with some authority about the crude stables (clubs) where black men are groomed and paced like thoroughbreds to run till they bleed or else are hacked up outright for Lepage's glue. I am about 28 years in these United States, which, in my estimation is one of the most vicious, racist social systems in the world—with the possible exceptions of Northern Rhodesia, South Africa, and South Viet Nam.

I am, for the moment, a helpless witness to the bloody massacre of my people on streets that run from Hayneville through Harlem. I watch them die. I pray that I don't die. I've seen the once children—now men of my youth get down on scag, shoot it in the fingers, and then expire on frozen tenement roofs or in solitary basements, where all our frantic thoughts raced to the same desperate conclusion: "I'm sorry it was him; glad it wasn't me."

I have seen the tragedy of perennially starving families, my own. I am that tragedy. I am the host of the dead: Bird, Billie, Ernie, Sonny, whom you, white America, murdered out of a systematic and unloving disregard. I am a nigger shooting heroin at 15 and dead at 35 with hog's head cheeses for arms and horse for blood.

But I am more than the images you superimpose on me, the despair that you inflict. I am the persistent insistence of the human heart to be free. I wish to regain that cherished dignity that was always mine. My esthetic answer to your lies about me is a simple one: you can no longer defer my dream. I'm gonna sing it. Dance it. Scream it. And if need be, I'll steal it from this very earth.

Get down with me, white folks. Go where I go. But think this: injustice is rife. Fear of the truth will out. The murder of James Powell, the slaughter of 30 Negroes in Watts, the wake of Chu-Lai are crimes that would make God's left eye jump. That establishment that owns the pitifully little that is left of me can absolve itself only through the creation of equitable relationships among all men, or else the world will create for itself new relationships that exclude the entrepreneur and the procurer.

Some of you are becoming a little frightened that we—niggers—ain't keepin' this thing simple enough. "The sound of surprise"? Man, you don't want no surprises from me.

How do I know that?

Give me leave to state this unequivocal fact: jazz is the product of the whites—the ofays—too often my enemy. It is the progeny of the blacks—my kinsmen. By this I mean: you own the music, and we make it. By definition, then, you own the people who make the music. You own us in whole chunks of flesh. When you dig deep inside our already disemboweled corpses and come up with a solitary diamond—because you don't want to flood the market—how different are you from the DeBeers of South Africa or the profligates who fleeced the Gold Coast? All right, there are niggers with a million dollars but ain't no nigger got a *billion* dollars.

I give you, then, my brains back, America. You have had them before, as you had my father's, as you took my mother's: in outhouses, under the back porch, next to black snakes who should have bitten you then.

I ask only: don't you ever wonder just what my collective rage will—as it surely must—be like, when it is—as it inevitably will be—unleashed? Our vindication will be black as the color of suffering is black, as Fidel is black, as Ho Chi Minh is black. It is thus that I offer my right hand across the worlds of suffering to black compatriots everywhere. When they fall victim to war, disease, poverty—all systematically enforced—I fall with them, and I am a yellow skin, and they are black like me or even white. For them and me I offer this prayer, that this 28th year of mine will never again find us all so poor, nor the rapine forces of the world in such sanguinary circumstances.

And you can tell Ira Gitler that he is a fool. "Repelled flies" indeed! What a thing it is to play God, snuff out yet born professional lives with impunity—worse, ignorance.

To Walmsley: one of the most thrilling musical experiences of my life was to play for the people of Chicago. You know it was amid cries of "MORE" that we were reluctantly allowed to leave that stage that night. You didn't seem to be able to muster the journalistic honesty to report that, though. Perhaps the jeers you heard were produced in that crabbed, frightened il-logicality of your own post-R&B consciousness. Your patent opinions were predictable, your tastes alarmingly similar: Stanley, Woody, and Gary.

I leave you with this for what it's worth. I am an antifascist artist. My music is functional. I play about the death of me by you. I exult in the life of me in spite of you. I give some of that life to you whenever you listen to me, which right now is never. My music is for the people. If you are a bourgeois, then you must listen to it on my terms. I will not let you misconstrue me. That era is over. If my music doesn't suffice, I will write you a poem, a play. I will say to you in every instance, "Strike the Ghetto. Let my people go."

note
Originally published in *DownBeat*, December 16, 1965.

The Jazz Pianist-Purist

HERBIE NICHOLS (*Rhythm*, 1946)

In this article I will tell you of a very rebellious person who has succeeded in reaching an enviable position among jazz musicians. This fellow aroused my interest many years ago when he first played at an uptown spot called Minton's. It is only now that I've sought a more personal contact with his greatness. This fellow happens to be the elusive Thelonious Monk, pianist, songwriter, and mad lover of jazz.

Dizzy Gillespie and Charlie Parker, whose musical offerings also en-tertain me quite fully, will also attest to the independent mind that Monk possesses. This in itself should arouse one's curiosity about the man's music.

I would claim that the reason why Monk does not play in any combination with these two gentlemen is all a matter of tempo. This fellow seems to find his greatest pleasure playing in a slow tempo. It almost borders on the lethargic and may well be a key to his total personality. Monk has to be in a great mood before he will swing out in a fast tempo, and he can swing as effectively as any I know. However, for the most part the faster tempos of Dizzy and Yardbird find him lost, without expression and constitutionally overwrought.

In his renditions he reminds me of Duke Ellington. His expressive and soulful figures are a reminder of Duke. This is where the similarity ends as you will find. Monk's rebellious spirit through the years has not permitted him to gain the all-around experience of an Ellington and so his enterprise has suffered.

It is strange to review how expressive such masters and lovers of slow tempos as Duke Ellington, Thelonious Monk, Louis Armstrong and Coleman Hawkins really are.

A few weeks ago I made a call at his 63rd Street apartment and found him practicing very thoughtfully on his Klein piano. I felt pretty good when I realized how satisfied he was with his instrument. He invited me to try it out. First I played one of his compositions which I learned a few weeks ago at the Spotlite which he had played with "Hawk." Later I played some of my tunes which he seemed to like. We promptly agreed to swap three piano arrangements of our tunes. I would arrange "Stratosphere," "Striving," and "Sailing" for him and he agreed to arrange "Ruby, My Dear," "Round Midnight," and another very expressive tune which he hadn't named or whose name he had forgotten. On the day of the proposed swap my tunes were the only ones completed. However, I haven't given up all hope of eventually learning his tunes which I will play morning, noon, and night.

One might say that Thelonious Monk is forever having a battle of music at the piano and always comes out the winner. This is probably true. His eyes light up when he speaks of instrumentalists getting the right "sounds" out of their instruments. He is forever searching for better "sounds," as he loves to say. He doesn't seek these effects elsewhere. He creates them at his Klein piano. This way of thinking throughout the years has resulted in the creation of a system of playing which is the strangest I have heard and may someday revolutionize the art of swing piano playing.

For the past few weeks Monk has been out of work and he let me know that he was completely dissatisfied with the meager gold offered him. He said that the leaders ought to "let everybody live. Pay a fellow a good price especially when someone can really blow." And there you have it, folks.

Whatever his plans happen to be, they are a complete mystery to me. Monk travels in his own little world getting a greater kick out of his Klein piano than he does out of the whole jazz industry.

Hearing his piano rendition of his composition, "Ruby, My Dear," is one of the greatest pleasures I've had listening to jazz. This song could be another "Body and Soul," if he would only put it down on paper and let a few other people learn it. Some of his other new and old compositions are "You Needn't," "What Now," and "Y Don't U Try Now." To my mind all of these tunes are strange and worthy creations.

Thelonious Monk is one more jazz purist who believes that the rhythm section is the most important section of the band. The recent Coleman Hawkins rhythm of Denzil Best, Monk, pianist, about Monk, he threw up his hands and said that he could only rationalize the man's strange oddness by speculating as to his foreign birth. As far as I know, Monk has been a New Yorker ever since he was a kid, although he might well tell you that he was born in Egypt. On the other hand this possible explanation might clear up quite a few things at that.

note

Originally published in *Rhythm*, July 1946.

Smack! Memories of Fletcher Henderson

REX STEWART (*DownBeat*, 1965)

Today's jazz listener is likely to be unaware of the huge debt that current music owes to James Fletcher Henderson. Ragtime, swing, bop, and Third Stream all stem from the same tree. Fashions in music happen and change with such speed that it becomes increasingly difficult to realize what an infant jazz still is, in comparison with other art forms.

Further, there exists an explainable—but notwithstanding, total—lack of communication between our current favorites—Charlie Mingus, John Coltrane, Thelonious Monk, Miles Davis, and Neophonic jazz—and what has gone on before—Jelly Roll Morton, Willard Robison, Bix Beiderbecke, etc.—which makes this contemporary scene possible.

Fletcher Henderson was a bridge between the earliest forms and what later evolved. I consider myself blessed to have been there and a part of the action in the '20s in New York, when musical history was being made.

By strange coincidence, the two giants who I believe played the biggest roles in the development of jazz—Henderson and Duke Ellington—had a great deal in common.

Henderson, fondly known as Smack, was a chemistry major in his native Cuthbert, Ga. He arrived in New York City scheduled to do postgraduate work at New York University. However, he soon found it took much more money for school in swift-paced New York than he had anticipated back in the red-clay country of Georgia. Fortunately, he knew W. C. Handy and other popular songwriters of the day from back home and was soon playing piano background for record dates. What started out to be just a means toward finishing his education turned into a life's career.

Duke, on the other hand, went to New York from Washington, D.C., a fine-arts major with a scholarship to Pratt Institute of Art. He turned it down to continue his career as a musician.

Duke and Smack were pianists and possessed middle-class family backgrounds. Ellington's father was a white-collar government worker while Henderson's was a high-school principal. The resemblance continued as both Henderson and Ellington became bandleaders, equally handsome, affable, and erudite. Henderson had preceded Ellington to New York by some years and was already a figure on the New York scene when Elmer Snowden, with young Ellington on piano, arrived in town.

New York at that period was piano crazy, perhaps because the combination of bootleg whisky and relief from the tensions of the war provided a happy-go-lucky atmosphere for most people. Harlem was the stomping ground for many pianists—Luckey Roberts, Willie (The Lion) Smith, James P. Johnson, and the up-and-coming Fats Waller.

Thomas (Fats) Waller always stood a bit apart from the other greats of the instrument, because somehow he thought in terms of an orchestra. At a party or social gathering, he'd play the rags, stomps, or blues like everyone else. But that was only one side of him. Often, sitting in a cafe musing at the piano, he would explain to his enraptured audience as he struck a chord "this is the sax section," another chord "now, here comes the brass." He always strove to weave some sort of musical fabric into a tune.

It was not strange, therefore, that Fats became both Duke's and Smack's tutor at about the same time.

Fats loved the big-band sound of our Roseland group, and he also enjoyed the imaginative smaller group that Duke led at the Kentucky Club. Fats sat in at Roseland, coaching Smack on orchestral speculations, and then went down to Duke's gig, where he also sat in.

Fletcher had a struggle with himself to start arranging—for one thing, he had Don Redman with his group who did arrangements and employed much of Fats' idiom in his writings.

Meanwhile, Duke absorbed Fats' teachings and proceeded to utilize them until he brought his own inventive mind to jazz. This is where Duke and Fletcher started going in divergent directions. Smack fell asleep at the switch, while Duke, perhaps under the prodding of his manager, Irving Mills, explored every possible angle to make his music identifiable. This is one reason that Ellington chose to write his own compositions.

In the mid-'20s, however, Henderson's band was the talk of the town among musicians. His was the second Negro orchestra to play an all-season engagement at Roseland Ballroom on New York's Gay White Way. All the famous musicians hung around in front of the railing of our bandstand at Roseland, eager to hear (and borrow) from Smack. It seems like only yesterday when Frank Skinner, Archie Bleyer, Joe Glover, Georgie Bassman—to name only a few—would haunt Roseland in order to learn from the master.

Smack was not only the boss of his own bailiwick—New York—but of the entire country, for that matter.

The main reason was our broadcasts from Roseland during the winter months we were in residence. Along with this, there were the eastern tours for booker Charlie Shribman, where we did tremendous repeat business, especially in the coalfields of Pennsylvania. As a matter of fact, we opened up the area for dance bands, and it was on one of those early tours that we met Pa and Ma Dorsey and their two lads, Tom and James.

Henderson's great popularity stemmed from the music, the many great musicians in the band, and the man himself. Smack was a man of imposing stature, about 6 feet 2 or so. His complexion was that of an octoroon, and in his youth he could have been mistaken for an Italian, as long as he was wearing his hat, because his hair was on the sandy side for his skin color. He was a pleasant man, gentle and thoughtful. He could be frivolous or serious, according to his mood. However, even in his zany moments, there would be overtones of gentility. His greatness also lay in his impeccable selection of sidemen . . . Louis Armstrong, Benny Carter, Coleman Hawkins, Don Redman.

Don played a most important role in the Henderson band. Short-statured, brown-skinned, this little giant arrived in New York in the mid-'20s from Piedmont, W.Va. At the time he joined Fletcher, the band was a Dixie-landish outfit, like most groups of the time. This loose approach did not satisfy Don, who, having been a music major in college, recognized the beauty that could be obtained if music were organized harmonically.

Redman set out to prove his point, over the objections of many musicians who felt that arranged music would take away from their creative ability. On the other hand, Don received a lot of encouragement from Smack, from Will Vodery (who gave the jazz flavor to the Flo Ziegfeld's shows), Will Marion Cook, and other leading Negro musicians.

The Henderson band assumed another dimension with Redman's arrangements. When Smack heard Louis Armstrong, in Chicago, playing licks that emphasized the dancing of a team called Dave and Tressie, this was quickly orchestrated the Redman way. The new concept (featuring figures made by the brass that paralleled the syncopation of the dancers) was copied immediately by other bands.

Later, another of Don's ideas was paraphrased and parlayed into a career by Tommy Dorsey and others. Remember *Marie*, *Blue Skies*, and the parody of *On the Sunny Side of the Street* utilizing an obbligato countermelody with lyrics? Redman was the originator.

Actually, the Henderson band was a group of jazz giants—and about the biggest assortment of characters ever assembled to produce magnificent music. I was in my early 20s when Armstrong picked me as his replacement in Fletch's band. I joined reluctantly, and it took me a long time to overcome my awe at sitting in Louis' chair, playing the very same music and trying vainly to spark that band as Satchmo had. I almost had a nervous breakdown at first.

But Smack's easygoing attitude toward the men soon made me feel at ease. This lack of aggressiveness in situations that called for a strong hand, however, was sometimes resented by the fellows.

To illustrate: Bobby Stark (my section mate on trumpet) developed the habit of demanding money from Fletch at any time of the day or night when he was in his cups. This often-repeated scene was more than a little humorous, as Bobby stood about 5 feet 1 and didn't weigh 145 pounds soaking wet. Bobby would charge Smack, head to chest, and in a belligerent manner snarl, "Goddammit, Smack, give me some dough. It's drinking time, and I'm thirsty." The guys would howl with laughter as little Bobby bearded the larger man. Fletcher would smile tolerantly and say, "No money for you, Bobby. You are drunk already, so head for home."

Later, on a road trip, Bobby outdid himself. This was in Tulsa, Okla., and we were living at a hotel. Suddenly, we were awakened by what sounded like somebody shooting into the side of the hotel. Everybody jumped up and looked out the window. There stood Bobby Stark hurling bricks at Fletcher's window, punctuating each volley with a demand. It went like this:

"Smack, you SOB. I know you hear me."

Crash.

"Throw me 20!"

Crash.

"Smack, you hear me? Throw me some dough. Make it 10!"

Crash.

By the time we reached Bobby, he was down to $5.

Bobby was a very quiet fellow until he got on the sauce, but Smack was undoubtedly reincarnated from another age or planet. He was just too gentle for his time. In my mind, he was the Mahatma Gandhi of the jazz age.

Redman had a pretty easygoing attitude toward life too. One time, he hit the Irish Sweepstakes for several thousand dollars. The Henderson band was playing a concert at the Renaissance Theater in Harlem, and the afternoon of the concert, Don bought a brand new Cadillac with the money and proudly parked it right in front of the theater. It seems to me that we had just started playing when the band boy frantically signaled from the wings. A drunken taxi driver, he said, had demolished the new Cadillac. Don paused for a few seconds but then continued playing, seemingly unruffled. When the concert was over, he didn't even go out to look at the damage but remarked with a shrug, "Well, I guess that buggy just wasn't for me." The next day, he bought a new Buick.

As a band, we were car crazy. Since there were so few good cars in Harlem during that period, our departures on a road trip took on the aspect of a three-ring circus.

Fletcher had a long black Packard roadster; Joe Smith, the trumpet player, had a chic, lean Wills St. Clair; drummer Kaiser Marshall sported a Buick. When these three beautiful cars were lined up in front of the Rhythm Club waiting for the rest of the guys, the pool players put down their cues, the poker games stopped, and all the other musicians gathered around to ooh and ah. I remember hearing Jelly Roll Morton, who seldom had a good word for anything, remark, "Damn, well, that's what I call a pretty sight."

Just about that time, Elmer Williams and Chu Berry, the tenor sax stars, rounded the corner of Seventh Ave. and 132nd St. on foot. Williams had his customary cigar in his mouth, but when he saw our classy caravan, he almost swallowed the cigar as he told Chu, "Now that's what I call the real big time. Those cats must be making *all* the money."

We weren't really making all the money, but everybody in the band was very well paid.

We all welcomed these road trips, because we were paid even more money on the road, and then, too, there were lots of new little chicks in each town dedicated to helping us pass the time away. But for Fletcher and his wife, Leora, these trips were a lot of hard work. Our tours preceded the days of booking agents. Therefore, the Hendersons wrote many letters, sent loads of telegrams, and telephoned all over the eastern seaboard to co-ordinate the trips and consolidate the bookings.

Even with all the advance planning, sometimes there would be a goof, such as the time we jumped from Louisville to New York, only to be met by Mrs. Henderson saying, "Fletcher, what are you doing here? You're booked in Lexington tomorrow night." So we gassed up immediately, stopped by the bootlegger's and got some whisky, and hit the road for Lexington, Ky. All of this in 2½ days, not over superhighways but bad roads. The guys in the band really earned the extra loot. We paid our dues.

Gradually, a few booking agents turned up on the scene. Along with Charlie Shribman, the next big operator was Ed Fishman, who started branching out from Harrisburg, Pa., and little by little more people entered the field. For groups that went on the road in later years with the aid and assistance of Music Corp. of America, Joe Glaser, and others, life was much simpler than for the Henderson band back in the '20s.

One experience I recall from our road tours is unforgettable.

We had given up the caravan of cars and were riding a chartered bus. We got caught in an early spring freeze in the mountains of New Hampshire. The bus was unheated, and we had no overcoats; so we improvised by using newspapers. We'd place a newspaper between the undershirt and shirt, and another layer between the shirt and jacket. It kept us warm, but when the bus broke down climbing a mountain, we had to get out and push. Unaccustomed as we were to exercise, it was a real back-breaker pushing that bus up that mountain. To climax the situation, the top of the mountain was covered with ice, and hot as we had become pushing the bus up, we cooled off with fright as the bus slithered down the other side of the mountain. (Luckily, the bus was unharmed, and we were soon off and away again.)

During those road tours, we were notorious for not writing back home. Redman was one of the worst offenders. Days faded into weeks, and Don's wife began sending him telegrams, complaining because she had not heard from him. So Don bought a pretty box and some fancy wrapping paper, proceeded to gift-wrap several sets of soiled underwear, and mailed the box home. The telegrams stopped arriving.

On our return to New York, there would always be a lot of record dates for us because of the snowballing of popularity on the road. Along with the emergence of bookers for tours, the recording business picked up, since the tours produced new markets for the music.

Curiously enough, although the Henderson band played a variety of music on the tours, the record executives categorized Smack's band as a stomp band. They didn't accept the fact that a Negro band could play sweet, though, as a matter of fact, we used to get tremendous applause at Roseland and other places for playing waltzes beautifully. How unfortunate that we never recorded any of these waltz arrangements, and posterity can never know the greatness of the Henderson band in that field.

Of course, the record business was very different in its early days. I can't imagine a record executive today not being delighted to capitalize on the music that was delighting the public. But in the days of primitive recording, when each instrument would record into a separate horn and no bass drums were used, a lot of the real flavor of the music could never be captured.

Smack was very disappointed at not being permitted to record his famous *Rose* medley. This consisted of *Roses of Picardy* arranged by Charlie Dixon, *Broadway Rose* arranged by Benny Carter, and several other popular songs of the day with the word *rose* in the title, all in waltz tempo. Fletcher's disappointment was not solely because his waltz medley had been vetoed, but also because he had a predilection for rose. He wore rose-colored shirts and ties and even bought a rose-colored Packard, or at least ordered one. Unfortunately, Detroit didn't make cars in those colors then. But then, they don't make musicians like Fletcher Henderson today.

There is no question about Fletcher being the real big time for his era, which spanned the years 1923 until approximately 1944. At that time, he made his last significant effort when his *Jazz Train* was presented in a Broadway night spot. This was an attempt to depict and portray the evolutionary sequence of jazz. It was a production complete with singers and dancers and Fletcher's music.

Not only did Henderson achieve popularity and success from his music, but he also was the catalyst for the birth of another star. Record producer and critic John Hammond influenced Smack to give his book of arrangements to an unknown but talented young clarinetist. In large measure because of Fletcher's book, Benny Goodman became an overnight sensation.

Goodman is not the only musician who owes a debt of gratitude to Fletcher Henderson.

Jazz would not exist in its form today were it not for the many innovations, creativity, and contributions of Fletcher Henderson. He took the fundamentals of early jazz and molded them into a more permanent structure, from which our myriad contemporary forms of jazz have grown. Although many of our present-day jazz exponents may have forgot, or never knew, what it was that Fletcher Henderson gave to jazz, there can be no doubt that this man shall be immortalized as one of the founding fathers of the only American art form.

note

Originally published in *DownBeat*, June 3, 1965.